PETERSON'S®

ACT®PREP GUIDE 36:
PREP FOR THE
PERFECT SCORE

About Peterson's®

Peterson's is everywhere that education happens. For over five decades, Peterson's has provided products and services that keep students and their families engaged throughout the pre-college, college, and post-college experience. From the first day of kindergarten through high school graduation and beyond, Peterson's is a single source of educational content to help families maximize their student's learning and opportunities for success. Whether a fifth-grader needs help with geometry or a high school junior could benefit from essay-writing tips, Peterson's is the ultimate source for the highest quality educational resources.

Since 2005, Peterson's has been the leading publisher of prep guides for the ACT. Over the past ten years, more than one million students across 60 countries have prepared for the ACT with Peterson's titles.

For additional information about Peterson's range of educational products, please visit http://www.petersons.com.

ACT® is a registered trademark of ACT, Inc., which did not collaborate in the development of, and does not endorse, this product.

ACT® is a registered trademark of ACT, Inc., in the U.S.A. and other countries.

For more information, contact Peterson's, 3 Columbia Circle, Suite 205, Albany, NY 12203, 800-338-3282 Ext. 54229; or find us online at www.petersons.com.

Peterson's ACT® Prep Guide 36
ISBN 978-0-7689-4120-3

Printed in the United States of America

10 9 8 7 6 5 4 3 2   18 17 16

First Edition

Petersonspublishing.com/publishingupdates

Check out our website at www.petersonspublishing.com/publishingupdates to see if there is any new information regarding the test and any revisions or corrections to the content of this book. We've made sure the information in this book is accurate and up-to-date; however, the test format or content may have changed since the time of publication.

TABLE OF CONTENTS

6 ACT® READING: SOCIAL STUDIES/NATURAL SCIENCES PASSAGES

7 ACT® READING: LITERARY NARRATIVE/PROSE FICTION AND HUMANITIES PASSAGES

8 DATA REPRESENTATION: INTERPRETING AND APPLYING EXPERIMENTAL RESULTS

9 RESEARCH SUMMARIES: ASSESSING EXPERIMENTAL DESIGN AND ANALYZING RESULTS

10 CONFLICTING VIEWPOINTS: INTERPRETING AND RELATING ARGUMENTS

11 THE ACT® WRITING TEST

CHAPTER 1:
ALL ABOUT THE ACT®

OVERVIEW

- The ACT®: An Overview
- Registering for the ACT®
- Scoring
- Getting Ready for Test Day
- Summing It Up

We know why you're here—you're an elite student with a very specific goal: a perfect score on the ACT. Your academic record likely reflects a long history of hard work, achievement, and success, and now you're focused on getting into your dream college or university. You probably feel confident in your chances of gaining admission to one of your target schools, but you're also aware that the competition is *intense*. There are top-notch students like you all over the country and abroad, some of whom are aiming for the exact same thing you are. You know that every facet of your application package is going to have to be strong if your dream is going to materialize into a reality. This includes a great score—ideally a perfect score—on your college admissions exams.

This book is the tool you need to completely conquer the ACT, and here's why—you get:

- **Extensive coverage and analysis** of the entire structure and format of the ACT, including everything you need to know to get ready for test day and be several steps ahead of the test-taking competition

- **Thorough and comprehensive review** of each section of the test along with proven tips, strategies, and advice for achieving your absolute best scores possible

- **Rigorous and challenging practice** that represents the very toughest of the tough questions you may encounter on test day to get you in superlative test-taking shape.

Why is a perfect score so important to you? You don't want to *just* impress the admissions committees at your target schools, you want to *dazzle* and *amaze* them. You don't want to *just* beat the competition, you want to *crush* them! You're a high achiever—you likely always have been and always will be—and nothing but perfection will satisfy you.

We get it, and we're here to help support your quest for perfection on the ACT. Keep reading. Everything you need to make your goal of a perfect score attainable is in the chapters that follow!

THE ACT®: AN OVERVIEW

We know you're eager to move forward and get to the heart of this book—the practice and review that will get you ready to ace the ACT. But let's spend a little time reviewing some ACT basics first. After all, knowledge is power, and the more you know about this high-stakes test, the better prepared you'll be.

Along with your GPA, resume of extracurricular activities, letters of recommendation, and application and essay, your score on the ACT will be among the most important factors that college admissions panels will use to decide whether or not to grant you admission. Your score on the ACT will give colleges a good idea of how strong your particular skills are in each tested area and will help your future advisors make decisions regarding class level placement.

NOTE: Make sure you're *fully* aware of the admissions requirements of each college or university that you're applying to. Nothing ruins an exceptional admissions application quite as effectively as a glaring omission.

The ACT is carefully designed by education experts to test your proficiency in the core subjects you've studied throughout your high school career: **English, mathematics, reading, science**, and **writing**. Most of the questions are multiple choice, the kind that require you to select the best option among several possible answer choices. There's also a written essay in the optional Writing test if you choose to take this test—and being an elite student, you likely never shy away from a challenge or an opportunity to show why you're a top student. We'll delve into an in-depth analysis of each section of the exam in subsequent chapters.

ACT Timing

The ACT is a **3-hour and 30-minute exam** consisting of **215 multiple-choice questions** (there's also a 30-minute break). Add in an extra 40 minutes if you're taking the optional Writing test.

Make sure you're comfortable with the format and timing of the ACT and each test section before test day. Practice working in simulated timed conditions to develop an effective test-taking pace.

The English Test

The English test is a 45-minute exam that consists of 75 questions. It's designed to test your skills in the core elements of effective writing, including **usage and mechanics** and **rhetorical skills**:

- **Usage and mechanics** questions test your knowledge and understanding of punctuation, grammar, and sentence structure.
- **Rhetorical skills** questions test your knowledge and understanding of writing strategy, organization, and style.

On the exam, you'll encounter five reading passages, each of which will contain various underlined portions that may include errors that you must recognize and fix. If there is an error or multiple errors, you will select the best correction offered from among the available answer choices for each question that accompanies a given passage. If there aren't any errors, you'll select the choice that reads NO CHANGE. The majority of usage and mechanics questions on the exam will adhere to this format.

The rhetorical skills questions will typically ask you to identify the best way to rethink, reorganize, or restyle a specific portion of each passage, or perhaps an entire passage. The relevant portion in the passage will be numbered, and that number will refer to the question number that relates to the portion.

The Mathematics Test

The Mathematics test is a 60-minute exam that consists of 60 questions. It is designed to test your ability in the following core subject areas that students typically encounter during high school:

- Pre-algebra/elementary algebra
- Intermediate algebra/coordinate geometry
- Plane geometry/trigonometry

Each question is multiple-choice; however, unlike the other ACT test sections, there are *five* possible answer choices for each question. If you're aiming for a perfect score on the ACT, your knowledge and skills in each of these topic areas need to be sharp.

While you'll have to know basic formulas and computations for the Mathematics test, you will *not* be expected to remember more complex ones—they'll be provided for you along with the questions. You'll also be permitted to use certain calculators on the Mathematics test, though a calculator is not required. You'll learn which kinds of calculators are permitted later on in this chapter.

THE READING TEST

The Reading test is a 35-minute exam that consists of 40 questions. You'll encounter four different kinds of passages in this test:

- **Literary Narrative/Prose Fiction** passages include portions of text from short stories, novels, memoirs, or personal essays.

- **Social Studies** passages discuss anthropology, archaeology, biography, business, economics, education, geography, history, political science, psychology, and sociology.

- **Natural Sciences** passages discuss anatomy, astronomy, biology, botany, chemistry, ecology, geology, medicine, meteorology, microbiology, natural history, physics, physiology, technology, and zoology.

- **Humanities** passages discuss architecture, art, dance, ethics, film, language, literary criticism, music, philosophy, radio, television, and theater.

The questions on the Reading test are multiple-choice, each with four possible answer choices. Reading test questions require you to determine meanings that are stated both explicitly and implicitly, recognize main ideas, and identify the meanings of words as they are used in context. You'll also have to locate and interpret significant details, understand the correct sequence of events, comprehend cause-and-effect relationships, analyze tone and mood, and draw generalizations.

Some passages will consist of a pair of shorter passages, and some of the accompanying questions will test your ability to analyze how those two passages relate to each other—including differences and similarities.

THE SCIENCE TEST

The Science test is a 35-minute exam consisting of 40 questions. The test includes various passages with key scientific information, each followed by multiple-choice questions with four possible answer choices. The science skills tested cover the following core topic areas: biology, chemistry, earth/space sciences, and physics.

You'll encounter three distinct question types:

1. **Data representation** questions require you to read and interpret information on graphs, scatterplots, and tables.

2. **Research summary** questions require you to read about experiments and draw conclusions about their designs and results.

3. **Conflicting viewpoints** questions feature pairs of contrasting hypotheses about data or premises and require you to understand, analyze, compare, and contrast those viewpoints.

 ALERT: Calculators are *not* allowed on the Science test because you will not be required to make any calculations.

THE WRITING TEST

The Writing test is an optional 40-minute exam consisting of a single essay writing task. You'll receive an essay prompt alongside three different perspectives on a particular issue. After reading the prompt and each perspective carefully, you'll compose an essay that evaluates the issue in the prompt and supports your distinct perspective on the issue, while also taking into account the other perspectives.

Your opinions will *not* affect your score; only the quality of your ideas and writing will.

Again, this is an optional exam section and not every college requires that you take it. You can find the Writing test requirements for your target colleges on the official ACT website: *www.actstudent.org/writing/*.

Perfect Score = Tough Practice!

The path to a perfect score on the ACT is *not* an easy one. Your skills in each section of the exam have to be razor sharp if you're going to achieve this goal. This book includes examples of the *toughest questions* for each of the sections that comprise the ACT. Good thing you're the type of student who likes a challenge!

Bottom line: Challenging practice under timed conditions will help you get closer to achieving your perfect score goal.

REGISTERING FOR THE ACT®

Registering online for the ACT is the quickest method—go to *www.actstudent.org regist/*, follow the instructions, and create an online account to get started and register.

You can use the official ACT website to request extended time to take the test if you have a disability, and you can request a standby online test if you missed the late registration deadline. You may also request an online test if you are homebound, confined, or not within 75 miles of a testing center (all of these arrangements can be made by visiting *www.actstudent.org/regist/online*).

If you are under age 13 or cannot pay with a credit card, don't worry! You can request a Register-By-Mail packet by filling out a form online at *www.actstudent.org/forms/ stud_req/*.

REGISTRATION FEES*

The fee for taking the ACT without the optional Writing test is $42.50, which includes having your score report sent to you, your high school, and as many as four colleges of your choice. If you're taking the optional Writing test, the total fee is $58.50 (the extra $16 fee is refundable in the event you either cannot make it to test day or you decide to take the ACT without the Writing test before the test begins).

* Registration fees at the time of publication. Go to *www.petersons.com/act* for up-to-date information.

If you decide to have your score report sent to a fifth and sixth college, there is a $12 fee for each additional school.

Other options and fees include:

- Standby testing: $51
- Late registration (available only in the US and Canada): $27.50
- International testing (outside the US and Canada): $41
- Changing the date of your test: $24
- Changing the location of your test: $25
- Requesting a copy of your test and answers (Test Information Release, or TIR): $20 (where available)

You may be eligible for a fee waiver to help cover the cost of the exam. To find out if you're eligible, and for additional fee information, check out the official ACT website: ***www.act.org/content/act/en/products-and-services/the-act/taking-the-test.html***.

Photo ID

For security purposes, you must provide a photo ID to register for the ACT. Your photo ID must be current, valid, and legal. Your ID must be hard plastic, such as a student ID or driver's license. If you do not have an acceptable photo ID, you must obtain an ACT Student Identification Letter with Photo from the ACT website here: ***http://www.act. org/content/dam/act/unsecured/documents/Identification-Letter-Form.pdf.***

You can learn how to upload a photo of yourself using your computer or mobile device on the official ACT website (***www.actstudent.org/regist/add-photo.html***). You can also learn how to submit a paper photo by visiting ***www.actstudent.org/regist/add-photo .html#paper***.

After you register for the ACT, you'll receive a registration ticket with your photo. You *MUST* bring this ticket, along with your photo ID, with you on test day!

Students taking the test on standby—those who missed the late registration date or requested a test date or test center change—must also bring a standby ticket with a photo of themselves on test day. (Find out more about obtaining this ticket on the ACT site: ***www.actstudent.org/regist/standbytest.html***).

SCORING

WHEN AND HOW OFTEN TO TAKE THE ACT

In the United States, its territories, and Canada, the ACT is given six times a year—in September, October, December, February (except in New York), April, and June. Select the test date that works best for you and your specific goals, and be sure to check out the registration deadlines on the official ACT website. In addition, if you require information for testing outside of the United States, visit the official ACT website.

If nothing short of a perfect score will satisfy you, you may decide to take the test more than once, which is an option that's available to you (you can take the exam up to twelve times). If you choose to retake the ACT, a separate record will be kept for each test date that you've taken the exam. When you request that ACT send a score report to a college, only the score record from the test date you request will be released. This means that you're in control of which scores colleges see and don't see.

You can also ask ACT to send more than one score report from more than one test date to a college. However, ACT will *not* create a new record for you by selecting and combining scores from different test dates—you can only send entire test date records as they stand. However, there is a process known as **superscoring**, which you can use to your advantage if you're applying to colleges that utilize the Common Application form. We will discuss how superscoring works a little later.

HOW THE ACT IS SCORED

Since you're on the hunt for a perfect score on the ACT, you should familiarize yourself with how the exam is scored. The ACT is a multiple-choice test (the optional Writing test is an essay-writing task) that does *not* penalize you for selecting a wrong answer. However, a blank answer *will* be marked as incorrect. Therefore, it is important to answer *every* question on the test, even if you only guess. *Never* leave a question blank!

Each of the four multiple-choice tests—English, Mathematics, Reading, and Science—is worth 36 points. Your total score, also known as your **composite score**, is the average score of these tests.

NOTE: The perfect score goal on the ACT is a composite score of 36.

The optional Writing test is scored a bit differently. Two official essay readers will score your essay independently on a scale from 1 to 6 in four writing domains: Ideas and Analysis, Development and Support, Organization, and Language Use. Each reader will assign your essay a score ranging from 4 to 24, based on how well you met the criteria for each domain. Your raw score is the sum of the scores from both readers, ranging from 8 to 48. The raw score is then scaled; the highest possible score you can earn for the Writing test is 36.

SUPERSCORING

Did you know that certain colleges (more than 500 as of this writing) allow you to take the ACT multiple times and average together your best scores on each of the multiple-choice tests? This is known as superscoring.

These colleges use the Common Application form, which gives you the option of entering your highest scores for the English, Mathematics, Reading, and Science tests. It does not matter if you earned each of these scores on different dates. The application averages these high scores, giving you your best possible score. Superscoring is a compelling reason to consider taking the ACT more than once, especially if you did great on a few of the test sections but fell short of your perfect score goal.

VIEWING YOUR SCORES

You'll be able to view your test scores online by logging into your account on the official ACT website. Scores are generally available for online viewing approximately two weeks after your test date, and score reports are typically released within five to eight weeks of your test date. If you've decided to take the optional Writing test, your score report (with writing score) will be released within 5 to 8 weeks of your test date.

We know you're eager to find out if you achieved your goal of a perfect score, but try to be patient when waiting for your score to be posted. Just keep checking back once a week, since scores are posted on a weekly basis. Writing test scores are posted approximately two weeks after multiple-choice test scores.

REPORTING YOUR SCORES

Once your score report is available, ACT will automatically send it to you and the schools you requested when registering (up to four at no extra charge). If there are additional institutions that you'd like to have your scores sent to, you can request additional reports.

You can request a regular report, which is processed within one week from receipt of request, for $12 per report (per test date), or a priority report (available only in the US), which is processed within two working days from receipt of request, for $16.50 per report (per test date).

You can request a report from the official ACT website by logging into your ACT account and completing a request form (payment must be made by credit card), by phone (319-337-1270), or by sending a letter of request (must include your full name; current mailing address and address used during registration if different; ACT ID; date of birth; phone number; test date; names and codes of additional institutions you'd like your score report sent to, including city and state; and your signature) and a check or money order payable to ACT to the following address:

> ACT Student Services—Score Reports
> PO Box 451
> Iowa City, IA 52243-0451

For complete information regarding ACT scoring policies and procedures, visit the official ACT website.

GETTING READY FOR TEST DAY

We know that on test day you'll be ready to attack every exam section and question, but knowing the test day fundamentals and preparing for the big day—including selecting a test day and location, what to expect when you arrive at your test center, what to bring, and what to leave home—will help you avoid surprises, reduce anxiety, and stay ahead of the competition. Preparing for the ACT is essential, but just as important is preparing yourself for what you'll encounter on test day, so keep reading!

CHOOSING YOUR TEST DATE AND LOCATION

On your quest for a perfect score on the ACT, be sure to choose a test day strategically—choose a day that allows you sufficient preparation time, is convenient for you, and will not conflict with other activities on your schedule. The last thing you want on the day of this important exam is to be overbooked or racing around to the point of exhaustion. There are a limited number of test administrations each year, and you're the type of student who knows just how important this test is, so choose wisely!

Also be sure that the location you choose to take the exam is convenient for you, and—this is important—make sure you know *precisely* how long it will take you to get to the testing center. Make a few practice runs of your route to the test location, have an alternate route just in case, and don't leave anything to chance. Be sure to take all possible factors into account to ensure you don't arrive late to the test center: traffic, adverse weather conditions, a detour to the gas station, etc. Showing up late for the test is the *quickest* way to derail your quest for a perfect score!

Visit the official ACT website to find the best test location for you—and register as early as possible to avoid having your preferred test location fill up before you sign up: ***http://www.act.org/content/act/en/products-and-services/the-act/taking-the-test/test-center-locator.html***.

WHAT TO EXPECT, WHAT TO BRING, AND WHAT TO LEAVE HOME

Test time *always* begins at 8:00 a.m., and by this time you should be present and in your seat. Plan to arrive early, giving you time to relax, get comfortable, and get settled into test-taking mode; you *definitely* don't want to have to deal with the stress of racing the clock to avoid missing the start of the test, and you will *not* be admitted to take the test if you arrive late.

When you arrive at your test center, the staff will check your photo ID and ticket, admit you into the room, bring you to your seat, and provide you with the required test materials.

The tests on the ACT are administered in the following order: English, mathematics, reading, science, and finally, writing. Your 30-minute break occurs after the Mathematics test. There is also an extra 10-minute break before the Writing test if you're taking it.

NOTE: Individuals taking the ACT are generally dismissed at 12:15 p.m. Those taking the ACT with Writing are generally dismissed at 1:15 p.m.

YOUR TEST DAY CHECKLIST

Make absolutely certain that you bring the following items with you on test day:

- A printed copy of your test ticket
- Acceptable photo ID (visit the official ACT website for what constitutes acceptable ID)
- Sharpened No. 2 pencils with erasers

Consider bringing the following optional items to help maximize your test-taking experience:

- Permissible calculator for the Mathematics test (see the guidelines that follow)
- A watch (without an alarm) to help pace yourself through each test section
- A sweater to help you adapt to the test center temperature

Do not bring the following items with you to the test room—you will absolutely not be able to use them:

- The following electronic devices: smartphone, cell phone, iPad or tablet, camera, and headphones
- Reading material, textbooks, reference materials (including dictionaries and other study aids), and outside notes
- Extra scratch paper
- Highlighters, colored pens and pencils, or correction tape/fluid
- Food or beverages (you will have a break opportunity outside of the test room)
- Tobacco

Calculators and the ACT Exam

Here's everything you need to know about using a calculator on test day:

- You may bring any 4-function, scientific, or graphing calculator for use on test day, as long as it does not violate any of the rules listed here.

- You'll be allowed to use a calculator only on the Mathematics test.

- If you bring or attempt to use a prohibited device on test day, you'll be dismissed from the exam and will not receive a test score.

- Sharing calculators during the ACT is prohibited.

- You will not be able to obtain a calculator from the test proctor—it is your responsibility to bring an acceptable device and know whether or not your calculator is permitted.

- You are responsible for the proper functioning of your calculator, and you are allowed to bring a spare calculator and batteries.

- An on-screen calculator may be provided in a computer-based testing environment.

- Accessible calculators, including audio/"talking" or Braille calculators, may be allowed under the accessibility policies for the ACT (visit the official website for details).

The following calculators are not permitted for use on the ACT:

- Any calculator with built-in or downloaded computer algebra system functionality
- Handheld, tablet, or laptop computers, including PDAs
- Calculators built into cell phones or any other electronic communication devices
- Calculators with a typewriter keypad (letter keys in QWERTY format; Letter keys not in QWERTY format are permitted)
- Electronic writing pads or pen-input devices
  - **Note:** The Sharp EL 9600 is permitted
- Any of the following brands:
  - **Texas Instruments**
    - All model numbers that begin with TI-89 or TI-92
    - TI-Nspire CAS (*Note:* The TI-Nspire (non-CAS) is permitted)
  - **Hewlett-Packard**
    - HP Prime
    - HP 48GII
    - All model numbers that begin with HP40G, HP49G, or HP50G
  - **Casio**
    - fx-CP400 (ClassPad 400)
    - ClassPad 300
    - ClassPad 330
    - Algebra fx 2.0
    - All model numbers that begin with CFX-9970G

The following types of calculators are permitted—but only after they are modified as indicated:

- Calculators that can hold programs or documents—remove all documents and remove all programs that have computer algebra system functionality
- Calculators with paper tape—remove the tape
- Calculators that make noise—turn off the sound
- Calculators with an infrared data port—completely cover the infrared data port with heavy opaque material such as duct tape or electrician's tape (includes Hewlett-Packard HP38G series, HP39G series, and HP48G)
- Calculators that have power cords—remove all power/electrical cords

SUMMING IT UP

- The ACT consists of four multiple-choice tests in **English, Mathematics, Reading, and Science,** with a total of 215 questions.
  - You will have 3 hours and 30 minutes to complete the test.
  - There is also an optional Writing test, which takes an additional 40 minutes to complete. Some colleges do not require the Writing test—make sure you know the requirements of the schools you're applying to.

- **Your ACT score is important.** It will be among the most important factors that college admissions panels will use to make admissions decisions. It also gives colleges a good idea of your skills in each tested area and will help guide decisions regarding class level placement.

- **The English test** lasts 45 minutes and consists of 75 questions that test your grammar and usage and rhetorical skills.

- **The Mathematics test** lasts 60 minutes and consists of 60 questions that test your knowledge of pre-algebra, elementary algebra, intermediate algebra, coordinate geometry, plane geometry, and trigonometry.

- **The Reading test** lasts 35 minutes and consists of 40 questions that test your ability to analyze and comprehend four distinct passages.

- **The Science test** lasts 35 minutes and consists of 40 questions that test your knowledge of biology, chemistry, earth/space sciences, and physics.

- **The optional Writing test** lasts 40 minutes and consists of an essay task, which requires you to evaluate a prompt and three perspectives on an issue, create your own perspective on that issue, and explain how your perspective relates to the ones provided.

- **Registering online for the ACT is the quickest method**—go to *http://www.act.org/ content/act/en/products-and-services/the-act/registration-information.html*, follow the instructions, and create an online account to get started and register.

- **Verify the cost of the test.** Make sure you're fully aware of all applicable test fees, based on your specific testing and reporting needs.

- **Choose the test date and location that works best for you,** and make sure you register before the deadline.

- **Plan your travel route.** Make sure you have at least one, and preferably an alternate, route to your test location that will get you there with plenty of time to spare.

- **The test begins at 8:00 a.m.** Arrive at the test center well before test time.
  - ○ Individuals taking the ACT without Writing are generally dismissed at 12:15 p.m. Those taking the Writing test are generally dismissed at 1:15 p.m.

- **Don't bring unnecessary items.** Make sure you're fully aware of what you *must bring*, *can bring*, and *cannot bring* with you on test day, including calculator guidelines.

- **The maximum score you can get on the ACT is a composite score of 36**, and that score is determined by averaging your score on each of the four multiple-choice tests.

- **The Writing test essay is scored on a scale from 1 to 6 in each of four writing domains.** The maximum raw score you can get is 48, which is the sum of your essay scores from two independent essay readers. The maximum scale score you can get is 36.

- **There is no penalty for choosing an incorrect answer on the ACT**, so you should answer every question. Unanswered questions are considered to be wrong answers.

- **ACT scores are generally available for online viewing approximately two weeks after your test date**, and score reports are typically released within three to eight weeks of your test date. If you're taking the optional Writing test, your score report (with writing score) will be released within five to eight weeks of your test date.

- **Be sure to request that ACT send your score report to each college that you're interested in applying to**; this includes the colleges you indicate while registering for the test (up to four), as well as any additional schools later on.

- **The path to a perfect score on the ACT exam is *not* an easy one.** Your skills on each section of the exam have to be razor sharp if you're going to achieve your goal. Your best approach is to get plenty of practice and review between now and test day and to target your weakest areas for improvement.

CHAPTER 2:
ACT® ENGLISH:
USAGE/MECHANICS REVIEW

OVERVIEW

- About Usage/Mechanics Questions
- Punctuation
- Grammar and Usage
- Sentence Structure
- Summing It Up

The ACT English test is always the first section you'll take. It tests your general English language skills, including grammar, usage, and organization. It's a fast-moving section, with 75 questions to answer in 45 minutes. Keep these numbers is mind as you make your way through the test: you have about 90 seconds to read each passage, and 30 seconds per question. So you need to be ready to read, digest, and answer questions pretty quickly.

Each English test contains five essays or passages, accompanied by 14–16 multiple-choice questions each. Each passage will be numbered throughout, many with corresponding underlined words, phrases, or sentences. The numbers in the passage correspond to the multiple-choice questions that follow. The questions may ask you to determine whether an underlined word or phrase is grammatically correct, or to make decisions about a paragraph or the passage as a whole.

The ACT English test assesses two general areas: **Usage/Mechanics** (which includes grammar usage, punctuation, and sentence structure) and **Rhetorical Skills** (which includes organization, strategy, and style within the passages). Although you'll receive individual subscores for both of these areas, it's best to focus on your overall English score.

NOTE: If spelling isn't your forte, don't worry! The ACT English test doesn't assess spelling or vocabulary. Instead, it focuses on general language skills, like punctuation, word usage, and grammar.

ABOUT USAGE/MECHANICS QUESTIONS

The Usage/Mechanics portion of the ACT English test assesses the nuts and bolts of your grammar skills. Grammar conventions, punctuation rules, appropriate word choice, and sentence construction all come into play in this section. Think of yourself as an all-powerful editor—you'll be reviewing the passages and figuring out how to make them better.

NOTE: Not every underlined item will need to be fixed. It can be tempting to assume that every question requires changes to the text. Being confident that you can identify when the writing is correct as written will help boost your ACT English score.

To get the highest possible Usage/Mechanics subscore, you'll need to have a solid grasp of standard English grammar and writing concepts. You won't need to know grammar rules verbatim or to remember every single thing you learned in high school English, but you *will* be expected to know generally how the rules work and be able to apply them in a given passage. Usage/Mechanics questions will ask you to look at particular words, phrases, or sentences in the passage and select "NO CHANGE" if the text is already correct or select the option that corrects the underlined text.

For example, here's a question you should not read too much into, as the sentence is correct as is:

The *Santa Maria,* Columbus's flagship, set sail for the New World in 1492.
                      1

1. **A.** NO CHANGE
   B. *Santa Maria.* Columbus's flagship
   C. *Santa Maria!* Columbus's flagship
   D. *Santa Maria* Columbus's flagship

The Usage/Mechanics question distribution on the English test breaks down like this:

- Punctuation (10–15%)
- Grammar and usage (15–20%)
- Sentence structure (20–25%)

The rest of the English test is made up of Rhetorical Skills questions, which we'll cover in Chapter 3:

- Strategy (15–20%)
- Organization (10–15%)
- Style (15–20%)

NOTE: Although this book tackles these two distinct question types in separate chapters, Rhetorical Skills and Usage/Mechanics questions appear *together* within the reading passages you'll encounter on test day. One of the challenges on the ACT exam is to recognize which type of question you're facing and which strategies you should utilize to arrive at the correct answers.

The skills assessed in the Usage/Mechanics questions on the English test include grammar building blocks: parts of speech (nouns, verbs, adjectives, etc.), as well as the various moving parts of sentences (clauses, fragments, coordination, etc.). To get a top score on the ACT, you'll need to be familiar with some advanced concepts as well—taking those building blocks to the next level.

Chances are, you're already familiar with the basics of how grammar works. That's why this section will not be a review of *all* of the potential Usage/Mechanics concepts you could see on test day—just the most difficult ones that may come your way. If you focus your studying energy on the strongest challenges that the ACT powers-that-be can throw at you, you'll be able to tackle these with confidence when the test is in front of you and time is short.

PUNCTUATION

Although punctuation questions account for only 10–15 percent of ACT English test questions, it's a crucial area to study if you want to get a top score. Punctuation is an essential part of writing—without correct punctuation, it can be very difficult to convey information clearly to a reader.

One of the most important punctuation questions to keep in mind as you prep for the ACT is, "Does this sentence need this punctuation?" Just because you see a comma or an apostrophe doesn't mean that the mark should be in the sentence. On test day, you should be just as open to taking punctuation out as you are to adding it or changing it to make the sentence correct. *Sometimes, the best punctuation is no punctuation at all.*

To maximize your ACT English test score, you should be very familiar with the types of punctuation and how they function within a given sentence.

COMMAS

Commas (,) do a lot of heavy lifting in the punctuation game. They join compound sentences, separate list items, set off independent clauses, and serve as visual pauses throughout a sentence.

I went to the park, but I forgot to bring my tennis racket.

Please be sure to pick up eggs, milk, and paper towels when you run to the store.

You know, I never looked at it that way, but you're right.

On the ACT, the comma is likely to be one of the most frequently tested parts of punctuation. Misused, misplaced, and missing commas are very likely to appear on your test. On the most basic level, the ACT English test requires you to be able to figure out how the commas are supposed to function and where they should be placed. Commas are present at every level of difficulty on the ACT English test. Some of the most challenging comma questions will ask you to examine the relationship between a sentence's meaning and the comma placement, untangle long sentences where commas represent false pauses, and determine whether essential or restrictive clauses require commas (or any other punctuation).

Commas and Sentence Meaning

An ACT English test question may require you to add commas—or delete them—to clarify the meaning of a sentence. Commas should always reduce ambiguity and help refine phrases and clauses so that they're clear and readable.

For example:

> I'm hungry; let's eat Margo.

Is the speaker suggesting that they eat Margo? Or is the speaker talking to Margo and suggesting that they both start eating? Two totally different interpretations of the sentence (especially if you're Margo!) mean that the comma is especially important in clarifying the purpose of the sentence.

> I'm hungry; let's eat, Margo.

Much better!

You will likely also see instances where there are too many commas in a sentence, confusing the meaning by adding unnecessary pauses. This is especially common in sentences where commas are used to set off items in a list. If the writer uses a comma to separate the items, it can be confusing to differentiate between the introductory phrase and the list itself.

> To make arroz con pollo, make sure you buy, chicken stock, tomatoes, rice, and boneless chicken.

In this example, the comma is unnecessary to set off the list of ingredients. There's no natural pause after *buy*. The way the commas are set up in this sentence, it looks like *buy, chicken stock, tomatoes, rice,* and *boneless chicken* are all equal items in the list, when in reality *chicken stock, tomatoes, rice,* and *boneless chicken* are objects of the verb *buy* here.

> To make arroz con pollo, make sure you buy chicken stock, tomatoes, rice, and boneless chicken.

One way to check for comma errors is to sound out the sentence quickly in your head. If a pause sounds unnatural and there's a comma in the underlined sentence, that's a red flag.

Commas and Appositives

Appositives are nouns or noun phrases that modify nouns.

> The classic novel Jane Eyre is a book club favorite.

> I'd like that cupcake, the one with blue frosting, please.

Appositives need commas only if they offer supporting information that is not essential to the meaning of the sentence. If the sentence's meaning would be different and unclear without the appositive phrase, no commas are necessary.

> My favorite actor, Tom Hanks, has won a number of Academy Awards.

> Actor Tom Hanks has won a number of Academy Awards.

In the first sentence, *Tom Hanks* isn't necessary to the meaning of the sentence, because "my favorite actor" is pretty specific, and the sentence can stand alone without the name. In the second sentence, *Tom Hanks* is necessary because it tells you which actor won a number of Academy Awards. On the ACT, you'll need to make a quick judgment call about whether a noun/noun phrase says enough on its own without the appositive phrase. If it conveys enough information, set off the appositive with commas. If the noun alone doesn't tell you enough to complete the sentence and make it clear, delete the commas.

Now try this quick exercise question on your own. Keep in mind that the English questions on the ACT will relate to a larger passage and not a standalone sentence like the examples you will see throughout the chapter.

. . . .

The Baseball Hall of Fame just admitted Ken Griffey, Jr. who was voted in almost
                                                                    2
unanimously.
    2

2.   **F.**   NO CHANGE
    G.   The Baseball Hall of Fame, who was voted in almost unanimously, just admitted Ken Griffey, Jr.
    H.   The Baseball Hall of Fame just admitted Ken Griffey, Jr., who was voted in almost unanimously.
    J.   Ken Griffey, Jr. who was voted in almost unanimously, was just admitted to the Baseball Hall of Fame.

The correct answer is H. "Who was voted in almost unanimously" is an appositive phrase that modifies *Ken Griffey, Jr.* It's not an essential clause, because removing it doesn't interfere with the main meaning of the sentence: *The Baseball Hall of Fame just admitted Ken Griffey, Jr.* Choice F is incorrect because a nonessential clause needs a comma (or other punctuation) to set it off. Choice G is incorrect because it shifts the appositive to describe *the Baseball Hall of Fame,* which changes the meaning of the sentence altogether. Choice H is correct because it adds the comma. Choice J is incorrect because it's still missing a comma after *Ken Griffey, Jr.*

. . . .

Commas and Complex Lists

On the ACT you may see sophisticated sentences that have complicated lists of ideas. As with the simple lists, commas may be the best way to set them off—but you need to be careful that in doing so, you're not setting up a run-on sentence. Lists are easy if the items are all clear: *The only fruit left in the basket are apples, bananas, and mangoes.* All of the list items are self-contained plural nouns, so it's not too difficult to see where the commas should go. Things get trickier when you start including complex phrases or compound nouns.

> *The most important qualities we're looking for include attention to detail professionalism ability to meet deadlines and punctuality.*

In this sentence, you need to decipher what the individual elements are, and then place commas after each one. One of the best ways to figure this out on the fly is to listen to how it sounds in your head. Wherever you hear the natural pauses, consider adding a comma.

> *The most important qualities we're looking for include attention to detail, professionalism, ability to meet deadlines, and punctuality.*

When a list contains compound nouns, it can be similarly confusing. As with the appositives, you'll need to make a judgment call about which words and phrases belong together and which ones need to be separated by commas.

> *The Olympic events I'm most looking forward to this year are water polo, the steeplechase, track, and field, and gymnastics.*

In this sentence, the extra *and* complicates things. Should *track, field*, and *gymnastics* all be separate list items? No, because *track and field* is one general sport, so there should be no comma within that phrase.

> *The Olympic events I'm most looking forward to this year are water polo, the steeplechase, track and field, and gymnastics.*

On test day, you should also be on the lookout for lists that contain complex ideas, not just separate objects.

> *F. Scott Fitzgerald's* The Great Gatsby *explores complex themes like what it means to achieve the "American dream," what costs come with wealth and power, whether love and infatuation are the same thing, and what it means to be a true friend.*

All of the items in the list are dependent clauses that are given equal weight in the writer's overview of the book, so it's okay to use commas. This gets tricky, though—you'll want to double check to make sure that the commas you're adding (or taking away) don't lead to fragments or a run-on sentence.

Now let's try this quick exercise question.

. . . .

According to the company's mission statement, <u>we value certain things very highly,</u>

3

<u>like honesty and commitment to customer service. There's also personal integrity,</u>

3

<u>which we value as well.</u>

3

3. A. NO CHANGE
   B. we value certain things very highly. Like honesty, commitment to customer service, and personal integrity.
   C. honesty is valued very highly, and also commitment to customer service and personal integrity.
   D. we value certain things very highly, like honesty, commitment to customer service, and personal integrity.

The correct answer is D. The two sentences in the question present three equal concepts that all describe the company's values: *honesty*, *commitment to customer service*, and *personal integrity*. These should be grouped into one concise list, separated by commas. Choice D does this, so it is correct. Choice A is incorrect because it has a partial list and an unnecessary extra sentence. Choice B is incorrect because it creates a sentence fragment containing the list of values. Choice C is incorrect because the three list elements are not presented in a straightforward list.

. . . .

COLONS

Speaking of lists, the colon (:) becomes the comma's perfect partner. If a list is long, consider using a colon to set it off, so that the sentence isn't bogged down by a confusing list of items. The colon should also be used if there's a complete sentence before the list begins.

> *I signed up for the following classes: English 101, Math 104, American History 200, and Physics 103.*

Note: Don't use a colon to set off a list if the list directly follows a verb or preposition that wouldn't normally require extra punctuation. For example, there should not be a colon after *for* in the following sentence.

> *I signed up for English 101, Math 104, American History 200, and Physics 103.*

Identifying how to use colons with lists is fairly common on the ACT English test. However, colons may also figure prominently in the more challenging questions. In addition to setting off easily identifiable lists of items, colons are also used as a pause to set off a related idea. Use a colon instead of a comma or semicolon between independent clauses if one of the clauses explains, illustrates, or clarifies the other one.

Kira was happy with the present she got for her birthday: she had needed a new watch ever since the old one broke a few months ago.

Joel's goofy jokes were welcome: the party really needed livening up.

It's easy to get to Baker Street from here: just take a left at Bramwell Avenue and drive for about 500 feet.

The colon is a way to balance independent clauses that complement each other without adding extra coordinating words or phrases. Colons are an effective way to introduce new information without having to break related clauses into chunky sentences.

 Use colons only after a complete sentence/independent clause. Never use a colon after a sentence fragment.

Colons are also used to introduce direct quotes (especially long ones with multiple sentences) to avoid an indistinct transition from the writer's voice to the speaker's voice.

Mr. Edwards had plenty to say on the issue: "I don't believe killer whales should be kept in captivity. They're born for the open seas, and yet we keep them in tiny tanks. I think we should release all of them back into their natural habitats."

In short, colons are the most effective way to give additional information to illustrate a point.

SEMICOLONS

Along with colons, semicolons (;) are the hard stops within sentences. They prompt the reader to pause longer than they would for a comma and indicate that there is a separation of ideas. Like colons, semicolons are often used to join two related independent clauses without forcing them into separate sentences.

The show doesn't start until 8 a.m.; if you leave now, you should make it in time.

To prepare for your vacation in Europe, be sure to renew your passport; you should also buy a travel guide.

 ALERT: Be extra careful not to confuse colons and semicolons. Some of the most challenging punctuation questions on the ACT English test will require you to know the nuances between colons, semicolons, and commas in sentences.

Semicolons are most commonly used to join two independent ideas that are thematically linked, but not necessarily describing one another. You can use semicolons to add variety to your sentences. For example, if a paragraph is made up of a number of short, choppy sentences, a semicolon to join at least two of them would help break up that monotony and improve the flow of the paragraph.

Semicolons can also be used in long or complicated lists of items, in place of commas. This can help untangle unwieldy lists and separate the elements very clearly for the reader.

> *The best man's toast touched on a number of memorable moments from his relationship with the groom: the time they met at summer camp; a disastrous double date they had in high school; their college graduation; and the time the best man introduced the groom to his eventual bride.*

Should I Use a Semicolon or a Colon?

Figuring out which type of punctuation you need can be challenging, especially in the gray area involving two independent clauses. If the second clause explains or describes the first, use a colon. If they're just two ideas that are related, but don't have a cause-effect relationship or a descriptive relationship, go with the semicolon. If you have only one independent clause, then leave both the colon and the semicolon behind and pick a comma.

Sentence Structure	Use	Example
Independent clause + explanatory independent clause	Colon	*I was all wet: it had been raining since morning.*
Independent clause + independent clause	Semicolon	*At the fair, Fred wanted to check out the dunking booth; I wanted to go see the animals.*
Independent clause + dependent clause	Neither (use a comma)	*Depending on how much time we have before the movie, we should stop at the mall.*
Independent clause + list	Colon	*Hit the buttons in the following order: red, blue, green, red, and then yellow.*

Try out an ACT-like question to test your skills.

· ·

I was so bored, <u>I'd forgotten</u> to bring a book or magazine with me to my appointment.
    4

4.   **F.**   NO CHANGE
　　　G.   I was so bored: I'd forgotten
　　　H.   I was so bored. I'd forgotten
　　　J.   I was so bored; I'd forgotten

The correct answer is G. Here you have two independent clauses, "I was so bored" and "I'd forgotten to bring a book or magazine with me to my appointment." The second independent clause explains the first: the speaker was bored because he or she forgot to bring reading material. This makes a colon (choice G) the best option. Using a comma (choice F) is incorrect because it creates a run-on sentence. A period (choice H) unnecessarily breaks up the sentence, so it is incorrect. A semicolon (choice J) is close, because of the two independent clauses, but the fact that one clause explains the other makes the colon a slightly better option.

· ·

PARENTHETICAL ELEMENTS

On the ACT English test, you will be asked to recognize parenthetical elements in sentences and punctuate them properly. A parenthetical element is similar to an appositive in that it offers extra information in the sentence. Yet unlike an appositive, a parenthetical element is *almost always nonessential*. Following the same rules as an appositive, a parenthetical element should be set off by punctuation so that the reader knows it's extra (and possibly helpful) information, but not necessary to understand the sentence.

Parentheses

The most common punctuation for a parenthetical element is its namesake, the parentheses: ( ). Parentheses are used to bracket the information to make it clearly separate from the main parts of the sentence. Parentheses usually contain one of the following pieces of information:

- Appositives *(the green one)*
- Relative clauses or phrases that typically start with *who/whom/whose, which, where,* or *when (which he knew would never happen)*
- Verb phrases that describe the preceding noun *(making it difficult to see the moon)*
- Prepositional phrases that describe the preceding noun *(by a large margin)*
- Examples *(for example, such as, e.g., i.e.)*

Em Dashes

The more advanced English questions on the ACT could ask you to use a variety of punctuation to set off parenthetical elements. The most basic is the comma, followed by actual parentheses. However, parenthetical elements can also be set off by em dashes (—). Em dashes are used for strong emphasis. When you really want to make sure that the additional information is clearly set off on its own, em dashes can be very effective.

These changes—effective immediately—apply to all students.

The election results—which are not yet final—show that the incumbent mayor has a large lead.

My brother—who was supposed to be grounded—snuck out of the house around 9 p.m. last night to see a movie with his friends.

All three types of punctuation (commas, parentheses, and em dashes) are correct for setting off parenthetical phrases. The one you choose depends on what kind of emphasis you want to put on the information being set aside. Parentheses and em dashes add more visual interest to a sentence and can elevate the flow of a sentence and paragraph.

Now try a quick sample question.

· ·

Mary Anne stopped at the mall to exchange <u>the blue sweater for the yellow one—</u>

                                                                                5

<u>(which was the one she wanted in the first place)</u>.

                                5

5.   **A.**   NO CHANGE
     B.   the blue sweater for the yellow one which was the one she wanted in the first place.
     C.   the blue sweater for the yellow one (which was the one she wanted in the first place).
     D.   (the blue sweater for the yellow one, which was the one she wanted in the first place).

The correct answer is C. The parenthetical information here should be a nonessential clause, and it should be set off by a comma, parentheses, or em dash. Choice A is incorrect because it uses both an em dash and the parentheses, which is not necessary. Choice B is incorrect because it removes all punctuation and turns "which was the one she wanted in the first place" into an essential clause. Choice C is correct because it places parentheses around the nonessential clause. Choice D is incorrect because the placement of the parentheses is off—"the blue sweater for the yellow one" is essential information and not part of the descriptive clause.

· ·

APOSTROPHES

The apostrophe is one of the trickier punctuation marks you'll encounter on the ACT. When you're reading text quickly (as you'll be doing on the test), apostrophes can be easy to miss in the flow of a sentence. Yet they're among the most crucial pieces of punctuation to know inside and out, as an apostrophe can change the entire meaning of a sentence. Knowing when to hold 'em (add an apostrophe) and when to fold 'em (delete an apostrophe) can really boost your punctuation confidence on test day.

Apostrophes have three basic jobs: forming contractions, showing possession, and forming (some) plurals.

- **Contraction:** *I hadn't thought of that.*

- **Possession:** *Mary's speech was by far the most stirring one of the evening.*

- **Plural:** *My report card had 3 A's and 2 B's this semester.*

The forms we're most concerned with here are possessives and plurals. Contractions may appear on the ACT, but basic contractions are considered a lower level of difficulty on the exam. If you know how to use apostrophes to show possession and when to use them (or, more specifically, when *not* to use them) in plural nouns, you'll be prepared for the more advanced apostrophe punctuation questions on test day.

Possession

Apostrophes are used to show who possesses what. For singular nouns (which don't end in *s*), the rule is simple: add *'s*.

> *Darryl's driving test didn't go so well.*

> *The survey's results were surprising.*

> *Monday's staff meeting has been rescheduled for Thursday.*

For singular nouns that *do* end in *s*, the rule is actually the same—you add *'s*, although that can feel a bit unnatural when you're writing it out.

> *The princess's fairy tale ending just doesn't ring true to me.*

> *Francis's spelling bee win was announced in the local newspaper.*

> *Jonathan Swift wrote about Mars's moons Phobos and Deimos in his novel Gulliver's Travels.*

For plural possessive nouns, add the apostrophe *after* the final *s*.

> *Julio organized the books' spines by color.*

> *Melvin was dismayed that all of the reviews' tones were negative.*

> *Jeremy spent an hour on Christmas morning picking up the girls' discarded wrapping paper.*

There's an important exception to the plural possessive rule: irregular plural nouns. These are nouns like *man, woman, person,* and *child,* where the plural form doesn't end in *s*. In the case of an irregular plural noun, you go back to *'s*, since the words don't end in *s* already.

Be on the lookout for irregular plural nouns when making possessive apostrophe decisions. Some of the most common are listed in the following table:

Singular Noun	Plural Noun	Plural Possessive
Child	Children	Children's
Goose	Geese	Geese's
Man	Men	Men's
Mouse	Mice	Mice's
Ox	Oxen	Oxen's

Singular Noun	Plural Noun	Plural Possessive
Person	People	People's
Tooth	Teeth	Teeth's
Woman	Women	Women's

Plurals

As a rule, apostrophes are not used in standard plural words. If you see a word with an apostrophe on the ACT and it doesn't appear to be possessive (e.g., followed by a noun), then that's a red flag. The only time apostrophes should be used in basic plural words is when *not* using an apostrophe would make for awkward and confusing construction.

Take, for example, single letters used in a sentence.

Incorrect: *I got all As on my report card*

Correct: *I got all A's on my report card.*

In cases like this, you need the apostrophe to tell the reader that the writer is talking about multiple instances of *A*. These instances are rare, however, and you should be on the lookout for extraneous apostrophes cluttering up plural nouns.

One commonly confused apostrophe area is plural dates, especially when one is talking about entire decades.

Incorrect: *My sister was born in the 1990's.*

Correct: *My sister was born in the 1990s.*

When referring to decades, think of it as a collection of years (plural years). Use an apostrophe only if the year happens to be possessive. Both of the following are correct:

The Shining *was one of 1980's most popular movies.*

The 1970s were the peak years of disco music.

The correct use of apostrophes in plural nouns is pretty rare. In order to focus your ACT prep on the concepts you're most likely to see on test day, work on identifying and removing apostrophes that don't belong, or moving misplaced apostrophes in possessive nouns.

Should I Use an Apostrophe Or Not?

On the ACT, you will likely be asked to determine whether some words need apostrophes or have apostrophes that will need to be deleted. To do this, you'll have to size up the underlined word (and the surrounding words) to figure out if the word is possessive, plural, or none of the above.

There are two quick checks you can perform to see what you need to do, apostrophe-wise.

1. **Is it possessive?** Look at the next word in the sentence. If it's a noun, the underlined word is likely possessive. Only nouns can be possessed, so if the next word is a preposition, verb, pronoun, article, or conjunction, you can rule out a possessive apostrophe. ***Bottom line: If the next word is a noun, go ahead and add the apostrophe.***

2. **Is it plural?** Be sure to check the number of the word in question. From the context of the sentence, you should be able to tell if the noun is singular or plural. If the word is a possessive pronoun, figure out whether it replaces a singular noun or a plural noun. ***Bottom line: If the possessive noun is singular, use 's. If the possessive noun is plural, use s'.***

Here's a quick reference for correct apostrophe usage.

Form	Apostrophe placement	Example
Singular possessive noun (not ending in s)	's	Carrie's scores were brag-worthy. Climbing Mt. Everest has always been a goal of my mother's.
Singular possessive noun (ending in s)	's	Myles's sneakers were stylish. The boss's speech at Phyllis's retirement party was very touching.
Regular plural noun	[none]	The Smiths went to Virginia Beach last summer. The 1980s featured some fashion that seems crazy by today's standards.
Plural possessive noun	s'	The players' uniforms are gray with blue pinstripes. I tripped over my skates' untied laces.
Irregular plural possessive noun (not ending in s)	's	The children's museum had an exhibit that tested people's knowledge of dinosaurs. I can't decide if I want to major in Women's Studies or Astronomy.

Form	Apostrophe placement	Example
Possessive adjective	[none]	*The last house on the left is ours.* *Hers is the only car left in the parking lot.*

Now, try out a test-like question to practice these skills.

. . . .

Having bought tickets to the Indianapolis <u>Childrens Choir's</u> holiday concert,

6

Hermione was looking forward to inviting Chris.

6. **F.** NO CHANGE
   G. Childrens' Choir's
   H. Childrens' Choirs'
   J. Children's Choir's

The correct answer is J. Look closely at the plurals and the possessives in this sentence. *Children* is an irregular plural noun, meaning it shouldn't end in *s* as a plural. The possessive form should end in *'s*. That eliminates choices F and G. *Choir* is possessive (the holiday concert belongs to the choir) and singular, so it too should end in *'s*. This makes choice H incorrect. Choice J correctly assigns the possessive apostrophes in *Children's* and *Choir's*.

. . . .

GRAMMAR AND USAGE

Grammar and usage questions test how well you can make the pieces of a sentence fit together. The more challenging questions will ask you to take complex sentences with multiple clauses and make decisions about whether the individual elements agree, where they should fit to make the sentence's meaning clear, and whether or not they should be joined in a sentence.

SUBJECT-VERB AGREEMENT

On test day, you'll likely see several different types of subject-verb agreement questions. However, these are not all constructed the same. Some may be basic noun-verb phrases that need to be made consistent. The more challenging questions come when there are words (or entire clauses) between the subject and the verb, and you need to figure out two things: 1) which subject goes with which verb, and 2) how to make them agree.

A singular subject always goes with a singular verb, and a plural subject always goes with a plural verb. That never changes.

Basic Subject-Verb Agreement

> *Three books make up the* Lord of the Rings *trilogy:* The Fellowship of the Ring, The Two Towers, *and* Return of the King.

The subject in the sentence, *books*, is plural, so the verb, *make* needs to be plural as well. The two words are located close together, so you can confirm their agreement pretty easily and quickly. The more advanced questions will ask you to pick out subjects and matching verbs in more complex sentences.

Complex Subject-Verb Agreement

> *The books in the* Lord of the Rings *trilogy,* The Fellowship of the Ring, The Two Towers, *and* Return of the King, *were made into award-winning movies.*

In this example, there's a lot going on. The subject is the same (*books*), but the verb comes significantly later in the sentence, after both a modifying clause (*in the* Lord of the Rings *trilogy*) and a list of book titles. The verb phrase "were made" should be plural to match the subject. Don't let the singular word *trilogy* distract you into thinking it might be the subject—it's part of a prepositional phrase modifying the actual subject, *books*.

Another tricky area to be aware of in your test prep is the compound subject. Two singular nouns can make it *seem* like the verb should be singular, especially when you're reading quickly. Don't fall for it! A compound subject is really plural.

> *Bert and Ernie have been roommates for a long time.*

Bert has been and Ernie has been—but together, both of them have been.

> *In my opinion, oatmeal and tomato juice make the best breakfast.*

The subject here is not *breakfast*, *oatmeal*, or *tomato juice* (all singular), but rather *oatmeal and tomato juice* (plural). The verb (*to make*) should match that plural subject. Taking the extra few seconds to make sure you've got the right subject matched up to the verb(s) can help you get ahead of very avoidable mistakes on test day.

PRONOUNS

Pronouns take the place of nouns and are an essential part of making writing more concise. They're a basic part of speech, but the reason you want to focus on them for advanced ACT prep is that there are many ways that pronoun use can go wrong, from disagreement between pronouns and antecedents (the nouns to which they refer) to reflexive, possessive, or relative pronouns gone awry. One of the most common pronoun issues is one that plagues students and lifelong writers alike: the *who* vs. *whom* battle. Feeling solid on pronoun usage will serve you well in the upper levels of ACT difficulty.

Pronoun Agreement

Pronouns should match the nouns they replace. That means matching them in all aspects: person, number, gender, and case (whether the pronoun is standing in for the subject or object of the sentence). There's a finite number of pronouns, so it's best to know them cold as part of your prep. Before we dive into the nuances of agreement, let's do a quick review of the pronouns you're likely to see on test day.

Subject pronouns stand in for a noun that acts as the subject of the sentence. These are the subject pronouns:

Singular Subject Pronoun	Plural Subject Pronoun
I	We
You	You
He	They
She	They
It	They
One	They

Object pronouns stand in for a noun that acts as the object of a sentence. These are the object pronouns:

Singular Object Pronoun	Plural Object Pronoun
Me	Us
You	You
Him	Them
Her	Them
It	Them
One	Them

Some of the more challenging pronoun-related questions on the ACT will require you to recognize pronoun-antecedent agreement in sentences that are complex—or in different sentences altogether.

When you spot a pronoun in a passage, look closely for the related noun to see how they match up. Sometimes you'll need to consider a group of sentences to make sure everything is shaking out properly.

> *Harry and Melissa bought a house last year in the suburbs. Now that spring is coming, they want to start planting in their garden.*

The plural pronoun in the second sentence, *they*, needs to match up with the closest subject. To check, you'll need to review the nouns to determine the antecedent and see if the pronoun is correct. In the first sentence, the nouns are *Harry, Melissa, house*, and *suburbs. House* is an object (it was bought), so it's not the antecedent. *Suburbs* is part of a prepositional phrase that is modifying the object *house*. So it's not the subject either. That leaves *Harry and Melissa*, which is a compound subject and therefore plural. The plural pronoun matches the plural subject.

> *Ginny called to let me know she'd be late, so I set aside her dinner so that I could warm her up once she got in.*

Because there are two independent clauses here (coordinated by *so*), there are actually two subjects in play (*Ginny* and *I*), and several pronoun combinations. So how do we know which pronouns are referring to which nouns? To determine this, you need to look at the meaning of the sentence and what makes the most sense. In the first half of the sentence, *she* clearly refers to *Ginny*, so that's fine. In the second part of the sentence, it's less clear. *I* serves as a stand-in for the first-person speaker's name, and that works. The problem comes in with *her* … will the speaker warm up Ginny, or will the speaker warm up the dinner? Here you need to make the judgment call, and it makes most sense that the dinner, not Ginny, is being warmed up. The pronoun needs to change to make the sentence clearer.

The revised sentence reads:

> *Ginny called to let me know she'd be late, so I set aside her dinner so that I could warm it up once she got in.*

To practice your pronoun agreement for the ACT, review complex or related groups of sentences you find in books, magazines—anywhere. Practice spotting the pronouns and matching them with the nouns they replace. The more familiar you get with parsing sentences that way, the easier it'll be for you to fall right into that process on test day, when you have a very limited amount of time to read.

Reflexive and Possessive Pronouns

Reflexive pronouns are a type of pronoun that refers back to the subject of the sentence—meaning the subject and object of the sentence are the same person. Each personal pronoun has a corresponding reflexive pronoun.

Personal Pronoun	Reflexive Pronoun
I	Myself
You (singular)	Yourself
He	Himself
Her	Herself
One	Oneself
It	Itself
We	Ourselves
You (plural)	Yourselves
They	Themselves

Reflexive pronouns are tricky because they're very often used incorrectly, when a regular personal pronoun would be the better option. People often use reflexive pronouns like *myself* to refer to themselves, thinking it sounds more grammatically sophisticated. In reality, regular old object pronouns are more effective—and grammatically correct.

Incorrect: *Please e-mail the report to Andrea and myself.*

Correct: *Please e-mail the report to Andrea and me.*

Reflexive pronouns should be used *only* if they can be connected directly to the subject of the sentence. If you see a *-self* suffix popping up in any questions or text on test day, you should automatically look around for the corresponding subject/noun. Similarly, keep an eye on other pronouns to make sure that regular personal or possessive pronouns shouldn't be reflexive instead.

Johann spilled grape juice all over him right before he left for work.

To make sure we understand exactly what has happened here, we first need to identify who *him* is in this sentence. If you take a quick look at the surrounding sentences and there's no indication that *him* could possibly refer to any other noun, it's safe to assume that Johann spilled the grape juice on himself. If you replace the personal pronoun with its corresponding reflexive pronoun, the sentence is much clearer.

Johann spilled grape juice all over himself before he left for work.

The proper use of reflexive pronouns can increase sentence clarity and make writing more efficient grammatically.

Relative Pronouns

The relative pronouns introduce relative clauses. These are dependent clauses that modify a word or phrase in the sentence's main clause. Relative pronouns serve the purpose of linking that clause with the nouns (or phrases) they modify. Relative pronouns may be part of essential or nonessential clauses.

The relative pronouns are:

- Who
- Whom
- Whose
- Which
- Where
- When
- That

The most important thing to remember about relative pronouns is that they're like any other pronouns: they need to agree with the noun(s) they're replacing. Each relative pronoun has limitations in what it can modify, so it's best to know what each one can and can't modify.

Relative pronoun(s)	Modified word	Example
Who/whom	People	Ella is the one who helped me with my geometry homework.
Where	Places	That's the salon where I get my hair cut.
When	Times	George reminded us of the time last year when we forgot to pick Gino up from soccer practice.
Which	Nonhuman nouns	Bob couldn't decide which answer choice to select.
That	Any noun	The orange kitten is the one that I want to adopt.
Whose	People or things (possessive)	Be sure to thank Mike, whose car we borrowed to drive to Milwaukee.

The most challenging relative pronoun questions on the English test are likely to call upon some of the most easily confused pairs of relative pronouns:

- who/whom
- which/that

Who vs. Whom

Of the relative pronouns, *who/whom* is the most commonly tested set. It's a pair that confounds not only many ACT test takers, but also many people in general. A lot of people use *whom* because they think it's more formal and grammatically correct, but this isn't always the case. In fact, you're better off going with *who* if you're unsure, contrary to that popular myth about *whom* being more correct. *Who* is by far the most common relative pronoun. There are very specific times when *whom* should be used instead of *who*, and with these tips you should be good to go.

Are you referring to a person who is doing something (the subject of the sentence)? If so, choose *who*. Are you referring to someone who's having something done to him or her (the object of the sentence)? If so, choose *whom*.

Incorrect: *Whom ate the piece of pie I was saving for dessert?*

Correct: *Who ate the piece of pie I was saving for dessert?*

The relative pronoun is the subject of the sentence and the eater of the pie, so it needs to be adjusted to *who*.

Incorrect: *To who am I speaking, please?*

Correct: *To whom am I speaking, please?*

This one's a little tricky because the subject comes later in the sentence. But if you look closely, the *who/whom* is not the subject here—the subject is *I*. The *who/whom* is the person the subject *I* is speaking to, so the pronoun is the object of the sentence. That means *whom* is the correct option.

If you're having trouble telling whether the *who/whom* is the subject or the object, you can try some simple pronoun replacement to see what sounds right. You can insert a personal pronoun (with the same case) into the sentence.

Who (subject) pronouns	*Whom* (object) pronouns
He	Him
She	Her
They	Them

If *he/she/they* works better in the sentence, use *who*. If *him/her/them* works better in the sentence, go with *whom*.

Mrs. Tate, who everyone loves, won the Teacher of the Year award.

In this case, Mrs. Tate is feminine and singular, so try rephrasing the meaning of the sentence and inserting the pronouns *she* and *her* into it.

> *everyone loves Mrs. Tate*

> *everyone loves she*

> *everyone loves her*

Her is the right option here. It's grammatically solid, but it also just *sounds* right. So the corrected sentence should be as follows:

> *Mrs. Tate, whom everyone loves, won the Teacher of the Year award.*

Now try your hand at choosing *who* or *whom* correctly.

. . . .

In this election, I plan to vote for the candidate <u>who</u> has the strongest record on

    7

environmental issues.

7. **A.** NO CHANGE
    B. whom
    C. that
    D. whose

The correct answer is A. The sentence is correct as written. If you try to rephrase the sentence with an alternative subject pronoun, it works: *He/she is the candidate with the strongest record on environmental issues.* The pronoun functions as a subject, so it's *who*. Choice B is incorrect because it uses *whom*. Choice C is incorrect because it uses the pronoun *that* (which usually refers to an object) to refer to a person. Choice D is incorrect because the pronoun *whose* is possessive.

. . . .

Don't be afraid to trust your ear in the great *who* vs. *whom* debate. If something sounds awkward to you, it's likely incorrect. Go with your instincts!

Which vs. That

To get that perfect score on the English test, you should also be prepared to tell the difference between *which* and *that*. Which option is correct?

> *The University of Nebraska, which is my alma mater, won the NCAA basketball tournament this year.*

> *The University of Nebraska, that is my alma mater, won the NCAA basketball tournament this year.*

The key to decoding *which* and *that* quickly and efficiently on test day is knowing how each one should fit into the sentence. There's actually a pretty simple way to break it down: use *that* before a restrictive clause, and use *which* before a nonrestrictive clause.

In the previous example, the relative pronoun appears in a nonrestrictive clause—the writer is giving additional information about the University of Nebraska, but the sentence works just fine without knowing that the university is the writer's alma mater. So because it's a nonrestrictive clause, *which* is correct.

> *The University of Nebraska, which is my alma mater, won the NCAA basketball tournament this year.*

Let's try another one.

> *The grocery store no longer stocks the brand of cookies which I love.*

> *The grocery store no longer stocks the brand of cookies that I love.*

Here, the clause is a restrictive one. The writer is talking about a specific brand of cookies. Without "____ I love," the reader has no idea what kind of cookies the writer is talking about. Because the clause is restrictive, the correct choice is *that*.

> *The grocery store no longer stocks the brand of cookies that I love.*

Remember: *who* and *whom* are the relative pronouns you use to modify people. *Which* and *that* should be used only to modify things or ideas. You'll never use *which* to describe a person. On test day, zero in on relative pronouns and do a quick check to see what (or whom) they're supposed to be modifying. If you keep the rules *who/whom* = person and *that/which* = thing in mind, that can help you work through pronoun errors quickly.

The quick and dirty way to remember *that* vs. *which*: ask yourself, "is this clause necessary?" If yes, *that* is your answer. If not, *which* is the way to go.

Which we ended up lost should be no surprise, considering we put the wrong address
into the GPS.

8. **F.** NO CHANGE
   G. We ended up lost should be no surprise,
   H. That which we ended up lost should be no surprise,
   J. That we ended up lost should be no surprise,

The correct answer is J. The relative pronoun at the start of the sentence (choice F) is confusing. The sentence starts with a restrictive clause, so *that* is the correct relative pronoun to use (choice J). Choice G is incorrect because it deletes the pronoun altogether. Choice H is incorrect because it doubles up on the relative pronouns.

COMMONLY CONFUSED WORDS

The ACT test makers love to sneak in commonly confused words to try to trip up even the savviest test takers. Everyone has a word pair that trips them up every once in a while—*affect* and *effect* have tortured many a writer over the years. And while *affect* and *effect* are among the most common words, you should also be on the lookout for the less common ones.

Here are some of the more challenging word choices you might need to evaluate on the ACT:

Word	Meaning	Word	Meaning
accept	to receive	except	not including
access	permission	excess	too much
addition	extra	edition	version
adopt	to take in	adapt	to change
advice	suggestion of what to do	advise	to make a suggestion
adverse	negative	averse	opposed to
afflict	to cause suffering	inflict	to impose
afterward	later, after an event	afterword	postscript
aisle	a lane	isle	an island
allude	to refer to something	elude	to escape

Word	Meaning	Word	Meaning
allusion	an indirect reference to something	illusion	perception that isn't real
altar	table used in religious services	alter	to change
a lot	a large number	allot	to assign something
ambivalent	having mixed feelings	ambiguous	something that has more than one interpretation/ meaning
amend	to change	emend	to edit text
amoral	having no morals one way or the other	immoral	against accepted morals
amused	entertained	bemused	bewildered
anecdote	personal story	antidote	solution or cure
angel	spiritual being	angle	space formed by the meeting of lines
apart	separate	a part	one piece
appraise	to judge the value of something	apprise	to take stock of a situation
ascent	rise	assent	agreement
assistance	help	assistants	people who help
auditory	pertaining to the ear/hearing	audible	hearable
aural	pertaining to the ear	oral	by mouth
bare	naked	bear	to carry (as in a burden)
bazaar	a market	bizarre	strange

Word	Meaning	Word	Meaning
berth	a bed on a train or ship	birth	the act of being born
born	brought into the world	borne	carried
bough	tree branch	bow	a weapon or a part of a ship
breath	air in the lungs	breadth	width
brake	to stop	break	to split into pieces
canvas	material	canvass	to go door-to-door
capital	wealth, or a city where government is centered	capitol	legislature
choose	to select	chose	already selected
climactic	describing a major event	climatic	describing climate or weather
coarse	rough	course	a route or part of a meal
collaborate	to work together	corroborate	to confirm
command	to lead	commend	to praise
complement	to supplement or enhance something	compliment	to praise someone
conscience	inner sense of right and wrong	conscious	awake or alert
contemptuous	feeling contempt toward something	contemptible	something deserving of contempt
corps	a group (as in an army)	corpse	dead body
council	governing body	counsel	to give advice

Word	Meaning	Word	Meaning
dairy	related to milk	diary	journal
descent	moving downward	dissent	opposition
desirous	wanting	desirable	wanted
dessert	treats or sweet food after a meal	desert	geographical region that is very dry
discreet	cautious	discrete	separate or apart from something
disinterested	having no stake in the matter	uninterested	having no personal interest in something
die	to stop living	dye	colored ink
dyeing	coloring	dying	ending life
elegy	poem or song	eulogy	funeral speech
elicit	to draw out or request	illicit	illegal or against the rules
eminent	of high rank, distinguished	imminent	about to happen
emit	to give out	omit	to leave out
exhaustive	comprehensive	exhausting	tiring
expandable	able to grow or expand	expendable	unnecessary
explicit	stated exactly	implicit	implied
farther	at a greater physical distance	further	at a greater figurative distance
flaunt	to show off	flout	to reject
formally	officially	formerly	previously

Word	Meaning	Word	Meaning
foreboding	dread	forbidding	scary
human	a person	humane	compassionate
implicit	implied	complicit	joined together in an activity (especially illegal)
imply	to suggest	implicate	to accuse
incur	to accumulate (as in fines)	occur	to happen
influence	power	affluence	wealth
ingenious	brilliant	ingenuous	straightforward
lightning	natural electrical pulse	lightening	making lighter
moral	a lesson or principle	morale	feeling of enthusiasm
passed	past participle of *to pass*	past	the time before the present
precede	to come before something	proceed	to keep going
precedent	a previous example	president	a leader
prescribe	to order the use of something	proscribe	to prohibit
principal	main	principle	a value or concept
quiet	not loud	quite	very
rain	wet weather	reign	ruling period
raise	to lift	raze	to destroy
rational	reasonable	rationale	an explanation

Word	Meaning	Word	Meaning
respectfully	with deference or respect	respectively	in order
stationary	not moving	stationery	writing paper
straight	not crooked or curved	strait	narrow channel between two bodies of water
suppose	to theorize	supposed to	obligated to do something
than	conjunction used in comparisons	then	adverb used to express order or time
their	possessive plural pronoun	there	place or location
through	continuing on a journey	threw	past participle of *to throw*
whose	possessive form of *who* or *which*	who's	contraction of *who is*
your	possessive pronoun	you're	contraction of *you are*

Now try this quick practice question.

. . . .

The correct answer alludes me, so I'm going to need some extra help figuring it out.
9

9. **A.** NO CHANGE
    B. allusion
    C. eludes
    D. illustrates

The correct answer is C. From the context, you can tell that the writer doesn't have the answer, so the meaning of the verb should back that up. Choice A is incorrect because *allude* means "to refer to something." Choice B is incorrect because *allusion* is a noun, not a verb, and the root word *allude* is still wrong. Choice C is correct because *elude* means "to escape," and the answer has escaped the speaker so far. Choice D is incorrect because an answer can't illustrate a person, so the meaning and purpose of the under-lined text wouldn't fit with the rest of the sentence.

. . . .

Idioms

In addition to using correct words in context, the ACT also tests your knowledge of common idioms. Idioms are phrases that are used commonly in everyday speech, writing, and culture, but that aren't necessarily part of the grammar cannon. They're often expressions that just sound familiar: *across from* something, *throw it out, on the clock.* Idioms are a special grammar case because rather than relying on a set of rules, you're relying on your own eyes and ears—does it *look* right? Does it *sound* right to you? More advanced test takers should be able not only to recognize idioms but also to make sure that the components of the phrase (especially prepositions) are correct.

Here, we're going to focus on prepositional idioms. Prepositional idioms are an essential part of getting top-tier points on the ACT. The test makers want to be sure that you can not only identify common phrases, but also assign the correct preposition to complete the phrase.

> How *about* it?
>
> How *on* it?
>
> How *with* it?

Of these, only one sounds correct. (When is the last time you turned to someone and said, "I could go for some nachos right now. How on it?") Because so much of idiom identification relies on personal instinct, you already have the tools to work through any idiom ID questions. It's just a matter of making sure you're familiar with some of the most common prepositional idioms so that you're reminding your brain about what sounds right.

The following table features some of the prepositional idioms you may see (or need to adjust) on test day:

About	bring about; complain about; curious about; think about; to be happy about; to be particular about; wonder about; worry about
Against	defend against; protect against; protest against; up against
At	be adept at; succeed at; to work at
Around	from miles around; right around; to go around; hang around
By	accompanied by; amazed by; awed by; confused by; demonstrated by; encouraged by; followed by; impressed by; motivated by; outraged by; perplexed by; predated by; puzzled by; shocked by; stunned by; surprised by
For	advocate for; blame for; celebrated for; compensate for; criticize for; endure for; famous for; have a tolerance for; known for; last for; look out for; make for; named for; necessary for; prized for; recognized for; responsible for; strive for; wait for; watch for

From	apparent from; apart from; benefit from; defend from; different from; far from; opposite from; protect from; refrain from
Into	enter into; have insight into; walk into
In	engage in; have confidence in; interested in; succeed in; take pride in
On	based on; draw on; insist on; focus on; rely on; reflect on; dwell on
Over	have power over; have control over; mull over; to be over it
Of	a command of; a knowledge of; a mastery of; a plethora of; a proponent of; a source of; a variety of; have an abundance of; have an understanding of; approve of; capable of; characteristic of; composed of; comprised of; consist of; convinced of; devoid of; disapprove of; have an appreciation of; in awe of; in recognition of; in the hopes of; incapable of; made up of; on the verge of; suspicious of; take advantage of; to be a native of; typical of
To	a threat to; allow to; as an alternative to; as opposed to; be native to; central to; choose to; come to; devoted to; exposure to; immune to; in addition to; in contrast to; in opposition to; listen to; parallel to; prefer something to; put questions to; similar to; try to; unique to
Toward	biased toward; a tendency toward; to work toward
With	associate with; familiar with; consistent with; cope/coping with; correlate with; identify with; inconsistent with; preoccupied with; problem with; sympathize with; unfamiliar with

Again, don't be afraid to rely on your instincts. If you see a phrase on the test like *biased to*, but you know you usually hear it as *biased toward*, go with your gut feeling. You don't have much time, so have confidence in your instincts. If you really can't choose a correct answer among similar options, rule out the ones that really don't sound right, pick from the remaining choices, and move on to the next question.

Let's take a look at a test-like example.

. . . .

"Shush," said Felix. "You're so loud that you're making a <u>spectacle on us.</u>"
                                                                       10

10. F. NO CHANGE
      G. spectacle over us
      H. spectacle between us
      J. spectacle of us

The correct answer is J. "Making a spectacle of" is a common expression. Choice J is correct because it uses the correct preposition, *of*. Choices F, G, and H are incorrect because the prepositions don't sound or read correctly.

 Even if you're having trouble picking the correct idiom, your instincts can at least help you rule out some of the incorrect ones, leaving you with a smaller field of choices.

SENTENCE STRUCTURE

Once you have the general usage rules and the punctuation rules under your belt, it's time to take a closer look at how those concepts come together in sentences. To get the highest possible score, focus your prep on complex sentences or multiple sentences that are grouped by a particular theme or idea. The ACT will be testing to see how well you can parse sentences of any length and whether you can apply the basic rules (subject-verb agreement, pronoun agreement, punctuation, etc.) while juggling various sentence pieces.

 ALERT: There will be approximately 18 sentence structure questions on the ACT English test, so this is where you want to focus a lot of your prep time.

In this section we'll look at some of the more complicated sentence structure topics you'll face on test day.

SUBORDINATION AND COORDINATION

One of your top goals on the English test is ensuring that the writing in the passage is not only correct but also clear and sophisticated whenever possible. Five passages of short, choppy sentences would drive you nuts after a while—and wouldn't be very reflective of real-world writing. As such, you should understand how to tame unwieldy (or just plain incomplete) sentences and smooth out rough transitions.

For basic coordination, you're probably already familiar with the FANBOYS list of coordinating conjunctions:

For
And
Nor
But
Or
Yet
So

These conjunctions link elements of equal importance—words, phrases, and clauses. You see them a lot in fairly basic sentences made up of two or more independent clauses that need to be joined.

*Martin wants to go to the movies on either Tuesday **or** Wednesday.*

*Lakesha's calendar is mostly open on Thursday, **but** she does have an appointment at 3:00.*

*I'm supposed to leave for Detroit early tomorrow morning, **yet** I haven't even packed.*

For elements and clauses that *aren't* equal, there are subordinating conjunctions (sorry, no handy mnemonic for this list):

after	once	until
although	provided that	when
as	rather than	whenever
because	since	where
before	so that	whereas
even if	than	wherever
even though	that	whether
if	though	while
in order that	unless	why

The subordinate conjunctions are your key to complex sentences. Subordinating conjunctions basically have two roles: transitioning between ideas and letting the reader know which ideas are most important in the sentence. As a transition, subordinate clauses show a time, place, or cause-effect relationship between the sentence elements. As a flag of importance, subordinating conjunctions signal a dependent clause that is related to the main clause, but not quite as important.

Although he's scared of dogs, Perry agreed to watch his sister's Chihuahua.

In this sentence, the main clause (and the main idea of the sentence) is clear: Perry agreed to watch his sister's Chihuahua. The subordinating conjunction *although* tells the reader that the opening clause contains information that is good to have, but that doesn't interfere with the main idea of the overall sentence.

Try this sample question to see what this might look like on the ACT.

. . . .

It's been 10 years since Jodie last ate meat. She still craves bacon sometimes. She'll

never actually give in to that impulse. ¹¹

11. **A.** NO CHANGE
    B. Even though it's been 10 years since Jodie last ate meat, she still craves bacon sometimes, but she'll never actually give in to that impulse.
    C. It's been 10 years since Jodie last ate meat, she still craves bacon sometimes, but she'll never actually give in to that impulse.
    D. It's been 10 years since Jodie last ate meat, when she still craves bacon sometimes, and she'll never actually give in to that impulse.

The correct answer is B. There are three sentences here, all of which are conveying related information. The best bet is to combine them, but also to make sure that they're coordinated properly to avoid a run-on. Choice B does this correctly by establishing a dependent clause with the conjunction *even though*, followed by two independent clauses coordinated by *but* (which shows the relationship between Jodie's temptation and whether or not she'll give in). Choice C is incorrect because the three clauses are still independent (despite the coordinating *but* thrown in), creating a run-on. Choice D is incorrect because *when* is not quite the right subordinating conjunction, and the coordinating conjunction *and* incorrectly sets up the relationship between the second and third clauses.

. . . .

Faulty Subordination and Coordination

The ACT is likely to throw a number of different coordination and subordination errors your way on test day. And for basic sentences like the examples in this section so far, it's usually pretty clear when there's an error in coordinating or subordinating various clauses. Things get a bit trickier when the sentences get longer. Because you're reading a "draft" passage with the writer's mistakes, you'll see everything from run-on sentences to short sentences that shouldn't really be standing on their own. There's no ideal sentence length, so you should be prepared for everything. The most complex questions will ask you to take a look at sentences with lots of moving parts, and determine whether those parts are coordinated correctly.

On test day, you should be looking for faulty subordination. This can be as simple as a conjunction that conveys the opposite of what the sentence means.

> *Because he's scared of dogs, Perry agreed to watch his sister's Chihuahua.*

The logic doesn't make sense—why would his fear of dogs motivate Perry to spend time with one? You should also be on the lookout across all of the passage's sentences to make sure that the coordination makes sense.

Shelly's leaving for vacation tomorrow, but unfortunately her dog sitter fell through at the last possible minute, leaving her in a crunch. Desperate to find someone to take care of Pedro for the week, and having exhausted her contacts list, she called her brother, Perry. Although he's scared of dogs, Perry agreed to watch his sister's Chihuahua.

From this passage, you know that Shelly is desperate. It makes sense that Perry's loyalty to his sister might outweigh his personal aversion to dogs, so the subordinating conjunction (*although*) makes sense here. However, on test day, you won't have the luxury of poring over the entire passage to review the consistency of the sentences. When a coordinating or subordinating conjunction comes up in underlined text, just reread the sentence immediately following or before the text. That can give you the context you need to determine whether the meaning matches up with the structure of the sentence.

In this example paragraph as a whole, how do you check for coordination and subordination issues? Look for the transition words (the conjunctions).

In the first sentence, the word *but* tells you that the sentence should have at least two independent clauses. Check! "Shelly's leaving for vacation tomorrow" and "her dog sitter fell through at the last possible minute."

Next sentence: The word *and* tells you that it should also be connecting two equal elements. Check! It's joining two related dependent clauses: "Desperate to find someone to take care of Pedro for the week" and "having exhausted her contacts list" both describe Shelly.

Third sentence: *Although* signals the dependent clause, so you'll automatically know to look for an independent clause to complete the thought. Check! "Perry agreed to watch his sister's Chihuahua" completes the sentence, and the conjunction sets up the appropriate comparison between Perry's fear and his agreement to watch the dog.

This is why knowing the coordinating and subordinating conjunctions is so important going into test day—you want to see the transition words and think, "Aha! This sentence should be a comparison. Is it?" Similarly, you want to be able to read a sentence and say, "Hmm, this is missing a conjunction that suggests a cause-and-effect relationship."

Try out this practice question.

· ·

We have no problem with you going to the concert on Saturday, <u>whereas</u> you
                                                                                                12
complete your chores (all of them) and your homework ahead of time.

12. F. NO CHANGE
  G. rather than
  H. provided that
  J. because

The correct answer is H. *Whereas* (choice F) means "in contrast with the fact that" which is confusing—it appears the writer/speaker is setting conditions for "you" to meet, so it doesn't make sense to make a contrast. *Rather than* (choice G) also sets up a comparison, so it is incorrect. *Provided that* is correct because it means "on the condition that" which makes sense within the broader sentence. *Because* (choice J) is incorrect because the list of conditions themselves doesn't necessarily justify going to the concert.

· ·

Weak Conjunctions

Having the ability to spot less-than-ideal conjunctions is an advanced skill for the ACT English test. Much of the test is based on finding glaring errors and fixing the immediate issue. This is a more subtle area, where you can demonstrate a real understanding of when things are fine, but could be better.

You can spot weak conjunctions pretty easily: they usually involve *for, as,* or *so*— conjunctions that usually show cause and effect.

> She had to walk, for she missed the 8:30 bus.

> Claire recruited Sunny to help her with her science fair project, as there were only two days left before the deadline.

> Matthew made sure to mop the floor right away, so as to avoid anyone slipping in the milk he'd spilled.

Are these sentences technically grammatically correct? Yes. Do they sound a little too formal and haphazardly connected? Also yes. Being direct makes for better, clearer writing. If you're trying to show a cause and effect, use the more straightforward *because.*

> Because she missed the 8:30 bus, she had to walk.

> Claire recruited Sunny to help her with her science fair project because there were only two days left before the deadline and she had a lot left to do.

For *so,* make sure that the cause-and-effect relationship is as clear as possible.

> So that no one would slip in the milk he'd spilled, Matthew made sure to mop the floor right away.

You don't need to analyze every single conjunction in a passage to determine whether it *could* be better, but if you come across a question that involves the conjunctions *for, as,* or *so,* definitely take a closer look.

For he will not be home on Saturday, we will reschedule the *Walking Dead* marathon
13
for Sunday instead.

13. A. NO CHANGE
   B. So
   C. Because
   D. Being as

The correct answer is C. The speaker is explaining the marathon rescheduling, so the conjunction needs to set up the *x is the reason for y* (cause-and-effect) relationship. The sentence is inverted, so it's a bit confusing, but that confusion can be cleared up by picking a stronger conjunction to kick off the sentence. Choice C is correct because *because* sets up that relationship and makes it clear from the outset. Choice B is incorrect because it uses another weak conjunction, and the sentence is still awkward. Choice D is incorrect because although *being as* is a common conjunction in casual speech, it's not grammatically correct.

MISSING AND MISPLACED MODIFIERS

You've likely covered basic misplaced modifiers in other grammar lessons, but on the ACT, some of the most challenging sentence questions will ask you to find them in long or complicated sentences. Don't worry, though: the same golden rule applies. Modifiers should be located as close to the modify-ee as possible. It should also be clear that the phrase is modifying an element actually in the sentence and not left dangling by information that never made it into the sentence.

Misplaced Modifiers

Can you spot the modifier issue in this sentence?

> *Visitors to Mt. Rushmore, having seen the sculpture so many times on TV or in movies, are often amazed by the sheer size of the memorial and are taken aback by its beauty in person.*

The modifying clause, "having seen the sculpture so many times on TV or in movies," describes *Mt. Rushmore*, right? Or does it modify the visitors? Or *memorial*? It's unlikely that Mt. Rushmore has watched much TV, so something is definitely off. The clauses themselves are fine, but they should be juggled so that the meaning is clearer.

> *Having seen the sculpture so many times on TV or in movies, visitors to Mt. Rushmore are often amazed by the sheer size of the memorial and are taken aback by its beauty in person.*

Dangling Modifiers

Sometimes, a modified noun will be absent from the sentence, and you'll need to evaluate whether the sentence is clear enough.

> *Visiting Mt. Rushmore, the monument is breathtaking in person and is even bigger than you might think, only having seen it in pictures.*

This sentence makes it look like the monument is visiting Mt. Rushmore. Also, it's entirely unclear who, exactly, is visiting Mt. Rushmore, because that element is totally missing from the sentence. There's also a bonus modifier error in the second part of the sentence: *only* is confusing. Does the subject only see pictures and nothing else, or has he or she seen Mt. Rushmore, specifically, only in pictures? Here's one way to solve all of the problems:

> *If you have seen Mt. Rushmore only in pictures, you will discover that the monument is breathtaking in person and is even bigger than you might think.*

Always be on the lookout for modifiers that cause confusion—and don't take for granted that there's only one error in the sentence. The best bet with problematic modifier questions, especially ones found in long sentences, is to find an answer choice that restructures the clauses clearly instead of changing just one or two words.

Try to determine if the sample sentence suffers from confusing modifier placement.

. . . .

Earning a black belt has been Kevin's goal ever since he started training in karate,
<u>   </u>
14

fifteen years ago, which is the highest honor that one can receive.
14

14. F. NO CHANGE

    G. Kevin's goal has been, fifteen years after training in karate, earning a black belt—which is the highest honor one can receive.

    H. Kevin's goal, the highest honor one can receive, is to earn his black belt after fifteen years of training in karate.

    J. Ever since he started training in karate fifteen years ago, Kevin's goal has been to earn his black belt—the highest honor that one can receive.

The correct answer is J. As written, the sentence has an incorrectly placed modifier ("which is the highest honor that one can receive"). The phrase describes the black belt, but the way it's placed makes it seem like it could be modifying *Kevin's goal* or even *karate*. Choice G is incorrect because it too has misplaced modifiers and odd clauses. In choice H, "after fifteen years after training in karate" is awkwardly spliced in, so that it looks like it describes *goal*. Choice J is correct because it shuffles the sentence so that "the highest honor that one can receive" is correctly located after *black belt*, and the other clauses flow together as well.

. . . .

Parallelism

Parallelism is another area that pops up at all levels of difficulty on the ACT English test. At the most basic level, you'll need to make sure that simple list elements match.

Incorrect: *I bought a dozen eggs, apple, a pound of cheddar cheese, and bread.*

Correct: *I bought a dozen eggs, one apple, a pound of cheddar cheese, and a loaf of bread.*

Incorrect: *Before games, I have a ritual of eating a peanut butter sandwich, text my dad, and be there 30 minutes before game time.*

Correct: *Before games, I have a ritual of eating a peanut butter sandwich, texting my dad, and arriving 30 minutes before game time.*

Consistency is important in *all* aspects of ACT English, so all elements in a series or list should match in number, tense, and tone. In some of the more complicated instances of parallelism, you'll be tasked with comparing several different parts of sentences. They may or may not be within the same sentence, or even the same paragraph. You'll read more about consistency and organization in the Rhetorical Skills chapter, but this applies in Usage/Mechanics questions as well.

For example:

> *First, soften the butter at room temperature. Then have mixed it with the brown sugar and two eggs. Third, add flour and salt. The cook should have preheated the oven first, so take out your cookie sheets at that point, and get them ready.*

At the start of the paragraph, *first* tips you off that this is a series of steps or events. That means that this pattern should carry throughout the paragraph. Also, the writer goes back and forth between tenses, as well as the subject (the implied subject *you* and *the cook*). At the highest level, the ACT wants you to be able to identify and create parallel structure not just between clear items in a list, but also across sentences, in a complex series of ideas. This paragraph needs to be adjusted so that the steps are clear to the reader and the sentences follow in a similar pattern.

> *First, preheat the oven. Second, soften the butter at room temperature. Third, mix it with the brown sugar and two eggs. Fourth, add flour and salt. Once these steps are complete, take out your cookie sheets.*

By making the sentences more uniform, you've wrangled a series of complex steps into a process that makes sense. Whether it's within a sentence or pertaining to a paragraph overall, look for ways to make sentences flow more smoothly.

SUMMING IT UP

- The **Usage/Mechanics questions test concepts in grammar conventions, punctuation rules, and sentence structure.** Usage/Mechanics questions make up about 50 percent of the ACT English test.

- The most challenging punctuation questions will focus on when to use **advanced types of punctuation** (like semicolons, colons, apostrophes, and parenthetical punctuation).

    ○ Use a **semicolon** when you want to join two independent clauses.

    ○ Use a **colon** if you need to join an independent clause with an independent clause that explains the first one or if you have an independent clause in front of a list.

    ○ **Apostrophes** should only be used in possessive words, not regular plurals.

    ○ For parenthetical statements (like appositives), use **parentheses** or **em dashes** to set them off.

- While the ACT doesn't test verbatim grammar rules or vocabulary, the most advanced questions will ask you to be familiar with various types of **pronouns, commonly known idioms**, and **challenging words** that may be similar to other words with different meanings.

    ○ Pronouns and antecedents should always be matched in number and case and should also be clearly related so that the reader can link the two.

    ○ For idioms, you can often rely on your sense of what sounds right, but be careful about using the correct prepositions (*to succeed at, up against*, etc.).

    ○ The ACT will never test you directly on the definitions of commonly confused words like *allude* and *elude*, but knowing the difference will get you through vocabulary questions with ease.

- **Sentence structure questions** will ask you to identify malfunctioning clauses and faulty subordination and coordination within complex sentences. On test day, you'll be tasked with deconstructing these clauses and coordinating them into clauses that work well together. You should be ready to spot wrong conjunctions, missing conjunctions, and weak conjunctions, as well as mismatched sentence elements that should be made parallel.

CHAPTER 3:
ACT® ENGLISH:
RHETORICAL SKILLS REVIEW

OVERVIEW

- About Rhetorical Skills Questions

- Style

- Strategy

- Organization

- Attacking Rhetorical Skills Passages and Questions for a Perfect Score

- Summing It Up

On your quest to achieve a perfect score on the ACT, you'll encounter questions within the ACT English test that are designed to assess your rhetorical skills. These types of questions assess your ability to analyze a written passage and make decisions regarding the author's deployment of strategy, organization, and style within the passage. You'll be tasked with determining whether the author made appropriate rhetorical choices within the context of the passage at various points in the piece of writing provided, as well as deciding if the alternative options provided in the answer choices of each question serve to enhance and improve the writing and make it more effective.

Why are rhetorical skills such a key part of the ACT? In order to effectively convey your intended meaning and craft an effective, compelling, and persuasive piece of writing, you'll need to properly utilize the core tenets of strategy, organization, and style. As an elite student, you've doubtless recognized that effective verbal and written rhetorical skills are important tools for success in your academic career, and they will continue to remain essential skills for success, both in the classroom and after you graduate and embark upon your chosen professional career path.

Furthermore, your goal of achieving a perfect score on the ACT is most likely tied to a desire to gain acceptance into an elite college or university—possessing effective rhetorical skills is critical for impressing admissions teams, who will be reading your application essays very carefully!

It should now be abundantly clear why you should devote a significant portion of your ACT study plan to building and practicing your rhetorical skills if you're aiming for a perfect score. Let's move forward!

ABOUT RHETORICAL SKILLS QUESTIONS

Compared to questions involving usage and mechanics, rhetorical skills issues can be a bit of a challenge to identify quickly in a piece of writing—even for elite students aiming for a perfect score—because the issues may not always be as immediately obvious as punctuation or spelling errors, for example. Issues of style, strategy, and organization are often more subtle and require a deeper level of reading analysis and comprehension. Factor in the pressure of the ticking clock on test day, and you'll quickly understand why it's in your best interest to come equipped with a proven set of test-taking strategies and plenty of advanced practice if you're going to achieve your perfect score goal.

Take a look at the following brief paragraph:

> *Have you ever heard the song of a nightingale? These wondrous birds are renowned for their powerful and beautiful song, which has been memorialized in myths, poems, operas, and odes throughout history. Owls are known for their large eyes and binocular vision. Scientists believe that the nocturnal song of the nightingale is designed to attract a potential mate.*

Grammatically speaking, there's nothing wrong with this paragraph. The punctuation is in the right place. The sentences are all well-constructed. However, upon closer analysis, there is something wrong with it. A sentence about owls in a paragraph devoted to highlighting the nightingale reflects ineffective writing strategy. In fact, it's downright distracting—it weakens the author's attempt to convince you that the nightingale's song is unique and enchanting. This is the kind of subtle error you will have to recognize when answering rhetorical skills questions on the ACT.

Obviously, all rhetorical skills questions do not deal with off-topic details. Rhetorical skills questions focus on improving the overall clarity and effectiveness of a piece of writing. They also involve making sure that the tone and mood of a piece of writing are consistent and appropriate, that the piece reflects effective organization, that the piece is free from off-topic and redundant details, that transitions between ideas are strong, that wordiness is avoided, and so on.

 Every decision you make on this section of the ACT should accomplish the following goal: improve the quality and effectiveness of the written passages.

In order to achieve a perfect score on the ACT, your ability to assess and make decisions on a wide array of rhetorical issues in a given piece of writing must be razor sharp. On test day (and in the practice you'll find in this book), you'll see various portions of underlined text within the passages provided, and the questions that you'll answer will refer to rhetorical issues related to the underlined text.

You'll be tasked with making decisions about adding, deleting, moving, and revising words, sentences, and phrases within the passage, with the goal being to improve the readability, appropriateness, and effectiveness of the author's work.

As mentioned in Chapter 2, you'll encounter five writing passages and 75 multiple-choice questions on the ACT English test, and you'll have 45 minutes to complete the test. Your Rhetorical Skills subscore will be comprised of how well you answer the following types of questions. We'll first take a brief look at each question type, and then delve deeper, with targeted analysis and practice.

STYLE

Approximately 15–20 percent of questions you'll see on the ACT English test is designed to assess issues of style, including effective word choice and images meant to support and enhance a piece of writing, the appropriateness of an author's tone and style, the level of rhetorical effectiveness achieved through the use of appropriate sentence elements, and the level of effective writing economy achieved through the proper avoidance of ambiguous and redundant words, phrases, or sentences.

Here's an example of a style question that you may encounter on the ACT. This question is designed to assess your ability to decide if an author's word choice is appropriate given the context:

· ·

Should individuals under 18 years of age be allowed to vote? There are boisterous

and passionate voices on both sides of this controversial debate. Opponents of the
                                                                        1
notion to allow individuals under the age of 18 to vote argue that young citizens

should be able to advocate for and support candidates who support their best

interests. Those against the idea of allowing individuals under the age of 18 to vote

contend that this is an uninformed and inexperienced demographic that's in no

position to make intelligent decisions regarding political leadership.

1.　**A.**　NO CHANGE
　　B.　Proponents
　　C.　Critics
　　D.　Majorities

The correct answer is B. Proponents are individuals who support an idea and would be the most appropriate word choice in this instance. Here, the word in question should effectively describe someone who *supports* the notion to allow individuals under the age of 18 to vote, since they are arguing in its defense. *Opponents* represents the opposite word choice. *Critics* (choice C) also describes individuals who would argue *against* an idea. Choice D represents an example of an inappropriate word choice. In the context of the sentence and passage, *majorities* doesn't fit and is also not supported by any evidence provided.

· ·

Context Is Key

Throughout the ACT English test, you'll be tasked with making writing and language decisions for existing passages. Understanding passage context is crucial for making correct decisions, ranging from grammar and word choice to the appropriateness of sentences and holistic organization and construction.

Before jumping on what may seem an obvious answer choice, make sure you *fully* comprehend the context of each question, as well as the author's perspective. On your quest for a perfect score, it will be time well spent!

TONE AND MOOD QUESTIONS

When you read a piece of writing, you should be able to determine how the writer feels about the topic and how he or she wants to make readers feel. Writers employ elements of tone and mood to create their intended effects. At its core, *tone* refers to the author's attitude toward the subject she or he is discussing, and *mood* refers to the emotions that the piece of writing makes readers feel.

Sometimes, it's easy to recognize the intended tone of a piece; at other times, the writer is more subtle or purposefully deceptive. On the ACT, rhetorical skills questions may ask you to identify the audience for a particular piece of writing or determine if the tone or mood of a passage is consistent.

Does a writer appear to be in favor of a particular topic, and then suddenly takes a negative stance without rhyme or reason? Does a writer seem to be establishing a cheerful mood, and then suddenly things get dark for no logical reason? These are the sort of logical inconsistencies that you'll need to be able to recognize and fix. To answer these types of questions, be sure to analyze the tone and mood of the passages provided.

Try to tackle the following question.

· ·

Our quiet little existence was about to completely change. When my mother told me she wanted to move in with my wife and me, I was knocked two ways from Sunday. Why? My wife and I had established a sleepy little life in our small suburban house. We were perfectly happy gardening, reading, and doing other mundane activities that would probably bore most normal people to tears. The idea of my tornado of a mom

2

living with us would basically take that happy existence and stomp all over its head!

2. **F.** NO CHANGE
   G. dear mother
   H. maternal caregiver
   J. most subdued family member

The correct answer is F. Let's think about the mood the writer is trying to establish here. It's clearly one of impending, stressful, and unwelcome upheaval. The author seems to think that the "sleepy little life" that he and his wife have created is about to evaporate with the arrival of his mother. What sort of qualities would his mother have to possess to have the power to completely upend their existence? The description of her as a *tornado*, as written, would be appropriate and is the correct answer here. The other answer choices would lead readers to think that the mother wouldn't be capable of a tumultuous disruption and are not appropriate, given the paragraph's tone.

. . . .

 ALERT: When making these decisions, your goal is *not* to revise the author's perspective or point of view to align it with yours. Remembering this when taking the test will help you save time and avoid some tricky answer choice traps that simply revise the author's intended meaning.

AMBIGUOUS PRONOUNS

We covered pronoun types in the previous chapter, and established that the general rule for pronouns is pretty simple: one pronoun, one antecedent. Sounds easy, right? Not so much, when the ACT starts throwing antecedents at you fast and furious. Ambiguous (or vague) pronouns are the result when a sentence has several potential antecedents, but only one pronoun.

> *After Jacob won first place and Matt won second place, he congratulated him.*

In this sentence, who is *he* and who is *him*? It's difficult to tell whether Matt is congratulating Jacob, or Jacob is congratulating Matt.

> *Have you seen the bad reviews online for the new sushi restaurants in town? No one goes there anymore.*

Is *there* referring to the sushi restaurants or to the town? Or even the review web site? The ACT may ask you to fix ambiguity. The most efficient way to do that is to replace vague pronouns with specific nouns to avoid confusion.

> *After Jacob won first place and Matt won second place, Matt congratulated him.*

> *Have you seen the bad reviews online for the new sushi restaurants in town? No one goes to those restaurants anymore.*

If you see ambiguous pronoun usage in a question or underlined text, quickly read through the answer choices and zero in on the nouns to see which specific nouns make the most sense or, given the context, make an inference about what the writer means.

Now try this quick exercise question.

. . . .

Making time in my schedule for homework is one of my top priorities; I don't want

them to suffer because I spend too much time hanging out with my friends or
‾‾
3
watching TV.

3. **A.** NO CHANGE
    B. it
    C. my grades
    D. us

The correct answer is C. As the sentence is written, the pronoun *them* in the second sentence is problematic. Does it refer to *schedule, priorities, homework,* or something else entirely? With that vagueness, it's difficult to figure out what the writer was trying to say. Choice B is incorrect because it swaps *it* for *them*, but the core problem remains the same—which noun is being modified? Choice C is correct because by replacing the ambiguous pronoun *them* with the words *my grades*, it straightens out the meaning of the sentence and removes the ambiguity about what would be suffering if the writer doesn't do her homework. Choice D is incorrect because *us* is another vague pronoun.

. . . .

WORDINESS QUESTIONS

Strong writing reflects a thorough understanding of word economy—making cogent, concise, and effective points in as few words as possible. Unnecessary words, phrases, and sentences can turn a lean and mean piece of well-structured writing into a bloated, rambling, and confusing mess.

On the ACT English test, you'll likely be tested on your ability to recognize and fix issues of verbosity and word redundancy in the passages provided. These types of questions are typically focused at the sentence level; you'll be tasked with identifying and eradicating wordiness to improve the flow of sentences and, as a result, improve the passages as a whole. However, you typically don't need to analyze the entire passage to handle these types of questions.

 If a question on the ACT English test involves the option to delete text, this is often a signal that there may be issues involving redundancy or wordiness to address.

Let's tackle a sample question.

· ·

Malcolm retrieved a cookbook from the top kitchen shelf and <u>opened the book of</u>
4

<u>recipes</u> to his Aunt Vera's favorite seafood recipe.
4

4. **F.** NO CHANGE
    G. opened the recipe pages
    H. opened another book
    J. opened it

The correct answer is J. If you read the sentence with your critical editorial eye, you may have got the sense that there's a bit of unnecessary wordiness going on. We're told early on that Malcolm retrieved a cookbook, so there's no reason to say that he "opened the book of recipes"—it's unnecessary and redundant. Choice J helps to tighten and refine the sentence by eliminating the wordiness: *Malcolm retrieved a cookbook from the top kitchen shelf and opened it to his Aunt Vera's favorite seafood recipe.*

· ·

Some tricky answer choices for wordiness questions may *seem* correct at first glance, because they correctly delete unnecessary words, yet they are actually incorrect because they delete necessary words as well. Correct answers will eliminate the wordiness *without* depriving the original sentence of key details and meaning.

PASSIVE VS. ACTIVE VOICE QUESTIONS

Another style judgment that writers must make is whether to utilize an **active voice** or a **passive voice** in their writing, as each produces a wholly distinct effect on a final written piece.

The active voice is typically employed in most forms of writing and demonstrates a clear and straightforward connection between the subject of a sentence and the action being performed—the subject directly performs the action. Sentences written in the active voice are typically less wordy, are more impactful and emotionally evocative, and better serve to support the central purpose of a piece of writing.

In contrast, sentences written in the passive voice typically describe the action of the sentence as indirectly happening to the subject. These sentences are typically wordier, more meandering and subtler, and have less of a direct impact on readers.

You may be asked to recognize the use of the passive voice as an ineffective option or be tasked with revising a sentence so that it employs an active voice.

Let's look at an example.

Shara spent the entire morning preparing for her upcoming trip to Australia.

Her passport was placed in her purse by Shara, and it was then put by her on the
                                                              5
kitchen table. She had to leave her house in an hour to go to the airport.
              5

5. **A.** NO CHANGE
    B. Her kitchen table held her purse, which was put there by Shara after she put her passport in the purse.
    C. After she placed her purse with the passport together, she went over to the kitchen table and put the purse onto it.
    D. Shara placed her passport in her purse and then put her purse on the kitchen table.

The correct answer is D. While reading the paragraph, your critical eye should have alerted you that something was not quite right. We have two succinct, concise sentences surrounding a somewhat awkward sentence. Although it's grammatically correct, it's overly long and a bit confusing, the result of using the passive voice. Is there a version among the answer choices that refines the key information in this sentence? Choices B and C seem equally long and meandering, perhaps even more confusing than how the sentence is currently written. What about choice D? All of the information in the original version is here, but it's more succinct, direct, and clear—the result of using the active voice. It's a better-written sentence and thus the correct answer.

STRATEGY

Approximately 15–20 percent of the questions you'll see on the ACT English test will assess your knowledge of sentence-specific issues of audience and purpose and the appropriate and relevant use of effective words, phrases, and sentences. Let's review some of the most widely used strategy question types on the ACT and how to tackle them effectively.

SUPPORTING EXAMPLES AND EVIDENCE QUESTIONS

As you already know, an effective piece of writing contains both a clear and compelling topic or central theme and supporting evidence designed to convince readers of the soundness of one's point of view. On the ACT English test, you'll be tasked with making decisions on adding, revising, and deleting material and determining how this affects (strengthens or weakens) the overall effectiveness of the passages.

 In some instances, the sentences in a paragraph will be numbered. These numbers in a passage are a good indicator that you will be dealing with rhetorical skills questions addressing strategy or organization issues.

Let's walk through an example of a strategy question that you may encounter on the ACT and how to effectively attack it.

. . . .

[1] Manatees are large, distinctive, and gentle aquatic mammals. [2] Often referred to as "sea cows," indigenous representations of these herbivorous creatures can be found in the Gulf of Mexico, the Caribbean Sea, West Africa, and the Amazon basin. [3] Dairy cows produce approximately 21 billion gallons of milk annually in the United States. [4] It has been determined that manatees utilize a wide range of sounds in their communication patterns, possess excellent long-term memories, and are capable of displaying behaviors through complex associative learning.

Which of the following sentences should be deleted to enhance the overall focus and effectiveness of the paragraph?

    F.   NO CHANGE
    G.   Sentence 2
    H.   Sentence 3
    J.   Sentence 4

Before deciding which answer choice is correct, let's take a step back and think about what's being asked here. Essentially, this question is asking you to make a judgment call regarding which sentence among the possible answer choices provides information that does not support the overall focus and intent of the paragraph, with the strategic goal being to reduce superfluous information, tighten the focus of the paragraph, and enhance word economy.

This is a common type of question on the ACT. An effective strategy for answering this type of question is to assess the main idea of the passage and the focus of the particular paragraph under analysis. In this example, *manatees* is the obvious topic.

Once you've identified the main idea, it's helpful to look for connecting elements among the answer choices in an effort to locate the word, passage, phrase, sentence, or idea that doesn't quite fit with the others. We've established that the main idea of this paragraph is manatees. Is there an answer choice that doesn't focus on manatees? The sentence in choice H takes the comment that manatees are often referred to as "sea cows" and veers off topic and onto a tangent involving dairy cows. **The correct answer is H**; the sentence about dairy cows should be deleted.

. . . .

CHECK FOR A STEM

Strategy questions on the ACT often appear with a question stem, asking you to make a key decision about specific text, either currently within the passage or within the question and/or answer choices. A typical strategy question stem could be as follows:

Which of the following sentences should be deleted to reinforce the author's point of view that baseball is still America's national pastime?

Use this signal to help you quickly identify this question type and determine the best approach for getting the correct answer.

Let's review a sample question that asks you to select relevant contextual information to provide targeted support to a particular point within a passage, another common question type on the ACT.

. . . .

[1] There is an ongoing debate about the use of practical special effects versus computer-generated effects in movies. [2] Practical effects are physical props and models built by expert craftspeople. [3] Computer-generated effects are complex visuals made by digital animators. [4] Supporters of practical effects feel that they bring a sense of realism to a film. [5] Those who prefer computer-generated effects do so because such effects are on the cutting edge of technology, and therefore, look more modern to their eyes. [6] Regardless of which form of effect you prefer, they each have their pros and cons.

Which of the following sentences, when inserted after Sentence 4, provides logically placed support of a statement made by the author?

    A. Practical effects are Steven Spielberg's chosen way to render special effects in his movies.

    B. Practical effects do not require actors and actresses to interact with animated characters and objects that are not really there, which can be awkward.

    C. Before computer-generated effects came into use in the 1980s, almost all movie special effects were created by practical means.

    D. Movies that contain computer-generated effects earn more money than movies with special effects created by practical means.

Let's analyze this question. You're being asked to insert a sentence into the narrative flow of an existing paragraph. For this and similar questions on the ACT exam, *where* you are being told to insert the sentence is your first context clue.

Here, you're being told to insert the new sentence after the fourth one. That should lead you to review the fourth sentence and how it fits into the context of the paragraph. This sentence discusses the feelings of those who support the use of practical effects in film. What sort of sentence should logically follow this one? A sentence that supports the use of practical effects, for the realism it brings, would be the most logical fit. Now you're ready to scan the answer choices for the correct answer. Choice B is the most logical fit: *Practical effects do not require actors and actresses to interact with animated characters and objects that are not really there, which can be awkward.* This choice provides clear evidence regarding why practical effects bring a sense of realism that computer-generated effects do not. Plug this sentence into the paragraph, and you'll see that it fits quite well.

Let's examine the other answer choices. Choices A, C, and D, which may or may not be true and which may or may not reflect your point of view on the issue, are incorrect because they don't provide logical, direct support of a statement made by the author of the passage. **The correct answer is B.**

· ·

 Pay attention to the precise location of details you are reviewing in a passage, which is typically provided in the question stem. This will provide you with crucial contextual cues for answering a question.

OFF-TOPIC AND REDUNDANT DETAILS QUESTIONS

Recognizing—and eradicating—the existence of irrelevant, tangential, or redundant information within a passage is a common question type on the ACT English test. Remember, your goal is to improve the passages you'll encounter, which includes word economy and focus.

 If you're reading a passage and something seems wrong to you, make note of it. Chances are, it's *not* a coincidence and you'll come across it again when you're answering the questions. If you're already familiar with an issue and are ready for it, you'll likely save yourself some time finding the correct answer.

Bring your best editing eye on test day, and when you read each passage, make note of anything that seems off, including redundant words and phrases and text that seems completely off-topic or just barely related to the central ideas of the passage.

Let's tackle another ACT question together.

· ·

[1] Thunderstorms, powerful winds, relentless rain, and dangerous ocean waves are all bi-products of tropical cyclones. [2] The cyclones themselves are storm systems that rotate with great speed. [3] They also bring strong rain and wind with them. [4] Cyclones usually form over warm bodies of water and gain their power as surface water evaporates and builds saturated storm clouds.

Which of the following sentences can be deleted from the paragraph without losing any key information?

F. Sentence 1
G. Sentence 2
H. Sentence 3
J. Sentence 4

You may have quickly figured out that the question is asking you to determine which information in the paragraph is off-topic or redundant and could—and should—be deleted. If you've read the paragraph critically, you may have also quickly noticed information that can easily be deleted. If so, answer the question and move on. Success on the ACT requires you to be able to work quickly within the given timeframe, so if you've uncovered an answer choice that you're confident in, act boldly!

However, if you're unsure of the answer or are trying to make a decision between two answer choices, take a deep breath and break down the question. The best strategy for questions like these is to first determine the central theme of the passage or paragraph, and then quickly examine how each sentence fits into the overall structure. Let's do some analysis. The central theme of this paragraph is *cyclones*. Now, let's try to quickly capture the purpose of each sentence.

- For Sentence 1, we can say: *Products of cyclones—winds, rain, and ocean waves.*
- For Sentence 2, we can say: *Cyclones are storm systems that rotate fast.*
- For Sentence 3, we can say: *Cyclones bring strong rain and wind.*
- For Sentence 4, we can say: *Form over warm water, and gain power as surface water evaporates.*

Has the correct answer become clearer? Using this process, it should be apparent that Sentence 3 contains much of the same information as Sentence 1, so you are dealing with a matter of redundancy. So which one should be deleted? Sentence 1 contains key information that is not in Sentence 3 (dangerous ocean waves), so it stands to reason that Sentence 3 is the one to delete. **The correct answer is H.**

· ·

Remember, this process of breaking down questions can all be done quickly in your head and should be saved for those challenging questions that you're unsure about.

Don't forget—elite students aiming for a perfect score don't run away from challenging questions; they tackle them head on! When you confront a tough question on the ACT, break it down, use your analytical skills, and hunt down the correct answer!

Appropriate Expressions Questions

We'll say it again because it's important—*context is king!* When you are plotting out a piece of writing, you have to think about the audience, which will help guide the appropriate presentation and tone. You shouldn't be using the same formal tone in a professional letter or formal essay as you would in a casual e-mail or friendly letter.

On the ACT English test, you may be tasked with answering questions that are designed to assess your ability to recognize appropriate and consistent writing, based on context. These questions will require you to recognize the audience given the type of writing. Typically, you'll be given a piece of formal or informal writing and will need to determine the overall tone that's appropriate and whether or not there are parts of the writing or answer choices that are inappropriate given the context.

The following table contains examples of the kinds of formal and informal writing categories that you may encounter on test day.

Formal	Informal
Technical journal	Blog post
Academic paper	Entertainment magazine article
Newspaper article	Fictional story
Scientific study	Novel
Professional correspondence	Personal essay
Educational textbook	Post on social media site
Professional presentation	Friendly e-mail or tweet

Passages on the ACT won't necessarily announce the kinds of writing they are, but you'll be able to tell if they require formal or informal language based on how they're written.

Try the following test-like sample question.

· ·

[1] Johnny, I'm looking forward to meeting up for the football game with you, Paulie, and Rick on Sunday afternoon! [2] I'm going to bring some extra blankets and snacks for the whole gang—I got us covered! [3] I'm supremely confident that the effective defensive skills of the Seagulls, with an approximate statistical success rate of 83%, will ultimately prevail on said game day. [4] We should decide if we want to all drive together or take separate cars; can you figure out when everyone is planning to leave and we'll go from there?

For the sake of unity and coherence, which of the following sentences does NOT belong in the paragraph?

- **A.** Sentence 1
- **B.** Sentence 2
- **C.** Sentence 3
- **D.** Sentence 4

By now you know that you should read *everything* on the ACT with a critical eye. Did any part of this paragraph stand out for you? Clearly, this is a friendly and informal exchange between friends. However, one sentence seems a bit odd when compared with the others. Sentence 3 seems strangely formal and stiff and just doesn't fit with the relaxed tone of the other sentences. **The correct answer is C.**

. . . .

Hone your ability to recognize differences in formal and informal writing between now and test day, and you'll be able to tackle questions like these with ease.

ORGANIZATION

Approximately 10–15 percent of the questions you'll see on the ACT English test will assess how well you can make decisions about effective grouping, distribution, and arrangement of ideas at the word, phrase, sentence, and paragraph levels.

Organization questions typically ask you to make holistic and paragraph-level decisions regarding appropriate sequencing of opening, transitional, and closing sentences, including adding, deleting, and rearranging text for maximum effectiveness.

Here's an example of an organization question that you may encounter on the exam:

. . . .

[1] It's true, potatoes can be used to generate small levels of electricity. [2] The water-soluble chemicals in potatoes can be used to create chemical reactions with opposing electrodes and produce electricity. [3] These two different electrodes, typically copper and zinc, can be connected to the potato on one end of the circuit and a small appliance like a clock or light bulb on the other end, and sufficient electrical output can be created to power the appliance. [4] Have you ever heard of a potato battery?

Which of the sentences within the paragraph would be the most effective introductory sentence?

F. Sentence 1
G. Sentence 2
H. Sentence 3
J. Sentence 4

Let's first determine what makes an effective introductory sentence. Typically, an effective introductory sentence introduces and establishes the main idea or topic of a piece of writing and serves to capture the readers' attention, enticing them to continue reading. Which of the sentences in the answer choices best accomplishes this? Choice F begins with "It's true," which provides a clue that it builds off of a prior sentence. Choices G and H don't seem to introduce a topic; instead, they serve as procedural sentences, describing a process that needs to be introduced first. Choice J seems to fulfill all of the requirements of an effective introductory sentence and is the correct answer choice—it effectively introduces the topic (potato batteries) and entices the reader to continue reading by posing a unique and curious question. **The correct answer is J.**

Beware of the Answer-As-You-Go Approach!

Some students, often the best and brightest ones, like to work fast and tackle each question as they encounter the relevant number or underlined portion while reading a given passage for the first time. While this can be a good way to save time and work quickly through the exam, this strategy usually is more effective on usage and mechanics questions, where context is less relevant.

On rhetorical skills questions, this answer-as-you-go approach may backfire, particularly if there are carefully designed answer distracters that may *seem* correct—until you've read and fully digested the passage and realize they were just cleverly designed traps. Be careful!

RECOGNIZING EFFECTIVE OPENING SENTENCES

You've no doubt learned during your academic career that starting a piece of writing with a powerful, effective opening sentence is critical. The opening sentence sets the tone for all the other sentences that follow. It's also the sentence that most needs to hook the reader's interest. If you fail to capture a reader's attention early on, he or she may stop reading before reaching your key points.

On the ACT English test, you may be tasked with identifying effective opening sentences for the writing passages provided. Typically, you'll be given a series of possible introductory sentences in a set of answer choices and will be asked to determine which is the most effective, given the context of the passage.

Here are a few tips for crafting and recognizing effective opening sentences:

- **State the topic of the piece succinctly, confidently, and clearly.** (Example: *Without question, Shakespeare was the finest playwright who has ever lived.*)

- **Use exciting words to garner interest and capture attention.** (Example: *Although William Shakespeare wrote his plays four hundred years ago, they still have the unbridled power to thrill and dazzle audiences today.*)

- **Pose an intriguing or provocative question.** (Example: *Who is generally considered to be the finest playwright who has ever lived?*)

- **Use a point-counterpoint structure.** (Example: *Most people think William Shakespeare is the finest playwright who has ever lived; however,….*)

- **Use a surprising fact or theory, or bit of interesting trivia.** (Example: *William Shakespeare is generally regarded as the finest playwright who has ever lived, but there is a pervasive theory that he didn't actually write some of his best-known plays*).

- **If appropriate, try using a bit of humor.** (Example: *If William Shakespeare is the great playwright everyone seems to think he is, why do I fall asleep every time I have to sit through one of his plays?*)

- **Start with a poignant quote.** (Example: *"The remarkable thing about Shakespeare is that he is really very good—in spite of all the people who say he is very good."* –poet Robert Graves in "Sayings of the Week," The Observer, 1964.)

Let's take a look at a sample ACT-like passage and question.

· ·

The problem began when the state decided to use butterfly ballots. These are paper ballots that require voters to punch out perforated dots known as *chads*. However, a lot of voters had difficulty punching out these chads, leaving the dots hanging out of the ballots. Consequently, the press questioned whether or not Florida had tallied its votes correctly. This was an important issue, since Florida's votes were the deciding factor in who would be the president of the United States in 2000.

The author wishes to open the essay with an effective opening sentence. Which of the following would be the most effective choice?

A. In 2000, United States voters had to decide who the next president would be, and their choice was either George W. Bush, a republican, or Al Gore, a democrat who'd been the Vice President of the United States for the past eight years.

B. Do you happen to have any friends or family members named Chad?

C. The 2000 presidential election was thrown into chaos when Florida decided to recount its votes, with the fate of the presidency on the line.

D. Politics is typically a dull and uninteresting subject for most people.

Remember the core tenets of effective introductory sentences. They need to capture the spirit, tone, and central idea of the writing and grab readers' attention. While reading this paragraph critically, you should've determined the central idea: *the voting problems that occurred in Florida during the 2000 presidential election.*

Let's look at the answer choices—do any of them serve the dual purpose of introducing this central theme *and* capturing the reader's attention? Choice A seems to be a bland regurgitation of basic facts, which would work better as text in a body paragraph. Choice B is engaging and tongue-in-cheek, but off topic. Choice D certainly wouldn't make anyone eager to continue reading. Choice C is an appropriate and correct choice—it succinctly captures the spirit and intent of the paragraph and uses some engaging language (*thrown into chaos, the fate of the presidency on the line*) to capture the reader's attention. **The correct answer is C.**

. . . .

RECOGNIZING EFFECTIVE CONCLUDING SENTENCES

How you conclude a piece of writing is just as crucial as how you begin it. Remember, you want your writing to have two key impacts: *a great first impression* and *a memorable final impression*.

A great **conclusion** serves to tie up the ideas in the writing and leave a lasting impression. It's the cap on a piece of writing, and it should leave the reader feeling satisfied.

Not surprisingly, a strong closing should include many of the same elements of a strong introduction:

- It reiterates key words or phrases from the passage.
- It features a memorable quote or question that encapsulates your main point(s).
- It redefines an important idea or detail in the passage.
- It captures your perspective or point of view regarding the topic.

Let's tackle another typical ACT question.

The Empire State Building is truly an architectural gem among skyscrapers. When construction of the Empire State Building concluded and Governor Al Smith declared it open on May 1, 1931, New York City had become home to the tallest building in the world. In subsequent years, several taller buildings would be constructed across the globe, stripping the Empire State Building of its premier height status.

The writer wishes to add an effective conclusion to this paragraph. Which of the following sentences would most effectively accomplish this?

- **F.** It's likely time to demolish the Empire State Building and replace it with a taller building.
- **G.** The Empire State Building began construction on March 17, 1930, two months after the excavation crew broke ground at the site.
- **H.** Regardless, the impact of this architectural treasure on culture and design is undeniable.
- **J.** These taller new buildings are also better looking and reflect a better design than the Empire State Building.

Which of these sentences make an effective conclusion for the paragraph? Obviously, the author thinks highly of the Empire State Building, referring to it as an "architectural gem." Therefore, we can eliminate choices F and J, which include derogatory points of view. Choice G doesn't work very hard to engage readers and would better serve as an informative sentence within the body of the paragraph. Choice H is the best option—it effectively concludes the piece and leaves a lasting and favorable impression on readers. **The correct answer is H.**

RECOGNIZING EFFECTIVE TRANSITION WORDS AND PHRASES

An important factor in effective writing and organization is how ideas *connect* to each other. The right use of impactful and appropriate transition words and phrases in a piece of writing can make all the difference, and without them a compelling piece with powerful ideas could devolve into a rambling and incoherent mess that lacks authority.

Different transition words and phrases perform different functions, and your ability to recognize when transitions are being used correctly—and when they're not—will likely be put to the test on the ACT English test. Review and master the following table, which will help you to be able to quickly and effectively tackle questions involving transitions on test day.

Function	Transition Words and Phrases
Introduction	*to begin, first of all, to start with*
An addition	*also, furthermore, in addition, moreover, secondly, additionally*
Clarification	*in other words, that is to say, to put it another way*
Passage of time	*afterwards, later, meanwhile, next, subsequently*
Examples	*for example, for instance, to demonstrate, specifically, to illustrate*
Cause	*because, since*
Effect	*as a result, consequently, therefore*
Comparison	*comparatively, in comparison, in similar fashion, likewise, similarly*
Contrast	*at the same time, however, in contrast, nevertheless, notwithstanding, on the contrary, yet*
Conclusion	*in conclusion, in short, to conclude, to sum up, to summarize, ultimately*

Sometimes, writers use entire sentences to transition between ideas, as in the following example:

> People currently understand that the earth is spherical. However, this was not always the case. The common belief used to be that the earth was flat.

Notice how the transitional sentence helps connect the contrasting ideas (*people now know the earth is spherical; people once thought the earth was flat*) in an effective way.

Read the following sample passage and answer the question that follows to put your knowledge of transitional words and phrases to the test.

. . . .

[1] There is an attitude in our culture that certain art forms qualify as "high art," while others qualify as "low art." [2] For example, some sophisticated and intellectual people consider European films as "high art," and comic books as "low art" aimed at children and people with average or below-average intelligence. [3] Many European films are

as silly and insubstantial as the worst American movies, and there have been comic books with incredibly rich characterizations and intricate plot development that rival the finest novels.

Which of the following sentences, if inserted between sentences 2 and 3, would provide the most effective transition?

- **A.** Subsequently, there has been a great explosion in the number of comic books on the market.
- **B.** In contrast, fine literature is considered to be a "high art" and is taught in classes around the world.
- **C.** For example, people who did not attend college might be thought of as average.
- **D.** However, a closer look at this stereotype reveals that it is short-sighted and untrue.

We're told that the key point in the passage is between sentences 2 and 3, so let's zero in on what's happening here. Sentence 2 is highlighting a specific belief system regarding high art and low art, and then Sentence 3 seems to abruptly contradict that notion. What's missing here? Clearly, a transition sentence that debunks the belief offered in Sentence 2 would serve well here. Do any of the sentences in the answer choices fit the bill? Choice D does exactly that, by attacking the stereotype that is at the heart of Sentence 2. **The correct answer is D.**

. . . .

ORGANIZATION FOR CLARITY AND EFFECT

No passage can simply rest on a powerful introduction, memorable conclusion, and strong transitions. For a piece of writing to be truly effective, every sentence and paragraph needs to be on target and well organized.

Effectively tackling these sorts of questions begins even before you reach the questions. While you're reading each passage, keep your "editor instincts" sharp. Note the type of organization it follows, and get a sense of the structure and flow of the piece, which will help you identify any inconsistencies or illogical organization. Here are some of the most common organizational formats:

- **Chronological:** Information is organized by the time that the events occurred (can be forward or reverse).

- **Sequential:** Often used when describing a process, information is organized by the order in which the steps or parts occur.

- **Order of importance:** Information is organized by its relative value or importance (can be most to least important, or vice versa).

- **Compare and contrast:** Often used when writing about two or more things, wherein one is discussed, then another compared to it, and so on.

- **Cause and effect:** Often used to describe a particular result, the events or reasons behind why a result occurred are discussed.
- **Issue/problem and solution:** In this type of organization, a central dilemma is discussed, followed by strategies for addressing/fixing the problem.

Let's tackle another sample ACT-like question and put your skills to the test.

. . . .

[1] Crack a few eggs into a bowl and whisk them together. [2] Remove your melet from the heat, garnish based on your preferences, and enjoy! [3] Let's talk about making an omelet. [4] Pour your eggs in a hot, greased pan and cook for a few minutes to your desired level of doneness, flipping occasionally.

Which of the following sequences will make the paragraph most logical?

    F.   NO CHANGE
    G.   2, 1, 4, 3
    H.   3, 1, 4, 2
    J.   3, 1, 2, 4

The key to answering this question is to first recognize the type of organization you're dealing with. Here, the process of making an omelet is being discussed, so you know you're dealing with sequential organization, and therefore must determine the correct order of steps in the omelet-making process. Sentence 3 seems to make an effective introductory sentence, so we can eliminate choices F and G. Cracking the eggs, Sentence 1, would be the next logical step. After cracking the eggs we need to cook them, so Sentence 4 is the next logical sentence. Therefore, we can eliminate choice J. To check and see if choice H is indeed correct, we need to determine if the remaining sentence, Sentence 2, logically follows, which it does. **The correct answer is H.**

. . . .

ATTACKING RHETORICAL SKILLS PASSAGES AND QUESTIONS FOR A PERFECT SCORE

Now that you have a better sense of the main types of Rhetorical Skills questions that you'll encounter on the ACT English test, let's tackle some practice questions in the context and format that you'll encounter on test day—in a complete passage.

We know you're gunning for a perfect score, and we know that *practice makes perfect*, so we'll also look at some ways to effectively attack the passages and rhetorical skills questions you'll encounter in this test section, using proven strategies and techniques.

The following passage includes six questions that are designed to test your understanding of effective and appropriate written rhetorical skills. Make your way through them, and then read on to walk through the best strategy for approaching each question.

Buckminster Fuller—Under the Dome

[1]

Various scholars have referred to Buckminster Fuller—known as "Bucky" to those closest to him—as a modern-day Edison of sorts, an unabashed creative thinker, inventor and creator of new things, designer, author of more than 30 books, and theorist. Fuller had made numerous contributions to twentieth-century arts and sciences during his life, but is perhaps best known for his contributions to architecture, popularizing the geodesic dome, distinct spherical structures that are often gigantic in scope, which reached new heights of wonder and popularity in the 1964 World's Fair in New York Ciy. [2]

1.
  A. NO CHANGE
  B. inventor,
  C. inventor, creator of new things,
  D. creator and inventor of new things,

[2]

Fuller was born at the end of the nineteenth century (1895) in Milton, Massachusetts, and from an early age displayed a keen interest in design. Buckminster Fuller was related to Margaret Fuller, a key figure in the American Transcendentalist movement. Before he reached his teenage years, he had reportedly created his own set of building tools and tinkered with designs for improving the propulsion systems of boats. Perhaps surprisingly to some, he

2. Which of the following sentences would make an effective transition between paragraphs 1 and 2?

  F. Buckminster Fuller is one of many significant twentieth-century thinkers in the United States.
  G. Let's review the origin and key events of the 1964 World's Fair in New York City.
  H. How did Fuller spend the final years of his eventful life?
  J. Let's take a closer look at the life of this fascinating individual.

had trouble focusing in the classroom; he struggled with accepted abstract properties of geometry in grade school and was expelled from Harvard University twice—for partying, general dependability, and lack of sufficient focus. [4]

3. **A.** NO CHANGE
   B. hunger
   C. irresponsibility
   D. astuteness

4. Which of the following sentences in Paragraph 2 can be deleted without affecting the theme of the passage?

   F. Fuller was born at the end of the nineteenth th century (1895) in Milton, Massachusetts, and from an early age displayed a keen interest in design.
   G. Buckminster Fuller was related to Margaret Fuller, a key figure in the American Transcendentalist movement.
   H. Before he reached his teenage years he had reportedly created his own set of building tools and tinkered with designs for improving the propulsion systems of boats.
   J. Perhaps surprisingly to some, he struggled with focus in the classroom; he struggled with accepted abstract properties of geometry in grade school, and was expelled from Harvard University twice—for partying, general dependability, and lack of sufficient focus.

[3]

While working as a professor at Black Mountain College in North Carolina, Fuller began reimagining and revitalizing the earlier work of German engineer Dr. Walter Bauersfeld on the geodesic dome, a structural concept that could sustain its own weight with no theoretical limits. His work in this area was widely recognized and quickly utilized throughout the fields of architecture and design, as well as by the United States military. As a boy, Fuller spent a significant portion of his time on Bear Island, in Maine. His contributions to architecture and design did not stop there, and during his life Fuller made numerous important contributions, mainly in the areas of cost-efficient shelter and transportation.

[4]

Fuller's later years were spent in academia, as well as working with designers and scientists across the globe on a wide array of architecture and design projects. He also maintained a full writing and lecture schedule. During his life, Fuller received numerous honors and accolades, including the Gold Medal award from the American Institute of

5. What is the best organizational strategy for this sentence?

A. Move to Paragraph 1.
B. Move to Paragraph 2.
C. Move to the end of Paragraph 3.
D. Move to the beginning of Paragraph 3.

Architects and the Presidential Medal of Freedom. Fuller's ultimate life goal, in his own words, until his death at the age of 87 in 1983, was "applying the principles of science to solve the problems of humanity." 6

6. Which of the following would make an effective concluding sentence to the passage?

   F. Fuller should have designed an ultra-modern football stadium.
   G. Fuller clearly devoted his life to achieving this noble goal.
   H. Fuller was clearly too busy to be interested in non-professional pursuits.
   J. Did Fuller ever wish he did something different with his life?

ATTACKING ACT READING PASSAGES

Yes, you're keenly aware that the clock is ticking on test day and that you have only 45 minutes to read and analyze five writing passages and answer 75 multiple-choice questions on this test section. But you're an elite student and can move quickly and efficiently on any given academic task—especially one that can help you achieve your goal of earning a perfect score.

Practice using your well-honed editorial skills and critical eye to analyze and break down the passages you'll encounter on the ACT exam, which will help you attack any and all questions you'll come across along your journey to a perfect score on test day!

Consider the following quick yet helpful steps for attacking ACT reading passages:

Step 1: Analyze the passage type.

After you read each passage, take quick but careful note of what type of passage it is and what the main ideas are. Was it informational? Was it a persuasive piece? Does it present opposing sides of a controversial issue? Did it cover a significant event in history or a seminal figure? This process will help you identify—and remember—the main purpose of the passage, which will help you save time in the long run as you attack the questions. *The passage we're working with here is an informational biographical snapshot of Buckminster Fuller, an influential twentieth-century designer, inventor, and thinker.*

Step 2: Note general essay construction and organization.

This step is especially useful for attacking rhetorical skills questions, which include issues of organization. Quickly note the general construction of the piece—this will really help you make determinations about proper placement and movement of new words, phrases, sentences, and paragraphs if the need arises in the questions that follow. *Paragraph 1 provides a general overview of the life of Buckminster Fuller. Paragraph 2 covers his early years and struggles in school. Paragraph 3 covers his most popular work (the geodesic dome) and general contributions to architecture and design. Paragraph 4 covers Fuller's later years in academia and design, his accolades, and a quote about his ultimate life goal.*

Step 3: Note any glaring rhetorical issues.

Does something strange jump out at you while reading a passage? Is there information that's clearly missing, strangely worded, or glaringly out of place? If so, consider making a brief mental or written note about it. The passages you'll encounter on test day are carefully designed with meticulous attention to detail, so you can be sure that any glaring errors are intentional—and that you'll be tasked with fixing them on test day. Did anything stand out for you while reading "Buckminster Fuller—Under the Dome?" If so, consider making a quick note of it.

Again, *don't* spend a great deal of time on these steps—you don't even have to write them down if you feel it throws off your test-taking pace (which you should have down cold before test day). However, it would be to your benefit to quickly go through these steps when attacking a reading passage, regardless of what it's about, so that you'll be well prepared to handle any type of rhetorical skills question that you may face.

ATTACKING ACT RHETORICAL SKILLS QUESTIONS

If you carefully break down and analyze the reading passages you encounter on the ACT English test, you'll be well prepared to attack any question type you'll encounter on test day, including the rhetorical skills questions.

Let's take a close look at the rhetorical skills questions associated with the reading passage "Buckminster Fuller—Under the Dome." These questions span the three main areas of strategy, organization, and style, and the strategies utilized to answer these questions will help you answer any questions you'll encounter on test day, on your quest to achieve a perfect score!

1. **A.** NO CHANGE
   B. inventor,
   C. inventor, creator of new things,
   D. creator and inventor of new things,

Attacking the question: This is a style question, and like every question you'll encounter on the ACT English test, you should first identify what's being asked of you before attempting to answer it. A good strategy for starting is to **quickly scan the answer choices.** Here, you'll see a series of related yet varied words, which should immediately signal you that you're being asked to make a word choice decision. Now we know what we're dealing with!

Perhaps while you first read the passage, you encountered the issue underlined here and quickly discovered the correct way to fix it—and know the correct answer. If so, that's great. Mark it and move on. If not, take a methodical approach. **Go back to the underlined portion and reread it.** Does the issue and answer reveal itself now? If so, you know what to do—mark it and move on. If not, keep reading.

Scan the answer choices and look for clues: There seems to be some variation in how the words *inventor* and *creator of new things* appear—or do not appear. That's a possible clue that this choice is at the heart of the question. Reread the underlined portion of the passage, and you may discover that this is a question of redundancy. Using both *inventor* and *creator of new things* is clearly redundant because they essentially mean the same thing. Which answer choice fixes this issue? This question is at the heart of a key strategy for attacking ACT English test questions; **the correct answer will always be the choice that best improves the passage**. Make all of your decisions with this in mind.

In this case, **the correct answer is B.** A quick way to test it is to plug in the correct answer and see if it works. Choice B eliminates the redundancy without affecting the author's intended meaning—thereby improving the passage. As written, choice A contains the original redundancy problem. Choices C and D simply shuffle around the word order and do not fix the redundancy.

A key point worth noting for this and other rhetorical skills questions: Don't try to select answer choices out of context! Some answer choices may *seem* to be the most appropriate or best choices when scanning the list of options, but you won't be able to confidently choose the correct answers unless you're fully aware of how it works within the context of the passage. On the ACT, context is key!

2. Which of the following sentences would make an effective transition between paragraphs 1 and 2?

    F. Buckminster Fuller is one of many significant twentieth-century thinkers in the United States.

    G. Let's review the origin and key events of the 1964 World's Fair in New York City.

    H. How did Fuller spend the final years of his eventful life?

    J. Let's take a closer look at the life of this fascinating individual.

Attacking the question: This is an organization question that is asking you to determine which sentence among the answer choices would make the best addition to the passage. Questions that involve adding transition sentences between paragraphs are common on the English test. The way we attack this particular question is a sound strategy for attacking these types of questions whenever they arise on the ACT.

Remember earlier in the chapter when we suggested making a few quick notes on the structure and organization of the reading passages you'll encounter? Those notes will really come in handy when attacking organization questions. We've already noted that this passage is *an informational biographical snapshot of Buckminster Fuller, an influential twentieth-century designer, inventor, and thinker.* We can quickly eliminate choice F, which veers off on a tangent to other significant twentieth-century thinkers, and choice G, which veers off on a tangent to the 1964 World's Fair.

The question here focuses on a transition sentence between paragraphs 1 and 2. When you see the term *transition sentence* in a question, it may help to think of a bridge. We've already noted that Paragraph 1 *provides a general overview of the life of Buckminster Fuller* and that Paragraph 2 *covers his early years and struggles in school.* Scan the answer choices (remember, we've already eliminated choice F)—would any of them serve as an effective bridge between these two concepts? **The correct answer is choice J.** We can check by plugging it into the passage and seeing that it works quite well. Choice H would be more appropriate at the beginning of Paragraph 4, which we've already noted covers Fuller's later years.

3. **A.** NO CHANGE
   B. hunger
   C. irresponsibility
   D. astuteness

Attacking the question: This is a style question; the varied selection of words among the answer choices should immediately signal you that you're dealing with a word choice question. Again, for these and other types of rhetorical skills questions, **context is key.** Let's examine the question that contains the underline in question. What's the main idea of the sentence? It highlights Fuller's struggle in school, culminating in him getting expelled from Harvard. The underlined word in question is among the reasons for his expulsion. Which word among the answer choices is a trait that would contribute to a student getting expelled? An *irresponsible* student could feasibly get expelled from school. A student would likely not get expelled for being *dependable* (choice A), *hungry* (choice B), or *astute* (choice D). **The correct answer is C.**

4. Which of the following sentences in Paragraph 2 can be deleted without affecting the theme of the passage?

   F. Fuller was born at the end of the nineteenth century (1895) in Milton, Massachusetts, and from an early age displayed a keen interest in design.
   G. Buckminster Fuller was related to Margaret Fuller, a key figure in the American Transcendentalist movement.
   H. Before he reached his teenage years he had reportedly created his own set of building tools and tinkered with designs for improving the propulsion systems of boats.
   J. Perhaps surprisingly to some, he struggled with focus in the classroom; he struggled with accepted abstract properties of geometry in grade school, and was expelled from Harvard University twice—for partying, general dependability, and lack of sufficient focus.

Attacking the question: This strategy question is trying to gauge your ability to recognize what information in a passage is critical and what is superfluous, based on its main idea. We've already established that this passage is *an informational biographical snapshot of Buckminster Fuller, an influential twentieth-century designer, inventor, and thinker.* We've also established that Paragraph 2 *covers his early years and struggles in school,* so we can quickly hone in on the correct answer. (Do you see how this strategy can prove valuable?) Which of these answer choices does not fit in with these established themes or is the *worst* fit? The information in choice G about a notable relative of Buckminster Fuller, while interesting, does not support or directly relate to the central theme (Buckminster's accomplishments) or his early years or struggles in school, which the other answer choices do. **The correct answer is G.**

5. What is the best organizational strategy for this sentence?

   A. Move to Paragraph 1.
   B. Move to Paragraph 2.
   C. Move to the end of Paragraph 3.
   D. Move to the beginning of Paragraph 3.

Attacking the question: This question is designed to analyze your ability to make an effective sentence reorganization within the passage. Once again, our initial prep work will come in handy here—we don't need to spend time again determining the gist of each paragraph because we've already done that. The sentence in question highlights Fuller's childhood and where he spent his time as a boy. Which of our paragraphs would this best fit into? Paragraph 2 *covers his early years* and would be the most logical fit, so choice B is correct. Paragraph 1 *provides a general overview of the life of Buckminster Fuller,* so choice A would not be the correct choice. Paragraph 3 *covers his most popular work (the geodesic dome) and general contributions to architecture and design,* and a sentence about his early years would not fit here, so choices C and D are incorrect. **The correct answer is B.**

6. Which of the following would make an effective concluding sentence to the passage?

   F. Fuller should have designed an ultra-modern football stadium.
   G. Fuller clearly devoted his life to achieving this noble goal.
   H. Fuller was clearly too busy to be interested in nonprofessional pursuits.
   J. Did Fuller ever wish he did something different with his life?

Attacking the question: Here's a classic strategy question that's asking you to make a decision on the best way to conclude the passage. A great first step for tackling this question is to quickly ask yourself, "What makes an effective essay conclusion?" A strong essay conclusion is often a poignant and memorable wrap-up of the main themes and ideas that lie at the core of the written piece. Referring back to our notes, this passage is an *informational biographical snapshot of Buckminster Fuller, an influential twentieth-century designer, inventor, and thinker.* The concluding paragraph *covers Fuller's later years in academia and design, his accolades, and a quote about his ultimate life goal.* Do any of the answer choices capture the spirit of these central ideas? The sentence in choice G refers to Fuller's lifelong goal, which is referenced in the concluding chapter and effectively ties back to the main idea of the passage. Choice F is merely a tangential opinion. Choice H is a claim that is not rooted in firm evidence, so it is not appropriate to include. Choice J, while provocative, does not align with the information in the passage. Fuller clearly had a concrete and focused life goal, and he dedicated his time and efforts toward achieving it. **The correct answer is G.**

USE WHAT WORKS—WITH PRACTICE

We can't say this enough: the tools in your test-taking arsenal that have served you well thus far will be among your best tools on the day you take the ACT. The *key h*ere is to practice before test day to make sure you're comfortable using your test-taking skills within the format and timing of the official exam.

Some skills are transferable for any test—some aren't. We recommend you work on combining your existing skills with the strategies provided in this book; with careful practice, you'll have an effective mix of resources to work with on test day!

SUMMING IT UP

- **Rhetorical skills** questions assess your ability to analyze a written passage and make decisions regarding the author's deployment of strategy, organization, and style. On the ACT, you'll be tasked with making decisions about adding, deleting, moving, and revising words, sentences, and phrases within the passage, with the goal being to improve the readability, appropriateness, and effectiveness of the author's work.

- **Tone** refers to the author's attitude toward the subject she or he is discussing; **mood** refers to the emotions that the piece of writing makes readers feel.

- **Wordiness questions** test your ability to recognize and fix issues of verbosity and redundancy. These questions are usually focused at the sentence level, and you typically don't need to analyze an entire passage to handle them.

- **The active voice** demonstrates a clear and straightforward connection between the subject of a sentence and the action being performed; sentences written in the **passive voice** typically describe the action of the sentence as indirectly happening to the subject.

- **Supporting examples** and **evidence questions** will test your ability to recognize and add clear and compelling supporting evidence to a passage to convince readers of the soundness of one's point of view.

- **An effective opening sentence sets the tone for all the other sentences that follow.** It's also the sentence that most needs to hook the reader's interest.

- **Impactful and appropriate transition words and phrases** in a piece of writing are crucial for connecting key ideas. For a piece of writing to be truly effective, every sentence and paragraph needs to be on target and well organized.

- **A great conclusion serves to tie up the ideas in the writing and leave a lasting impression.**

- **Follow the four steps to successfully attacking rhetorical skills questions:** 1) break down and analyze the reading passages, 2) identify each type of question you encounter, 3) make sure you're fully aware of what you're being asked, and 4) take into account the entire context of the passage when you select an answer.

- **Context is key.** Understanding passage context is crucial for making correct rhetorical decisions on the ACT English test.

- **Retain the perspective.** When making rhetorical decisions on test day, your goal is *not* to revise the author's perspective or point of view to align it with yours.

- **Always read critically and bring your best editing eye on test day;** when you read each passage, make note of anything that seems off, including redundant words and phrases and text that seems completely off-topic or just barely related to the central ideas of the passage.

- **Pay attention to the precise location of details you are reviewing in a passage,** which is typically provided in the question stem. This will provide you with crucial contextual cues for answering a question.

- **The answer-as-you-go approach may backfire on rhetorical skills questions,** particularly if there are carefully designed distracters that may *seem* correct—until you've read and fully digested the passage and realize they were just cleverly designed traps.

- **Practicing and reviewing *before* test day is the best strategy** for getting good at identifying each question type, using the appropriate tools to get the right answers, and getting closer to your perfect score goal.

- **Understanding your strengths and weaknesses** is essential for creating an effective ACT study plan. Focus your time between now and test day on eradicating your weaknesses!

- **Use what works.** The existing tools in your test-taking arsenal that have served you well thus far in school will be among your best tools on test day.

- Every decision you make on the ACT English test should **improve the quality and effectiveness of the written passages.**

CHAPTER 4:
INTERMEDIATE ALGEBRA AND COORDINATE GEOMETRY

OVERVIEW

- Deceptive Percentages and Sneaky Averages
- Exponential and Radical Expressions
- Rational Expressions
- Factoring and Solving Quadratic Equations
- Absolute Value and Inequalities
- Direct and Inverse Variation

- Arithmetic and Geometric Sequences
- Systems of Equations
- Functions
- Complex Numbers
- Overlapping Groups
- Logarithms
- Matrices
- Working with Linear Equations
- Slope of Parallel and Perpendicular Lines

- Midpoint Formula
- Distance Formula
- Interpreting Graphs
- Graphing Quadratics
- Graphing Circles
- Graphing and Interpreting Inequalities
- Graphs of Ellipses
- Summing It Up

We know that, for years, you've been working hard and logging long hours to learn the ins, outs, and upside-downs of the toughest math concepts you've been able to get your hands on. Therefore, in this chapter we'll jump right into the most advanced intermediate algebra and coordinate geometry skills you'll see on the ACT Mathematics test.

We're not going to review foundational pre-algebra and elementary algebra concepts in this book, but we're expecting you're in tip-top shape regarding all the nuances in these areas. (If you're having a tough time remembering if 1 is a prime number or how to calculate percentage increase, you should do some additional reviewing of pre-algebra and algebra using *Peterson's ACT® Prep Guide*.) But even though this guide focuses only on the toughest concepts, we will quickly review some important formulas that you probably had in your back pocket a few years ago, but may not have seen since then.

Moving quickly and smoothly through the ACT will be easiest if you have a command of the formulas and procedures that give the most direct path to the correct answers. However, what will truly determine the difference between an excellent score and a perfect 36 is the ability to think outside of the box. If you want to ace the toughest questions the ACT throws at you, it is critical to do lots of ACT-type question practice in order to gain a nimbleness of mind. The toughest questions will not be testing your recall of obscure skills, but instead, they'll test your ability to problem solve by integrating several different skills.

The math chapters in this book contain a very broad array of content. It's not often that the ACT will test your ability to multiply matrices, FOIL complex numbers, or condense a long logarithmic expression into a single term, but if you do get tested on some of these challenging areas, you want to be prepared for them! Although we won't wax poetic on these less-frequently asked topics, we *will* let you know the most important concepts you need to be aware of to avoid getting stunned by a *zinger* question.

We'll start with a review of the toughest Intermediate Algebra and Coordinate Geometry concepts. These two concepts make up 30 percent of the entire ACT Mathematics test—that's about 18 total questions. Folded into this review are pre-algebra and elementary algebra concepts you need to know on their own and also to solve the multi-step questions presented here. Let's begin!

DECEPTIVE PERCENTAGES AND SNEAKY AVERAGES

We know that percentages and averages aren't intermediate algebra concepts, but since you will encounter hard questions testing these fundamental concepts, this seems like a great place to start.

DECEPTIVE PERCENTAGES

For the most part, the percentage questions won't faze you. You know how to take the percent of numbers, how to calculate tax, and how to calculate sale prices. But one concept that regularly tricks students is what happens when a number is increased and then decreased by the same percentage (or vice versa). At first glance, one might think that a stock that drops 20% on Monday, and then increases by 20% on Tuesday, is back at 100% of its Monday starting price. However, this is not the case! When you need to use two or more percentage manipulations to determine a final percentage value, use a starting point of 100. This way the final result translates easily into a percentage, since you'll be comparing it to the initial value of 100.

 When you need to use two or more percentage manipulations to determine a final percentage value, use a theoretical starting point of 100.

Here's how a question might look on the ACT:

Example:

Starting at 9 a.m., the temperature increases by 30% until 2 p.m. Then it drops by 40% until 9 p.m. The temperature at 9 p.m. is what percentage of the morning temperature at 9 a.m.?

Solution:

Start this question by assuming that the starting temperature was 100°. After a 30% increase during the day, the temperature would be 130°. Then a 40% decrease in the evening would mean a 52° drop (40% of 130 is 52). Subtracting 52° from 130° leaves us at 78°. Since the starting temperature we chose was 100°, the final temperature of 78° is 78% of the original temperature.

Use this technique to answer the following question:

· ·

Kai buys 70 shares of Hypolux stock on Friday afternoon. The following Monday his investment drops by 20%. On Tuesday, the value of Hypolux increases by 20%. The final value of Kai's investment on Tuesday is what percent of his initial investment?

- **A.** 70%
- **B.** 80%
- **C.** 94%
- **D.** 96%
- **E.** 100%

The correct answer is D. The number of shares that Kai bought is inconsequential, so ignore the 70. Assume that the total value of Hypolux stock on Friday was $100. A 20% decrease on Monday would be a $20 drop in price, which would bring the value to $80. Then, a 20% increase of $80 would be $16, bringing the stock up to $96 by Tuesday. The final value of Kai's investment on Tuesday is 96% of the starting value. Choice A resembles the number of shares he bought, which is insignificant. Choice B is the value of the stock after only the 20% decrease. Choice C is 2 percentage points too low. Choice E resembles the value that the stock would have been if it decreased and increased by 20 *dollars* instead of by 20 percentage points.

· ·

SNEAKY AVERAGES

Finding the average of numbers is easy, but there are a few different types of sneaky average questions that the ACT likes to use to trick clever students like you! Be on the lookout for questions like these:

What rational number is halfway between $\frac{3}{5}$ and $\frac{7}{9}$?

Don't let the fractions scare you. The average of any two numbers is always halfway between them, so simply take the average of these two fractions. (We'll let you do the work on that, but you should arrive at $\frac{31}{45}$.)

Here's another example of how you might have to deal with averages:

Example:

Parker is performing in a gymnastics meet where her competition score will be the average of her scores on high beam, uneven bars, vault, and floor. After receiving the following scores, what must she score on her floor routine in order to have a competition score of 9.2?

Event	Score
High beam	8.9
Uneven bars	9.3
Vault	9.1
Floor	

Solution:

When asked to find the last number needed to arrive at a particular average, students make a common mistake of taking the average of the given data and then weighing that average equally with the missing data point. *Do not* start this problem by taking the average of 8.9, 9.3, and 9.1! This approach would weight her floor performance as equally important as the other three events combined, which is incorrect. Instead, set up an average equation with 4 events, allowing *f* to be her score on floor, and then solve for *f*:

$$\frac{8.9+9.3+9.1+f}{4}=9.2$$

(Solving for *f*, you should get 9.5.)

 ALERT: When finding the last value needed to arrive at a desired average, do *not* first take the average of the known values. Instead, set up an average equation for all the given values plus your unknown. Represent the missing value with a variable, and then solve for that variable.

Let's look at another example. Think it through before you try to solve it.

Example:

Guests at Sierra's Serene Urban Oasis rate their hotel experience on a starring system that ranges from 1 to 7 stars. What is the average number of stars Sierra's Serene Urban Oasis receives to the nearest 0.1 stars?

Number of Stars	Number of Reviews with These Stars
1	0
2	2
3	3
4	5
5	7
6	12
7	8

Solution:

This is a weighted average problem! Don't just take the average of the numbers in the left or right columns! First add an additional column to the right side of the table and use that column to record the products of each row: (*number of stars*) × (*number of reviews*):

Number of Stars	Number of Reviews with These Stars	Subtotals of Stars Earned
1	0	$1 \times 0 = 0$
2	2	$2 \times 2 = 4$
3	3	$3 \times 3 = 9$
4	5	$4 \times 5 = 20$
5	7	$5 \times 7 = 35$
6	12	$6 \times 12 = 72$
7	8	$7 \times 8 = 56$

The sum of the values in the right-most column shows us that 196 stars were earned in total. The sum of the values in the middle column indicates that there were 37 reviews. Now divide the 196 number of stars earned by the 37 reviews to determine that the average review was 5.3 stars.

NOTE: When given a frequency table and asked to calculate any measure of center (mean, median, or mode), remember that each row with a frequency greater than 1 represents multiple data entries. It's easy to make careless mistakes with frequency tables. Whenever asked to find the average by using a frequency table, make sure to find the *weighted* average.

EXPONENTIAL AND RADICAL EXPRESSIONS

We imagine you find simplifying rational expressions like $\dfrac{(4x^2y^3)(8x^5y)}{20x^6y^5}$ soothing and meditative. You know the rules for multiplying and dividing like bases, so you hop along combining variables and coefficients. In this section, we want to make sure you remember how to handle rational exponents like $\left(16x^8\right)^{\frac{3}{4}}$ and radical expressions like $\left(\sqrt[3]{125h^{12}}\right)^2$. We also want to ensure that you won't panic when you're asked to solve for x in a feisty looking equation like $8x^{-1} = 32^{5-x}$.

Rules of Exponents

Let's begin with a review of the rules of exponents in the table below. Make sure you pay special attention to the common mistakes that students often make while rushing in a timed test environment. Be certain you understand how each example was simplified to the given answer:

Original Expression	Equivalent Expression	Common Mistake	Example
$y^a \cdot y^b$	$y^{(a+b)}$ (Add the exponents.)	$y^a \cdot y^b \neq y^{ab}$ (Don't multiply the exponents!)	$4^{5x} \cdot 4^{x+2} = 4^{6x+2}$
$\dfrac{y^a}{y^b}$	$y^{(a-b)}$ (Subtract the exponents.)	$\dfrac{y^a}{y^b} \neq y^{\left(\frac{a}{b}\right)}$ (Don't divide the exponents!)	$m^{6x} \div m^{2x} = m^{4x}$
$(y^a)^b$	y^{ab} (Multiply the exponents.)	$(y^a)^b \neq y^{a^b}$ (Don't raise the exponent to the outside power!)	$(a^4)^3 = a^{12}$

Original Expression	Equivalent Expression	Common Mistake	Example
$(2y^a z^b)^c$	$2^c y^{ac} z^{bc}$ (Raise each inside factor to the power of c.)	$(2y^a z^b)^c \neq (2c)y^{ac} z^{bc}$ (Don't multiply the coefficient by the exponent!)	$(3y^3 z^4)^2 = 9y^6 z^8$
y^0	1 (Anything to the power of zero equals 1!)	$y^0 \neq 0$ (Don't confuse this with $y \cdot 0 = 0$.)	$-(-4)^0 = -1$ (Notice that $(-4)^0 = 1$, so the final answer is negative.)
y^{-a}	$\dfrac{1}{y^a}$ (Move the base and its power to the denominator and turn the exponent positive.)	$y^{-a} \neq -y^a$ (Negative exponents *do not* make answers negative!)	$(4x)^{-2} = \dfrac{1}{(4x)^2} = \dfrac{1}{16x^2}$
$\sqrt{a}\sqrt{b}$	$\sqrt{ab}$ (Multiply the radicands under a single radical sign.)	$\sqrt{a}\sqrt{b} \neq ab$ (Don't forget the radical sign.)	$\sqrt{2}\sqrt{3} = \sqrt{6}$
$\left(\sqrt[a]{y}\right)^b$	$y^{\frac{b}{a}}$	$\left(\sqrt[a]{y}\right)^b \neq y^{\frac{a}{b}}$ (Don't mix up a and b!)	$\left(\sqrt[5]{32}\right)^3 = (2)^3 = 8$
$y^{\frac{a}{b}}$	$\left(\sqrt[b]{y}\right)^a$ or $\sqrt[b]{y^a}$ (Take the bth root of y and raise that to the power of a.)	$y^{\frac{a}{b}} \neq \left(\sqrt[a]{y}\right)^b$ (Don't mix up a and b!)	$(16x^8)^{\frac{3}{4}} = 8x^6$

If the last example in the table was cause for alarm, watch how to simplify $(16x^8)^{\frac{3}{4}}$ step by step:

Example:

Simplify $(16x^8)^{\frac{3}{4}}$.

Solution:

First, apply the power of $\dfrac{3}{4}$ to both factors inside the parentheses: $16^{\frac{3}{4}}\left(x^8\right)^{\frac{3}{4}}$.

Compute the coefficient: $16^{\frac{3}{4}} = \left(\sqrt[4]{16}\right)^3 = 2^3 = 8$.

Simplify the exponent for the variable: $\left(x^8\right)^{\frac{3}{4}} = x^{\left(\frac{8}{1}\right)\left(\frac{3}{4}\right)} = x^6$.

The final answer is $8x^6$.

USING EQUIVALENT BASES

A tricky type of exponent question on the ACT will require you to solve for x when it is used in the exponents of two equivalent expressions.

What is the solution of the equation $8^{x-1} = 32^{5-x}$?

Whenever you see an equation with a variable being used as an exponent, look to see if you can turn the bases into equivalent bases. In this case, the two bases are 8 and 32. Since these are both powers of 2, we can rewrite the equation replacing 8 with 2^3 and 32 with 2^5:

$$8^{x-1} = 32^{5-x} \text{ becomes } (2^3)^{x-1} = (2^5)^{5-x}$$

Next, use the rule that $(y^a)^b = y^{ab}$ to simplify both sides (don't forget to use the distributive property):

$$(2^3)^{x-1} = (2^5)^{5-x} \text{ becomes } (2)^{3x-3} = (2)^{25-5x}$$

Now that both sides of the equation have the same base, it must be true that their exponential expressions are equivalent. (*Note:* If $x^a = x^b$, then $a = b$.) Disregard the bases and set the exponential expressions equal to each other:

$$2^{3x-3} = 2^{25-5x} \text{ means that } 3x - 3 = 25 - 5x$$

Solving this equation yields $x = \dfrac{28}{8} = \dfrac{7}{2}$.

 **TIP** When an equation uses variables in different exponential expressions, like $4^{3x} = 8^{2x-1}$, rewrite the bases as equivalent bases before proceeding. Once an equation is in the form $x^a = x^b$, disregard the bases and set $a = b$.

Use this method to approach the following question.

....

If for all real numbers r and b, $16^r = \sqrt[b]{8}$, what is the value of rb?

    F. -1

    G. $\dfrac{1}{2}$

    H. $\dfrac{4}{3}$

    J. $\dfrac{3}{4}$

    K. $\dfrac{3}{2}$

The correct answer is J. First, change 16 and 8 to powers of 2: $\left(2^4\right)^r = \sqrt[b]{2^3}$. Simplify both sides into exponential form: $2^{4r} = 2^{\frac{3}{b}}$. Disregard the like bases and set the exponents equal to each other: $4r = \dfrac{3}{b}$, so $rb = \dfrac{3}{4}$. Choice F had an error when solving $4rb = 3$; 4 was incorrectly subtracted from both sides to isolate rb, but it needed to be divided. Choice G is the quotient of 8 and 16, but it does not correctly work with the exponents. Choice H is the reciprocal of the correct answer. Choice K is the quotient of the cubed root of 8 and the fourth root of 16, but it does not work correctly with the exponents.

....

GENERALIZING EXPONENTIAL PROPERTIES

Exponential questions can be difficult when they require you to generalize facts about exponential properties that you have never seen before.

Example:

For all real numbers w, x, and y, such that $w \neq x \neq y$, if $w^x = 4$ and $y^x = 3$, then what is the value of 12 in terms of w, x, and y?

Solution:

The ACT loves questions like this because you can't just plug values into your calculator to solve this question. First, recognizing that $4 \cdot 3 = 12$, you can substitute the exponential equivalents for 4 and 3 into the equation: $w^x \cdot y^x = 12$. That part was easy, but what if $w^x \cdot y^x$ is not one of the available answer choices? You're accustomed to multiplying *like bases* with *different exponents*, but in this equation you have *different bases* with *like exponents*. Notice that $w^x y^x$ is the result of raising the product wy to the power of x: $w^x y^x = (wy)^x$. You see that $(wy)^x$ is indeed an answer choice, and you do a small victory dance in your seat!

NOTE: Some of the toughest questions on the ACT cannot be solved on a calculator and require more abstract thinking. This is especially true with properties of exponents.

OPERATIONS WITH RADICALS

Here are two more skills to keep sharp when working with radicals. In the following question, you need to add fractions with radical denominators by finding a common denominator. Don't be intimidated—unlike radicals can be combined through multiplication, just *not* through addition!

Example:

Find the sum: $\dfrac{3}{\sqrt{5}} + \dfrac{3}{\sqrt{3}}$

Solution:

Use a common denominator of $\sqrt{15}$ to add these two fractions:

$$\frac{3}{\sqrt{5}} + \frac{3}{\sqrt{3}} = \frac{3}{\sqrt{5}}\left(\frac{\sqrt{3}}{\sqrt{3}}\right) + \frac{3}{\sqrt{3}}\left(\frac{\sqrt{5}}{\sqrt{5}}\right)$$

$$= \frac{3\sqrt{3}}{\sqrt{15}} + \frac{3\sqrt{5}}{\sqrt{15}}$$

$$= \frac{3\sqrt{3} + 3\sqrt{5}}{\sqrt{15}}$$

It's also a good idea to remember how to *rationalize the denominator* of a fraction. This involves multiplying the numerator and denominator by the conjugate of the radical expression in the denominator.

Example:

Find an equivalent expression to $\dfrac{4}{2-\sqrt{5}}$.

Solution:

$$\dfrac{4}{\left(2-\sqrt{5}\right)} \cdot \left(\dfrac{2+\sqrt{5}}{2+\sqrt{5}}\right) = \dfrac{8+4\sqrt{5}}{-1} = -8-4\sqrt{5}$$

Note that we used FOIL to simplify the denominator $\left(2-\sqrt{5}\right)\left(2+\sqrt{5}\right) = 4-5 = -1$.

EXPONENTIAL EXPRESSIONS WITH FRACTIONAL BASES

Consider the expression $y = a^x$ for any real number $a > 0$. Will y always get larger as x increases? Students often fall for this misconception, but it's a trap! If a is a positive fraction less than 1 ($0 < a < 1$), then as x increases from 0 to ∞, y will actually *decrease*.

Conversely, y will *increase* as x decreases from 0 to $-\infty$. If this is confusing to grasp, look at the graph of $y = \left(\dfrac{1}{2}\right)^x$ pictured here and observe what happens to y as x moves in both directions:

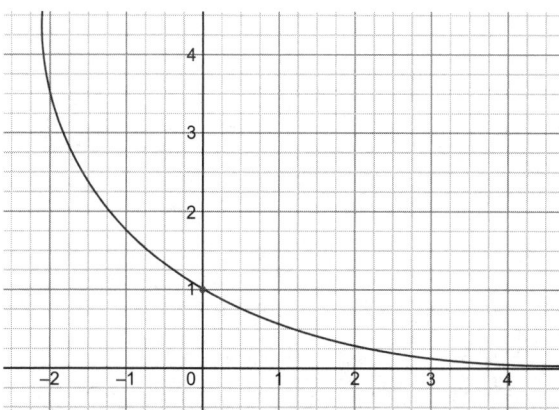

 ALERT: Remember that given the expression $y = a^x$, y will not *always* increase as x increases. If $0 < a < 1$, then y will decrease as x increases from 0 to ∞. Conversely, y will *increase* as x decreases from 0 to $-\infty$. Beware of fractional bases!

BEING POSITIVE ABOUT NEGATIVE BASES

It's a good idea to have a sound proficiency in identifying fractions with perfect square denominators as integers with negative exponents. For example, $\frac{1}{2}$ is equivalent to 2^{-1} and $\frac{1}{3}$ is 3^{-1}. We'll get you started with these five examples, but don't stop here—you should be just as comfortable converting $\frac{1}{25}$ and $\frac{1}{27}$ into their exponential equivalents of 5^{-2} and 3^{-3}, respectively!

Fraction	Exponential Equivalent
$\frac{1}{2}$	2^{-1}
$\frac{1}{4}$	2^{-2}
$\frac{1}{8}$	2^{-3}
$\frac{1}{3}$	3^{-1}
$\frac{1}{9}$	3^{-2}

Your problem-solving skills will be stronger if you are fluent in converting fractions with perfect square denominators, such as $\frac{1}{9}$ and $\frac{1}{4}$, into their equivalent expressions with negative bases (respectively, 3^{-2} and 2^{-2}).

RATIONAL EXPRESSIONS

Rational expressions are lots of variables jumbled together into what can look like an intimidating fraction. The good news is that these questions are normally much easier than they look. We think you can muscle your way through these questions without too much help, so we won't spend a lot of time here, but we do want to show you the different types of rational expression questions you can expect on the ACT.

SIMPLIFYING RATIONAL EXPRESSIONS

You might be able to do these questions with your eyes closed, but if it's been a while, recall that in order to simplify rational expressions, you will need to find the GCF of two terms or maybe factor quadratics into the product of two binomials. Once your numerator and denominator have been fully factored, see which factors can be canceled out in the expression.

Example:

For all x in the domain of the expression, $\dfrac{4x^2+8x}{x^2-x-6}$, find an equivalent expression.

Solution:

Factor the numerator and denominator and cancel out like factors:

$$\frac{4x^2+8x}{x^2-x-6} = \frac{4x(x+2)}{(x+2)(x-3)} \text{ Now the } (x+2) \text{ factors cancel out}$$

$$= \frac{4x}{x-3}$$

 ALERT: When simplifying rational expressions, remember that you can only cancel out *factors* and you may not cancel out individual *terms*. For example, in $\dfrac{5x-3}{10x-3}$, you may not reduce the 5 and 10, nor may you cancel out the 3's on the top and bottom. $\dfrac{5x-3}{10x-3}$ is fully simplified.

ADDING AND SUBTRACTING RATIONAL EXPRESSIONS

You will not be asked to add or subtract the same gnarly rational expressions you've surely done in your math class, but this is still good to review. Remember to find a common denominator and, if subtracting, don't forget to distribute the subtraction to *both* terms in the numerator of the second expression.

Example:

For all x in the domain of the function $\dfrac{3}{x-2} - \dfrac{4}{x}$, find an equivalent function.

Solution:

We will use a common denominator of $x(x-2)$:

$$\frac{3}{x-2} - \frac{4}{x} = \frac{3}{x-2}\left(\frac{x}{x}\right) - \frac{4}{x}\left(\frac{x-2}{x-2}\right)$$ This step gets common denominators.

$$= \frac{3x}{x(x-2)} - \frac{4x-8}{x(x-2)}$$ Distribute the minus sign to both $4x$ and 8!

$$= \frac{3x - 4x - (-8)}{x(x-2)} = \frac{-1x + 8}{x(x-2)}$$

IDENTIFYING CHANGES IN EXPRESSIONS

Sometimes, students can get tricked when asked to determine how a rational expression changes when one of the variables increases or decreases by a certain factor.

Example:

Let $P = \dfrac{100c + cd}{3bc + b}$ represent the price of a bond. What happens to the value of P when the value of b is doubled?

Solution:

It's tempting to say that the value of P will also double when b is doubled, but instead of jumping to hasty conclusions, replace b with $2b$ and see how that changes the value of P:

Let $b = 2b$:

$$P = \frac{100c + cd}{3(2b)c + 2b} = \frac{100c + cd}{6bc + 2b}$$

Now you can factor out a 2 from the denominator and rewrite this as $\dfrac{1}{2}$ times the original expression:

$$P = \frac{100c + cd}{2(3bc + b)} = \frac{1}{2} \cdot \frac{100c + cd}{3bc + b}$$

This helps you determine that the value of P will be cut in half when the value of b is doubled.

When asked how a change in the value of one variable will impact an entire expression, use substitution to replace the altered variable with its new value. Then, use algebraic manipulations to rewrite the new expression as a product of the original expression and a new factor. This new factor illustrates how the value of the original expression has changed.

FACTORING AND SOLVING QUADRATIC EQUATIONS

Recall that a quadratic is an equation that can be written in the form $y = ax^2 + bx + c$, such that $a \neq 0$. You've probably gotten enough practice with the quadratic formula to last you a lifetime, so you'll be happy to know that we're not going to hit you over the head with it. You should know that the quadratic formula is $x = \dfrac{-b \pm \sqrt{b^2 - 4ac}}{2a}$, and this formula gives you the x solutions to a quadratic that has been set to zero: $ax^2 + bx + c = 0$. But we don't think you're really going to need to use this formula on the ACT.

The majority of the quadratics you might see on test day will be easy to factor. If you get thrown a challenging quadratic, you can determine its factorization by working backwards with the answer choices. The ACT won't challenge you with absurdly difficult factoring puzzles, but it *will* push you to apply your knowledge about factoring and quadratics in nonstandard ways.

FACTORING NONSTANDARD QUADRATICS

Although you can often work backward to determine the factorization of quadratics on the ACT, it's usually more time-efficient to do the factoring directly. Recall that factoring $ax^2 + bx + c$ is pretty easy when $a = 1$. Your two factors must *multiply* to c and must *add* to b as indicated below:

For all real numbers b and c

$1x^2 + bx + c = (x + m)(x + n)$

as long as $mn = c$ and $m + n = b$.

When $a \neq 1$, things get a little more interesting. Usually on the ACT, if $a \neq 1$, you will be able to factor out a GCF, so that a is then equal to 1. But if this isn't possible, you can either use the quadratic equation to find your factors or work backward from the given answers.

Let's take a look at some factoring questions that might initially give you pause, but are actually more straightforward than they appear.

Example:

Factor completely: $4x^2 - 32x + 60$.

Solution:

Since $a \neq 1$, you may start to panic, but notice that 4 can be divided out as the GCF, which will leave a as 1:

$$4x^2 - 32x + 60 = 4(x^2 - 8x + 15)$$

Next, factor $x^2 - 8x + 15$ using factors -3 and -5:

$$4(x^2 - 8x + 15) = 4(x - 3)(x - 5)$$

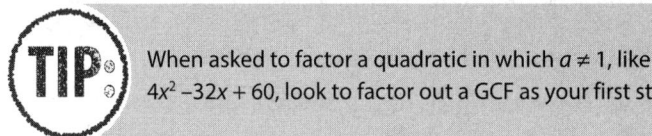 When asked to factor a quadratic in which $a \neq 1$, like $4x^2 - 32x + 60$, look to factor out a GCF as your first step.

Notice how the following question doesn't *ask* you to factor, but that is what must be done in order to solve it.

Example:

Find the largest value of m such that $21m = -m^2 + 100$.

Solution:

Since this equation has an m^2 as well as an m, solve it by moving everything over to one side of the equation and setting it equal to zero. It's important to note that it's always a good idea to keep the leading coefficient positive; rather than moving the $21m$ to the right side of the equation, move the $-m^2$ and 100 to the left side and write it in standard $ax^2 + bx + c = 0$ form:

$$21m = -m^2 + 100 \text{ becomes } 21m = m^2 + 21m - 100 = 0$$

$$m^2 + 21m - 100 = 0 \text{ factors into } (m - 4)(m + 25) = 0$$

You were asked to find the largest value of m. This is the point at which some students will get tricked. It might look like 25 is the largest answer, but -4 and 25 are not the *solutions* to the equations. Your solutions are the values of m that will make $(m - 4)(m + 25) = 0$, namely, $m = 4$ and $m = -25$. Therefore, the largest value of m is 4.

ALERT: Factoring a quadratic is different from *solving* it! When asked to solve a quadratic equation, remember that getting it into factored form $(x + w)(x + v) = 0$ is just the first step! Don't forget to set each binomial equal to zero individually—$(x + w) = 0$ and $(x + v) = 0$—to solve for the correct x-values.

SPECIAL QUADRATICS

You must be well versed in factoring quadratics that are the *difference of perfect squares*. These types of quadratics do not have a *bx*-term, but instead are one perfect square subtracting another perfect square. They have the following shortcut for factoring:

Factoring the difference of perfect squares:

$$x^2 - y^2 = (x + y)(x - y)$$

Notice that the two binomials in the factored form are $(\sqrt{x^2} \pm \sqrt{y^2})$. For example, the quadratic $4x^2 - 25$ factors into $(\sqrt{(4x^2)} \pm \sqrt{25})$, which is $(2x + 5)(2x - 5)$.

SOLVING QUADRATICS WITH EXTRANEOUS VARIABLES

The hardest quadratic questions you might see on the ACT are the nonstandard questions that include extra variables. We'll walk you through two examples and then give you a sample question to try on your own:

Example:

If -3 is a solution to $x^2 + kx + 12 = 0$, then what is the value of k?

Solution:

A great distracter that many students might select is -7. Students know that -3 times -4 equals 12, and since $-3 + -4 = -7$, at first glance, it seems that -7 is the correct value for k. Here's why it's not: If -3 is a *solution* to $x^2 + kx + 12 = 0$, it means that $(x + 3)$ is a factor, and *not* $(x - 3)$. Therefore, the other factor would need to be $(x + 4)$, since $3 \cdot 4 = 12$. Now we have $(x + 3)(x + 4) = x^2 + 7x + 12$, and we can correctly determine that $k = 7$.

Example:

Suppose that $x = 5$ is the only solution to the equation for $x^2 + 2wx + v = 0$, where w and v are real numbers. What is the value of $w + v$?

Solution:

This is a question that looks really confusing, but it can be solved without too much hassle by working backward. If $x = 5$ is the only solution, we know that $(x - 5)$ must be a repeated factor of the original quadratic:

$$(x - 5)(x - 5) = x^2 + 2wx + v$$

FOIL the left side of the equation: $x^2 - 10x + 25 = x^2 + 2wx + v$.

It is clear now that $v = 25$. Notice that $-10 = 2w$, which means that $w = -5$. The value of $w + v$ is $-5 + 25 = 20$.

Hopefully, now you don't think it's too intimidating when random variables are inserted into quadratic equations. Give this sample ACT-type question a try:

. . . .

Determine the value of $e \cdot f$, if $(x + 3)$ and $(x - 2)$ are the only factors of the following quadratic expression: $x^2 + (5 - f)x + e - f$.

   A. −2
   B. 4
   C. 2
   D. 8
   E. −8

The correct answer is E. Working backward, use the given factors to determine that $(x + 3)(x - 2) = x^2 + 1x - 6$. Set this trinomial equal to the given expression: $x^2 + 1x - 6 = x^2 + (5 - f)x + e - f$. Notice that $(5 - f) = 1$, which means that $f = 4$. Next, note that $e - f = -6$, and replace f with 4: $e - 4 = -6$, which gives $e = -2$. The value of $e \cdot f$ is −8. Choice A is the value of e, and not the value of $e \cdot f$. Choice B is the value of f, and not the value of $e \cdot f$. Choice C is the value of $e + f$, and not the value of $e \cdot f$. Choice D has the wrong sign of $e \cdot f$, which should be −8 and not 8.

. . . .

ABSOLUTE VALUE INEQUALITIES

An inequality is a mathematical relationship that has an inequality symbol, like > or <, instead of an equal sign. The ACT probably won't trick you with absolute value or inequality questions, but you *do* need to be completely comfortable solving absolute value inequalities and graphing their solution sets on number lines.

One step that students often forget with inequalities is to change the direction of the inequality symbol when the inequality is *divided* or *multiplied* by a negative number. For example, $-3x > 6$ will have the solution set $x < -2$ after both sides are divided by -3.

ALERT: It's easy to forget to switch the direction of the inequality symbol when dividing or multiplying by negatives. Check your answer by testing a value from your solution set in the original inequality!

A tricky aspect of the solutions to absolute value inequalities is that they will either be bounded on two sides ($4 < x < 10$) or they will go on for infinity in two opposite directions ($x < -2$ and $x > 6$). Let's look at one example of each type.

Example:

Graph the solution set for the inequality $|5 - 2x| < 13$.

Solution:

First, realize that if $|5 - 2x|$ is less than 13, it must also be greater than -13. This is because the absolute value of any number less than -13 will end up being greater than 13. So to start solving this equation, rewrite the equation with its lower bound included:

$$-13 < |5 - 2x| < 13$$

Now that the lower bound is included, remove the absolute value symbol and solve for x by performing the identical operations on all three parts of the inequality for each step:

$$-13 < 5 - 2x < 13$$
$$\underline{-5 \quad -5 \qquad -5}$$
$$-18 < -2x < 8$$
$$\underline{\div -2 \div -2 \div -2}$$
$$9 > x > -4 \text{ (switch the direction of the inequality symbol)}$$
$$-4 < x < 9$$

In order to graph this solution, circle -4 and 9 on a number line. Keep the circles open to show that they are not part of the solution set and shade the space between them:

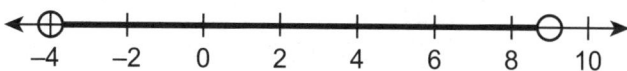

 Absolute value inequalities will always involve two solutions, but don't just memorize a technique for setting them up. As long as you *think* about the significance of the absolute value brackets, you should be able to construct both equations to uncover the full solution set.

If the absolute value portion of an equation is mixed with other terms, the first step is always to isolate the absolute value expression before considering how to construct the upper and lower solutions.

Example:

Graph the solution set for the inequality $\left(\left|\dfrac{2}{3}x\right| - 11\right)^2 \geq 49$.

Solution:

$\left(\left|\dfrac{2}{3}x\right| - 11\right)^2 \geq 49$ looks a lot more complicated than the previous example, but just approach it step by step and you will see that it is not as scary as it appears. First, take the square root of both sides:

$$\sqrt{\left(\left|\dfrac{2}{3}x\right| - 11\right)^2} \geq \sqrt{49}$$

$$\left|\dfrac{2}{3}x\right| - 11 \geq 7$$

Next, add 11 to both sides to isolate the absolute value-term:

$$\left|\dfrac{2}{3}x\right| \geq 18$$

Now recognize that the second part of our solution comes from realizing that $\left|\dfrac{2}{3}x\right|$ will be greater than 18 when $\dfrac{2}{3}x$ is less than −18. (The absolute value of any number less than −18 is greater than 18.) Rewrite $\left|\dfrac{2}{3}x\right| \geq 18$ as two separate inequalities since there will be no overlap between these two solutions (a number cannot be simultaneously greater than 18 and less than −18). Solve both inequalities by dividing by $\dfrac{2}{3}$:

$$\dfrac{2}{3}x \geq 18 \quad \text{and} \quad \dfrac{2}{3}x \leq -18$$

$$x \geq 18\left(\dfrac{3}{2}\right) \qquad x \leq -18\left(\dfrac{3}{2}\right)$$

$$x \geq 27 \qquad \qquad x \leq -27$$

27 and −27 are the starting points of each part of the solution set, which will expand outward toward positive and negative infinity. The circles at −27 and 27 will be filled to show they are part of the solution set:

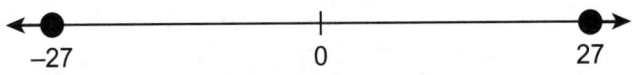

DIRECT AND INVERSE VARIATION

Direct and inverse variation is one of those topics that you may have covered only briefly in math class. Although these variation questions are not frequently on the ACT, if you *do* get one, it could be a score buster if you haven't reviewed variation! Although the following questions may sound like secret code at first, once you understand the jargon of direct and inverse variation, they will be easy points to put toward your score.

The formula for direct variation is $y = kx$, where k is a real number called the *constant of variation*. The *constant of variation*, k, doesn't have to be multiplied to a linear term, like x. It can be multiplied to a quadratic or cubic, such as w^2 or z^3, or by a radical term, like $\sqrt{v}$. For example, the phrase, "y varies directly as the product of m and c^2," is written as $y = k \cdot mc^2$.

The formula for inverse variation is $y = \dfrac{k}{x}$, where the constant of variation, k, is being divided by a variable term. For example, "y varies inversely with the square root of the sum of x and 5" should be represented with the equation $y = \dfrac{k}{\sqrt{x+5}}$. Look over the variation examples in the following table to make sure you have a handle on how to translate the language of variations into equations:

Variation Language	Equivalent Variation Equation
A varies directly with the square of *r* and the constant of variation is π.	$A = kr^2$ becomes $A = \pi r^2$
L varies directly as the root of *c* and inversely as the cube of *d*.	$L = \dfrac{k\sqrt{c}}{d^3}$
z varies inversely as the product of 3 and *x*. If $z = 4$ when $x = 2$, what is the constant of variation, *k*? Write an equation for the variation.	$z = \dfrac{k}{3x}$ becomes $4 = \dfrac{k}{3 \cdot 2}$, so $k = 24$ and the variation is expressed as $z = \dfrac{24}{3x}$

Notice in the second example that a single equation can have both direct and inverse variation at the same time. Also take note that in the third example, we were able to solve for k given the additional information that $z = 4$ when $x = 2$. If you are given a variation question, you will most likely need to perform this task and then use k to solve for a missing piece of information.

Example:

In a scientific experiment, the width, W, of a bacteria colony starts at 75 millimeters and grows wider as it is incubated. The growth rate of the colony varies directly with the square of the number of hours, h, it is incubated. If the colony is 165 millimeters wide after 3 hours, what will the width of the colony be after 5 hours?

Solution:

Since the growth rate of the colony varies directly with the square of the number of hours, h, we know that the growth rate is kh^2. Since the starting width is 75 millimeters, we can model the width W as $W = 75 + kh^2$. Given that $W = 165$ when $h = 3$, substitute in these values and solve for k:

$$W = 75 + kh^2$$
$$165 = 75 + k(3^2)$$
$$90 = 9k \text{ and } k = 10$$

Now determine the width of the colony after 5 hours by substituting $k = 10$ and $h = 5$ into the equation and solving for $W = 325$ millimeters after 5 hours of incubation.

$$W = 75 + kh^2, k = 10, \text{ and } h = 5:$$
$$W = 75 + 10 \cdot 5^2$$
$$W = 75 + 250 = 325$$

Direct variation models a relationship where the constant of variation, k, is multiplied by a factor: $y = kx$. Inverse variation models a relationship where the constant of variation is divided by a factor: $y = \dfrac{k}{x}$.

ARITHMETIC AND GEOMETRIC SEQUENCES

The ACT generally has one arithmetic or geometric sequence question on each test. It's critical to keep these two different types of sequences straight. Students sometimes confuse the formulas for sequences, and they aren't *needed* for the ACT questions, so instead of asking you to memorize formulas, we'll demonstrate a visual way we call "counting the gaps" that can be used to conquer sequence questions.

ARITHMETIC SEQUENCES

An arithmetic sequence is a string of numbers that moves from one term to the following term by adding the same value each time. For example, 10, 15, 20, 25, ... and –3.5, –6, –8.5, –11, ... are both arithmetic sequences. 10, 15, 20, 25, ... starts at 10 and adds 5 to each term, while –3.5, –6, –8.5, –11, ... starts at –3.5 and adds –2.5 to each term. (Notice that adding a negative makes a decreasing sequence.)

In order to test if a series of numbers is an arithmetic sequence, subtract each term from the following term to see if there is a common difference between all the terms. The common difference in arithmetic sequences is referred to as d. A must-have skill with algebraic sequences is to be able to determine the d when given two nonconsecutive numbers from the sequence. Let's walk through a problem together.

Example:

> The 5th term of an arithmetic sequence is 23 and the 9th term is 29. Find the sum of the first three terms of this sequence.

Solution:

Rather than get you all tied up with funny looking recursive sequence formulas, we are going to show you our "count the gaps" technique. First, make a quick sketch of 9 spaces for your first 9 terms of this sequence. Put 23 in the fifth position and 29 in the ninth slot:

$$\underline{\quad}\ \underline{\quad}\ \underline{\quad}\ \underline{\quad}\ \underline{23}\ \underline{\quad}\ \underline{\quad}\ \underline{\quad}\ \underline{29}$$
$$1^{st}\ \ 2^{nd}\ \ 3^{rd}\ \ 4^{th}\ \ 5^{th}\ \ 6^{th}\ \ 7^{th}\ \ 8^{th}\ \ 9^{th}$$

Next, notice that in order to get from the 5th to the 6th terms you would need to add d, the common difference. The same goes for moving from the 6th term to the 7th term, and so on. Label each of the four gaps going from position 5 to position 9 each as "$+d$":

$$\underline{\quad}\ \underline{\quad}\ \underline{\quad}\ \underline{\quad}\ \underline{23}\ \underline{\quad}\ \underline{\quad}\ \underline{\quad}\ \underline{29}$$
$$1^{st}\ \ 2^{nd}\ \ 3^{rd}\ \ 4^{th}\ \ 5^{th}\ \ 6^{th}\ \ 7^{th}\ \ 8^{th}\ \ 9^{th}$$

$$+d\ \ +d\ \ +d\ \ +d$$

$$+4d$$

Since it will take four repeated additions of d to get from 23 to 29, we can represent this relationship as $23 + 4d = 29$. Make sure you understand how we arrived at this equation, since you'll need to be comfortable deriving these patterns on your own! Now solve for the common difference, d:

$$23 + 4d = 29$$

$$4d = 6, \text{ so } d = 1.5.$$

Confirm that $d = 1.5$ by starting with the 5th term, 23, and adding 1.5 to it four times. This will have us arrive perfectly at the 9th term of 29:

$$\underline{\quad}\ \underline{\quad}\ \underline{\quad}\ \underline{\quad}\ \underline{23}\ \underline{24.5}\ \underline{26}\ \underline{27.5}\ \underline{29}$$
$$1^{st}\ \ 2^{nd}\ \ 3^{rd}\ \ 4^{th}\ \ 5^{th}\ \ 6^{th}\ \ 7^{th}\ \ 8^{th}\ \ 9^{th}$$

$$+1.5\ \ +1.5\ \ +1.5\ \ +1.5$$

Next, in order to uncover the first three terms, we must move *left* from the 5th term, by *subtracting* 1.5 from each term:

$$\underset{\substack{1^{\text{st}}}}{17}\ \underset{\substack{2^{\text{nd}}}}{18.5}\ \underset{\substack{3^{\text{rd}}}}{20}\ \underset{\substack{4^{\text{th}}}}{21.5}\ \underset{\substack{5^{\text{th}}}}{23}\ \underset{\substack{6^{\text{th}}}}{24.5}\ \underset{\substack{7^{\text{th}}}}{26}\ \underset{\substack{8^{\text{th}}}}{27.5}\ \underset{\substack{9^{\text{th}}}}{29}$$

$$-1.5\ -1.5\ -1.5\ -1.5$$

Now we can see that the first three terms of this arithmetic sequence are 17, 18.5, and 20. The sum of the first three terms is therefore 55.5.

A potential pitfall when solving problems like these is counting the *numbers* that fall between set terms, rather than counting the *gaps* that exist between the given terms.

 ALERT: When you have an arithmetic sequence set up as follows, make sure you count the *gaps* and *not* how many numbers fit between the two terms.

GEOMETRIC SEQUENCES

A geometric sequence is a string of numbers where each new term is found by *multiplying* the same value to each term. For example, 1, –2, 4, –8, ... is a geometric sequence that starts at 1, and each new term is found by multiplying by –2. Notice how multiplying by a negative number makes the sequence oscillate between negative and positive terms. A geometric sequence will have decreasing terms when the multiple is a value between 0 and 1: Notice that 200, 100, 50, 25, ... starts at 200 and multiplies by $\frac{1}{2}$ to get each new term.

Divide any term in a geometric sequence by its previous term to get the *common ratio*, referred to as *r*. For example, the geometric sequence that starts off 12, 15, 18.75... has an *r* of 1.25, since $\frac{15}{12} = 1.25$. Let's see how to use the "count the gaps" method to find the *r* in a geometric sequence when nonconsecutive terms are given.

Example:

If the 4th term in a geometric sequence is 2 and the 8th term is –512, find the 2nd term in the sequence.

Solution:

First, make a quick sketch of 8 spaces for your first 8 terms of this sequence. Put 2 in the 4th position and 512 in the 8th position:

$$\underset{\substack{1^{\text{st}}}}{\underline{\hspace{1.5em}}}\ \underset{\substack{2^{\text{nd}}}}{\underline{\hspace{1.5em}}}\ \underset{\substack{3^{\text{rd}}}}{\underline{\hspace{1.5em}}}\ \underset{\substack{4^{\text{th}}}}{\underline{2}}\ \underset{\substack{5^{\text{th}}}}{\underline{\hspace{1.5em}}}\ \underset{\substack{6^{\text{th}}}}{\underline{\hspace{1.5em}}}\ \underset{\substack{7^{\text{th}}}}{\underline{\hspace{1.5em}}}\ \underset{\substack{8^{\text{th}}}}{\underline{512}}$$

Notice that in order to get from the 4th to the 5th term you would need to multiply by r, the common ratio. The same goes for moving between all the other terms. Label the 4 gaps going from the 4th term to the 8th term each as a "$\cdot r$" as shown here:

$$\underset{\text{1st}}{\underline{}}\ \underset{\text{2nd}}{\underline{}}\ \underset{\text{3rd}}{\underline{}}\ \underset{\text{4th}}{\underline{2}}\ \underset{\text{5th}}{\underline{}}\ \underset{\text{6th}}{\underline{}}\ \underset{\text{7th}}{\underline{}}\ \underset{\text{8th}}{\underline{512}}$$

$$\underbrace{\cdot r \quad \cdot r \quad \cdot r \quad \cdot r}_{\cdot r^4}$$

Since it will take four repeated *multiplications* of r to get from 2 to 512, we can represent this relationship as $2 \cdot r^4 = 512$. Looking at the illustration, can you see why this equation makes sense? Now solve for the common ratio, r:

$$2 \cdot r^4 = 512$$
$$r^4 = 256, \text{ so } r = 4$$

We can confirm that $r = 4$ by starting with the 4th term, 2, and multiplying it by 4, four times, to bring us to the 8th term, 512:

4th term: 2

5th term: $2 \times 4 = 8$

6th term: $8 \times 4 = 32$

7th term: $32 \times 4 = 128$

8th term: $128 \times 4 = 512$

Use division to move backwards in a geometric sequence. Starting with the 4th term, divide by r two times to determine the 2nd term:

4th term: 2

3rd term: $2 \div 4 = \dfrac{1}{2}$

2nd term: $\dfrac{1}{2} \div 4 = \dfrac{1}{8}$

The 2nd term in the sequence is $\dfrac{1}{8}$.

The *common difference, d,* in an arithmetic ratio is found by subtracting a term from its following term. The *common ratio, r,* in a geometric ratio is found by dividing a term by its previous term.

Now apply the "count the gaps" method on your own, to solve this question:

. . . .

Find the sum of the first two terms in a geometric sequence that has –5 as its 4th term and 135 as its 7th term.

    F. $\dfrac{20}{27}$

    G. $\dfrac{5}{27}$

    H. $-\dfrac{5}{9}$

    J. $-\dfrac{10}{27}$

    K. $\dfrac{5}{3}$

The correct answer is J. Since this is a geometric series, the 4th term must be multiplied by r three repeated times to arrive at the 7th term:

$$\underline{}\ \underline{}\ \underline{}\ \underline{\overset{-5}{}}\ \underline{}\ \underline{}\ \underline{\overset{135}{}}$$
$$\ ^{1st}\ \ ^{2nd}\ \ ^{3rd}\ \ ^{4th}\ \ ^{5th}\ \ ^{6th}\ \ ^{7th}$$
$$\qquad\qquad\quad \vee\ \ \vee\ \ \vee$$
$$\qquad\qquad\quad \bullet r\ \ \bullet r\ \ \bullet r$$

Therefore the equation $-5 \cdot r^3 = 135$ can be used to solve for r:

$$-5 \cdot r^3 = 135$$
$$r^3 = -27$$
$$r = -3$$

To find the 1st, 2nd, and 3rd terms, start with the 4th term and divide by –3 each time:

    4th term: -5

    3rd term: $-5 \div -3 = \dfrac{5}{3}$

    2nd term: $\dfrac{5}{3} \div -3 = -\dfrac{5}{9}$

    1st term: $-\dfrac{5}{9} \div -3 = \dfrac{5}{27}$

Now find the sum of the first two terms: $-\dfrac{5}{9} + \dfrac{5}{27} = -\dfrac{10}{27}$. Choice F was the sum of $\dfrac{5}{9}$ and $\dfrac{5}{27}$, rather than the sum of $-\dfrac{5}{9}$ and $\dfrac{5}{27}$. Choice G was the first term, and not the sum of the first two terms. Choice H was the second term, and not the sum of the first two terms. Choice K was the third term, and not the sum of the first two terms.

. . . .

FINDING THE SUMS OF SEQUENCES

You may need to find the sum of terms in sequences. Questions wanting the sum of terms in a finite or infinite geometric sequence will give you the formula to do so. However, if you're asked to determine the sum in an arithmetic sequence, you will not be given a formula. You will need to determine the last required term in the sequence and then apply the formula:

> The sum of a fixed number of terms in an arithmetic sequence is:
>
> **(the average of the first and last terms) × (# of terms)**

Let's put this formula to work in the following problem:

Example:

Yeimi puts $37 of savings from her job in a bank account on the first week of the year. Her goal is to deposit $3 more, each successive week, than what she deposited the week before. Considering that there are 52 weeks in a year, how much money will Yeimi save if she meets her goal?

Solution:

Use the summation technique formula above since it would take too much time to determine and sum all 52 deposits by hand! We already know that there will be 52 terms and that the first term is $37. Let's determine the final deposit on week 52 so that we can apply the formula, (the average of the first and last terms) × (# of terms). Determine Yeimi's deposit on week 52 by finding the pattern for each week. Illustrate the first 5 weeks of Yeimi's saving as such:

$$
\begin{array}{ccccc}
\underline{\ 37\ } & \underline{\quad} & \underline{\quad} & \underline{\quad} & \underline{\quad} \\
\text{Week} & \text{Week} & \text{Week} & \text{Week} & \text{Week} \\
1 & 2 & 3 & 4 & 5 \\
& +3 & +3 & +3 & +3 &
\end{array}
$$

Notice that in order to get the deposit amount for week 5, we'd add $3, four times. We can apply this type of reasoning to week 52 by realizing that her final deposit will be her initial $37 plus $3 added 51 times:

$$
\begin{array}{cccc}
\underline{\ 37\ } & \underline{\quad} & \underline{\quad} & \underline{\ ?\ } \\
\text{Week} & \text{Week} & \cdots\cdots & \text{Week} & \text{Week} \\
1 & 2 & & 51 & 52
\end{array}
$$

$3 added 51 times

Evaluate $37 + $3(51)$, to determine that Yeimi's final deposit on week 52 will be $290. The average of her first and last deposit is $\dfrac{37 + 290}{2} = 163.50$, which we'll put into the formula:

(the average of the first and last terms) × (# of terms)

$$(163.50) \times (52)$$
$$= \$8{,}502$$

So if Yeimi meets her goal, she will save $8,502 over the course of a year.

SYSTEMS OF EQUATIONS

The ACT loves systems of equations. Sometimes, you'll be asked directly to solve a system of equations, like, "What is $x + y$ if $3x + 2y = -1$ and $5x - 3y = 11$?" (Notice that this question doesn't advertise that it was a system of equations. It didn't ask you to find the (x, y) solution. Remember, this is the ACT, so it has to be at least a *little* creative in how it asks its questions!) Many times you will need to answer systems of equations problems that are in the form of a word problem, so let's look at some tips for that. (Note the answer from above: $x = 1$ and $y = -2$, so $x + y = -1$.)

SYSTEMS OF EQUATIONS WORD PROBLEMS

Quite often a system of equations will be dressed up in a long word problem with lots of fascinating information. Key information to look for includes:

- *The starting point:* the number that doesn't get influenced when other factors change (such as the one-time sign-up fee to join a fitness club—this won't be doubled if you keep your membership for 2 months)

- *The rate of change:* a factor what will cause an increase or decrease in the final value of a relationship as one of the conditions changes (such as the fee per month of a fitness club—you will pay this fee three times after 3 months of membership)

In general, you will pull information out from the problem and organize it as such:

y = starting point + (rate of change) x

In this equation, x is the *independent variable* that fluctuates (*number of months of gym membership*) and influences the value of the dependent variable, y (*total money spent on gym membership*).

The standard linear equation, $y = mx + b$, can be reconstructed to easily model the information you'll be given in word problems: $y =$ starting point + (rate of change)x. Instead of using y and x, choose variables that clearly represent the real-world content of the problem, like m for months and d for dollars spent.

Once you have pulled the information out of a word problem and correctly put it into two linear equations, you can solve the system of linear equations by whichever method you prefer. The methods that will be most useful are:

- *Equal values method:* Cancel out one of the variables by setting the two equations equal to each other.

- *Elimination method:* Cancel out one of the variables by adding/subtracting the two equations. (This method is also called combination.)

It won't hurt to be familiar with the substitution method as well, but that method might not be used as frequently on the ACT.

We are not going to get into the nitty-gritty of the algebra involved in solving systems of equations, but we'll instead focus on the tricky part of setting equations up and recognizing special case systems. If you aren't 100 percent comfortable with the algebra required to solve systems of equations, then please brush up on this since you'll see at least one or two systems of equations questions on the ACT! Let's take a look at one of the challenging types of questions you might see.

· ·

Kayla leaves to drive from Dillon, Colorado, to Moab, Utah, at an average speed of 60 miles per hour. When Kayla is 50 miles into her trip, Ryland calls to say that he also is going to drive from Dillon to Moab. He has just left and will average 70 miles per hour. Which equation would determine the number of hours it will take Ryland to catch up to Kayla if she continues toward Moab at 60 mph?

A. $(70 - 50)h = 60h$
B. $70h = (50 + 60)h$
C. $60h = 50 + 70h$
D. $70h = 50 + 60h$
E. $0 = 50 + 60h + 70h$

The correct answer is D. Use *distance = rate × time* to model Kayla's distance from Dillon: $d = 60h$. Since Ryland is traveling at 70 miles per hour, his distance from Dillon can be represented as $d = 70h$. Next, incorporate the fact that Kayla was already 50 miles from Dillon when Ryland left Dillon by adding 50 to her original distance: $d = 50 + 60h$. (This shows that when Ryland has traveled h hours, Kayla will have travel $60h$ miles in addition to her initial 50 miles.) Ryland will catch up to Kayla when their distances are equal, so set the two equations equal to each other: $70h = 50 + 60h$. Choice A is incorrect because it models Ryland going 20 miles per hour. Choice B is incorrect because it models Kayla going 110 miles per hour. Choice C is incorrect because it adds Kayla's initial 50 miles travels to Ryland's distance. Choice E is incorrect because Kayla's and Ryland's speeds should not be added together.

· ·

NOTE: Sometimes, the ACT will not ask you to *solve* a system of equations, but instead it will ask you to identify a system of equations that correctly models the system of equations. It can be tempting to work backwards and work through all the answers to see which one makes sense, but it's actually more time-efficient to come up with the system of equations on your own and then look for it among the answer choices.

SPECIAL CASE SYSTEMS OF EQUATIONS

When two lines are parallel, they will never intersect. Therefore, a system of equations consisting of two parallel lines has no solution and is called inconsistent. You will be able to tell that two lines are parallel by putting them both into $y = mx + b$ form and comparing their slopes, m. (We will talk more about slope later in this chapter.) Or, if you attempt to solve an inconsistent system of linear equations algebraically, the x-terms will cancel out and you will end up with a false statement like $-4 = 8$.

Example:

Find the solution to the system of equations:

$$\begin{cases} 2x + 4y = 32 \\ -5x - 10y = 40 \end{cases}$$

Solution:

Putting both of these into $y = mx + b$ form shows us that this system is two linear equations both with the same slope. They are parallel and there is no solution:

$$\begin{cases} y = -\dfrac{1}{2}x + 8 \\ y = -\dfrac{1}{2}x - 4 \end{cases}$$

And if we solved this system algebraically, we would have ended up with the false statement $-4 = 8$, showing that there is no solution.

If two linear equations simplify into equivalent equations, they are the same line and will therefore have infinite solutions. You can recognize that two lines are equivalent by putting them both into $y = mx + b$ form; the m and b will be the same values in both equations. A system of equations will have infinite solutions if when solved algebraically, the x-values cancel out and the resulting statement is true, such as $-4 = -4$.

The ACT may ask you find the value of a variable coefficient that would give a system of infinite solutions. Take a look at the next question and the two different ways to solve it.

Example:

For what value of k would there be an infinite number of solutions to the following system of linear equations?

$$\begin{cases} 15x - 12y = -8 \\ -5x + 4y = 6k \end{cases}$$

Solution:

A system of equations has infinite solutions when the equations are equivalent. Find a factor that when multiplied by one equation sets its x- and y-coefficients equal to those of the other. Multiply the second equation by -3:

$$-5x \cdot (-3) + 4y \cdot (-3) = 6k \cdot (-3)$$
$$15x - 12y = -18k$$

Now, compare the equation $15x - 12y = -18k$ with the first equation, $15x - 12y = -8$.

Notice that -8 must equal $-18k$ in order for there to be infinite solutions: $-8 = -18k$, so

$$k = \frac{-8}{-18} = \frac{4}{9}.$$

An alternate way to solve this question is to get both of the equations into $y = mx + b$ form and then set the constant terms equal to each other. However, if you can multiply one equation by an integer in order to arrive at identical coefficients with the other equation, use this faster method!

NOTE: A system of equations has *infinite* solutions when the two equations are the same line. A system of equations has *no* solution when the two lines are parallel but have different y-intercepts.

FUNCTIONS

The ACT will contain a good amount of questions about functions. These are the following function subtopics with which you will need to be most familiar:

- Function notation and evaluating functions at given values of x
- Compound functions
- Determining the domain of a function
- Vertical and horizontal asymptotes
- Odd and even functions

Function Notation

Some students get intimidated by function notation. Stay calm and remember that $f(x)$ is really just a fancy way to say "the value of y at x." Therefore, $f(8)$ means "the value of y when $x = 8$." To find the value a function at $f(8)$, replace all the x's in the equation with 8 and evaluate the expression using the correct order of operations.

The easiest way to trick students with function notation is to ask them to substitute a negative value into an equation that contains $-x^2$. Read on carefully and avoid this pitfall!

Example:

What is the value of $f(-5)$ if $f(x) = -x^2 - 2x + 5$?

Solution:

First replace all the x's with -5: $f(-5) = -(-5)^2 - 2(-5) + 5$. Now, *many* students will make the mistake of thinking that the negative signs in $-(-5)^2$ cancel out and result in 25. This is incorrect since $-(-5)^2$ expands to $-(-5 \cdot -5)$, which is equivalent to -25. Thus $f(-5) = -25 + 10 + 5 = -10$.

 ALERT: Whether x is replaced with a positive or negative number, the value of $-x^2$ will *always* be negative. Do not make the mistake of canceling out all the negative signs when computing a term like $-(-5)^2$, which equals -25!

Compound Functions

A compound function is created when one function is substituted into another function. You may be asked to calculate an exact value for a compound function.

Example:

$$\text{If } h(x) = \sqrt{x} \text{ and } g(x) = \frac{1}{x} + x \text{, find the value of } g\left(h\left(\frac{1}{4}\right)\right).$$

Solution:

This problem is actually a lot friendlier than it looks. Work from the inside out to evaluate $g\left(h\left(\frac{1}{4}\right)\right)$. First evaluate the $h(x)$ function for $x = \frac{1}{4}$:

$$h\left(\frac{1}{4}\right) = \sqrt{\frac{1}{4}} = \frac{\sqrt{1}}{\sqrt{4}} = \frac{1}{2}$$

Now, put that value of $\dfrac{1}{2}$ into $g(x)$:

$$g\left(\frac{1}{2}\right) = \frac{1}{\frac{1}{2}} + \frac{1}{2} = 2 + \frac{1}{2} = 2\frac{1}{2}$$

$$\text{So } g\left(h\left(\frac{1}{4}\right)\right) = 2\frac{1}{2}.$$

A more challenging compound function question will require you to determine the equation for the compound function.

Example:

If $h(x) = (x - 3)$ and $g(x) = x^2 - x + 9$, find the expression that represents $g(h(x))$.

Solution:

This question is asking you to substitute the $h(x)$ function in for all the x-values in the $g(x)$ function, and then to simplify the expression. (Remember that $(x - 3)^2 \neq x^2 - 9$. You will need to use FOIL to expand this.)

$$g(h(x)) = g(x - 3)$$
$$g(h(x)) = (x - 3)^2 - (x - 3) + 9$$
$$g(h(x)) = x^2 - 7x + 21$$

 ALERT: When working with compound functions, remember that $(a - b)^2 \neq a^2 - b^2$! You will need to use FOIL to expand $(a - b)^2$ into $a^2 - 2ab + b^2$.

Perhaps the trickiest compound function question will ask you to use compound functions to solve for an unknown variable in one of the functions.

Example:

Functions $h(x) = \sqrt{x + 1}$ and $g(x) = 5x - b$ exist such that the graph of the $h(g(x))$ passes through the point $(2, 4)$. What is the value of b?

Solution:

This question looks like a real doozy! Keep your wits about you and start with the information that $h(g(x))$ passes through the point (2, 4). This means that $h(g(2)) = 4$. For starters, let's determine $h(g(x))$:

$$h(g(x)) = \sqrt{(5x+b)+1}$$

Now use $h(g(2)) = 4$ to write:

$$4 = h(g(2)) = \sqrt{(5(2)-b)+1}$$
$$4 = \sqrt{11-b}$$

Next, square both sides:

$$4^2 = \left(\sqrt{11-b}\right)^2$$

$$16 = 11-b, \text{ so } b = -5$$

DETERMINING THE DOMAIN OF A FUNCTION

The domain sets restrictions on the input values that can be used in a function. The domain of any function will be *all real numbers* except any *x-values* that would make the function undefined or equal to an imaginary number. In general, you want to avoid three unruly situations:

1. **The bottom of a fraction may never equal zero.** Keep this from happening by setting the denominator equal to 0 and solving for the *x*-values that would make that happen. Omit these *x*-values from the domain.
2. **An expression within a square root may never be negative.** Find the domain of functions with square roots by setting the expression *within* the square to ≥ 0, and solve for *x*. That will be your domain.
3. **If the bottom of a fraction is a square root expression, that root may never be less than *or* equal to zero.** Find the solution set of *x*-values that make a square root denominator > 0, and this will be your domain.

Find the restrictions on the domain of a function that has a fraction by omitting any *x*-values that would cause the denominator to equal zero. Find the domain of functions with square roots by setting the expression within the square to be $\mathbb{R} 0$ and solve for *x*.

Take a look at each of the functions and their associated domains in the following table:

Function	Domain	Explanation
$f(x) = \dfrac{5}{x^3 - 16x}$	All real numbers except 0, 4, and –4	The denominator factors into $x(x^2 - 16) = x(x + 4)(x - 4)$. This will equal 0 when $x = 0$, 4, and –4, so these are omitted from your domain.
$h(x) = \sqrt{-8 - x}$	All real numbers such that $x \le -8$	Set $-8 - x \ge 0$ to find that $x \le -8$.
$g(x) = \dfrac{x}{\sqrt{3 + x}}$	All real numbers such that $x > -3$	Since $\sqrt{3 + x}$ is in the denominator, $3 + x$ must be greater than 0 and cannot equal 0. Solve $3 + x > 0$ to determine the domain.

 ALERT: A common mistake students make when solving for restrictions in the domain is to think that the *numerator* of a fraction cannot equal 0, which is not true. A fraction is undefined only when the *denominator* equals 0, so do not add unnecessary restrictions to the domain of a function.

VERTICAL AND HORIZONTAL ASYMPTOTES

Know your asymptotes! Asymptotes are values that functions approach, but never reach. On a graph, a function will look like it is flattening out at the asymptote.

A vertical asymptote occurs at any x-value that is not in the domain of a function. 0 is not in the domain of $f(x) = \dfrac{1}{x}$, but as x gets closer and closer to 0, the value of $f(x) = \dfrac{1}{x}$ gets larger and larger and approaches infinity. Since x approaches a value of 0, but can never exist at $x = 0$, the line $x = 0$ is a vertical asymptote of the function $f(x) = \dfrac{1}{x}$.

 Vertical asymptotes have the equation $x = k$ for all real numbers k omitted from the domain of a function. For example, $g(x) = \dfrac{1}{x - 2}$ has a vertical asymptote at $x = 2$.

A horizontal asymptote is a *y*-value that a function will approach but never reach. For example, consider what happens to the *y*-value of $f(x) = \dfrac{1}{x}$ as *x* gets bigger and bigger. The height of the curve will approach 0 as *x* gets infinitely large, but it will never actually *reach* zero (remember that a fraction equals zero only when its *numerator* equals 0). Therefore, $f(x) = \dfrac{1}{x}$ has a horizontal asymptote at *y* = 0.

Finding the horizontal asymptotes is a little more involved than finding the vertical asymptotes. There are four cases that are used to determine the horizontal asymptotes of functions, and you will need to know three of these cases. You will need to identify the *degree* of the expressions in the numerator and denominator, and you may need to identify the *leading term,* so let's review these definitions:

- **The degree of a single-variable expression is the largest exponent.**
  - For example, $5x^2 + 8x$ is a second-degree expression.

- **The leading term of an expression is the term with the largest exponent.**
  - For example, $5x^2$ is the leading term in $5x^2 + 8x$.

The following table organizes the three cases for determining the horizontal asymptote, along with examples:

Case	Horizontal Asymptote	Examples
The degree of the denominator is larger than the degree of the numerator.	$y = 0$	$f(x) = \dfrac{5}{1-x}$ and $h(x) = \dfrac{4x+8}{3x^2}$
The degree of the denominator is equal to the degree of the numerator.	The horizontal asymptote is the quotient of the leading terms.	If $g(x) = \dfrac{8x^2+2}{4x^2-3}$, divide $\dfrac{8x^2}{4x^2}$ to find $y = 2$ as the horizontal asymptote.
The degree of the denominator is larger than the degree of the numerator.	No horizontal asymptote exists.	$f(x) = \dfrac{-4x^3}{9-x^2}$ has no horizontal asymptote.

Given the functions $h(x) = \dfrac{1}{2x}$ and $g(x) = 4x + b$, if the function $h(g(x))$ has a vertical asymptote at $x = 3$, what is the value of b?

    A.   –4
    B.   –8
    C.   8
    D.   12
    E.   –12

The correct answer is E. To find the function $h(g(x))$, replace the x in $g(x)$ with $4x + b$:

$$h(g(x)) = \frac{1}{2(4x + b)} = \frac{1}{8x + 2b}.$$ If $h(g(x))$ has a vertical asymptote at $x = 3$, then 3 is not in the domain of $h(g(x))$. Therefore, we can conclude that the denominator of $h(g(x))$ must equal 0 when $x = 3$. Set $8x + 2b = 0$, plug in $x = 3$, and solve for b: $8(3) + 2b = 0$, so $b = -12$. Choice A is the opposite of the coefficient of x in $g(x)$, but this value for b does not make the denominator of $h(g(x))$ equal to 0 when $x = 3$. Choice B is the opposite of the coefficient of x in $h(g(x))$, but this value for b does not make the denominator of $h(g(x))$ equal to 0 when $x = 3$. Choice C is the coefficient of x in $h(g(x))$, but this value for b does not make the denominator of $h(g(x))$ equal to 0 when $x = 3$. Choice D is the negative value of the correct answer.

ODD AND EVEN FUNCTIONS

The ACT test makers will probably provide you with the function notation definitions of odd or even functions if they ask you a question on these characteristics. But function notation definitions can be confusing to the untrained eye, so let's review what it means for a function to be *odd* or *even*.

The question will most likely state "a function is odd if for all values of x in its domain $f(-x) = -f(x)$." This means that for any (x, y) coordinate pair in the function, there also exists the coordinate pair $(-x, -y)$. For example, if an odd function contains the point (5, 8), it will also contain (–5, –8). Odd functions that are defined at 0 must always pass through the origin, (0, 0), and they are symmetrical about the origin. The following graphs show odd functions:

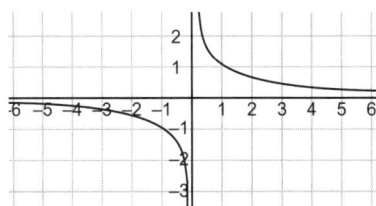

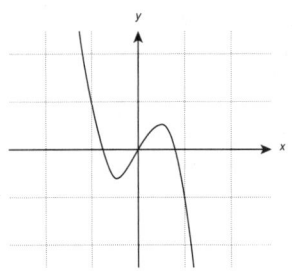 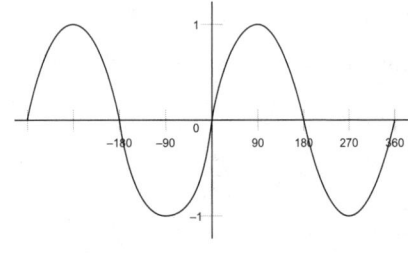

The ACT will probably also inform you that "a function is even if for all values of x in its domain, $f(-x) = f(x)$." This means that in even functions, x and $-x$ will produce the same y-value. For example, if an even function contains the point (5, 8), it will also contain the point (–5, 8). Even functions do not need to pass through the origin, (0, 0), and they are symmetrical about the y-axis. The following graphs depict even functions:

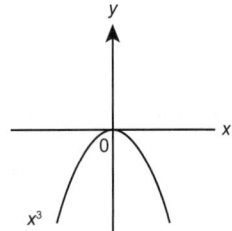 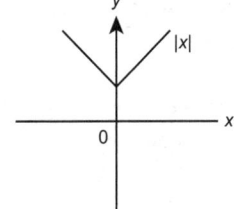 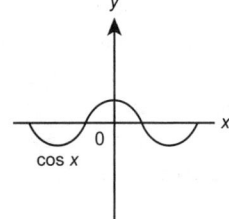

COMPLEX NUMBERS

The family of complex numbers includes all imaginary numbers that are the result of taking the square root of a negative number. The imaginary number i is used to represent $\sqrt{-1}$. The standard form for complex numbers is $a + bi$, where a and b are real numbers and $i = \sqrt{-1}$. The first four powers of i are important to know since the values for i^n repeat in a cycle once $n > 4$:

- $i = \sqrt{-1}$
- $i^2 = \left(\sqrt{-1}\right)^2 = -1$, since squaring cancels out the square root
- $i^3 = i^2 \cdot i = -1 \cdot i = -i$
- $i^4 = i^2 \cdot i^2 = -1 \cdot -1 = 1$

 Complex numbers are written in the form $a + bi$, where a and b are real numbers, $i = \sqrt{-1}$, and $i^2 = -1$.

The ACT will probably remind you that $i = \sqrt{-1}$ or that $i^2 = -1$, but it's helpful to have these facts committed to memory. As long as you feel comfortable with the following two problems, you should be ready for any of the complex number questions you'll see on the test.

Examples:

1. For $i^2 = -1$, find the value of $(8 - i)^2$.
2. If j and k are complex numbers, find the value of jk if $j = -6i + 3$ and $k = 6i + 3$.

Solutions:

1. Use FOIL to expand $(8 - i)^2$: $64 - 16i + i^2$. Then replace i^2 with -1 and simplify:

$$64 - 16i + i^2 = 64 - 16i + (-1) = 63 - 16i.$$

2. When rewriting jk, keep each complex number in parentheses and use FOIL to expand the product. Remember to replace i^2 with -1:

$$
\begin{aligned}
(-6i + 3)(6i + 3) &= -36i^2 - 18i + 18i - 9 \\
&= -36(-1) + 0i - 9 \\
&= 36 - 9 \\
&= 27
\end{aligned}
$$

OVERLAPPING GROUPS

There's not an incredibly high chance you'll see an overlapping group question on test day, however, these questions can be score busters. Overlapping group questions will make your head hurt if you don't know the handy formula to solve them:

Total = (Group 1 + Group 2 + Neither) – Both.

Let's see how to apply this.

Example:

A group of students was surveyed about their activities last weekend. 52 students said they played sports. 35 students said they went to the movies. If 16 students said they did both activities and 22 students said they did neither of those activities, how many students were surveyed in total?

Solution:

Use this formula for these mind-twisters:

Total = (Group 1 + Group 2 + Neither) – Both

Total = (Sports + Movies + Neither) – Both

Total = (52 + 35 + 22) – 16

Total = 93 students

 To solve word problems that have overlapping groups, use the formula:

Total = (Group 1 + Group 2 + Neither) – Both.

Now try an overlapping group problem on your own.

. . . .

In a survey at a music conservatory, 80 professors were asked if they were professionally trained in piano and classical guitar. 68 responded that they were professionally trained in piano, and 56 responded that they were professionally trained in classical guitar. If 5 professors said they'd never been professionally trained in piano or guitar, how many professors at the conservatory had been professionally trained in *both* piano and classical guitar?

    A.   12
    B.   39
    C.   44
    D.   49
    E.   56

The correct answer is D. Plug the given responses into the formula and solve for *Both*:

$$\text{Total} = (\text{Group 1} + \text{Group 2} + \text{Neither}) - \text{Both}$$
$$80 = (68 + 56 + 5) - \text{Both},$$

which shows that "Both" equals 49. Choice A is the difference between the professors who were professionally trained in piano and guitar. Choice C is the sum of the piano- and guitar-trained professors, minus the total number of professors, but it doesn't consider the 5 "neither" professors. Choice E is the number of professors trained in guitar, but it doesn't reflect the other categories.

. . . .

LOGARITHMS

There's about a 50 percent chance that you'll get a logarithm question on the ACT. The tough thing about logarithm questions is that they don't pop up on every test, but when they do, they span a very wide range of logarithm-solving skills.

You might get a simple question testing your understanding of the language of logs and how to convert a logarithm into exponential form:

- Evaluate $\log_2\left(\dfrac{1}{4}\right)$
- Solve for x: $\log_{27} x = -\dfrac{2}{3}$

You might get a more theoretical question testing your understanding of the properties of logarithms:

- What is the value of $\log_8 8^{\frac{7}{3}}$?
- What is an equivalent expression to $\log_c\left(c^m \cdot c^n\right)$?

The toughest type of log question you could see would require you to expand or condense logarithmic expressions or equations:

- Solve for w: $\log_3 36 - \log_3 4 = \log_8 w$
- If $\log_v 4 = c$ and $\log_v 3 = d$, then $\log_v\left(\dfrac{4}{3}\right)^2$ is equivalent to:

If reading through these sample questions has gotten your heart rate up a bit, then you might need to log some time with logs. We'll give you all the facts you need to know right here, but really, the trick to being a logarithm rock star is *practice*. If it's been a little while since you worked with logarithms, find some other resources to get your practice on, so that you're fully prepared for test day. Let's get all the facts out in the open and then work our way through the sample problems presented above.

First, remember that logarithms are just fancy ways to express exponential relationships. In the following relationship, we refer to *b* as the *base*.

Logarithm Definition:

$\log_b y = x$ is equivalent to $b^x = y$

Note: If there is no base noted, then the log is base 10. The ACT doesn't seem to use base 10 very often, but this is still important to know. Let's review how to use the definition of logs to solve the two problems posed at the beginning of this section. First:

Examples:

1. Evaluate $\log_2\left(\dfrac{1}{4}\right)$.

---

2. Solve for x: $\log_{27} x = -\dfrac{2}{3}$

Solutions:

1. The expression $\log_2\left(\dfrac{1}{4}\right)$ is asking you to find the exponent that will cause 2 to become $\dfrac{1}{4}$. Set the log expression equal to x and rewrite it in exponential form: $\log_2\left(\dfrac{1}{4}\right) = x$, so $2^x = \dfrac{1}{4}$. Hopefully, you recall from earlier in this chapter that when the exponent is a variable, you should look to rewrite the expression with identical bases. Since $\dfrac{1}{4}$ is 2^{-2}, rewrite $2^x = \dfrac{1}{4}$ as $2^x = 2^{-2}$, and determine that $x = -2$. Therefore, $\log_2\left(\dfrac{1}{4}\right) = -2$.

2. Rewrite this equation in exponential form: $27^{\frac{2}{3}} = x$. This is the same as $\left(\sqrt[3]{27}\right)^2$. Since $\sqrt[3]{27} = 3$, we can determine that $\left(\sqrt[3]{27}\right)^2 = 9$.

Let's review some of the basic properties of logarithms to answer the next two questions:

Basic Logarithm Properties

$$\log_b b = 1$$

$$\log_b b^y = y$$

$$\log_b = x^y = y \cdot \log_b x$$

$$\log 10^x = x$$

Examples:

1. What is the value of $\log_8 8^{\frac{7}{3}}$?

2. What is an equivalent expression to $\log_c\left(c^m \cdot c^n\right)$?

Solutions:

1. Use the property $\log_b b = 1$ to determine that $\log_8 8^{\frac{7}{3}} = \dfrac{7}{3}$. That's not too bad, right? The next problem just has one additional step.

2. First use the properties of exponents to add the exponents of the c-terms: $\log_c\left(c^m \cdot c^n\right) = \log_c c^{(m+n)}$. Now apply the property $\log_b b = 1$ to determine that $\log_c c^{(m+n)} = m+n$.

The toughest log questions on the ACT require competence using the following properties in both directions. This means you may need to expand a single log into two separate logs (moving left to right in the properties below), or you may have to condense two (or even three) logs into a single expression (moving from right to left).

Expansions for Logs of Products and Quotients

Log of a product: $\log ab = \log a + \log b$

Log of a quotient: $\log\dfrac{a}{b} = \log a - \log b$

Log of a product to a power: $\log(ab)^c = c(\log a + \log b)$

Log of a product within a quotient: $\log\dfrac{ab}{c} = \log a + \log b - \log c$

Note that the third property above is a combination of two log properties, $\log ab = \log a + \log b$ and $\log x^y = y \cdot \log x$ (Similarly, the previous illustration combines two log properties). As you will see in the next question, sometimes multiple properties can be combined to make a monster question!

Example:
════════════════

Solve for w.
$$\log_3 36 - \log_3 4 = \log_8 w$$

Solution:
════════════════

First condense the left side of the equation into a single log using the log of a quotient rule:

$$\log_3 36 - \log_3 4 = \log_8 w$$
$$\log_3\left(\frac{36}{4}\right) = \log_8 w$$
$$\log_3 9 = \log_8 w$$

Now it seems like we're stuck! The bases on both sides are not equal, making this question tougher than normal. Look to see if $\log_3 9$ can be simplified. Since $3^2 = 9$, we can replace $\log_3 9$ with 2:

$$2 = \log_8 w$$

This can now be translated into exponential form: $8^2 = w$, so $w = 64$.

Get ready to use that third rule to solve this practice question.

. . . .

If $\log_v 4 = c$ and $\log_v 3 = d$, then $\log_v \left(\dfrac{4}{3} \right)^2$ is equivalent to:

A. $2c - d$

B. $2c - 2d$

C. $2(c + d)$

D. $\left(\dfrac{c}{d} \right)^2$

E. $\dfrac{c}{d}$

The correct answer is B. Like a barking Chihuahua, this question sounds so much tougher than it really is. Since you are given information about $\log_v 4$ and $\log_v 3$, do *not* change $\left(\dfrac{4}{3} \right)^2$ into $\dfrac{16}{9}$ (You don't know anything about $\log_v 16$ or $\log_v 9$ so that's your clue to *not* do that!) Instead, rewrite $\log_v \left(\dfrac{4}{3} \right)^2$ as $2 \cdot \log_v \left(\dfrac{4}{3} \right)$. Now use the *log of quotient* rule to expand this to $2(\log_v 4 - \log_v 3)$ Lastly, replace $\log_v 4$ with c and $\log_v 3$ with d: $2(c - d) = 2c - 2d$. Choice A is equivalent to $\log_v \left(\dfrac{4^2}{3} \right)$ because the 2 is only being multiplied to the c and not the d. Choice C is equivalent to $\log_v (4 \cdot 3)^2$ because the *product* of a log is the sum of the two individual logs. Choices D and E are incorrect because you may not simply insert $\log_v$ into the numerator and denominator of $\dfrac{4}{3}$.

. . . .

MATRICES

Matrices are rectangular arrays of numbers (or variables) that are organized into *r* rows by *c* columns. The following is a [3 × 2] matrix (said "three by two"). Notice that it has 3 rows and 2 columns:

$$\begin{bmatrix} 1 & A \\ 2 & B \\ 3 & C \end{bmatrix}$$

ADDING AND SUBTRACTING MATRICES

Only matrices with the same dimensions may be added and subtracted. Perform the addition or subtraction on the corresponding entries:

$$\begin{bmatrix} 1 & A \\ 2 & B \\ 3 & C \end{bmatrix} + \begin{bmatrix} 10 & 4A \\ 11 & 5B \\ 12 & 6C \end{bmatrix} = \begin{bmatrix} 11 & 5A \\ 13 & 6B \\ 15 & 7C \end{bmatrix}$$

The ACT will pair the easy task of matrix addition with some algebra:

Example:

What is the value of w in terms of x?

$$\begin{bmatrix} 1 & 4 & 8x+6 \\ 2 & 5 & 7 \end{bmatrix} + \begin{bmatrix} -3 & 9 & w \\ 12 & 6 & 13 \end{bmatrix} = \begin{bmatrix} -2 & 13 & -2x-4 \\ 14 & 11 & 20 \end{bmatrix}$$

Solution:

Add the corresponding entries on the left and set them equal to the sum on the right. Then solve for w in terms of x:

$$8x+6 + w = -2x - 4$$
$$w = -2x - 8x - 4 - 6$$
$$w = -10x - 10$$

SCALAR MULTIPLICATION

Scalar multiplication is when a single multiple is multiplied by every entry in a matrix.

$$\text{Find } -\frac{1}{2}A \text{ if } A = \begin{bmatrix} 18 & -6 \\ -2 & 11 \end{bmatrix}$$

$$-\frac{1}{2}A = \begin{bmatrix} -\frac{1}{2} \cdot (18) & -\frac{1}{2} \cdot (-6) \\ -\frac{1}{2} \cdot (-2) & -\frac{1}{2} \cdot (11) \end{bmatrix} = \begin{bmatrix} -9 & 3 \\ 1 & -5.5 \end{bmatrix}$$

MATRIX MULTIPLICATION

This concept is another score-buster for some students! Matrix multiplication is much more involved than scalar multiplication, but it occurs only once-in-a-blue moon on the ACT Mathematics tests, so lots of students don't review it properly. To multiply matrices, you will need to match up the 1st, 2nd, *nth, rows* of the first matrix with the corresponding 1st, 2nd, *nth columns* of the second matrix. It gets worse . . . . You must multiply each entry in the *nth row* of the first matrix by each corresponding entry in the *nth column* of the second matrix. *Then* the sum of these products will be the entry for the product in the resulting matrix. Take a look at the example here:

$$\begin{bmatrix} A & B & C \\ W & X & Y \end{bmatrix} \begin{bmatrix} 1 & 4 \\ 2 & 5 \\ 3 & 6 \end{bmatrix} = \begin{bmatrix} (1A + 2B + 3C) & (4A + 5B + 6C) \\ (1W + 2X + 3Y) & (4W + 5X + 6Y) \end{bmatrix}$$

Notice that the top entry in the first column of the product matrix is $(1A + 2B + 3C)$. This was the result of mapping the first *row* of the first matrix $\begin{bmatrix} A & B & C \end{bmatrix}$ onto the first *column* of the second matrix $\begin{bmatrix} 1 \\ 2 \\ 3 \end{bmatrix}$: The entries matched up as follows: A corresponded with 1, B corresponded with 2, and C corresponded with 3. Therefore, to find the product of $\begin{bmatrix} A & B & C \end{bmatrix}$ and $\begin{bmatrix} 1 \\ 2 \\ 3 \end{bmatrix}$, we multiplied A by 1, B by 2, and C by 3, and the sum of these products was $(1A + 2B + 3C)$.

If this is not making complete sense to you, then put "matrix multiplication" on your list of concepts to review. It's *unlikely* you will get a matrix multiplication question on your ACT, but you want to be prepared for the worst-case-scenario!

TO MULTIPLY OR NOT TO MULTIPLY?

The good thing about matrix multiplication is that the ACT usually tests only to see if you know *what types of matrices can be multiplied*, rather than asking you to perform the actual multiplication. To determine if two matrices can be multiplied, first express the dimensions of each matrix in $[r \times c]$ form and then use the following rule:

When can matrices be multiplied?

Let $A = [r \times c]$ and $B = [R \times C]$. The matrix product is defined if and only if the number of columns in A is equal to the number of rows in B. Thus, AB is defined if $c = R$ and AB will have dimensions $[r \times C]$.

Use the matrices to determine which of the following statements are true:

$$A = \begin{bmatrix} 1 & 4 \\ 2 & 5 \\ 3 & 6 \end{bmatrix}, \quad B = \begin{bmatrix} 10 & 40 & 70 \\ 20 & 50 & 80 \end{bmatrix}, \quad C = \begin{bmatrix} E & F \\ G & H \end{bmatrix}, \quad D = \begin{bmatrix} X \\ Y \\ Z \end{bmatrix}$$

    I.   Products AB and BA are defined.

    II.   Products AB and CA are defined.

    III.   Product BD is defined and will yield a $[1 \times 2]$.

F.   I

G.   II

H.   III

J.   II and III

K.   None of the statements are true.

The correct answer is K. None of the given statements are true. In order for the product $[r \times c] \cdot [R \times C]$ to be defined, c must equal R. Therefore, AB is defined, but BA is not defined, so Statement I is not true. Similarly, CA is not defined, so Statement II is false. The product BD is defined but it will yield a product with dimensions $[2 \times 1]$ rather than $[1 \times 2]$, so Statement III is also false.

Now that we've wrapped up our investigation of the trickiest intermediate algebra questions the ACT will throw at you, let's look at what you should expect to see in the world of coordinate geometry.

WORKING WITH LINEAR EQUATIONS

Coordinate geometry is the body of concepts relating to graphing points, lines, and curves in the standard (x, y) coordinate plane. We're going to move pretty quickly through most beginning concepts because we imagine you know them inside and out!

CALCULATING SLOPE

The slope between any two points is the rate of change between them. It is the ratio of the *rise*, or vertical change, compared to the *run*, or horizontal change:

> The slope between any two points (x_1, y_1) and (x_2, y_2) $= \dfrac{y_2 - y_1}{x_2 - x_1}$

What is the slope of the line connecting the points (–2, 8) and (6, –4)?

Let $(x_1, y_1) = (-2, 8)$ and let $(x_2, y_2) = (6, -4)$.

$$\text{Slope} = \frac{y_2 - y_1}{x_2 - x_1} = \frac{-4 - 8}{6 - (-2)} = \frac{-12}{8} = -\frac{3}{2}$$

 ALERT: The most common error made while calculating slope is to put the x-coordinates in the numerator of the fraction instead of in the denominator. Make sure that the y-coordinates are always on top!

Sometimes, you will encounter a slope question that requires you to blend algebra and coordinate geometry skills.

• •

Line q contains points G (4, –4) and H (–6, 2w). What is the value of the y-coordinate of point H if the slope of line q is $-\frac{6}{5}$?

    A. –8
    B. 8
    C. 4
    D. –4
    E. 16

The correct answer is B. Plug the given points into the slope formula:

$$\text{Slope} = \frac{y_2 - y_1}{x_2 - x_1} = \frac{-4 - 2w}{4 - (-6)} = \frac{-4 - 2w}{10}.$$

Now set $\frac{-4 - 2w}{10}$ equal to the given slope of $-\frac{6}{5}$ and solve for w:

$$\frac{-4 - 2w}{10} = \frac{-6}{5}$$
$$-60 = -20 - 10w$$
$$w = 4$$

Since $w = 4$, and H (–6, 2w), the y-coordinate of H is 8. Choice A is what the value of the y-coordinate of point H would be if the slope of the line was $\frac{6}{5}$ instead of $-\frac{6}{5}$. Choice C is the value of w but not the value of the y-coordinate of H. Choice D is the opposite of the value of w. Choice E is double the value of the y-coordinate of H.

• •

FINDING LINEAR EQUATIONS

It is not uncommon when taking the ACT to have to find the equation of a line going through two given points. To do this, use the slope-intercept equation for lines, $y = mx + b$, where m is the slope and b is the y-intercept. Here's a quick review of the steps:

1. Calculate the slope, m.
2. Plug m and one of the (x, y) coordinate pairs into the slope-intercept equation, $y = mx + b$.
3. Solve for b.
4. Write the final equation in $y = mx + b$ form, replacing m and b with the found values, but leaving x and y as variables.

Let's see these steps in action.

Example:

What is the equation of the line connecting the points $(-2, 8)$ and $(6, -4)$?

Solution:

First, we find the slope between two points. (In the previous example, we determined the slope between these two same points is $-\frac{3}{2}$.) Next, plug $-\frac{3}{2}$ in for m along with the point $(-2, 8)$ into $y = mx + b$ and solve for b:

$$8 = -\frac{3}{2}(-2) + b$$
$$8 = 3 + b, \text{ so } b = 5$$

$y = -\frac{3}{2} + 5$ is the equation of the line connecting $(-2, 8)$ and $(6, -4)$.

SLOPE OF PARALLEL AND PERPENDICULAR LINES

A commonly tested concept on the ACT is determining if lines in the standard (x, y) coordinate plane are parallel or perpendicular. Recall that parallel lines never intersect, while perpendicular lines intersect to form right angles. Here's a summary of the slopes of parallel and perpendicular lines:

- **Parallel lines:** Parallel lines in the coordinate plane have *identical slopes*.

  $y = \frac{2}{3}x + 5$ and $y = \frac{2}{3}x - 7$ are parallel lines.

- **Perpendicular lines:** Perpendicular lines in the coordinate plane have *negative reciprocal slopes*.

  $y = 4x + 3$ and $y = -\frac{1}{4}x + 2$ are perpendicular lines.

Sometimes, linear equations will be presented in standard form, $Ax + By = C$, where A, B and C are all integers and A is non-negative. Don't be fooled into thinking that the coefficient of x, A, is the slope of a line presented in the form. Instead, use algebraic manipulations to rework the equation into $y = mx + b$ form, and identify the slope as m.

Try to identify the slope in this sample question.

· ·

What is the slope of a line that is perpendicular to $9x - 8y = 144$ in the standard (x, y) coordinate plane?

    F. -9

    G. $-\dfrac{1}{9}$

    H. $\dfrac{9}{8}$

    J. $\dfrac{8}{9}$

    K. $-\dfrac{8}{9}$

The correct answer is K. Rewrite $9x - 8y = 144$ so that it is in slope-intercept form,

$y = mx + b$: $9x - 8y = 144 \rightarrow y = -\dfrac{9x}{-8} + \dfrac{144}{-8} \rightarrow y = \dfrac{9}{8}x - 18$. The slope of the given line is

$\dfrac{9}{8}$, so a perpendicular line will have a negative reciprocal slope of $-\dfrac{8}{9}$. Choice F is the

opposite of the Ax-term in $9x - 8y = 144$, but standard form does not represent the slope

of the line. Choice G is the negative reciprocal of the Ax-term in $9x - 8y = 144$, but standard form does not represent the slope of the line. Choice H is the slope of lines that will be parallel to the original line. Choice J is the reciprocal of the slope of the original line, but not the negative reciprocal.

· ·

MIDPOINT FORMULA

The midpoint between two coordinate pairs in the standard (x, y) coordinate plane is the point that is equal distance from the two given points. The midpoint formula should be easy for you to recall since the midpoint will always be the average of x-coordinates, followed by the average of y-coordinates:

The midpoint between (x_1, y_1) and $(x_2, y_2) = \left(\dfrac{x_1 + x_2}{2}, \dfrac{y_1 + y_2}{2} \right)$.

NOTE: Sometimes, you'll be given the midpoint along with one of the endpoints and asked to solve for the missing endpoint. Also, be prepared to do something creative with the x- and y-coordinates you determine, like finding the sum, $x + y$, or the product, xy.

Point C is the midpoint of line segment $\overline{LD}$ and has the coordinates $(-2, 5)$. Endpoint L is the coordinate pair $\left(-4\dfrac{1}{3}, 9\dfrac{3}{4} \right)$, and the other endpoint D is the coordinate pair (v, w). What is the sum of $v + w$?

A. $\dfrac{1}{3}$

B. $\dfrac{1}{4}$

C. $\dfrac{7}{12}$

D. $\dfrac{1}{12}$

E. $\dfrac{4}{3}$

The correct answer is C. The average of the x-coordinates of the endpoints must equal

-2, so set up the equation $\dfrac{-4\frac{1}{3}+v}{2}=-2$. Multiplying both sides by 2 gives $-4\frac{1}{3}+v=-4$,

so $v=\dfrac{1}{3}$. Similarly, the average of the y-coordinates of the endpoints must equal 5, so

set up the equation $\dfrac{9\frac{3}{4}+w}{2}=5$. Multiplying both sides by 2 gives $9\frac{3}{4}+w=10$,

so $w=\dfrac{1}{4}$. Therefore, $(w,v)=\left(\dfrac{1}{3},\dfrac{1}{4}\right)$ and $v+w=\dfrac{7}{12}$. Choice A is the value of v.

Choice B is the value of w. Choice D is the value of vw. Choice E is the value of $\dfrac{v}{w}$.

··

DISTANCE FORMULA

Although the distance formula looks rather intimidating, it is really just an application of the Pythagorean theorem to the standard (x, y) coordinate plane.

> The distance between (x_1,y_1) and $(x_2,y_2) = \sqrt{\left(x_2-x_1\right)^2+\left(y_2-y_1\right)^2}$.

Having a deeper understanding of where the distance formula comes from will prevent you from making the common mistake of inverting the addition and subtraction signs within this long formula! Investigate the following illustration to see how $(x_2 - x_1)$ and (y_2-y_1) are expressions that represent the lengths of the legs of a right triangle where d is the hypotenuse. Notice that the long square root symbol comes from taking the square root of both sides of the equation $d^2 = (x_2 - x_1)^2 + (y_2 - y_1)^2$ to solve for the distance, d.

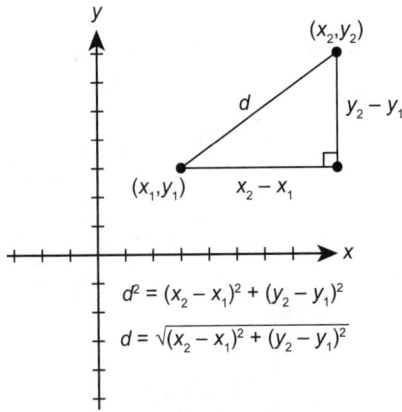

On test day, you might be asked to simply find the distance between two points, or you may get a more challenging question such as the following one that requires you to apply the midpoint and distance formulas together.

Camp Whitsett has a girls' cabin, boys' cabin, pool, and cafeteria. In the figure shown, each of these is represented on a standard (x, y) coordinate plane, using meters east of the entrance as the x-coordinates and meters north of the entrance as the y-coordinates. The camp wants to build an amphitheater halfway between the boys' cabin at point B and the girls' cabin at point G. Approximately how many meters will the new amphitheater be from the cafeteria that is located at point C?

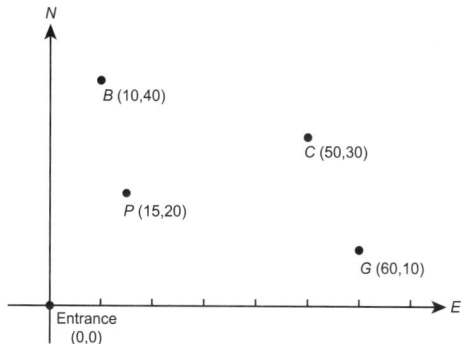

F.   10 meters
G.   16 meters
H.   18 meters
J.   21 meters
K.   25 meters

The correct answer is G. First, find the midpoint between points B (10, 40) and G (60, 10):

$$\text{Midpoint} = \left(\frac{x_1 + x_2}{2}, \frac{y_1 + y_2}{2}\right) = \left(\frac{10 + 60}{2}, \frac{40 + 10}{2}\right) = (35, 25)$$

The amphitheater will have a location at (35, 25). To find out how far this will be from the cafeteria at (50, 30), use the distance formula:

$$d = \sqrt{(x_2 - x_1)^2 + (y_2 - y_1)^2} = \sqrt{(50 - 35)^2 + (30 - 25)^2} = \sqrt{225 + 25} = 15.8 \text{ m}$$

The amphitheater will be approximately 16 meters from the cafeteria. Choice F is the difference between the coordinates of the location of the amphitheater which will be at (35, 25). Choice H is too large of an approximate since the actual distance was closer to 15.8 meters. Choice J is the approximate distance from the amphitheater to the pool at point P. Choice K is the y-coordinate of the location of the amphitheater, which will be located at (35, 25).

INTERPRETING GRAPHS

Graphs provide useful information quickly to the well-trained eye! Whether the relationships shown are linear equations with constant slope, or curved quadratic equations with varying rates of change, graphs can be used to make conclusions about how the two variables relate to each.

Remember that functions use the *x*-axis to chart their independent variable (like a baby's age in weeks), while the *y*-axis displays the data for the dependent variable (like the baby's weight gain). When presented with a single function illustrated in a coordinate plane, the important features to look for are the starting point, break-even point, and rate(s) of change.

STARTING POINT

The starting point of a graph is the value of the *y*-coordinate when $x = 0$. It will be the *y*-intercept, which can be negative, positive, or zero:

- A new business would likely have a negative starting point because there are costs associated with starting a business before any sales of goods or services have been made.

- A relationship correlating the weight gain of a newborn baby to her age in weeks would have a positive starting point because at birth she has a positive weight.

- The relationship between minutes jogging and miles run would have 0 as a starting point.

BREAK-EVEN POINT

The *x*-intercept marks the break-even point, since this is where the *y*-values are transitioning from negative values to positive values or vice-versa.

- A company needs to sell 1,000 smart phone apps to pay for its start-up costs, and after that it will be making a profit. In this case, 1,000 would be the *break-even point*.

- The height trajectory of a ball thrown up into the sky off a roof will look like an upside down parabola. The curve's *break-even* point on the *x*-axis illustrates when the ball is no longer in the air and is zero feet from the ground.

Rate of Change

The rate of change is the slope of a function. The steeper a line or curve is, the *faster* its rate of change is. You will be expected to compare and contrast rates of change based on graphical representations.

- Straight lines have a constant rate of change, while curved functions (including parabolas) have rates of change that increase and decrease based on steepness.

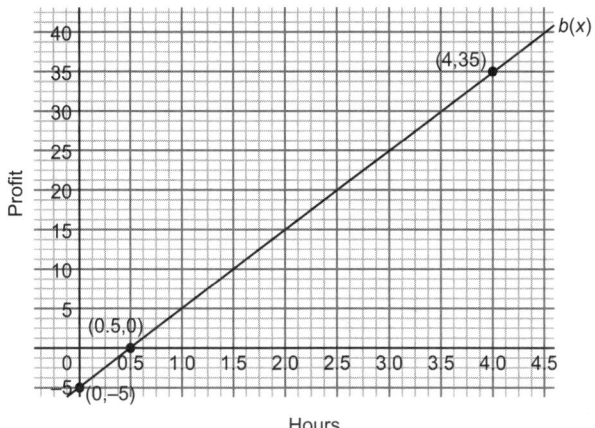

Hours

Let's use the following graph to illustrate these three features. This graph shows the relationship between Willa's babysitting hours worked and profit she earned:

- **Starting point:** The starting point here is at –5. This might seem odd for a job, but maybe she has to pay $5 for her transportation, so when she has worked zero hours, her profit is actually –$5.

- **Break-even point:** The break-even point here is at 0.5 hours, or 30 minutes. This is the point at which her profit is at $0, and it is transitioning from negative profit to positive profit.

- **Rate of change:** The rate of change here is constant because it is a straight line with an unchanging slope. Using the coordinate pairs (0, –5) and (1, 5) in the slope formula shows that the slope is 10. This means that Willa earns $10 per hour.

When two different relationships are graphed in the same coordinate plane, another important feature to identify and interpret is the points of intersection of the functions. You might also be asked to compare the *values* of two functions:

- **Point(s) of intersection:** Any point at which two functions intersect is a unique coordinate pair where both functions have the same output value (*y*) for a particular input value (*x*).

- **Values:** In coordinate geometry, the word *value* is used as shorthand for *y*-value. So when a question asks, "which function has the greater value," it is referring to the *y*-values or *height* of the function.

Let's suppose that instead of babysitting, Willa gets an offer to get paid for taking her neighbor's dog on a hike. We've added the function representing that opportunity to her original babysitting graph, so let's take a look at the useful information we can get out of analyzing the point of intersection. (Note that the function $b(x)$ represents her babysitting profit, while $d(x)$ represents her dog hiking profit.)

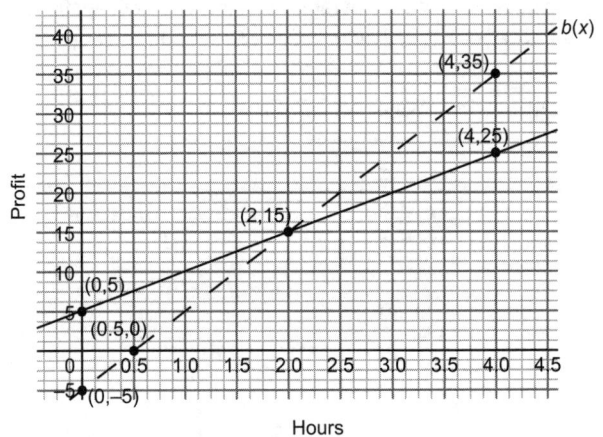

Let's look at a few different types of questions you could see regarding a graph like this.

Examples:

1. If Willa only has 90 minutes free to work on Saturday afternoon, would it be more profitable for her to babysit or take her neighbor's dog for a hike?

2. For how many hours of work would Willa receive the same amount of pay for either job?

3. If Willa plans to work for more than 2 hours on Saturday and less than 2 hours on Sunday, which jobs should she book for these days?

Solutions:

1. Looking at $b(x)$, we can see that when $x = 1.5$, $y = \$10$, so her babysitting profit would be $10. The y-value of $d(x)$ is $12 when $x = 1.5$, so she would actually make a little more money with her neighbor's dog.

2. The point of intersection shows us that at 2 hours, both of these jobs would earn Willa $15.

3. Notice that after the point of intersection at $x = 2$ hours, the $b(x)$ line is above the $d(x)$ line. This indicates that Willa would be better off babysitting on Saturday since she plans to work for more than 2 hours. Since the $d(x)$ line has a greater y-value when x is less than 2 hours, Willa should plan a doggie hike for Sunday when she has less than 2 hours available for work.

The ACT will include at least one grouping of three questions that all relate to the same illustration. Be prepared to apply a range of skills to answer these questions, which often involve relationships displayed on a coordinate plane. See how well you can work through the following question set.

· ·

Thy's Tees wants to produce either tank tops or long-sleeve shirts to sell at a local music festival this summer. He does not have enough money to produce both types of shirts, so he must decide which style will be better for this festival. *Number* represents the number of shirts he would sell, and *Profit* is the amount of money he would earn from sales of *x* shirts. The following graph shows his projections for profits from the production and sale of tank tops, $T(x)$, versus long-sleeve shirts, $L(x)$.

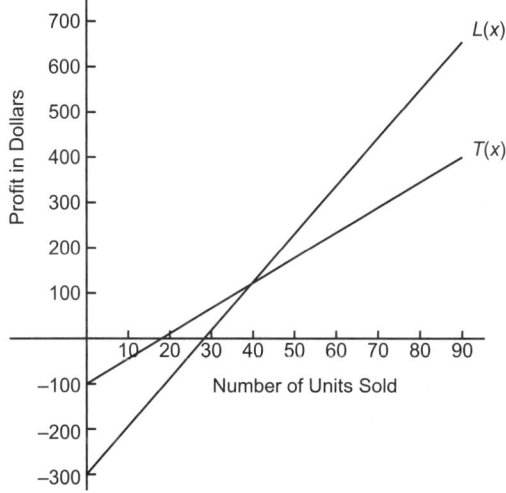

Whether he decides to produce the tank tops or the long-sleeve shirts, Thy does not want to lose any money on this project and he wants to be sure he breaks even (does not lose, but does not gain money). If he decides to make long-sleeve shirts, approximately how many *more* long-sleeve shirts would he need to sell, compared to tank tops, in order to break even?

    A.   10
    B.   18
    C.   28
    D.   40
    E.   125

The correct answer is A. The *x*-intercept of $T(x)$ shows that at around 18 shirts, Thy's Tees would break even. The *x*-intercept of $L(x)$ shows that at around 28 shirts, Thy's Tees would break even. Therefore, he would need to sell about 10 more long-sleeve shirts to break even. Choice B is the number of tank tops that Thy would need to sell to break even. Choice C is the number of long-sleeve shirts that Thy would need to sell to break even. Choice D is the point of intersection that shows that Thy would make the same amount of money whether he sold 40 tank tops or 40 long-sleeve shirts. Choice E is the profit Thy would make from selling 40 tank tops or 40 long-sleeve shirts.

Which of the following statements is true?

    I. If he produces the long-sleeve shirts, Thy will need to sell at least 40 shirts in order for them to be more profitable than the tank tops.

    II. The long-sleeve shirts are more expensive to produce and have a lower selling price per shirt.

    III. If Thy were to sell 80 shirts, he would earn about $550 more profit if he produced long-sleeve shirts instead of tank tops.

F. I
G. II
H. II, III
J. I, III
K. None of the statements are true.

The correct answer is F. Statement I is true, since after 40 shirts sold, the $L(x)$ function has a higher profit value than the $T(x)$ function. Statement II is false: Although it is true that the long-sleeve shirts are more expensive to produce, the $L(x)$ function has a steeper slope than the $T(x)$ function, which shows that the price per shirt is higher for the long-sleeve shirts, making Statement II false. Statement III is also false: If Thy were to sell 80 tank tops, his profit would be approximately $350. If instead he sold 80 long-sleeve shirts, his profit would be approximately $550. Therefore, his additional profit from the long-sleeve shirts would be $200, and not $550, so Statement III is false. Since only Statement I is true, choice F is the correct answer.

· ·

GRAPHING QUADRATICS

A quadratic function graphed in the coordinate plane makes a parabola, or *u*-shaped curve, that opens upward or downward. Quickly, let's review a few important quadratic vocabulary terms:

- The **vertex** is the turning point of a parabola.
  - ○ In parabolas that open upward (and look like a smiley face), the vertex is the **minimum**. Conversely, in downward-facing parabolas, the vertex is called the **maximum**.

- All parabolas have a vertical line of symmetry that goes through the vertex. The parabola is symmetrical when reflected over this vertical line.

Standard Form: $y = ax^2 + bx + c$

The standard form for a quadratic equation is $y = ax^2 + bx + c$, for all real numbers a such that a ≠ 0 (a can't be zero and cancel out the x^2-term because the x^2-term makes a function a parabola). The most basic quadratic, $y = x^2$, has the following appearance with its vertex at the origin:

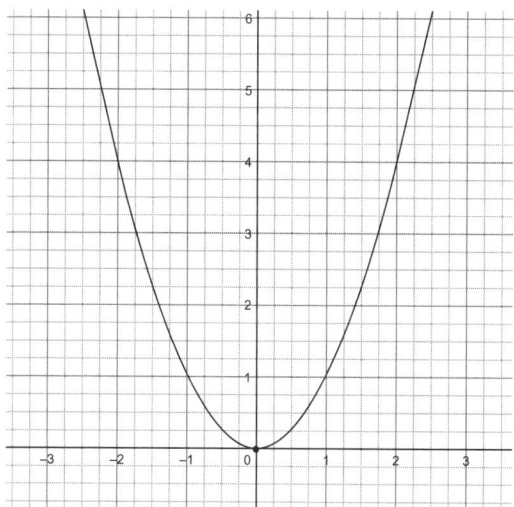

The equation of the parabola above is $y = ax^2 + bx + c$, such that $a = 1$, $b = 0$, and $c = 0$. What happens to the appearance of the curve when these numbers change? It's important that you have a clear understanding of how a, b, and c affect the graphs of parabolas.

How does a impact the graph of a parabola?

The leading coefficient, a, determines the direction that the parabola opens. (It also determines the steepness of the parabola, but this concept isn't something the ACT focuses on.)

- When a is positive, the parabola will face upward.
- When a is negative, the parabola will face downward.
- The larger a is, the steeper its sides will be.

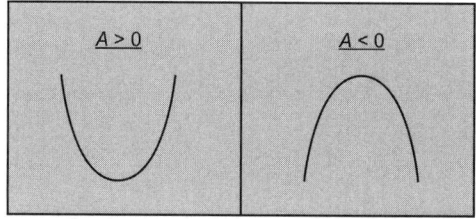

 The leading coefficient, *a*, determines which way the parabola will open. A positive *a* makes an upward, "smiley-face" parabola and a negative *a* makes a downward, "frowny-face" parabola.

How does *b* impact the graph of a parabola?

When $b = 0$, the parabola has the form $y = ax^2 + c$. In this case, the parabola's vertex and the line of symmetry are on the *y*-axis.

 The constant, *c*, is always the *y*-intercept of all parabolas. Know that when $b = 0$, and the parabola is in the form $y = ax^2 + c$, the vertex will sit at *c* on the *y*-axis.

How does *c* impact the graph of a parabola?

There are two important aspects to know about *c*:

- The constant, *c*, is *always* the *y*-intercept of the parabola.
- When *c* is altered, it will vertically shift the parabola up or down, which will change both the intercepts and the vertex, but the overall shape will be the same.

These facts are illustrated below. Notice how the *y*-intercept of $y = x^2 - 3x + 2$ is 2 and the *y*-intercept of $y = x^2 - 3x - 1$ is -1. Also notice how changing *c* from -1 to 2 keeps the shape of the curve the same, but changes the values of the vertex and the *x*-intercepts.

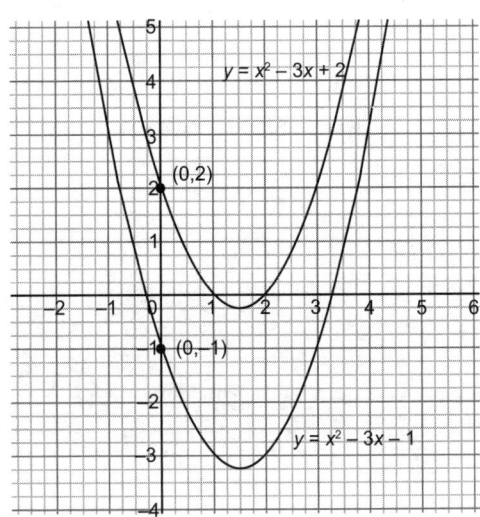

The ACT may test your general understanding of the coefficients in quadratics with a question such as the following.

· ·

Evelyn throws a ball off the roof of a building. Its height in feet, h, is measured over time in seconds, t, and is shown in the following graph.

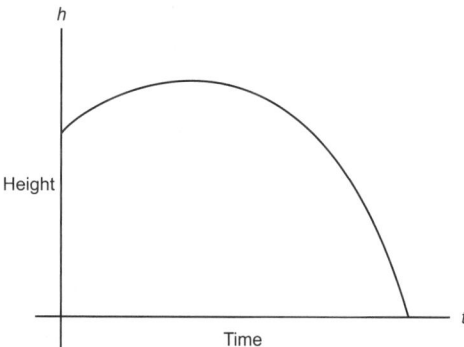

If the graph has the equation $h = at^2 + bt + c$, which of the following must be true statements?

    I. a is negative.

    II.   If c is changed, it will affect the maximum height as well as the t-intercept.

    III.   If c is changed, it will affect the h-intercept, but the maximum height and the t-intercept will stay the same.

    A.   I
    B.   I, II
    C.   II, III
    D.   I, III
    E.   I, II, III

The correct answer is B. Statement I is true since downward facing parabolas have a negative leading coefficient, a. Statement II is true because if c is changed, it will shift the entire curve vertically, which will change both t-intercept and the maximum height (vertex) of the curve. Statement III is false because if c is changed, it will shift the entire curve vertically, which will change all three features mentioned: the h-intercept, the maximum height (vertex), and the t-intercept. Since only Statements I and II are true, choice B is the correct answer.

· ·

Don't be surprised by an ACT trajectory question where a quadratic model is used to show the height of a flying object over time. Be familiar with these parts of the graph:

- The *y*-intercept is the height from which the object fell or was thrown.
- The *x*-coordinate of the vertex is the *time at which the object reached maximum height,* and the *y*-coordinate of the vertex is the *maximum height reached.*)
- The *x*-intercept shows the time at which the object hit the ground.

FINDING THE LINE OF SYMMETRY AND VERTEX

To determine line of symmetry, use the coefficients *a* and *b* in the following formula:

$$\text{Line of Symmetry: } x = \frac{-b}{2a}$$

Since the line of symmetry goes *through* the vertex, the vertex is found by plugging that *x*-value back into the equation to solve for the *y*-coordinate of the vertex. It looks confusing at first, so take the time to familiarize yourself with the formula used for calculating the vertex:

$$\text{Vertex formula for a parabola in the form } y = ax^2 + bx + c: \left(\frac{-b}{2a}, f\left(\frac{-b}{2a} \right) \right)$$

 When presented with a quadratic, remember that the vertex is always the minimum or the maximum! Questions on the ACT will often ask you to find the *minimum* or *maximum* of quadratic functions.

You may be asked to solve for the vertex in an equation that is not presented in standard form.

Example:

State if the function has a maximum or a minimum and determine its coordinates:

$$p(x) = -6x - 3x^2$$

Solution:

Notice that the ax^2-term in this equation is $-3x^2$. This tells you that it is a downward-facing parabola, so therefore it will have a *maximum.* Since *bx* is $-6x$, put $a = -3$ and $b = -6$ into the vertex formula: $x = \frac{-b}{2a} = \frac{6}{2 \cdot (-3)} = -1$. Now put -1 into $p(x)$ to solve for the *y*-coordinate $p(-1) = -6(-1) - 3(-1)^2 = 3$. The maximum is at $(-1, 3)$.

VERTEX FORM: $y = a(x - h)^2 + k$

You might be presented with a special vertex form for quadratics on the test. (You won't have to complete the square to rewrite a parabola in vertex form, but it's helpful to be familiar with this form.)

> Vertex Form of Parabola: $y = a(x - h)^2 + k$, where (h, k) is the vertex.

In this form, a is the same a from the standard vertex form, and it still determines if the parabola is upward- or downward-facing. It's convenient that (h, k) is the vertex of the formula, but it's inconvenient that h and k are preceded by two different signs (subtraction and addition).

 ALERT: Be careful when determining the vertex from $y = a(x - h)^2 + k$! The vertex of $y = 4(x + 3)^2 - 2$ is at $(-3, -2)$, not $(3, -2)$.

DETERMINING SOLUTIONS FROM GRAPHS

Remember the quadratic factoring we sped through earlier in this chapter? Factoring is an important skill with quadratics because it helps us identify the *solutions* or *x*-intercepts of a quadratic. For example, factor $y = x^2 + x - 6$ into $y = (x - 2)(x + 3)$. Now if we set $y = 0$, we can find the *x*-intercepts for the graph: $y = (x - 2)(x + 3)$ when $x = 2$ and $x = -3$. (Note that in order to find these solutions, you have to set each individual factor, $(x - 2)$ and $(x + 3)$, equal to zero.) The *x*-intercepts are referred to as the *solutions* to any quadratic in the form $0 = ax^2 + bx + c$. You will often find questions that cannot be solved on a graphing calculator on the ACT Mathematics test.

· ·

A quadratic equation is graphed in the standard (x, y) coordinate plane as shown. Which of the equations represents the correct factored form of this parabola?

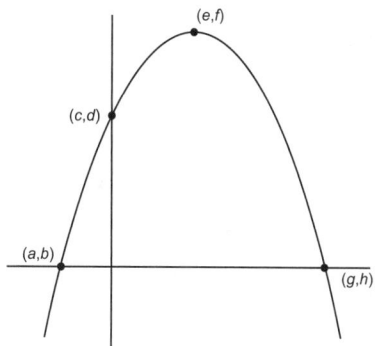

F. $y = (x + a)(x + g)$
G. $y = (x + e)(x + f)$
H. $y = (x - a)(x - g)$
J. $y = (x - b)(x + h)$
K. $y = (x - a)(x + g)$

The correct answer is H. The x-intercepts, a and g, are the values that make $y = 0$. Therefore, $(x - a)$ and $(x - g)$ are the two factors of this function and $y = (x - a)(x - g)$ represents this parabola. Choice F is incorrect because $y = (x + a)(x + g)$ would result in x-intercepts at $-a$ and $-g$, but the intercepts are a and g. Choice G is incorrect because $y = (x + e)(x + f)$ would result in x-intercepts at $-e$ and $-f$, but (e, f) is the vertex, which is not used to write the equation of a quadratic. Choice J is incorrect because b and h equal 0, since b and h are the y-coordinates of the x-intercepts. Choice K is incorrect because $y = (x - a)(x + g)$ would result in x-intercepts a and $-g$, but the intercepts are a and g.

. . . .

GRAPHING CIRCLES

More often than not, the ACT will have at least one question requiring you to apply the formula for graphing circles in the standard (x, y) coordinate plane. All you need to know to represent a circle in this form is the length of the radius and the coordinates of the center of the circle:

Circle-radius form of a circle with center (h, k) and radius r:

$$(x - h)^2 + (y - k)^2 = r^2$$

Most of the questions regarding circles are pretty straightforward, but here's one with a little twist:

What is the equation for a circle that has a center at $(-1, -3)$ and passes through the point $(2, 1)$?

We are given the center coordinates, but not the radius. Find the radius by using the distance formula with the center point and the point on the circumference:

$$d = \sqrt{(x_2 - x_1)^2 + (y_2 - y_1)^2} = \sqrt{(-1-2)^2 + (-3-1)^2} = \sqrt{25} = 5$$

The radius equals 5, so the equation for the circle is $(x + 1)^2 + (y + 3)^2 = 25$.

Think carefully as you work your way through the following practice question.

The circle drawn below in the standard (x, y) coordinate plane has its center at (a, b), passes through the point (c, d), and is tangent to the y-axis. Which of the following is an equation for this circle?

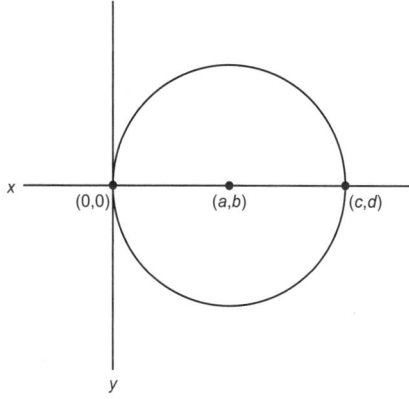

A. $(x + a)^2 + (y + b)^2 = c^2$

B. $(x - a)^2 + (y - b)^2 = c^2$

C. $(x - a)^2 + (y - b)^2 = \left(\dfrac{1}{2}c^2\right)$

D. $(x + a)^2 + (y + b)^2 = \left(\dfrac{1}{2}c^2\right)$

E. $(x - a)^2 + (y - b)^2 = \left(\dfrac{1}{2}c\right)^2$

The correct answer is E. The center, (h, k), for the circle illustrated is (a, b) and the radius is $\dfrac{1}{2}c$. Putting this information into the center-radius form, $(x - h)^2 + (y - k)^2 = r^2$, yields $(x - a)^2 + (y - b)^2 = \left(\dfrac{1}{2}c\right)^2$. Choice A cannot be correct because the center is at (a, b) and not $(-a, -b)$. Choice B is incorrect because the radius is $\dfrac{1}{2}c$ and not c. Choice C is incorrect because the radius of $\dfrac{1}{2}c$ should be squared, but instead, only c is squared. Choice D cannot be correct because the center is at (a, b) and not $(-a, -b)$.

 ALERT: Remember that the equation for the circle-radius form of a circle with center (h, k) and radius r is *the sum of squared differences*, and *not* the sum of squared sums: $(x - h)^2 + (y - k)^2 = r^2$.

GRAPHING AND INTERPRETING INEQUALITIES

We talked about absolute value inequalities with one variable earlier in this chapter. Now we'll review graphic solutions of inequalities with two variables. Inequalities are graphed in the standard (x, y) coordinate plane and then shaded *above* or *below* the function.

Remember that the inequality sign will determine whether a dotted or solid line is appropriate:

- **> or <:** Use a **dotted line** to show that the solution set does *not* include the values on the line or curve.

- **≥ or ≤:** Use a **solid line** to show that the solution set includes the values on the line or curve.

The most common mistake students make is shading to the *right* or *left* of the line instead of *above* or *below* it. The following problem is an example of what to avoid.

Example:

What is the inequality represented by the following graph?

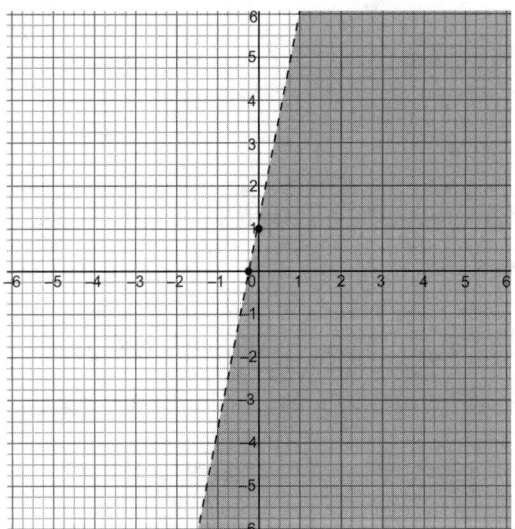

Solution:

The line graphed has a y-intercept at 1 and a slope of 5, so we know the *line* representing this inequality is $y = 5x + 1$. The line is dotted, so we know that it will be < or > , and not < or >. The untrained eye would read this shading as *to the right* of the line and would therefore see this incorrectly as $y > 5x + 1$. However, the shading is *below* the line, indicating that all the shaded values are *less than* the y-coordinates on the line. Therefore, the inequality that represents this is $y < 5x + 1$.

 Remember inequalities are shaded *above* or *below* the line or curve and not to the right or left of it!

Several inequalities can be graphed together on the same standard (x, y) coordinate plane to model the constraints placed on a real-world situation. It is common for students to have to draw conclusions based on these illustrations.

Consider the following figure, which shows the constraints the management has for their nonprofit animal shelter, which takes in homeless dogs and cats and seeks to find them permanent homes. The management has a minimum number of dogs and cats that they want at all times, as well as a maximum number of animals they can house at once. Try to answer the following questions before looking at their solutions!

Examples:

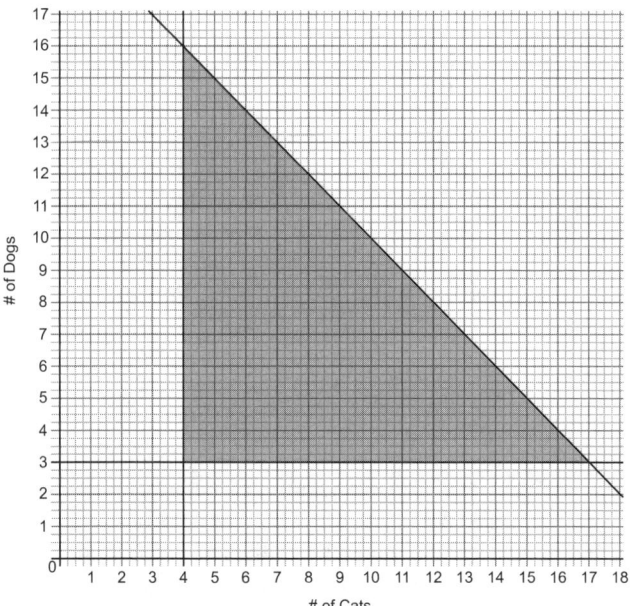

1. What is the lowest number of dogs the shelter wishes to have at all times?
2. What is the lowest number of cats the shelter wishes to have at all times?
3. What are the fewest and the greatest number of animals the shelter can house at any single time?
4. If the shelter has 12 cats on a given day, what are all the possible numbers of dogs it may have?

Solutions:

1. Since *# of Dogs* is on the y-axis, the constraint $y > 3$ represents the shelter's dogs. They wish to house at least 3 dogs at all times.

2. Since *# of Cats* is on the x-axis, the constraint $x > 4$ represents the shelter's cats. They wish to house at least 4 cats at all times.

3. Since the shelter plans on housing at least 3 dog and 4 cats at all times, the fewest number of animals they would have at any time would be 7. The diagonal line, represented by the inequality $y < 20 - x$, illustrates that the greatest number of animals they can shelter at one time is 20.

4. If the shelter has 12 cats on a given day, it may have anywhere from 3 to 8 dogs, based on the constraints represented in the graph.

Lastly, you might receive an inequality question that asks you to make conclusions about how linear functions compare with nonlinear functions:

The functions $y = (x + 2)^4$ and $y = -x - 2$ are shown on the standard (x, y) coordinate plane. What are the real values of x that satisfy the inequality $-x - 2 > (x + 2)^4$?

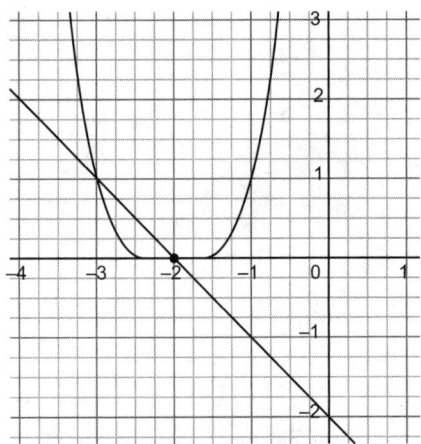

This inequality $-x - 2 > (x + 2)^4$ is looking for the x-values that make the point on the linear relationship, $-x - 2$, *greater than* the corresponding point on the quartic relationship, $(x + 2)^4$. Look for the parts of the graph where the line is *above* the parabolic curve. This occurs only when x is between -3 and -2, but these end values are not included since the values are equal. The correct solution is $-3 < x < -2$.

GRAPHS OF ELLIPSES

Very rarely, you will see an ellipse question on the ACT. If you committed the formulas for ellipses to memory, that would be great, but if you have a brain freeze and forget them, you should be able to solve the question correctly by working backward and plugging points from the graph into the given equations.

Before we spring the formulas on you, let's review a few things about the ellipse:

- An ellipse has **two lines of symmetry**: a vertical and a horizontal line that would each cut the ellipse in half.

- The **major axis** is the longer line segment that cuts the ellipse in half.

- The **minor axis** is the short line segment that that cuts the ellipse in half.

- The **center, (h, k)**, sits at the intersection of the major axis and the minor axis.

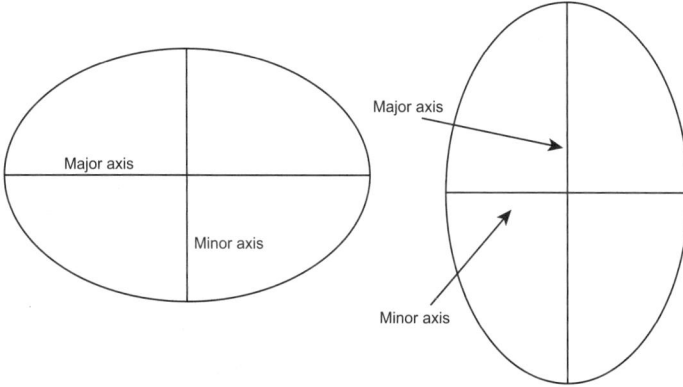

The distance from the center of the ellipse to the endpoint of the major axis is called a. Similarly, the distance from the center of the ellipse to the endpoint of the minor axis is called b. In other words, a is *half the length of the major axis* and b is *half the length of the minor axis*. In the formula for an ellipse, the placement of a and b changes, depending on whether the ellipse is *wide* or *tall*. Notice below that a is paired with the x-coordinate when the ellipse is wide, and conversely, a is paired with the y-coordinate when the ellipse is tall (and the b-value changes accordingly).

Formula for a *wide* ellipse: $\dfrac{(x-h)^2}{a^2} + \dfrac{(y-k)^2}{b^2} = 1$

Formula for a *tall* ellipse: $\dfrac{(y-k)^2}{a^2} + \dfrac{(x-h)^2}{b^2} = 1$

Aside from the placement of a and b above, it is also important to notice that both of these values are squared. So remember that after you cut the lengths of the minor and major axes in half, you must square those values before using them in the formula for the ellipse.

SUMMING IT UP

- When given the task of taking a percentage of a number, chose a starting point of 100.

- If asked to find the average of data presented in a frequency table, you will need to find the weighted average.

- When an equation has variables as exponents, like $4^{3x} = 8^{2x-1}$, rewrite the bases as equivalent bases and then set the exponential expressions equal to each other.

- Given $y = a^x$, y will not *always* increase as x increases. If $0 < a < 1$, then y will decrease as x increases from 0 to ∞ and y will *increase* as x decreases from 0 to ∞.

- For all real numbers b and c, $1x^2 + bx + c = (x + m)(x + n)$, as long as $mn = c$ and $m + n = b$.

- Solve a quadratic $ax^2 + bx + c = 0$ by getting it into its factored form $(x + m)(x + n) = 0$ and finding the values of m and n that make this true.

- The shortcut for factoring the **difference of perfect squares is** $x^2 - y^2 = (x + y)(x - y)$.

- The inequality symbol must change directions when the inequality is *divided* or *multiplied* by a negative number. For example if $-1x > 9$, then $x < -9$.

- The formula for direct variation is $y = kx$ and inverse variation is $y = \dfrac{k}{x}$, where k is the constant of variation.

- An **arithmetic sequence** is a string of numbers that moves from one term to the following term by adding the same value each time.

  ◦ The *common difference, d*, in an arithmetic sequence is found by subtracting a term from its following term.

  ◦ The sum of a fixed number of terms in an arithmetic sequence is (the average of the first and last terms) × (# of terms).

- A **geometric sequence** is a string of numbers where each new term is found by multiplying the same value to each term. The *common ratio, r*, in a geometric sequence is found by dividing a term by its previous term.

- A **system of linear equations** will have infinite solutions if, for $Ax + By = C$ and $Ex + Fy = G$, $\dfrac{A}{E} = \dfrac{B}{F} = \dfrac{C}{G}$ and the equations produce the same line.

- A system of equations has *infinite* solutions when the two equations are the same line. A system of equations has *no* solution when the two lines are parallel but have different y-intercepts.

- $f(x)$ means "the value of y at x." To find the value of a function at $f(8)$, replace all the x's in the equation with 8 and evaluate the expression using the correct order of operations.

- After substituting a value in for x, the value of $-x^2$ will *always* be negative. Do not cancel out all the negative signs when computing a term like $-(-1)^2$.

- When working with compound functions, remember that $(a - b)^2 \neq a^2 - b^2$! Use FOIL to expand $(a - b)^2$ into $a^2 - 2ab + b^2$.

- The **domain** sets restrictions on the input values that can be used in a function. A function can never have a denominator that equals zero or take the square root of a negative number.

- A **vertical asymptote** occurs at any x-value that is not in the domain of a function. Vertical asymptotes have the equation $x = k$ for all real numbers k omitted from the domain of a function.

- A **horizontal asymptote** is a y-value that a function will approach but never reach.

- **A function is odd if for all values of x in its domain, $f(-x) = -f(x)$.** For example, if an odd function contains the point (5, 8), it will also contain (−5, −8).

- **A function is even if for all values of x in its domain, $f(-x) = f(x)$.** For example, if an even function contains the point (5, 8), it will also contain the point (−5, 8).

- **Complex numbers** are written in the form $a + bi$, where a and b are real numbers, $i = \sqrt{-1}$, and $i^2 = -1$.

- **Logarithims** are expressions of exponential relationships. Keep these definitions and properties in mind:

  ○ $\log_b y = x$ is equivalent to $b^x = y$.

  ○ $\log_b b = 1$

  ○ $\log_b x^y = y \cdot \log_b x$

  ○ Log of a product: $\log ab = \log a + \log b$

  ○ Log of a quotient: $\log \dfrac{a}{b} = \log a - \log b$

- A **matrix** is an array or variables organized into r rows by c columns. The illustrated [3 × 2] matrix has 3 rows and 2 columns:

$$\begin{bmatrix} 1 & A \\ 2 & B \\ 3 & C \end{bmatrix}$$

  ○ Add or subtract matrices by combining their corresponding entries.

  ○ **Scalar multiplication** is performed by multiplying the scalar factor to every entry in the matrix:

$$k\begin{bmatrix} 1 & A \\ 2 & B \\ 3 & C \end{bmatrix} = \begin{bmatrix} 1k & Ak \\ 2k & Bk \\ 3k & Ck \end{bmatrix}$$

  ○ Let $A = [r \times c]$ and $B = [R \times C]$. The matrix product AB is defined if and only if the number of columns in A is equal to the number of rows in B. Thus, AB is defined if $c = R$ and AB will have dimensions $[r \times C]$.

- The **slope** between any two points (x_1, y_1) and (x_2, y_2) = $\frac{y_2 - y_1}{x_2 - x_1}$.

- The **slope-intercept equation for lines is y = mx + b,** where m is the slope and b is the y-intercept. **Standard form of a linear equation is Ax + By = C,** where A, B, and C are all integers and A is non-negative.

- **Parallel lines** in the coordinate plane have *identical slopes*. **Perpendicular lines** in the coordinate plane have *negative reciprocal slopes*.

- The **midpoint** between (x_1, y_1) and (x_2, y_2) = $\left(\frac{x_1 + x_2}{2}, \frac{y_1 + y_2}{2} \right)$.

- The **distance** between (x_1, y_1) and (x_2, y_2) = $\sqrt{(x_2 - x_1)^2 + (y_2 - y_1)^2}$.

- Any point at which two functions intersect is a unique coordinate pair where both functions have the same output value (y) for a particular input value (x).

- **Standard form of a quadratic is y = ax² + c,** and when $a > 0$, its graph will be an upward u-shaped curve, but when $a < 0$, the u-shaped curve will be downward.
  - Given a quadratic, $y = ax^2 + bx + c$, the intercept will always occur at c.

- The **line of symmetry** of the u-shaped parabola will be at $x = \frac{-b}{2a}$.

- The **vertex of a parabola** is the minimum or maximum of the curve.
  - The vertex of a parabola in the form $y = ax^2 + bx + c$ is $\left(\frac{-b}{2a}, f\left(\frac{-b}{2a} \right) \right)$.
  - Vertex Form of Parabola: $y = a(x - h)^2 + k$, where (h, k) is the vertex.

- Circle-radius form of a circle with center (h, k) and radius r: $(x - h)^2 + (y - k)^2 = r^2$.

- Inequalities graphed in the standard (x, y) coordinate plane are shaded *above* or *below* the function.

- The formula for an ellipse with center (h, k), where a is half the length of the *major axis* and b is half the length of the *minor axis* is $\frac{(x - h)^2}{a^2} + \frac{(y - k)^2}{b^2} = 1$ when the ellipse is "wide" and $\frac{(y - k)^2}{a^2} + \frac{(x - h)^2}{b^2} = 1$ when the ellipse is "tall."

Chapter 5:
Plane Geometry and Trigonometry

OVERVIEW

- Angles Within Parallel and Perpendicular Lines

- Properties of Triangles

- Properties of Quadrilaterals and Polygons

- Properties of Circles

- Area and Perimeter with Polygons, Circles, and Composite Shapes

- Surface Area

- Volume

- Transformations

- Trigonometric Relations in Right Triangles

- Circle Trigonometry, Radian Measure, and Polar Coordinates

- Graphing Trigonometric Functions

- Working with Trigonometric Identities

- Laws of Sines and Cosines

- Summing It Up

In this chapter, we will investigate plane geometry and trigonometry. Plane geometry covers the properties of two-dimensional shapes that exist in a plane, such as lines, angles, circles, and polygons. We'll also review ways to calculate the area, perimeter, volume, and surface area of two- and three-dimensional shapes. Trigonometry is the arm of mathematics that studies the relationships between the sides and angles in triangles. The ACT Mathematics test will include approximately 14 questions dealing with the plane geometry topics we will cover in this chapter. The test normally contains about four trigonometry questions.

Remember that you should try to solve *every* question *independently* in this chapter, whether it's an example question or a model ACT question. If you can't answer a question on your own, put a star next to the question and keep a running list of pages to revisit in the front of this book. Your success on the ACT depends on your mastery of all the question types in this book.

ANGLES WITHIN PARALLEL AND PERPENDICULAR LINES

Before we dive into parallel and perpendicular lines, let's buzz through some basic definitions regarding angles just to make sure that we're speaking the same language. You must know all of these terms:

Term	Definition	Illustration
Straight Angle	An angle that measures 180°. Notice that this doesn't look like an angle but is instead a straight line.	180°
Right Angle	An angle that measures 90°. Notice that it is represented with a square in the corner.	right angle x $x = 90°$
Acute Angle	An angle that measures more than 0° but less than 90°.	acute angle x $0° < x < 90°$
Obtuse Angles	An angle that measures more than 90° but less than 180°.	obtuse angle x $90° < x < 180°$
Vertex	The point at which two lines (or line segments or rays) meet to form an angle.	D F E Vertex

Term	Definition	Illustration
Congruent	Two angles are congruent when they have the same measure. The symbol $\cong$ is used to identify congruent angles, as is hatch marking.	$\angle F \cong \angle E$
Complementary Angles	Two angles that have a sum of 90°. They can be adjacent (sharing a common side), or they can be two separate angles (as pictured). When adjacent, complementary angles form a right angle.	20° 70°
Supplementary Angles	Two angles that have a sum of 180°. They can be share a common side, or they can be two separate angles. When adjacent, supplementary angles form a straight angle (as pictured).	a b D
Vertical Angles	The non-adjacent angles formed when two lines, or line segments, intersect. Vertical angles are congruent ($\cong$).	Pictured are two congruent vertical angle pairs: $\angle 1 \cong \angle 2$ and $\angle 3 \cong \angle 4$ 3 1 2 4

Use the concepts reviewed above to answer the following question. Get out your ruler, because you're going to need to create your own illustration.

NOTE: The ACT will often provide you with illustrations for the plane geometry questions, but expect to get some questions requiring you to create your own drawing to model the information given.

Example:

Line segments $\overline{WE}$ and $\overline{US}$ intersect at point E, which sits between points U and S. If m$\angle WES = 2x - 40$, find $m \angle UEW$ in terms of x.

Solution:

Draw line segments $\overline{WE}$ and $\overline{US}$ so that they intersect at point E and label m$\angle WES$ as $2x - 40$:

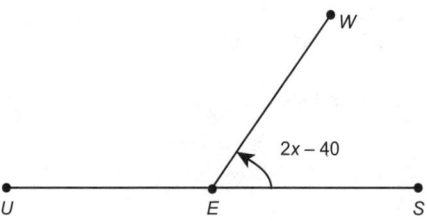

We can see that $\angle UEW$ and $\angle WES$ are supplementary, so we can write an algebraic equation and solve for m$\angle UEW$ in terms of x:

$$m\angle UEW + 2x - 40 = 180$$

$$m\angle UEW = 220 - 2x$$

After drawing an illustration to represent the information given in a problem, re-read the problem carefully while looking over your drawing to make sure that you have constructed it correctly.

ANGLES WITHIN PARALLEL LINES

Be prepared to see a question involving parallel lines on the ACT Mathematics test. Let's do a brief review of the properties shared by special angles formed when a transversal intersects parallel lines. (A *transversal* is a line that intersects two or more lines, but this term is most frequently used for a line that intersects parallel lines.) Use the given illustration to review the names and properties of the special angle pairs formed by parallel lines:

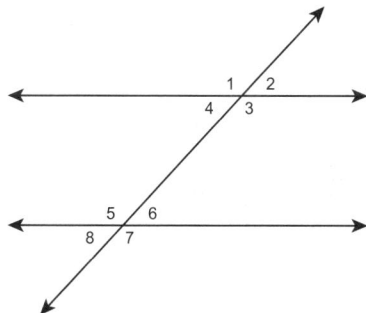

Corresponding angles are angles that are in the same relative position at each of the intersections. For example, the *top right* angle at the upper intersection of lines ($\angle 2$), corresponds to the *top right* angle at the lower intersection of lines ($\angle 6$).

- Corresponding angles are congruent.
- Corresponding angle pairs above are as follows:

$$\angle 1 \cong \angle 5; \angle 2 \cong \angle 6; \angle 3 \cong \angle 7; \angle 4 \cong \angle 8.$$

Alternate interior angles are angle pairs that sit *inside* the parallel lines but on opposite sides of the transversal. For example, $\angle 5$ and $\angle 3$ are alternate interior angles.

- Alternate interior angles are congruent.
- Alternate interior angle pairs above are $\angle 5 \cong \angle 3$ and $\angle 4 \cong \angle 6$.

Alternate exterior angles are angle pairs that are *outside* the parallel lines, on opposite sides of the transversal. For example, $\angle 7$ and $\angle 1$ are alternate exterior angles.

- Alternate exterior angles are congruent.
- Alternate exterior angle pairs above are $\angle 7 \cong \angle 1$ and $\angle 8 \cong \angle 2$.

Obtuse and acute angle pairs in parallel lines: Any pair of angles above, consisting of one acute and one obtuse angle, is supplementary.

Often, you will need to come up with algebraic equations to solve the plane geometry questions on the ACT. When writing these equations, don't think that you must use *all* of the given information at once. Keep this in mind as you do the following question. (Remember that "bisect" means to cut in half.)

In the figure below, $\overline{AC} \parallel \overline{WY}$, point B sits on $\overline{AC}$, and point X sits on $\overline{WY}$. If $\overline{BY}$ bisects $\angle CBX$, $\overline{BX}$ bisects $\angle ABY$, and $\overline{BW}$ bisects $\angle ABX$, what is the m$\angle WBX$?

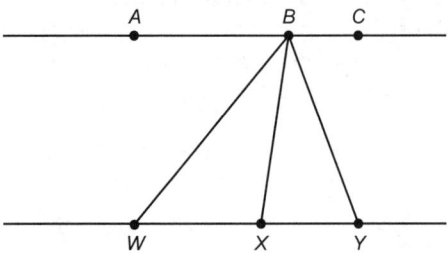

Start by just using the first two pieces of given information: $\overline{BY}$ bisects $\angle CBX$ and $\overline{BX}$ bisects $\angle ABY$. Since $\overline{BY}$ bisects $\angle CBX$, start by labeling $\angle CBY$ and $\angle YBX$ as x. Then since $\overline{BX}$ bisects $\angle ABY$, conclude that $\angle ABX$ must also equal x since it is equal to $\angle YBX$. Conclude that $\angle CBX$, $\angle XBY$, $\angle ABX$ must all be congruent.

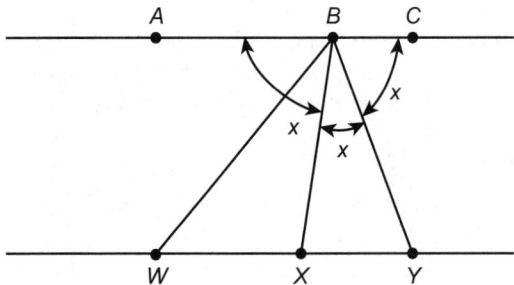

Therefore, $3x = 180°$ and $x = 60°$. Since $\overline{BW}$ bisects $\angle ABX$, it can be determined that m$\angle WBX = 30°$.

Watch out for competing transversals! Expect it to be more challenging to solve a parallel line question when more than one transversal is shown. It's a good idea to use your pencil to darken *one* of the transversals and *both* of the parallel lines so that you can see the corresponding angles made by one of the transversals. Don't get those angles confused with the angles made by the *other* transversal.

NOTE: Parallel line questions get more difficult when there are two transversals involved! Darken *one* of the transversals and *both* of the parallel lines with your pencil in order to be able to distinguish between the angles that are formed by each transversal.

In the following illustration, lines *m, n, a,* and *b* exist in the same plane such that *m* ∥ *n* and lines *a* and *b* intersect with lines *m* and *n* at points *p, q,* and *r.* If angles *x* and *y* exist as illustrated, which expression below must define the measure of angle *z*?

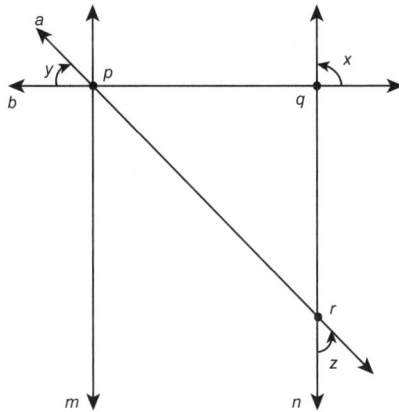

- **A.** ∠*y*
- **B.** 90° – ∠*y*
- **C.** 180° – ∠*x*
- **D.** 180° ∠*y* – ∠*x*
- **E.** It cannot be determined with the given information

The correct answer is D. Work backward to see that ∠*z* ≅ ∠4 (vertical angles) and ∠4 ≅ ∠3 (corresponding angles), so therefore ∠*z* ≅ ∠3 . (This could also have been determined using alternate exterior angles.) Proceed by finding ∠3 . Since *m* ∥ *n,* ∠*x* is a corresponding angle to ∠2. ∠*y*, ∠2, and ∠3 make a straight line, so represent this relationship with the equation:

$$\angle y + \angle 3 + \angle 2 = 180°$$

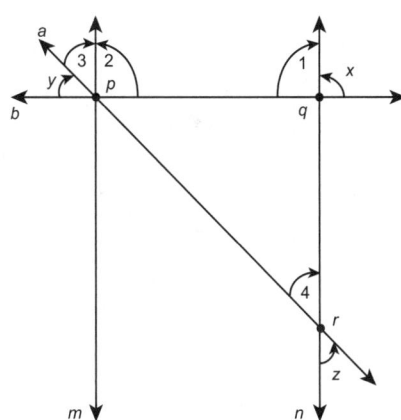

Since $\angle x \cong \angle 2$, replace $\angle 2$ with $\angle x$:

$$\angle y + \angle 3 + \angle x = 180°$$

Now, isolating $\angle 3$ brings us to $\angle 3 = 180° - \angle y - \angle x$. Since $\angle z \cong \angle 3$, determine $\angle z = 180° - \angle y - \angle x$. Choice A is not correct because $\angle y$ is an angle made from transversals a and b, while $\angle z$ is made from transversal a and parallel line n; therefore, they do not make up a special angle pair. Choice B cannot be correct because there are no given 90° angles, so we cannot assume that any angle is right. Choice C is not correct because $\angle x$ and $\angle z$ are from two different transversals, so you cannot make assertions using just these angles alone.

PROPERTIES OF TRIANGLES

Triangles have lots of fantastic features, so it's easy for the ACT to test your knowledge of them in many ways. Here are the subtopics we will review in this section:

- Triangle sum rule and triangle inequality theorem
- Types of triangles
- Pythagorean theorem
- Special triangles
- Remote angles
- Similar triangles

TRIANGLE SUM RULE

The triangle sum rule is just the principle that the interior angles of a triangle have a sum of 180°. We know you already knew that, but it just had to be said!

TRIANGLE INEQUALITY THEOREM

The triangle inequality theorem states that *the sum of any two sides of a triangle must be greater than the third side*. If that is not something you're already familiar with, make sure you understand how to work through the following problem.

Example:

In $\triangle ABC$, $\overline{AB} = 12.3$ and $\overline{BC} = 8.7$. Write a compound inequality to represent the possible side lengths of $\overline{AC}$.

Solution:

Since the sum of any two sides of a triangle must be greater than the third side, $12.3 + 8.7 > \overline{AC}$ so $\overline{AC} < 21$. But there has to be a *minimum* length that $\overline{AC}$ could be. (Realize that if $\overline{AC} = 1$, then $8.7 + 1$ would not be larger than 12.3.) Use the *smaller* side to create the inequality, $\overline{AC} + 8.7 > 12.3$, and solve for $\overline{AC} > 3.6$. Therefore $\overline{AC}$ must be bigger than 3.6 but less than 21, and the inequality solution is $3.6 < \overline{AC} < 21$.

TYPES OF TRIANGLES

You must know these three triangle types for the ACT:

1. **Equilateral triangles** are triangles with three equal sides and three equal angles that each measure 60°.
2. **Isosceles triangles** are triangles that have two congruent angles, called *base angles*, and two congruent sides, called *legs*. The third side is called the *base* and the angle opposite the base is called the *vertex*.

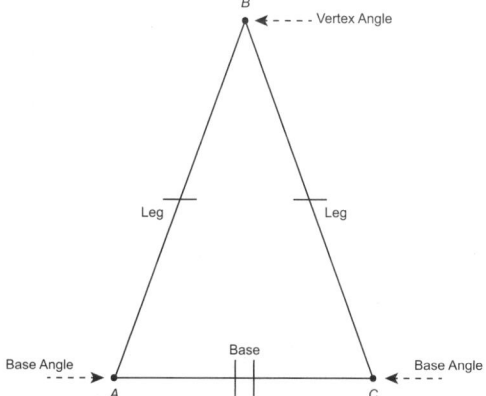

3. **Right Triangles** are triangles with exactly one 90° angle.

Pythagorean Theorem

The Pythagorean theorem is used to solve for missing side lengths in right triangles. The two shorter sides of right triangles are called the *legs,* and they intersect at a 90° angle. The *hypotenuse* is always the longest side and will always be opposite the 90° angle.

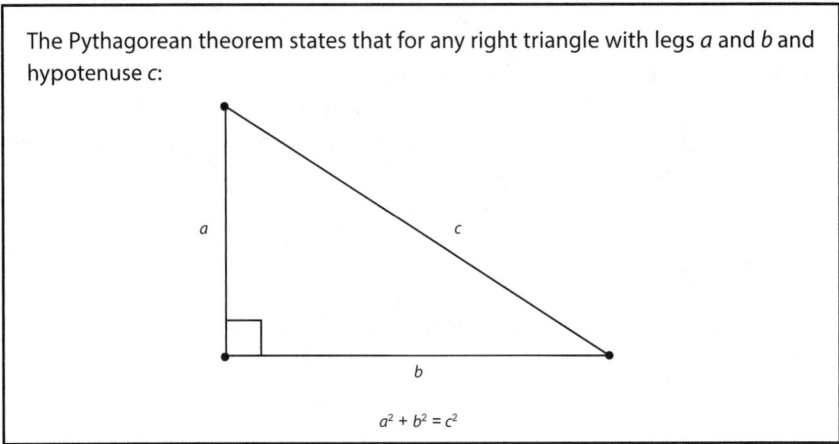

The Pythagorean theorem states that for any right triangle with legs *a* and *b* and hypotenuse *c*:

$$a^2 + b^2 = c^2$$

The Pythagorean theorem questions on the ACT will usually require straightforward solutions for missing sides. You will also need to use the Pythagorean theorem to solve many of the trigonometry questions, as you will see later in this chapter. Try this one that involves some higher-level skills:

Example:

What is an expression for *y* in terms of *x*?

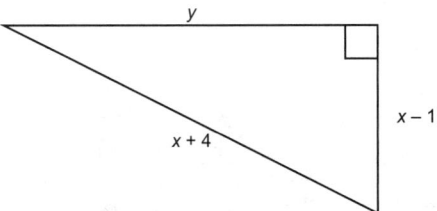

Solution:

Using substitution into the Pythagorean theorem, replace *a* and *b* with the legs, *y* and *x* – 1, and replace the hypotenuse, *c*, with *x* + 4. Then square all the terms (use FOIL for the binomials) and isolate *y*:

$$a^2 + b^2 = c^2$$
$$y^2 + (x-1)^2 = (x+4)^2$$
$$y^2 + x^2 - 2x + 1 = x^2 + 8x + 16$$
$$y^2 = 10x + 15$$
$$y = \sqrt{10x + 15}$$

 ALERT: When working with the Pythagorean theorem, don't expect to always be solving for the hypotenuse: plug the legs and hypotenuse into the equation carefully. Also, don't forget the last step of taking the square root of both sides.

Pythagorean Triples

There are a few useful common ratios that are found in right triangles. The most widely used is the 3–4–5 triangle, which has side lengths in the ratio of 3:4:5. For example, if a given right triangle has legs that measure 6 and 8, you can determine that the hypotenuse will be 10, since both of the legs were twice as large as the legs in the 3–4–5 triangle. Another useful Pythagorean triple is the 5–12–13 triangle. You will not need to *memorize* these special ratios, but knowing how to use them will allow you to work more quickly and save your time for the tougher questions.

SPECIAL TRIANGLES

There are two special triangles that are commonly referenced for their unique side relationships: the 30–60–90 and the 45–45–90 triangles. (These numbers refer to the interior angle measures of each of these two right triangles.) Before reading about these triangles, remember this fact about side-angle relationships in all triangles:

 In all triangles, the shortest side is always opposite the smallest angle, and the longest side is always opposite the largest angle.

- **30–60–90:** In this triangle, the hypotenuse is twice the length of the shortest leg and the longer leg is $\sqrt{3}$ times the shortest leg. You can create a visual for this relationship by labeling the shorter leg x, the hypotenuse $2x$, and the longer leg $x\sqrt{3}$:

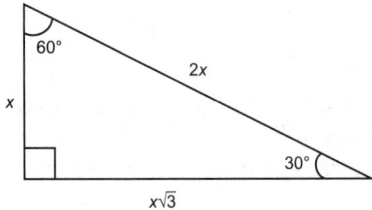

- **45–45–90:** This is an isosceles triangle, since the two base angles are congruent. Therefore, the two legs are also congruent. In a 45–45–90 triangle, the hypotenuse is $\sqrt{2}$ times the length of the legs. You can create a visual for this relationship by labeling the legs as x and the hypotenuse as $x\sqrt{2}$:

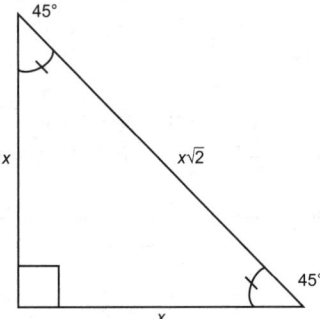

- You can often use the Pythagorean theorem as a workaround in the event that you forget the side-angle relationships of these two triangles. However, similar to our recommendation regarding the Pythagorean triples above, if you are familiar with these side-angle relationships, it will improve your speed and give you more time to crack the harder questions.

Example:

The area of a trapezoid is given by the formula $A = \dfrac{1}{2}(h)(b_1 + b_2)$, where h = height, and b_1 and b_2 equal the lengths of the two parallel bases. Find the area of the following right trapezoid:

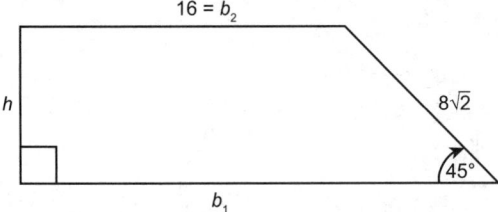

Solution:

In order to be able to use the formula $A = \frac{1}{2}(h)(b_1 + b_2)$, we need to find the length of height, h, as well as the length of base, b_1. This at first might seem like a task that requires more than the given information. However, use the 45°angle to make a 45–45–90 triangle by drawing a perpendicular leg as follows:

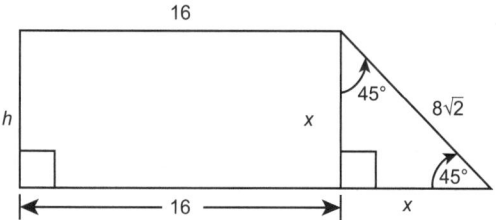

Now, using the side-angle relationships of 45–45–90 triangles, conclude that $x = 8$. This means that the height will be 8 and that b_1 equals 24. Use the given formula to get the area: $A = \frac{1}{2}(8)(24 + 16) = 160$.

Whenever you are working with right triangles that have a 30°, 45°, or 60° angle, immediately apply the side ratios of 30–60–90 or 45–45–90 triangles to give yourself more information about the side lengths. Sometimes, you can draw an altitude into a quadrilateral to create one of these special triangles.

Remote Angles

There is an important theorem that relates a triangle's *exterior* angle to the *remote interior* angles. The remote angles are the nonadjacent interior angles.

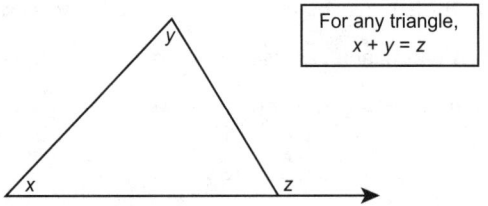

For any triangle,
$x + y = z$

The measure of an exterior angle of a triangle is equal to the sum of the two remote interior angles.

You can apply this theorem to answer a question such as this:

Example:

What is the sum of angles *w*, *v*, and *u*?

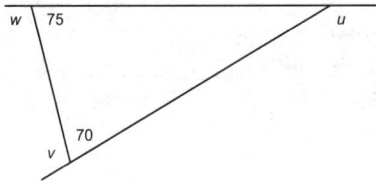

Solution:

Angles *w* and *v* are supplements to their adjacent angles, so m∠w = 105° and m∠v = 110°. Angle *u* is the exterior angle that is equal to the sum of the remote interior angles, so 75° + 70° = 145°. Therefore, ∠w + ∠v + ∠u = 105° + 110° + 145° = 360°.

Similar Triangles

The ACT Mathematics test asks questions dealing with similar triangles quite frequently, so you need to know what they are, how to recognize them, and how to find the proportional relationship between them. In general, similar triangles have the same shape, but are different sizes.

Similar triangles have two properties:

1. Their corresponding angles are congruent.

2. The ratios of their three corresponding side-pairs are proportional.

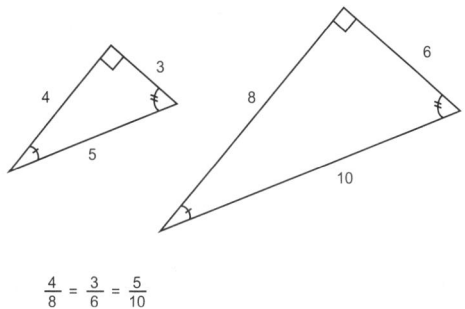

$$\frac{4}{8} = \frac{3}{6} = \frac{5}{10}$$

Angle-Angle → *Similarity*

If you know that two triangles have two pairs of congruent corresponding angles, then it suffices to know that they are similar. (This is because if we know the value of *two* angles in a triangle, there is only one possible measure for the third angle.) So, in short, **angle-angle congruency guarantees similarity**.

If you know that two triangles are similar, then both of the properties above will be true. However, all you need to know is *one* of the properties above to determine that triangles are similar and that the other case *must* be true. Notice that in the following model question, you are not *given* the fact that the triangles are similar, but you must deduce this in order to answer the question.

$\triangle ABC$ and $\triangle AEF$ exist such that E is on $\overline{AB}$, F is on $\overline{AC}$, $\overline{EF} = 4$, $\overline{AF} = x$, and $\overline{AC} = 9$. Determine the value of x.

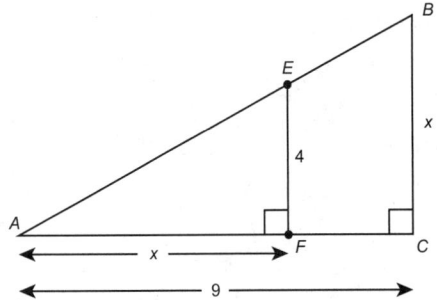

F. 5.5

G. 5.8

H. 6

J. 6.2

K. 7

The correct answer is H. Since both triangles have a right angle and both triangles share angle A, we know that these triangles are similar. Set up a proportion of the corresponding sides and solve for x:

$$\frac{x}{4} = \frac{9}{x}$$
$$x^2 = 36$$
$$x = 6$$

Choice F is not correct since $\frac{5.5}{4} \neq \frac{9}{5.5}$. Choice G is not correct since $\frac{5.8}{4} \neq \frac{9}{5.8}$.

Choice J is not correct since $\frac{6.2}{4} \neq \frac{9}{6.2}$. Choice K is not correct since $\frac{7}{4} \neq \frac{9}{7}$.

PROPERTIES OF QUADRILATERALS AND POLYGONS

A polygon is any two-dimensional figure that has at least three straight sides. A quadrilateral is a four-sided polygon. For the ACT, the most important concepts you must know are:

1. The special properties of various quadrilaterals
2. The sum of the interior angles in a polygon with n sides

SPECIAL PROPERTIES OF QUADRILATERALS

Begin by reviewing the features of the quadrilaterals listed in the table below, paying special attention to the less-commonly discussed traits of the diagonals.

Name	Features	Example
Rectangle	• Two pairs of opposite congruent sides • Two pairs of parallel sides • Four congruent right angles • Congruent diagonals bisect each other	
Rhombus	• Four congruent sides • Two pairs of parallel sides • Two pairs of opposite congruent angles • Diagonals bisect each other • Diagonals intersect at right angles • Looks like a "squished" square	
Square	• Four congruent sides • Four congruent right angles • Two pairs of parallel sides • Congruent diagonals bisect each other • Diagonals intersect at right angles • A square is a rhombus *and* a rectangle	

Name	Features	Example
Parallelogram	• Two pairs of opposite congruent sides • Two pairs of parallel sides • Diagonals bisect each other, but are not congruent	
Trapezoid	• Exactly one pair of parallel sides • Noncongruent diagonals do not bisect each other	
Isosceles Trapezoid	• Exactly one pair of parallel sides • Exactly one pair of congruent opposite sides, called *legs* • Two pairs of adjacent congruent angles • Congruent diagonals do not bisect each other	$\overline{AC} = \overline{BD}$

Know the features in the above table forward and backward. If you are asked, "What type of quadrilateral has diagonals that do not bisect?" you can answer with confidence, "trapezoid!"

Pay special attention to the properties of diagonals in quadrilaterals. The diagonals of squares, rectangles, rhombuses, and parallelograms all bisect each other. The diagonals of squares, rectangles, and isosceles trapezoids are congruent, but the diagonals of rhombuses and parallelograms are not! The diagonals of squares and rhombuses intersect at right angles.

INTERIOR ANGLE SUMS IN POLYGONS WITH *N* SIDES

You already know that a triangle's interior angles sum to 180° and that a quadrilateral's exterior angles sum to 360°. What you need to also know is that every additional side added to a polygon will increase the sum of the interior angles by 180°. This relationship is expressed in the following formula:

> The sum of the interior angles of a polygon with *n* sides is $(n - 2) \times 180°$.

Although you could always figure this out by dividing a given polygon into non-overlapping triangles, this is a convenient formula to know by heart. Use it to solve the following question.

Example:

In the pentagon *NICER*, $m\angle I = 130°$. What is the sum of the other four angles?

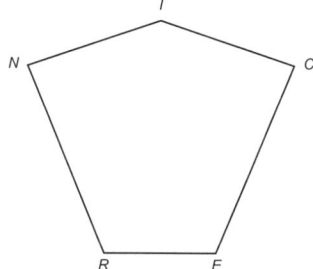

Solution:

Use the formula to determine the total sum of all five angles in a pentagon: $(5 - 2) \times 180° = 540°$.

Since $m\angle I = 130°$, the remaining four angles must have a sum of 410°.

A regular polygon is a polygon where all angles are equal in measure and all sides are equal in length. In order to find the measure of a *single* interior angle of a regular polygon, use this formula:

> The measure of an interior angle of a regular polygon with *n* sides is $\dfrac{(n - 2) \times 180°}{n}$.

TIP The sum of the interior angles of a polygon with n sides is $(n-2) \times 180°$. A regular polygon will have all equal angles, so the measure of a single interior angle in a regular polygon with n sides is $\frac{(n-2) \times 180°}{n}$.

Use this formula to answer the following question:

Given the regular hexagon below, what is the measure of the angle indicated by x?

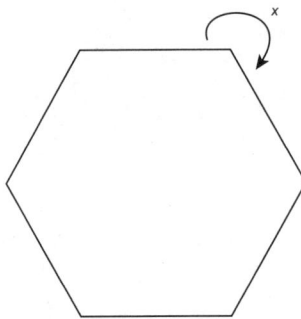

- **A.** 120°
- **B.** 232°
- **C.** 240°
- **D.** 252°
- **E.** 720°

The correct answer is C. The measure of an interior angle of a regular 6-sided polygon is $\frac{(6-2) \times 180°}{6} = 120°$. Therefore, the measure of $\angle x$ will be 360° − 120° = 240°. Choice A is incorrect because this is the measure of one of the interior angles of the given hexagon, but it is not the measure of the indicated angle x. Choice B is incorrect since this would be the approximate measure of $\angle x$ if this were a regular 7-sided polygon. Choice D is incorrect since this would be the measure of $\angle x$ if this were a regular pentagon. Choice E is incorrect because this is the sum of the interior angles of a hexagon.

PROPERTIES OF CIRCLES

In this section we are going to discuss the following aspects of circles:

- Tangent lines to circles
- Angles, arcs, and chords
- Circumference and chord length

TANGENT LINES TO CIRCLES

When a line is tangent to a circle, it intersects the circle at only *one* point and forms a 90° angle with the radius that terminates at that point. Use this definition to construct an illustration to model the information given in the following question.

Example:

Circle P has a radius of 10. Line m is tangent to circle P at point Q. Point R sits on line m such that $\overline{PR}$ = 16 units. Find the length of $\overline{QR}$ rounded to the nearest tenth.

Use the given information to construct the following illustration:

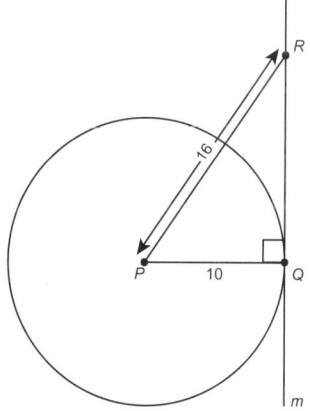

Solution:

Since line m is tangent to circle P at point Q, we know $\overline{PQ}$ is perpendicular line m. Therefore, this is a right triangle and the Pythagorean theorem can be used to solve for $\overline{QR}$:

$$10^2 + \left(\overline{QR}\right)^2 = 16^2$$
$$\overline{QR} = \sqrt{156} = 12.5$$

The term *tangent* can also be used to describe the relationship between circles. If two circles are tangent to each other, it means that that they touch at only one point. The following illustration shows two smaller tangent circles that are tangent to a larger circle.

Notice that the radii of the smaller circles could combine to form the diameter of the larger circle.

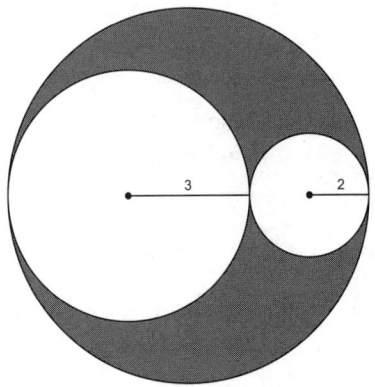

Whenever you are given information that a line is tangent to a circle, you should immediately draw a radius out to the point of intersection and draw in a 90-degree right angle. This might help you unlock the next steps you need to take to answer the question.

ANGLES, ARCS, AND CHORDS

Before we discuss angles within circles, let's recall that a *chord* is a line segment whose endpoints sit on the circumference of the circle. (When a chord passes through the center of the circle, it's a *diameter*.) There are several types of angles that can be formed within, outside, or adjacent to circles, but there are only two types that you need to know for test day:

- A **central angle** is formed by two radii that intersect to create the vertex at the center of the circle.

- An **inscribed angle** is formed by two intersecting chords and has its vertex on the circumference of the circle.

It is critical to know the relationships that central angles and inscribed angles have with the intercepted *arcs* they form along the circumference of the circle. (An **intercepted arc** is the distance along the circumference between two points on the circle. Intercepted arcs are notated with a small curve over their endpoints, such as $\overarc{AB}$.)

Type of angle	Relationship to arc formed	Example
Central angle	A central angle has the same measure as its intercepted arc.	$\angle ABC = 30°$ and $\overset{\frown}{AC} = 30°$
Inscribed angle	An inscribed angle has a measure that is half its intercepted arc. (Conversely, the intercepted arc has a measure that is twice the measure of its inscribed angle.)	$\angle ABC = 45°$ and $\overset{\frown}{AC} = 90°$

Example:

Circle K has diameters $\overline{VW}$ and $\overline{PQ}$ and chord $\overline{PW}$. If $\angle VWP = 38°$, find the measure of $\overset{\frown}{VQ}$.

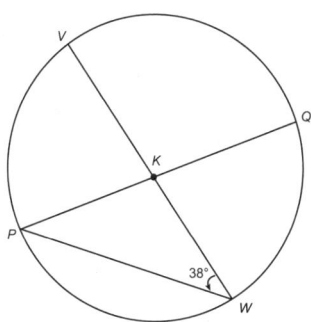

Solution:

Since $\overline{KW}$ and $\overline{KP}$ are both radii of circle K, conclude that $\triangle PKW$ is isosceles and therefore $m\angle QPW = 38°$:

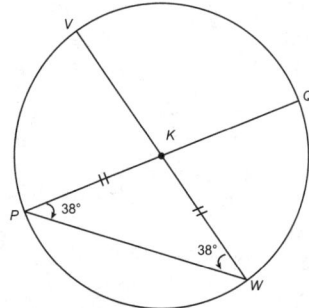

Therefore, it can be determined that the vertex angle, $\angle PKW$, of $\triangle PKW$ is equal to 104°. Since central angle $\angle VKQ$ is a vertical angle with $\angle PKW$, the measure of both $\angle VKQ$ and $\overset{\frown}{VQ}$ are 104°.

A central angle has its vertex at the center of the circle and a measure that's equal to its intercepted arc. An inscribed angle has its vertex on the circumference of the circle and has a measure that is half of its intercepted arc. Whenever you see chords within a circle, use this information to label all the associated arcs and angles before starting the question.

INTERSECTING CHORDS

Any time two chords intersect in a circle, they create four separate line segments that have a special relationship.

When two chords intersect within a circle, the products of their segments are equal. Given the following chords that intersect to form segments a, b, w, and y, it stands that $a \times b = w \times y$:

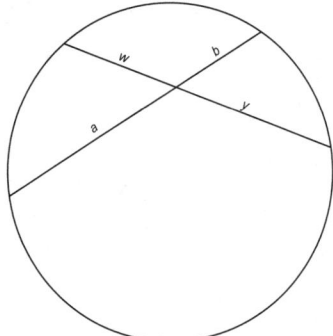

The theorem would be used to determine that $x = 6$ in the following figure, since $4(x) = 3(8) = 24$:

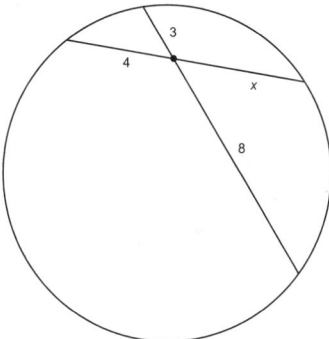

CIRCUMFERENCE AND CHORD LENGTH

One of the toughest questions about circles you may encounter will ask you to determine the unit length of an arc made by a central angle (as opposed to its measure in degrees). Of course it's easy to use the previously mentioned theorem to determine the measure of an arc in *degrees*, since it's always equal to the central angle, but converting degree measurement to a unit length takes a little more effort.

Recall that the *circumference* of a circle is the distance around it, which is found with the formula $C = 2\pi r$. When we need to find the *length* of an arc, we are finding a fraction of the circumference. That fraction of the circumference is defined as the ratio $\dfrac{\text{degrees of central} \angle}{360°}$.

For instance, let's start with a circle has a circumference of 20 feet. In order to find the length of the intercepted arc formed by a 90° central angle, multiply the circumference of 20 by the fractional circumference $\dfrac{90}{360}$:

$$20 \times \frac{90}{360} = 20 \times \frac{1}{4} = 5$$

Investigate the formula below and then apply it to the question that follows.

In a circle with radius r, the length of an arc formed by a central angle θ is:

$$\text{Arc Length} = 2\pi r \times \frac{\theta}{360}$$

Rye maintains a circular garden plot at his local park that has a diameter of 40 feet. He needs to fence off a section of the plot so that the vegetables he plants for the community will be protected from the hungry deer and bunnies that frequent the park. If he plans on using a central angle of 130° to make the edibles section of the garden plot, how many feet of fencing, to the nearest whole foot, must he purchase in order to surround the shaded region in the following illustration?

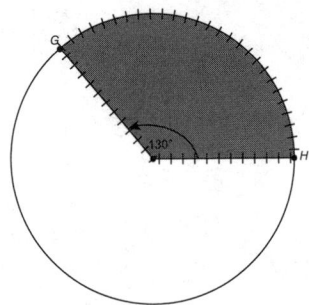

F. 68 feet
G. 80 feet
H. 82 feet
J. 86 feet
K. 243 feet

The correct answer is J. First, use the arc length formula with $r = 20$ and $\theta = 130$:

$$\text{Arc Length} = 2\pi(20) \times \frac{130}{360} \approx 45.4 \text{ feet}$$

Since Rye needs 45.4 feet for the arc and 20 feet for each radii, he will need a total of 85.4 feet. Round up to 86 feet since 85 feet of fencing would be 0.4 feet short. Choice F is incorrect because this would only be enough fencing to cover the two radii and an arc made by an 80-degree angle. Choice G is incorrect because this is only enough fencing for the two radii, but not enough to line the arc. Choice H is incorrect because this would only be enough fencing to cover the two radii and an arc made by an 120-degree angle, not a 130-degree angle. Choice K is incorrect because this would be the fencing needed if the *radius* was 40 feet, however, it is the *diameter* that is 40 feet.

An angle θ represents a portion of the full 360 degrees there are in a circle. Once you comprehend that, the following formula should be easy to re-create (instead of memorize) on test day:

$$\text{Arc Length} = 2\pi r \times \frac{\theta}{360}$$

AREA AND PERIMETER WITH POLYGONS, CIRCLES, AND COMPOSITE SHAPES

The topics of area and perimeter are the most frequently tested plane geometry concepts on the ACT. Be prepared to answer at least 3 or 4 questions on area and perimeter. The difficult part about perimeter and area questions is the multi-step problem solving involved. You'll be able to do the easier perimeter and area questions in your sleep, but the best method to prepare for the most challenging questions in this area will be practice, practice, and more practice! We're going to spend less time on the formulas in this section (we know you know those) and more time working through the following types of problems:

- Problems with similar shapes
- Problems involving symmetrically divided two-dimensional figures
- Problems requiring algebraic modeling
- Problems with composite shapes
- Problems presenting shapes within shapes

IMPORTANT FORMULAS

The **perimeter** is the distance *around* a figure and is the sum of all of its sides. Although not always necessary, the perimeter formulas for rectangles and squares are useful if you're working with side lengths that are presented as algebraic expressions. (Remember that circumference is like the perimeter of a circle!) **Area** is the measure of the space *within* a shape and will always require multiplication. Area is always expressed in squared units, such as cm^2, $ft.^2$, or m^2. It's critical to remember that in the last three area formulas that require h, or *height*, the height must be *perpendicular* to the base!

Measure of Shape	Formula	Illustration
Perimeter of rectangle	$P = 2l + 2w$ or $P = 2(l + w)$	$p = 2l + 2w$ or $p = 2(l + w)$

Measure of Shape	Formula	Illustration
Perimeter of square	$P = 4s$	
Circumference of circle	$C = 2\pi r$ or $C = \pi d$	
Area of square	$A = s^2$	
Area of rectangle	$A = l \times w$	

Measure of Shape	Formula	Illustration
Area of parallelogram	$A = b \times h$	area = base (b) × height (h)
Area of triangle	$A = \dfrac{1}{2}bh$	Area = $\dfrac{1}{2}$base × height
Area of trapezoid	$A = \dfrac{1}{2}(h)(b_1 + b_2)$	
Area of circle	$A = \pi r^2$	

 ALERT: Remember that the *height* or *altitude* of a polygon is always the *perpendicular* line segment that connects the *base* with the opposite angle (in triangles) or opposite side (in quadrilaterals). Don't use the slant heights by mistake in your calculations.

PROBLEMS WITH SIMILAR SHAPES

Earlier we discussed similarity in triangles. Polygons can be similar as well, as long as their corresponding angles are equal and their corresponding side-pairs are proportional. Let's consider two similar shapes A and B. If shape A has side lengths that are twice as long as those in shape B, how will the perimeter and area of shape B be different from shape A?

- The perimeter of shape B will be twice as large as that of shape A.

- The area of shape B will be four times as large as that of shape A.

The first bullet above didn't shock you, but we think you may have found the second one counterintuitive! Since *area* requires you to *multiply* the length of two dimensions together, if *both* dimensions are twice as long, then (2 × *length*) × (2 × *width*) will result in an area that is 4 × (*length* × *width*).

Work carefully as you apply this concept to the following question.

Example:

$\triangle ABC$ is similar to $\triangle XYZ$ such that $\overline{AB} = 4$ and $\overline{XY} = 12$. If the perimeter of $\triangle ABC$ is equal to P and the area of $\triangle ABC$ is equal to Q, what is the perimeter and area of $\triangle XYZ$?

Solution:

Since $\overline{AB} = 4$ and $\overline{XY} = 12$, all of the dimensions of $\triangle XYZ$ will be three times the length of the dimensions in $\triangle ABC$. Assuming that the side lengths of $\triangle ABC$ are s_1, s_2, and s_3, perimeter $P = s_1 + s_2 + s_3$. It follows that the side lengths of $\triangle XYZ$ are $3s_1$, $3s_2$, and $3s_3$ and that its perimeter is $3s_1 + 3s_2 + 3s_3 = 3(s_1 + s_2 + s_3)$. Therefore, the perimeter of $\triangle XYZ$ is $3P$.

Similarly assuming that base and height of $\triangle ABC$ are b and h, area $Q = \frac{1}{2}bh$. It follows that the side lengths of $\triangle XYZ$ are $3b$ and $3h$ and that its area is $\frac{1}{2}(3b)(3h) = 9 \times \frac{1}{2}bh$. Therefore, the area of $\triangle XYZ$ is $9Q$.

 ALERT: Although the *perimeter* of the larger polygon will be k times the perimeter of the smaller polygon, this is not true for the area. The area of the larger polygon will be k^2 times larger than the area of the smaller polygon.

Problems Involving Symmetrically Divided Two-Dimensional Figures

The ACT likes to test your ability to deconstruct a shape into smaller shapes, and then draw conclusions about the areas or perimeters of a portion of the included shapes. The following question does this and also tests your fluency with fractions.

Example:

Luke has designed a flag for a country he invented for a school project. The flag is a rectangle divided vertically into 4 columns of equal area. He divides the first and fourth columns into two triangles of equal area. He divides the second column into three squares of equal area. To finish, he divides the third column into four rectangles of equal area. All the spaces labeled G will be painted green. What fraction of the Luke's flag will be green?

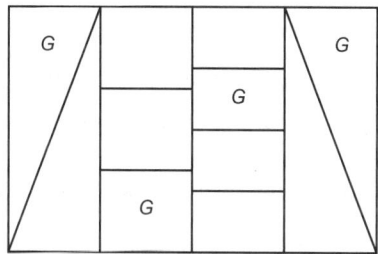

Solution:

Each column represents $\frac{1}{4}$ of the entire flag. Since each column is divided into regions of equal area, we can determine that the shapes within the first and fourth columns represent halves of each quarter, the squares within the second column represent thirds of each quarter, and the rectangles in the third column represents fourths of each quarter. Calculate the fraction of the whole each G region represents column by column:

$$\text{Column 1: } \frac{1}{2} \text{ of } \frac{1}{4} \text{ is } \frac{1}{2} \times \frac{1}{4} = \frac{1}{8}$$

$$\text{Column 2: } \frac{1}{3} \text{ of } \frac{1}{4} \text{ is } \frac{1}{3} \times \frac{1}{4} = \frac{1}{12}$$

$$\text{Column 3: } \frac{1}{4} \text{ of } \frac{1}{4} \text{ is } \frac{1}{4} \times \frac{1}{4} = \frac{1}{16}$$

$$\text{Column 4: } \frac{1}{2} \text{ of } \frac{1}{4} \text{ is } \frac{1}{2} \times \frac{1}{4} = \frac{1}{8}$$

So now we know how much of the whole each *G* region represents. To finish the question, find their sum: $\frac{1}{8}+\frac{1}{12}+\frac{1}{16}+\frac{1}{8}=\frac{19}{48}$. So $\frac{19}{48}$ of Luke's flag will be green.

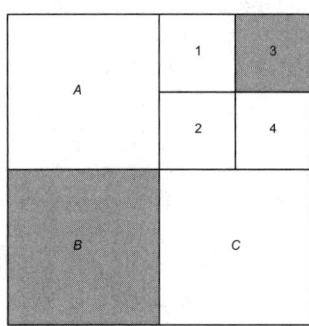

When given a subdivided geometric shape, look for symmetries in the main shape, but even within the *shapes within the shapes*! In this square, regions *A*, *B*, and *C* are each equivalent to $\frac{1}{4}$ of the square, but regions *1, 2, 3*, and *4* are each equal to $\frac{1}{4}$ of $\frac{1}{4}$ of the square. Therefore, the smaller regions are each $\frac{1}{16}$, and the shaded regions would be $\frac{1}{4}+\frac{1}{16}=\frac{5}{16}$ of the total square.

PROBLEMS REQUIRING ALGEBRAIC MODELING

It's likely that you'll need to use a good deal of algebraic modeling and equation solving when working with perimeter and area questions. Your key will be to look for the questions that don't give you concrete dimensions.

Example:

Square *DEFG* is inside square *ABCD* such that vertex *E* is on $\overline{AD}$ and vertex *G* is on $\overline{CD}$. The area of *DEFG* is 16 and $\overline{AE} = x$. What is the value of *x* if the area of *ABCD* is $x^2 + 36$?

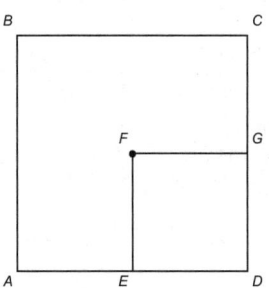

Solution:

First determine that since the area of square *DEFG* is 16, $\overline{ED} = 4$. Since $\overline{AE} = x$, we can determine that $\overline{AD} = (x+4)$. Since *ABCD* is a square, all sides are equal to $x + 4$, and the area of *ABCD*, $x^2 + 36$, must be equivalent to $(x + 4)(x + 4)$. Set up an equation to solve for *x*:

$$(x+4)(x+4) = x^2 + 36$$
$$x^2 + 8x + 16 = x^2 + 36$$
$$8x + 16 = 36$$
$$x = \frac{20}{8} = 2.5$$

Problems with Composite Shapes

A composite shape is a complex figure that can be divided into two or more different common shapes. Expect to calculate the areas and perimeters of composite shapes.

Example:

The following illustration shows the entryway to a European train depot that is 40 feet wide by 8 feet tall. There are plans to hire a local artist to create and install semicircular stained glass mosaics to the left and right of the entryway, as well as above it. If the artist charges a total of $80 per square foot for her design, materials, and labor, what would be the cost of this installation?

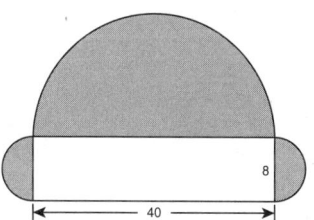

Solution:

First determine that the left and right semicircles would combine to form one circle with a diameter of 8 feet and a radius of 4 feet: $A = -\pi r^2 = \pi(4)^2 \approx 50.24$ ft.². The installation on top would be a semicircle with a diameter of 40 feet and a radius of 20 feet: $A = \frac{1}{2}\pi r^2 = \frac{1}{2}(20)^2 = 628.32$ ft.². These two areas combined to 678.56 ft.², so at $80 per square foot, this installation would cost $678.56 \times \$80 = \$54,284.80$.

Problems Presenting Shapes within Shapes

The last type of area and perimeter problem we'll look at is one that has shapes nested within each other. You will be given information about one of the shapes and will be required to make a determination about the perimeter or area of the second shape. When doing questions such as the one that follows, it's important that you label the given illustration as much as possible, which will help you make connections between the given information and the steps you need to take to answer the question.

· ·

Square *ABCD* has an area of 12 square units and is inscribed into circle *P*. Which of the following is the closest approximation of the area of circle *P*?

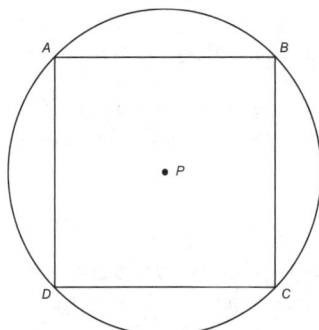

A. 5
B. 19
C. 24
D. 38
E. 75

The correct answer is B. In order to find the area of circle *P*, we need to find its diameter or radius. Notice that the diagonal $\overline{DB}$ of square *ABCD* is also the diameter of the circle, so start with the information given about the square. If square *ABCD* has an area of 12, then $A = s^2 = 12$, and we can determine that $s = \sqrt{12}$. Use $\sqrt{12}$ in the Pythagorean theorem to find the square's diagonal:

$$a^2 + b^2 = c^2$$
$$\left(\sqrt{12}\right)^2 + \left(\sqrt{12}\right)^2 = \left(\overline{DB}\right)^2$$
$$24 = \left(\overline{DB}\right)^2$$
$$\sqrt{24} = \overline{DB}$$

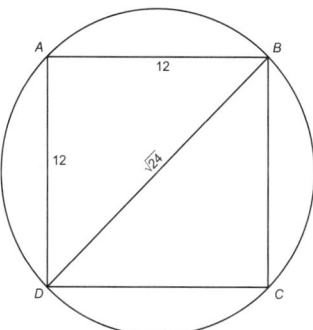

So the diameter of circle P is $\sqrt{24}$ and the radius is $\dfrac{\sqrt{24}}{2}$. Put this into the formula for area of a circle:

$$A = \pi r^2 = \pi \left(\frac{\sqrt{24}}{2} \right)^2 = \pi \left(\frac{24}{4} \right) \approx 18.84$$

Choice A is the approximate diameter of the circle. Choice C is incorrect because 24 is the radicand of the diameter of the circle, but it is not the area of this circle. Choice D is incorrect because it is the area of a circle that has a diameter of 24 and not $\sqrt{24}$. Choice E is incorrect because it is the area of a circle that has a radius of $\sqrt{24}$ and not $\dfrac{\sqrt{24}}{2}$.

• •

 ALERT: Don't overuse your calculator! It is sometimes better to keep calculations as fractions or radicals rather than simplifying them to decimal estimates on the calculator.

SURFACE AREA

Surface area seems to make an appearance on about only 50% of the ACT tests, and these questions are normally fairly straightforward. If asked to find the surface area for any shape other than a cube, you will be provided with the appropriate formula. You should know the formula for surface area for a cube:

> Surface Area of a cube with side length s is $SA = 6s^2$.

It's not likely you'd get a question this hard, but test your skills on this tricky question that requires algebraic modeling and solving quadratics.

When the side length of a sample cube is increased by 2 inches, the new surface area will be 216 square inches. What is the surface area, in square inches, of the original sample cube?

- **F.** 64
- **G.** 72
- **H.** 96
- **J.** 108
- **K.** 384

The correct answer is H. Create an algebraic model to uncover how the surface area will changes when the unknown side length is increased by 2. The original sample cube has a surface area of $6s^2$, which means that after all the side lengths have been increased by 2, the new cube will have a surface area of $6(s + 2)^2$. Set this expression equal to the surface area of the new cube, which is 216 square inches. Then solve for s:

$$6(s+2)^2 = 216$$
$$\left(s^2 + 4s + 4\right) = 36$$
$$s^2 + 4s - 32 = 0$$
$$(s+8)(s-4) = 0$$

Since $s = -8$ or 4, and side lengths must be positive, conclude that $s = 4$. The surface area of the original sample cube is $SA = 6s^2 = 6(4)^2 = 96$. Choice F is the volume of the original cube, but not the surface area. Choice G is the quotient of 216 and 3, but not the surface area of the original cube. Choice J is half of the new cube's surface area but does not relate to the original cube. Choice K is the result of using an edge length of 8 to find the surface area, but −8, and not 8, is a solution to the quadratic model.

Although the following formulas will most likely be provided to you, it is good for you to be familiar with the surface area formulas for rectangular prisms and for cylinders. This way you don't have to take too much time on test day deciphering the formulas.

Surface Area of a Rectangular Prism with length *l*, width *w*, and height *h:*

$$SA = 2lw + 2lh + 2wh$$

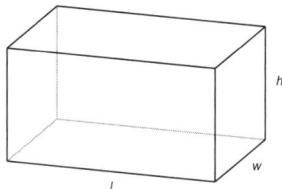

Surface Area of a Cylinder with radius *r* and height *h*:

$$SA = 2\pi rh + 2\pi r^2$$

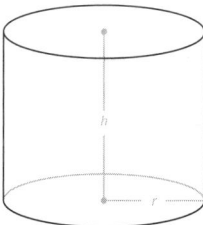

Notice that the formula for the surface area of a rectangular prism is made up of the areas of the bottom and top (2*lw*), plus the areas of the front and back (2*lh*), plus the areas of the left and right (2*wh*).

The surface area formula for a cylinder can similarly be deconstructed: the $2\pi r^2$ is the area of both circles on the top and bottom. The $2\pi rh$ is the circumference ($2\pi r$) times the height. This is akin to calculating the *length* times *width* of the flattened out cylinder part. Having a deeper understanding of these formulas will make it easier for you to apply them and reduce the chance of making a careless error as you plug the values into the formulas.

VOLUME

Volume is the measure of space *within* a three-dimensional object and is always expressed in cubed units, such as cm^3, ft^3, or m^3. Be prepared to see one or two volume questions on the test and be ready for one of them to make you squirm at least a bit. (The test makers get creative with their volume questions!)

Before we get started with some sample questions, take a minute to review the formulas for the volume of cubes, rectangular prisms, and cylinders (you will be given the formulas for any other three-dimensional object, such as a sphere):

Figure	Volume formula	Illustration
Cube	$V = a^3$	
Rectangular Prism	$V = l \times w \times h$	
Right Cylinder	$V = \pi r^2 h$	

Fractional Volume Relationships

Similar to the questions on perimeter and area, volume questions can sometimes require you to convert given information about one type of measurement to another, like finding the volume of a figure when given the surface area. Another type of application within volume questions is one that asks you to consider the fractional volumes of a three-dimensional object, which we will explore next.

Example:

Last winter, the Eng family emptied, cleaned, and repainted their pool. The weather is getting warmer, so Ms. Eng is getting the pool ready to enjoy. She puts a hose in the pool for a few hours one afternoon; before going to sleep for the night, she sees that it is $\frac{1}{6}$ full. The hose runs overnight and puts an *additional* 900 cubic feet of water to the pool, and it is $\frac{2}{3}$ full when Ms. Eng checks the depth in the morning. What is the full volume, in cubic feet, that the pool holds?

Solution:

Remember that finding the fractional value of something is as easy as multiplying that quantity by that fraction. For example, if the pool's full volume is p, then the expression $\frac{1}{6}p$ represents the pool when it is $\frac{1}{6}$ full. Similarly, $\frac{2}{3}p$ represents a pool that is $\frac{2}{3}$ full.

Once we've made note of these expressions, we can set up an equation that illustrates "900 gallons of water added to $\frac{1}{6}$ of the pool's full volume results in a pool that is $\frac{2}{3}$ full". $\frac{1}{6}p + 900 = \frac{2}{3}p$. Solving for p brings us to $900 = \frac{3}{6}p$ and $p = 1,800$ cubic feet.

The ACT often features questions that require converting from one type of measurement (like volume) to another type of measurement (like surface area). Using the formula for the given measurement (i.e., volume), work backwards to determine the dimensions needed to calculate the new type of measurement (i.e., surface area).

Changing Dimensions

How does the volume of a cube change when all the side lengths are all doubled? Express the new side length using an algebraic expression (such as $2s$), and put it into the original formula in order to analyze its impact. We've practiced this a few times now, so see if you can get through the next question on your own the first time around.

Example:

Rani is filling helium balloons for a New Year's Eve party. She has rented a helium tank and wants to fill enough balloons to make her house look festive. She loves the extra large balloons that Party Central sells, but she's worried she won't be able to fill enough of them for her party. The extra large balloons have a radius that is 3 times larger than the small balloons that are also for sale. How many times larger is the volume of the extra large balloons than the volume of the small balloons? (Note: The balloons are spherical, and the volume for a sphere is $V = \frac{4}{3}\pi r^3$.)

Solution:

The fastest way to handle problems like this is to create an algebraic expression to model the change and then substitute that expression into the equation. Since the radius of the extra large balloons is three times larger than a small balloon's radius, use b as the radius for the small balloons and $3b$ as the radius for the extra large balloons. The volume for the small balloons would be $\frac{4}{3}\pi b^3$, and the volume for the extra large balloons would be $\frac{4}{3}\pi(3b)^3 = \frac{4}{3}\pi b^3 \times 27$. This shows that the volume of the extra large balloons is 27 times larger than the volume of the small balloons.

VISUALIZING VOLUME AS LAYERS

Some questions will demand a keen visual ability along with a comprehensive understanding of volume that goes *beyond* the formula. You should feel comfortable deconstructing volume formulas and picturing the volume of an object as *layers* of unit cubes. Consider a box that is 6 inches long, 4 inches wide, and 3 inches tall. Each flat layer of this box can hold 6 rows of 4 1-inch cubes. In order to cover the bottom of the box entirely, you would need 24 cubes as pictured below:

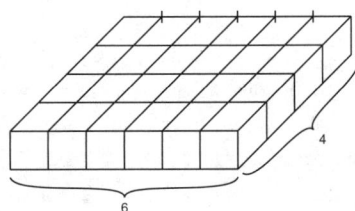

Since the box is 3 inches tall, we can picture the volume as being 3 layers of 24 1-inch cubes, which sums to a total of 72 cubes:

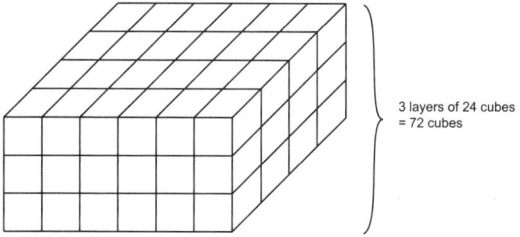

3 layers of 24 cubes = 72 cubes

Let's consider this box when its empty, but still has a bottom that is 4 by 6 units and the height is 3 units. Suppose enough paint were to get poured into this box, so that it was $\frac{1}{2}$ inch full. What is the volume of the paint that was poured into the box? Hopefully, you can see that each of the 24 1-inch cubes on the first layer, would be $\frac{1}{2}$ inch full, so the volume of paint would be $\frac{1}{2}$ of 24, which would be 12 cubic inches. See if you can exercise this type of logic with the following question.

Example:

Cam has a koi fish tank in his school that is 6 feet long, 3 feet wide, and 4 feet tall. One month has passed since the tank was filled to its optimal level. Cam realizes that since then, the water level has decreased by 3 inches due to evaporation. How many cubic feet of water have evaporated over the course of a month?

Solution:

First, we need to notice that the tank dimensions are given in feet, but the water loss is reported in inches. Both measurements *must* be in the same units, so convert 3 inches to $\frac{1}{4}$ of a foot. Since the fish tank is 6 feet long by 3 feet wide, each vertical foot of water represents a volume of 18 cubic feet. Since $\frac{1}{4}$ of a foot evaporated, this means that $\frac{1}{4}$ of 18 ft³ has evaporated: $\frac{1}{4} \times 18 = 4.5 \text{ft}^3$.

TRANSFORMATIONS

A transformation is a uniform change performed on a shape in a two-dimensional plane or on a standard (x, y) coordinate plane. After a point has undergone a transformation, it is written as the *prime* of that point, which is notated with an apostrophe: point P becomes P' after being transformed. A transformation question seems to appear on about half of the ACT tests. There are two types of transformations you may encounter: rotations and reflections.

ROTATIONS

Either clockwise or counterclockwise rotations can occur on standard (x, y) coordinate plane. Generally, you will be asked to identify the new coordinates of a point that has been rotated 90° or 180°. To determine this, you can apply the rules below, which illustrate how a coordinate pair, (x, y), changes after three different types of rotations:

Type of Rotation	(x, y) becomes...	Illustration
90° **clockwise**	(x, y) becomes $(y, -x)$	(4, 2) becomes (2, −4)
90° **counterclockwise**	(x, y) becomes $(-y, x)$	(1, 3) becomes (−3, 1)
180°	(x, y) becomes $(-x, -y)$	(−2, 3) becomes (2, −3)

Notice that for each rotation, x and y change places. When a point is rotated 180°, both coordinates change signs. When rotated 90°, only one of the coordinates will change signs. As long as you remember to switch the order of the coordinates, it should be easy for you to determine the signs of each coordinate without needing to memorize these formulas!

The x- and y-coordinates of a point will always switch places when the point is rotated 90° or 180°. For 180° rotations, both coordinates will also change signs, but for 90° rotations, only one coordinate will reverse signs.

Now try your hand at a rotation problem.

. . . .

Triangle ABC sits in the standard (x, y) coordinate plane as pictured. What will be the coordinates of vertex A after the triangle is rotated 90° counterclockwise?

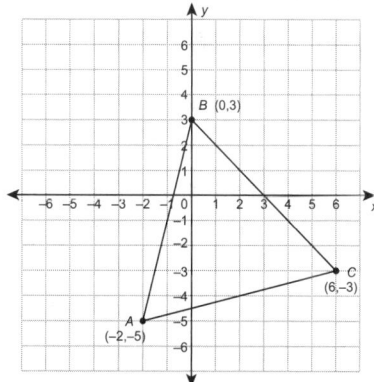

A. (–5, –2)
B. (2, –5)
C. (5, 2)
D. (2, 5)
E. (5, –2)

The correct answer is E. When a coordinate pair (x, y) is rotated 90° counterclockwise, its new coordinates become (–y, x). Therefore, (–2, –5) will become (5, –2). Choice A does not show the coordinates for any standard rotation since at least one of the coordinates needs to change signs. Choice B shows the coordinates of A' after being reflected over the y-axis. Choice C would be a rotation greater than 90° since it has skipped over the fourth quadrant. Choice D shows the coordinates of A' after being rotated 180°.

. . . .

REFLECTIONS

Points or shapes can be reflected over an axis or over a line in the standard (x, y) coordinate plane.

- A point that's reflected *horizontally* will keep its y-coordinate, but have a different x-coordinate. For example, when the point A at $(2, 5)$ is reflected over the line $x = 10$, it becomes A' at $(18, 5)$ since the x-coordinate will still be 8 away from the line $x = 10$, but on the *other* side.

- Conversely, a point that is reflected *vertically* will have a change in its y-coordinate, but its x-coordinate will remain the same. For example, if point B at $(-5, 7)$ is reflected over the x-axis, then B' will be $(-5, -7)$.

At times you will be asked to reflect a given shape over one of its sides in order to create a new shape.

· ·

Right triangle ABC is graphed on a standard (x, y) coordinate plane. If it is reflected over $\overline{BC}$ to form square $ABA'C$, find the area of $ABA'C$.

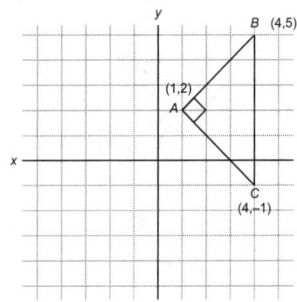

A. 9

B. 18

C. $6 + 6\sqrt{2}$

D. $12\sqrt{2}$

E. 36

The correct answer is B. Since reflected polygons have equal area, the easiest way to find the area of square $ABA'C$ is to find the area of $\triangle ABC$, and multiply that by two. Use $\overline{BC}$ as the *base* of $\triangle ABC$. $\overline{BC} = 6$. The perpendicular height from $\overline{BC}$ to vertex A goes from $(4, 2)$ to $(1, 2)$, so it is 3 units long. Therefore, the area of $\triangle ABC$ is $A = \dfrac{1}{2}bh = \dfrac{1}{2}(6)(3) = 9$ units^2. $\triangle BA'C$ also has an area of 9 units^2, so the total area of $ABA'C$ is 18 units^2. Choice A is the area of $\triangle ABC$ and not the area of $ABA'C$. Choice C is the perimeter of $\triangle ABC$ and not the area of square *ABA'C*. Choice D is the perimeter of square *ABA'C* and not its area. Choice E is twice the area of square *ABA'C*.

. . . .

Nice work! You just finished the review of plane geometry. Now you're ready to move on to a review of the trigonometry content that will be on the ACT. On average, the ACT asks about 4 trig questions on each test. The good news is that although you might think these will be your toughest questions, the trig content on the ACT isn't too obtuse. (Pun intended!) Our discussion will start with trigonometric relations in right triangles, which is the most commonly tested trig concept on the ACT.

TRIGONOMETRIC RELATIONS IN RIGHT TRIANGLES

The Pythagorean theorem is used to find the missing side length in a triangle when two sides are known. The magic of trigonometry allows us to solve for a missing side length when just one side and one angle are known. When given two side lengths in a right triangle, trigonometry can also be applied to determine the unknown angles. Expect to see two or more questions applying trigonometric ratios to right triangles.

USING TRIG RATIOS TO FIND SIDE LENGTHS

There are three principal functions that define the relationships between the angles and sides in right triangles: sine, cosine, and tangent. (You won't see the reciprocal functions secant, cosecant, and cotangent on the ACT.) The sides are always named *relative* to one of the angles in the right triangle. Notice that in the following triangle, side *a* is *opposite* θ, side *b* is *adjacent* to θ, and side *c* is the *hypotenuse*. You should have complete fluency with how these sides are used in the trig ratios in the table provided.

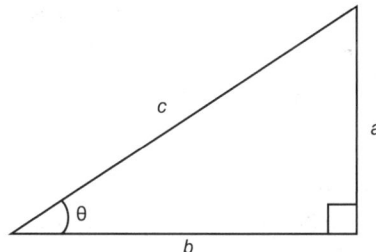

Function (Abbreviation)	Side Ratio	Example from Illustration
Sine (sin)	$\sin\theta = \dfrac{\text{opposite}}{\text{hypotenuse}}$	$\sin\theta = \dfrac{a}{c}$
Cosine (cos)	$\cos\theta = \dfrac{\text{adjacent}}{\text{hypotenuse}}$	$\cos\theta = \dfrac{b}{c}$
Tangent (tan)	$\tan\theta = \dfrac{\text{opposite}}{\text{adjacent}}$	$\tan\theta = \dfrac{a}{b}$

You may have learned the side ratios represented by sine, cosine, and tangent using the mnemonic SOH-CAH-TOA, where:

SOH represents $\sin\theta = \dfrac{\text{opposite}}{\text{hypotenuse}}$,

CAH represents $\cos\theta = \dfrac{\text{adjacent}}{\text{hypotenuse}}$, and

TOA represents $\tan\theta = \dfrac{\text{opposite}}{\text{adjacent}}$.

This is a useful trick to getting your ratios correct on test day!

Be prepared to dust off your Pythagorean theorem skills for this section! Also, you may need to create your own illustrations modeling the given information.

 ALERT: When you know only two side lengths in a trig relation question, it is very uncommon that these are the sides you'll need to use for your final answer. It is more likely that you will need to solve for the third side length to complete your trig ratio.

Example:

The two shorter sides of a right triangle are 17 inches and 22 inches. Which expression represents the sine of the triangle's smallest interior angle?

Solution:

First, draw a right triangle with two legs that are 17 and 22 units long with a hypotenuse of c. The angle opposite the smallest side, 17, is the smallest angle, so label that angle θ:

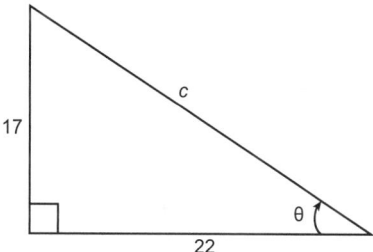

We know $\sin\theta = \dfrac{\text{opposite}}{\text{hypotenuse}}$, but we need the value of the hypotenuse. Use the Pythagorean theorem, but keep the hypotenuse as a radical expression since it is an irrational number:

$$(17)^2 + (22)^2 = c^2$$
$$c = \sqrt{(17)^2 + (22)^2}$$

Now we can determine that $\sin\theta = \dfrac{17}{\sqrt{(17)^2 + (22)^2}}$.

Notice that the solution to the example question includes the radical expression, $\sqrt{(17)^2 + (22)^2}$. Testing your ability to set up the solution, rather than your ability to work through the final arithmetic steps, is common on the ACT.

Similar to how one half can be written as $\dfrac{14}{28}$, 0.5, or 50%, there are multiple ways that just one angle can be expressed in terms of trig functions. We bet that your initial solution to the next question is not one of the answer choices provided. When this happens, step back, and determine what other information can be uncovered to solve the question from a different angle. (Again . . . pun intended!)

Test your understanding with the following question.

. . . .

The illustration below shows a right triangle where two side lengths are shown in inches. Which expression is equivalent to the value of x?

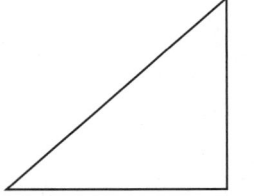 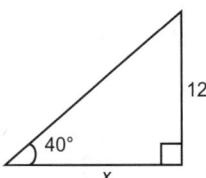

- **A.** 12 sin 50
- **B.** 2 sin 40
- **C.** 12 tan 50
- **D.** 12 cos 40
- **E.** 12 tan 40

The correct answer is C. The obvious solution is $\dfrac{12}{\tan 40}$, but since this is not an answer choice, approach the solution using the other acute angle. The second acute interior angle is 50°. Use tangent: $\tan 50 = \dfrac{\text{opposite}}{\text{adjacent}} = \dfrac{x}{12}$, which leads to $x = 12 \tan 50$. Choice A cannot be correct because sine is the ratio between *opposite* and *hypotenuse,* and the hypotenuse is unknown. Choice B cannot be correct because sine is the ratio between *opposite* and *hypotenuse,* and the hypotenuse is unknown. Choice D cannot be correct because cosine is the ratio between *adjacent* and *hypotenuse,* and the hypotenuse is unknown. Choice E cannot be correct because if the 40°angle were used, x would equal the quotient, $\dfrac{12}{\tan 40}$, and not the product $12 \tan 40$.

. . . .

USING TRIG RATIOS TO FIND ANGLES

When two sides of a right triangle are given, trig ratios can be used to solve for the angles of the triangle. This is done by using the inverse of basic trig functions. There are two notations for inverse functions: one of them uses the prefix *arc* in front of the trig abbreviation and the other uses an exponent of –1. Notice that when inverse notation is used, it is not followed by an *angle,* but is instead followed by a *side ratio.* This is because the inverse functions are taken of side ratios in order to *determine* angles. Use the table below to review how inverse functions would be used to solve for the missing angle, θ, in the following 3–4–5 triangle.

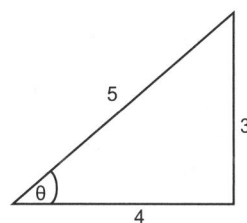

Inverse Function	General Arc Notation	Inverse Notion from Example
Inverse of sine	$\theta = \arcsin\left(\dfrac{\text{opposite}}{\text{hypotenuse}}\right)$	$\theta = \sin^{-1}\dfrac{3}{5}$
Inverse of cosine	$\theta = \arccos\left(\dfrac{\text{adjacent}}{\text{hypotenuse}}\right)$	$\theta = \cos^{-1}\dfrac{4}{5}$
Inverse of tangent	$\theta = \arctan\left(\dfrac{\text{opposite}}{\text{adjacent}}\right)$	$\theta = \tan^{-1}\dfrac{3}{4}$

Remember that whenever you see inverse trig functions like $\arcsin\left(\dfrac{9}{13}\right)$ or $\cos^{-1}\left(\dfrac{17}{22}\right)$, these functions are referring to *angle measurements* that have the side ratios expressed.

Try to stay calm if you get an expression that looks like $\cos\left[\sin^{-1}\left(\dfrac{3}{5}\right)\right]$. This function is really just asking, "What is the cosine of the *angle* that has a sine of $\dfrac{3}{5}$?" If we use the given 3-4-5 triangle to answer this question, we could determine that θ is the angle that has a sine of $\dfrac{3}{5}$, and since $\cos\theta = \dfrac{4}{5}$, we could determine that $\cos\left[\sin^{-1}\left(\dfrac{3}{5}\right)\right] = \dfrac{4}{5}$.

Example:

What is the value of $\tan\left[\arctan\left(\dfrac{12}{17}\right)\right]$?

Solution:

This question is asking, "What is the tangent of the *angle* that has a tangent of $\frac{12}{17}$?"

The only possible solution is $\frac{12}{17}$, since you would need to apply the same trig function (tangent) to the original angle.

Many of the trigonometry questions will be in the form of word problems, accompanied by illustrations.

Example:

A 12-foot wheelchair accessibility ramp runs alongside a staircase that is 3 feet high, as pictured below. Find an expression that represents the measure of angle θ that is formed between the ground and the ramp.

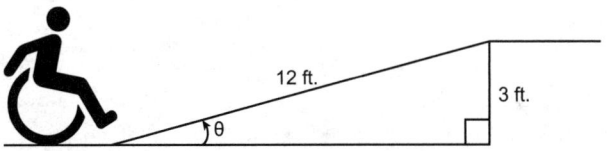

Relative to angle θ, the two given side lengths are the *opposite* and the *hypotenuse*. Therefore, use the sine relationship to determine the requested angle: $\theta = \sin^{-1}\frac{3}{12}$, which simplifies to $\theta = \sin^{-1}\frac{1}{4}$. (This is what the correct answer choice will look like on the test; you will not be required to evaluate it.)

NOTE: The ACT will not ask you to evaluate trig functions or inverse trig functions. You will commonly see answer choices written as the product of a constant and a trig function, such 8sin40, or as an inverse function like $\sin^{-1}\left(\frac{3}{5}\right)$.

Hopefully, those first two problems were easy for you. Here's a trickier one:

. . . .

In the right triangle below with sides a, b, and c, one of the angles has a measure of $\sin^{-1}\left(\dfrac{b}{c}\right)$. What is the value of $\cos\left[\sin^{-1}\left(\dfrac{b}{c}\right)\right]$?

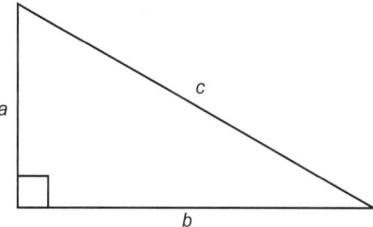

F. $\dfrac{c}{b}$

G. $\dfrac{a}{b}$

H. $\dfrac{b}{a}$

J. $\dfrac{c}{a}$

K. $\dfrac{a}{c}$

The correct answer is K. First use $\sin^{-1}\left(\dfrac{b}{c}\right)$ to determine that the angle in question is the one formed in the top left, between sides a and c, since from that angle, b is the *opposite* side and c is the hypotenuse. The cosine of that same angle is $\dfrac{a}{c}$. Choice F is just the reciprocal of the ratio provided. Choice G is the tangent of the other acute angle in the triangle. Choice H is the tangent of the correct angle in question. Choice J is the reciprocal of the correct answer.

. . . .

Angles of Elevations and Depression

You are probably familiar with these two types of angles that occur frequently in trigonometric word problems, but we just want to quickly review them.

- An **angle of elevation** is the angle formed from a subject's horizontal line of
  sight, *up* to an object that is higher than the subject. Here's a 65° angle of
  elevation up to the top of a giant redwood tree:

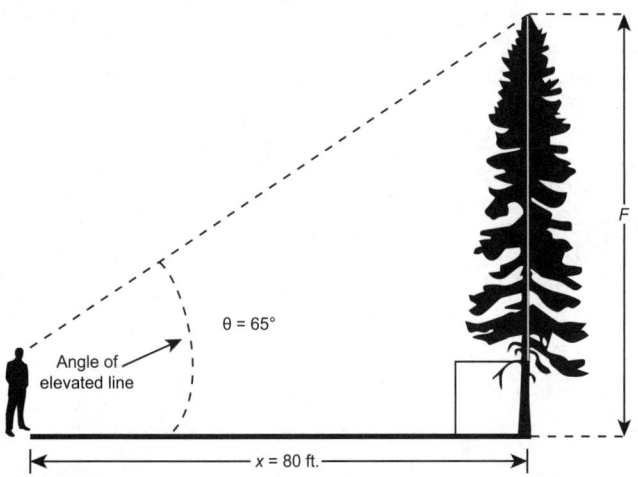

- An **angle of depression** is the angle formed from a subject's horizontal line
  of sight, *down* to an object that is lower than the subject. Here's a 40° angle
  of depression from someone looking down from the top of a building to a
  car on the street:

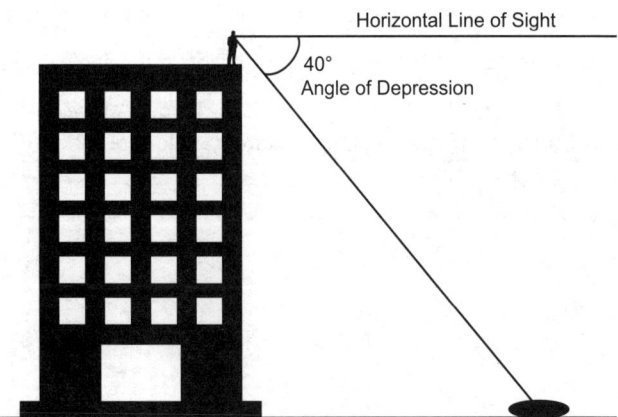

Put these concepts into practice with the next question.

· ·

Olivia is a lifeguard on duty in a lifeguard stand that is 18 feet tall. She notices a swimmer that is struggling in the lake at an angle of depression of 30°. Which of the following is the best estimate for the horizontal distance, over land and water, from the lifeguard stand to the struggling swimmer?

(Note: sin30° = 0.50, cos30° ≈ 0.87, and tan30° ≈ 0.58)

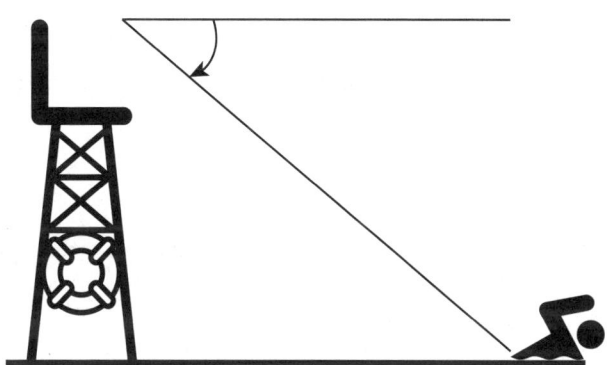

A. 15 feet
B. 16 feet
C. 21 feet
D. 31 feet
E. 36 feet

The correct answer is D. The angle given is *adjacent* to the side we want to determine,

which is the horizontal distance out from the lifeguard stand to above the swimmer.

The height of the lifeguard stand represents the *opposite* side to the angle. Therefore,

use $\tan 30 = \dfrac{\text{opposite}}{\text{adjacent}} = \dfrac{18}{d}$ to solve for the horizontal distance to the swimmer: $d = \dfrac{18}{\tan 30}$.

Substituting in tan30° ≈ 0.58 gives the solution $d = 31$ feet. Choice A is the value of

18sin30. Choice B is the value of 18cos30. Choice C is the value of $\dfrac{18}{\cos 30}$. Choice E is

the value of $\dfrac{18}{\sin 30}$.

· ·

When the answer choices to a trig question are in numerical form, you will be given the decimal value equivalents of all the trig functions for the given angle, such as sin30°= 0.50. cos30° ≈ 0.87, and tan30° ≈ 0.58. Use these decimal estimates to evaluate your final answer.

SKETCHING RIGHT TRIANGLES FROM TRIG RATIOS

Here is the last type of right triangle trig question you could see on the test. This style of question will never be accompanied by an illustration, but drawing one yourself will make solving this type of question a snap!

Example:

Angle θ is in a right triangle such that $\sin\theta = \dfrac{6}{145}$ and $\tan\theta = \dfrac{6}{125}$. What is the value for $\cos\theta$?

Solution:

Start this question by sketching a right triangle and labeling one of the acute angles as θ. Next, since $\sin\theta = \dfrac{6}{145} = \dfrac{\text{opposite}}{\text{hypotenuse}}$, you know that the side *opposite* θ is 6 and the *hypotenuse* is 145. Add these dimensions to your triangle:

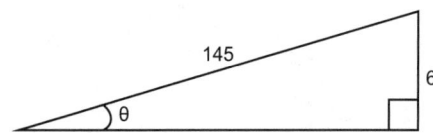

$\cos\theta = \dfrac{\text{adjacent}}{\text{hypotenuse}}$, so we need to find the unknown *adjacent* side to θ. (Shocking that you didn't get the two sides you needed, right? Be prepared for this!) Using the Pythagorean theorem, we find that the other leg is 125, so $\cos\theta = \dfrac{125}{145}$.

CIRCLE TRIGONOMETRY, RADIAN MEASURE, AND POLAR COORDINATES

In addition to being represented in degrees, angles can also be expressed in radian measure, such as $\dfrac{7\pi}{4}$. The good news is that the ACT won't assess you on all the ins and outs of radian measure—you just need the very basics of converting between radian measure and degrees, and vice versa. In order to convert an angle from radian measure into degrees, just replace π with 180° in the expression and evaluate it: $\dfrac{7\pi}{4} = \dfrac{7 \times 180}{4} = 315°$.

Conversely, to convert an angle from degrees to radian measure, multiply the angle by $\frac{\pi}{180}$, reduce the constants, and keep pi as π. Using this method, let's convert 270° into radians: $270° \times \frac{\pi}{180} = \frac{270\pi}{180} = \frac{3\pi}{2}$.

To convert radian angle measure into degrees, replace π with 180° and evaluate the expression. To convert degrees into radian measure, multiply the angle by $\frac{\pi}{180}$, and then reduce the constants, but keep pi as π.

TRIGONOMETRY IN THE COORDINATE PLANE

In trigonometry, an angle is in standard position in the (x, y) coordinate plane when its vertex is at the origin and its initial side is on the positive x-axis. The second side of the angle is called the **terminal side**. Sometimes, the ACT asks a question about what other angle measurements share the same terminal side with a given angle.

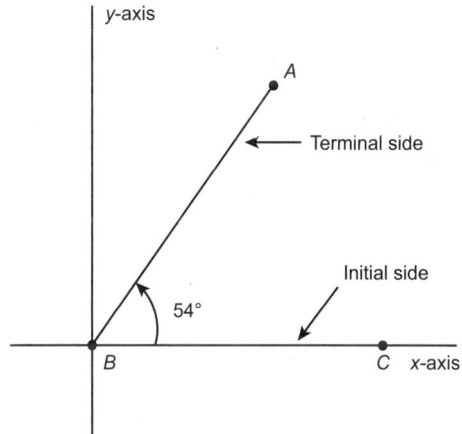

If graphed on a standard (x, y) coordinate plane, with its vertex on the origin and its initial side on the positive x-axis, which of the following angles will *not* have the same terminal side as $-\frac{5\pi}{12}$?

F. $-75°$
G. $285°$
H. $435°$
J. $645°$
K. $-435°$

The correct answer is H. An angle with a radian measure $-\dfrac{5\pi}{12}$ will equal $-\left(\dfrac{5\times180}{12}\right) = -75°$.

Any angle in the form $-75 \pm 360n$, for all integers n, will have the same terminal side

as $-\dfrac{5\pi}{12}$. 435° is the only angle measure that cannot be written in the form $-75 \pm 360n$

for an integer value of n. Choice F will have the same terminal side as $-\dfrac{5\pi}{12}$

since $-75° = -75 \pm 360n$, when $n = 0$. Choice G will have the same terminal side as $-\dfrac{5\pi}{12}$

since $-75° = -75 \pm 360n$, when $n = 1$. Choice J will have the same terminal side as $-\dfrac{5\pi}{12}$

since $-75° = -75 \pm 360n$, when $n = 2$. Choice K will have the same terminal side as $-\dfrac{5\pi}{12}$

since $-75° = -75 \pm 360n$, when $n = -1$.

. . . .

CIRCLE TRIGONOMETRY

You should already by familiar with the unit circle, which has a radius of 1 and its center on the origin. As a radius moves around the circle, with its endpoint (x, y) on the circumference, an angle θ is formed between the positive x-axis and the radius. A right triangle can be drawn with the radius as the hypotenuse, a horizontal leg as the length of x extends right or left from the origin, and the vertical leg as the length of y extends up or down from the x-axis.

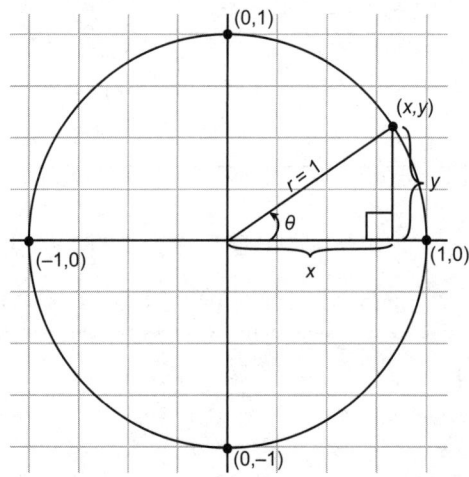

Notice that as (x, y) moves around the circle, the lengths of the two legs change, but the hypotenuse remains 1 unit. One of the most important concepts to know in circle trigonometry is that the coordinate pair (x, y) on the circumference of the circle can be expressed as $(\cos\theta, \sin\theta)$. Therefore, when $\theta = 30$ in the unit circle, the (x, y) coordinate pair is equivalent to $(\cos 30, \sin 30)$ which is $\left(\dfrac{\sqrt{3}}{2}, \dfrac{1}{2}\right)$.

In terms of the unit circle, $\cos\theta$ is the x-coordinate of the point on the circumference, and $\sin\theta$ is the y-coordinate, but what is $\tan\theta$? It is important to know that $\tan\theta = \dfrac{\sin\theta}{\cos\theta}$.

There are five key angles in the first quadrant that are often used in trig questions. We're sure you are already familiar with these from your math class, but if not, you should learn the sine, cosine, and tangent values of these following angles, backward and forward:

θ	$\cos\theta$	$\sin\theta$	$\tan\theta$	Unit Circle (x, y) Coordinate Pair
$0°$	$\cos\theta = 1$	$\sin\theta = 0$	$\tan\theta = 0$	$(1, 0)$
$30°$	$\cos 30 = \dfrac{\sqrt{3}}{2}$	$\sin\theta = \dfrac{1}{2}$	$\tan\theta = \dfrac{\sqrt{3}}{3}$	$\left(\dfrac{\sqrt{3}}{2}, \dfrac{1}{2}\right)$
$45°$	$\cos\theta = \dfrac{\sqrt{2}}{2}$	$\sin\theta = \dfrac{\sqrt{2}}{2}$	$\tan\theta = 1$	$\left(\dfrac{\sqrt{2}}{2}, \dfrac{\sqrt{2}}{2}\right)$
$60°$	$\cos\theta = \dfrac{1}{2}$	$\sin\theta = \dfrac{\sqrt{3}}{2}$	$\tan\theta = \sqrt{3}$	$\left(\dfrac{1}{2}, \dfrac{\sqrt{3}}{2}\right)$
$90°$	$\cos\theta = 0$	$\sin\theta = 1$	undefined	$(0, 1)$

REFERENCE ANGLES

You may be given an angle θ outside of the first quadrant and asked to find the coordinates of a point sitting on the terminal side of θ. Consider the following illustration:

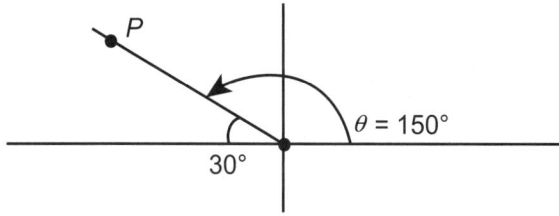

Notice that $\theta = 150°$ and that its supplement is $30°$. The smallest angle between the terminal side of a given angle, θ, and the x-axis is called the **reference** angle to angle θ. In this case, $30°$ is the reference angle to $150°$. If Point P is one unit from the origin, it will have the same coordinate values as if it were on a 30° angle. The only difference is that the signs of the x-coordinate and y-coordinate must be reevaluated and adjusted since it's in a different quadrant. For example, since x-coordinates are negative in the second quadrant but y-coordinates are still positive, the coordinate pair associated with

30°, $\left(\dfrac{\sqrt{3}}{2}, \dfrac{1}{2}\right)$, would translate into $\left(-\dfrac{\sqrt{3}}{2}, \dfrac{1}{2}\right)$ to represent point P formed by $\theta = 150°$.

Look at the patterns that occur in this unit circle, which contains all the angles of special interest.

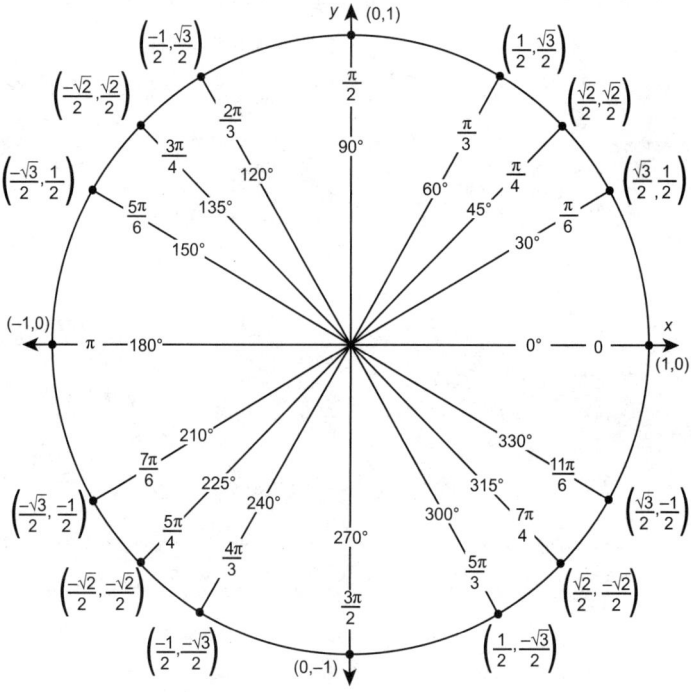

You can use the mnemonic *All Students Take Calculus* to remember which functions are positive when moving counterclockwise through quadrants I to IV:

- All in quadrant I.
- Sine in quadrant II.
- Tangent in quadrant III.
- Cosine in quadrant IV.

Remember that each coordinate pair shown is (cosθ, sinθ). Notice the sign changes in *cosine* and *sine* as you move through the different quadrants:

- Cosine is positive in quadrants I and IV.

- Sine is positive in quadrants I and II.

- Tangent is positive in quadrants I and III (since it's the quotient of sine and cosine).

You should be able to recall these angles and their associated coordinates on test day. (We've also included the radian angle measures since these are helpful to be familiar with.)

> To determine the (x, y) coordinate pair defined by an angle in a unit circle, first identify its reference angle. Then adjust the signs of the reference angle's coordinate pair to reflect the quadrant that θ terminates in.

It will be easier to answer the following question if you are very familiar with the radian measurements and their associated coordinate values from the *angles of special interest* illustration above.

Example:

Find the values of θ, in radian measure, where $\cos\theta = -\dfrac{\sqrt{3}}{2}$, given $0 \le \theta \le 2\pi$.

Solution:

$\cos\theta$ represents all the x-coordinates of points moving around the unit circle. In quadrants II and III, x is negative, so θ will be in those quadrants. Since $\cos 30 = \dfrac{\sqrt{3}}{2}$, the reference angle for all values of θ will be 30°. Since the x-axis between the second and third quadrants represents the terminal side of a 180° angle, if we add and subtract 30° to and from 180°, we will find two angles that both have 30° as their reference angle: 180° + 30° = 210° and 180° − 30° = 150°. So 210° and 150° both have a reference angle of 30° and will therefore have a cosine of $-\dfrac{\sqrt{3}}{2}$. Convert these angles to radians:

$$210° \times \dfrac{\pi}{180} = \dfrac{7\pi}{6} \text{ and } 150° \times \dfrac{\pi}{180} = \dfrac{5\pi}{6}.$$

In the next question, you will be given the angle and asked to come up with the coordinates.

. . . .

$\angle CAT$ is in the standard (x, y) coordinate plane such that T is on the positive x-axis, A is at the origin, and C is on $\overline{CA}$ such that $\overline{CA} = 1$ unit. If the measure of $\angle CAT = 240°$, what are the coordinates of C?

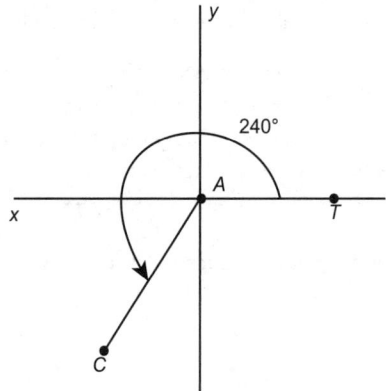

A. $\left(-\dfrac{\sqrt{3}}{2}, \dfrac{1}{2} \right)$

B. $\left(-\dfrac{\sqrt{3}}{2}, -\dfrac{1}{2} \right)$

C. $\left(-\dfrac{\sqrt{2}}{2}, -\dfrac{\sqrt{2}}{2} \right)$

D. $\left(-\dfrac{1}{2}, \dfrac{\sqrt{3}}{2} \right)$

E. $\left(-\dfrac{1}{2}, -\dfrac{\sqrt{3}}{2} \right)$

The correct answer is E. Since 240° is in the third quadrant, we know that both coordinates will be negative. The reference angle for 240° will be 240° – 180°= 60°. Since the coordinates for 60° are $\left(\dfrac{1}{2}, \dfrac{\sqrt{3}}{2} \right)$, we can determine that the coordinates for 240° are $\left(-\dfrac{1}{2}, -\dfrac{\sqrt{3}}{2} \right)$. Choice A is the coordinate pair for 150°. Choice B is the coordinate pair for 210°. Choice C is the coordinate pair for 225°. Choice D is the coordinate pair for 120°.

. . . .

Polar Coordinates

Although not frequently on the ACT, a polar coordinate question can be a real party stopper if you're not familiar with this format. A polar coordinate combines a *length instruction* with an *angle instruction*. For example, the polar coordinate (5, 90°) refers to a point in the (*x, y*) coordinate plane that is on the terminal side of a 90° angle (in standard position), 5 units from the origin. In the unit circle, a point at 90° has the coordinates (0, 1), so we can therefore determine that (5, 90°) will translate to (0, 5).

The general form for polar coordinates is (*r, θ*), where *r* represents the radius of the circle the point is on and *θ* is the angle the radius makes with the positive *x*-axis. Luckily, it's simple to convert from polar notation to coordinate notation:

. . . .

Polar coordinate (8, 120°) is equivalent to which of the following standard (*x, y*) coordinate pairs?

The polar coordinate (r, *θ*) is equivalent to (*r* • cos*θ*, *r* • sin*θ*) in the standard (*x, y*) coordinate plane.

F. $\left(-\dfrac{1}{2}, \dfrac{\sqrt{3}}{2}\right)$

G. $\left(-4\sqrt{3}, 4\right)$

H. $\left(-4, 4\sqrt{3}\right)$

J. $\left(-4\sqrt{3}, 2\sqrt{6}\right)$

K. $\left(4, 4\sqrt{3}\right)$

The correct answer is H. A polar coordinate (*r, θ*) is equivalent to *r* • cos*θ*, *r* • sin*θ* in a standard (*x, y*) coordinate plane. Therefore, (8, 120°) =

$(8 \cdot \cos 120, 8 \cdot \sin 120) = \left(8 \times -\dfrac{1}{2}, 8 \times \dfrac{\sqrt{3}}{2}\right) = \left(-4, 4\sqrt{3}\right)$. Choice F is the coordinate pair

for 120° on a unit circle, but it doesn't take into consideration the *r* of 8. Choice G is the coordinate pair for 150°, and not 120°. Choice K is the coordinate pair for 60°, not 120°.

. . . .

GRAPHING TRIGONOMETRIC FUNCTIONS

Let's not mince words . . . graphing trig functions can be a real beast! Thankfully, the trig graphing questions on the ACT will probably be a walk in the park compared to what you've been asked to graph in class. You will probably see questions only on the graphs of sine and cosine. You might see a tangent function as one of the answer choices, but it's unlikely you'll be given a graph of $y = \tan\theta$. Also, it's unlikely that you'd ever get more than one trig graphing question per test. Lastly, there's a chance you'll only be asked to identify the *altitude* of a graph either from an equation or a graph.

Let's begin by reviewing the graphs of $y = \cos\theta$ and $y = \sin\theta$. Remember that the x-axis in trig graphs is labeled with angle measurements in radians, and that the y-axis is measured in units.

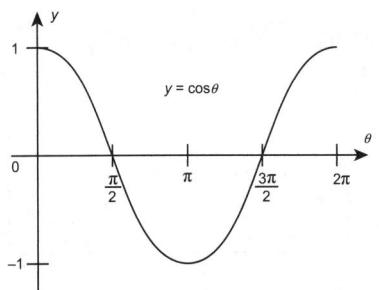
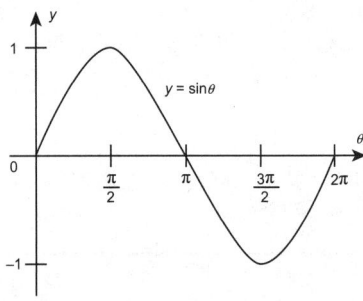

Notice that $y = \cos\theta$ is symmetric over the y-axis and that $\cos(\theta) - \cos(-\theta)$. This means that cosine is an *even* function. Similarly, notice that $y = \sin\theta$ is symmetric about the origin and that $\sin(-\theta) = -\sin-\theta$. Therefore $y = \sin\theta$ is an *odd* function. (Remember that odd functions cross through the origin, so $y = \sin-\theta + D$, for all non-zero values of D, is neither even nor odd.)

Let's review some of the terms used to discuss the graphs of trig functions:

- **Amplitude:** This refers to the average *height* of a trig function and is found by subtracting the minimum value (lowest point) from the maximum value (highest point) and dividing that difference by 2.
  - Amplitude $= \dfrac{\text{max} - \text{min}}{2}$.
  - The amplitude of $y = \cos\theta$ and $y = \sin\theta$ is 1.
  - When a function has a negative amplitude, its graph will be reflected over the x-axis.

- **Period:** This is a radian measure of how long it takes for one full cycle of the function to be completed.
  - The period of $y = \cos\theta$ and $y = \sin\theta = \pi$.

- **Frequency:** This is the number of times the function completes a full cycle in its normal period
  - The frequency of $y = \cos\theta$ and $y = \sin\theta$ is 1.

- **Vertical shift:** This is the number of vertical units up or down the graph of a trig function is shifted.

- **Phase shift:** This is the number of radians left or right a trig function is horizontally shifted.

Now let's see how we can identify these traits in the general sine and cosine formulas:

Given the functions $y = A\sin(B\theta - C) + D$ and $y = A\cos(B\theta - C) + D$:

- The amplitude is A.
- The frequency is B.
- The period is $\dfrac{2\pi}{B}$.
- The phase shift is $\dfrac{C}{B}$.
- The vertical shift is D.

If you know *all* of these facts about the sine and cosine functions, then you will be well prepared to handle the graphing questions on the ACT.

NOTE: Knowing the graphs of $y = \cos\theta$ and $y = \sin\theta$ is a must for the ACT. If you also understand how to identify the amplitude, vertical shift, frequency, and phase shift of the sine and cosine graphs, then you are set for the questions on trig graphs.

WORKING WITH TRIGONOMETRIC IDENTITIES

Although infrequently found on the ACT, this wouldn't be a proper trig review without discussing the most important trig identities. We know that a student like you is already familiar with the infamous Pythagorean identity that comes from the unit circle:

$$\cos^2\theta + \sin^2\theta = 1$$

You are probably also familiar with the following two identities that come out of the Pythagorean identity:

$$\cos\theta = \sqrt{1 - \sin^2\theta} \text{ and } \sin\theta = \sqrt{1 - \cos^2\theta}$$

It wouldn't hurt to know the double angle identities for sine and cosine. Although we don't think you need to have them memorized for the test, if they are provided to you in the context of a question, it will be helpful to not waste time deciphering them!

$$\sin(2\theta) = 2\sin\theta\cos\theta$$
$$\cos(2\theta) = \cos^2\theta - \sin^2\theta$$

An identity question might look like this:

Example:

Add and then simplify the sum $\dfrac{\sqrt{1-\sin^2\theta}}{2\sin\theta} + \dfrac{\sqrt{1-\cos^2\theta}}{2\cos\theta}$.

(Note that $\sin(2\theta) = 2\sin\theta\cos\theta$).

Solution:

First, replace $\sqrt{1-\sin^2\theta}$ with $\cos\theta$ and replace $\sqrt{1-\cos^2\theta}$ with $\sin\theta$. Then find common denominators and add:

$$
\begin{aligned}
\frac{\sqrt{1-\sin^2\theta}}{2\sin\theta} + \frac{\sqrt{1-\cos^2\theta}}{2\cos\theta} &= \frac{\cos\theta}{2\sin\theta} + \frac{\sin\theta}{2\cos\theta} \\
&= \frac{\cos^2\theta}{2\sin\theta\cos\theta} + 2\frac{\sin^2\theta}{\sin\theta\cos\theta} \\
&= \frac{\cos^2\theta + \sin^2\theta}{2\sin\theta\cos\theta} \\
&= \frac{1}{\sin(2\theta)}
\end{aligned}
$$

LAWS OF SINES AND COSINES

Up until now, we've only been applying trigonometry to *right triangles*. We are going to finish our review of trigonometry with two laws that are used told solve for missing angles and side lengths in non-right triangles! (Exciting, right?)

There are 6 parts to every non-right triangle: 3 angles and 3 sides. We can solve for *all* the angles and sides if we are given any of the following three cases of information:

1. An angle and its opposite side length, along with any other side length or angle
2. Two side lengths and the angle they form (called the *included angle*)
3. Side lengths for all 3 sides and no angles

Let's review how to apply the laws of sines and cosines to determine the missing measures in a non-right triangle.

Law of Sines with "Case 1"

When you are given the measure of an angle and its opposite side length in a non-right triangle, use the law of sines. Here's an illustration of it:

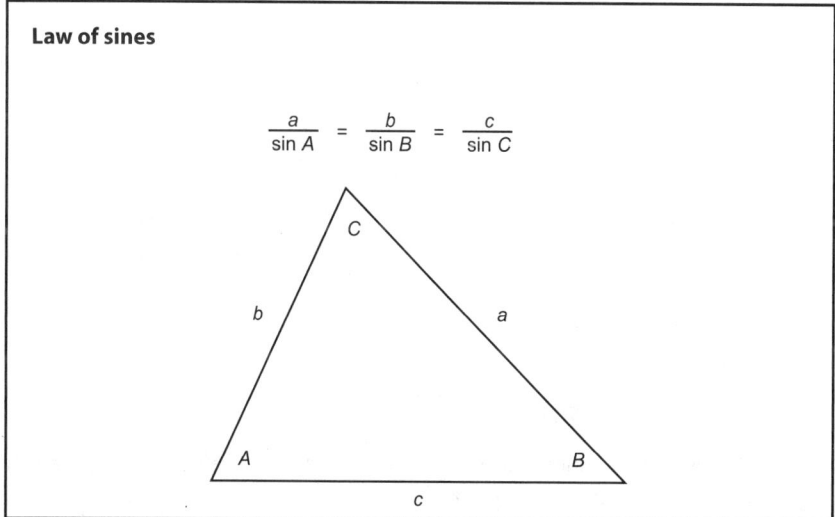

You won't be using *all three* of the ratios at that same time, but instead you will set up a proportion of just two ratios, such as: $\dfrac{a}{\sin 80} = \dfrac{12}{\sin 38}$. Also, it is inconsequential if your proportion puts the values of sine in the numerators or the denominations of all the fractions. As long as you are consistent with both ratios, you will get the correct answer.

Let's see what a law of sines question will look like in the following questions.

· ·

In given triangle $\triangle ABC$, m$\angle A$ = 30°, m$\angle C$ = 100°, and AC = 2. Which expression represents the length in units of $\overline{BC}$?

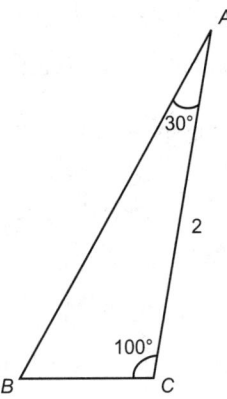

F. $\dfrac{2\sin 30}{\sin 50}$

G. $\dfrac{2\sin 50}{\sin 30}$

H. $\dfrac{2\sin 100}{\sin 50}$

J. $\dfrac{2\sin 50}{\sin 100}$

K. $\dfrac{2\sin 100}{\sin 30}$

The correct answer is F. Since there is not an angle-side pair given, use the two known angles to solve for angle B so that it can be paired with $\overline{AC}$ in the law of sines. m$\angle B$ = 50°. Now in order to find an expression for $\overline{BC}$, use its opposite angle A in the law of sines:

$$\frac{\overline{AC}}{\sin B} = \frac{\overline{BC}}{\sin A}$$

$$\frac{2}{\sin 50} = \frac{\overline{BC}}{\sin 30}$$

$$\frac{2\sin 30}{\sin 50} = \overline{BC}$$

Choice G is incorrect because the angles were flipped and not used with their opposite sides while setting up the law of sines. Choice H is the expression of $\overline{BA}$. Choice J cannot be correct because 2 and sin100 must be a quotient and not a product since they are an opposite angle-side pair. Choice K cannot be correct because 2 and sin30 should not be a quotient since they are not an opposite angle-side pair.

· ·

 ALERT: Don't just force the information you are given into a formula. You will often need to unfold the question a little, solving for the other unknowns before having all the information you need to proceed!

Did you notice in the previous question that you were not initially given an angle-side opposite pair? Don't be lulled into laziness and use whatever information is presented in your final answer.

Sometimes the law of sines results in the ambiguous case, where it is possible for two triangles to exist with the given information. This will not be tested on the ACT. (If you haven't ever heard of the ambiguous case, then forget we even mentioned it, but if you know what we're talking about, you can breathe a large sigh of relief!)

Law of Cosines with "Case 2"

Use the law of cosines when you are given two side lengths and their included angle. (The angle formed by the two sides.)

The law of cosines is certainly a little more intimidating looking than the law of sines, but working with it is no more difficult.

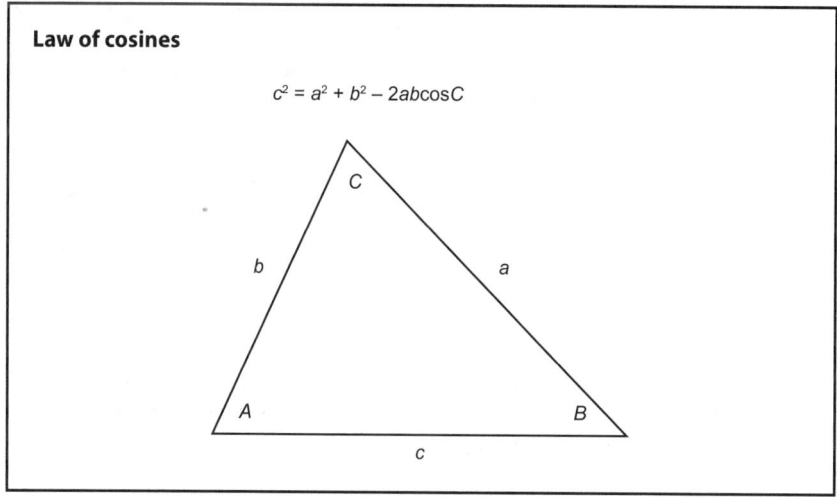

Law of cosines

$$c^2 = a^2 + b^2 - 2ab\cos C$$

An important feature to remember in the law of cosines is that the side squared that sits alone will have its opposite angle at the end of the formula. The law of cosines as set up in the box will solve for side *c*, so notice how cos *C* is the last part of the formula. Let's apply it to the following question. We like to think of the law of cosines as looking like a sandwich, where the same variables (an opposite side-angle pairing) act as the left and right bookends of the equation.

Example:

In the given triangle *ABC*, m∠*C* = 40°, $\overline{BC}$ = 6 units, and $\overline{AC}$ = $6\sqrt{2}$ units. Write an expression that represents the length in units of $\overline{BA}$; do not evaluate it.

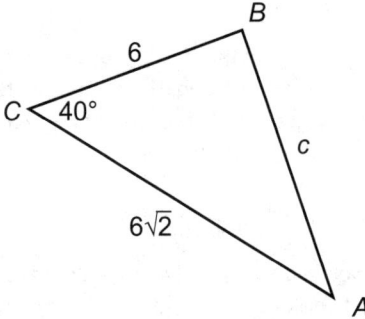

Solution:

Now for the last step, we need to take the square root of the entire expression on the right-hand side to solve for *c*. Don't make the mistake of thinking you can evaluate individual squares under the radical sign; keep it as one long expression.

$$c^2 = a^2 + b^2 - 2ab\cos C$$

$$c^2 = 6^2 + \left(6\sqrt{2}\right)^2 - 2(6)\left(6\sqrt{2}\right)\cos 40$$

$$c = \sqrt{6^2 + \left(6\sqrt{2}\right)^2 - 2(6)\left(6\sqrt{2}\right)\cos 40}$$

NOTE: Keep your calculators turned off when working with the laws of sines and cosines! You will not have to determine decimal or degree values for angles or sides, but will instead just need to set up the answer correctly.

LAW OF COSINES WITH "CASE 3"

Use the law of cosines when you are given all three side lengths and no angles.

We have not seen this application of the law of cosines tested on the ACT, but it's good to see what an example question could look like.

Example:

$\triangle XYZ$ is a non-right triangle such that $\overline{XY} = 4$, $\overline{XZ} = 9$, and $\overline{YZ} = 12$. Find an expression that represents the measure of the largest angle.

Solution:

Remember that the largest angle in a triangle is always opposite the largest side. Therefore, we will find the angle opposite the side of 12 units. In the law of cosines, the angle on the right side of the formula is the angle opposite the side on the left side of the formula. Therefore, put the largest side, 12, in for c and solve for the largest angle, C.

$$c^2 = a^2 + b^2 - 2ab \cos C$$

$$12^2 = 4^2 + 9^2 - 2(4)(9) \cos C$$

Now carefully get C alone:

$$\frac{12^2 - 4^2 - 9^2}{-2(4)(9)} = \cos C$$

Now for the last step, take the inverse of $\cos C$ to get an expression that represents the measure of angle C.

$$C = \cos^{-1}\left(\frac{12^2 - 4^2 - 9^2}{-2(4)(9)}\right)$$

You can see why that last problem isn't something typically on the ACT, which keeps its trig answers in uncalculated form—that final answer is quite a handful!

Nice work! You're finished with the review of plane geometry and trigonometry. We've put the most important facts in the summary below, but remember that your best preparation will not be simply reading through these chapters, but revisiting the problems that gave you trouble until they become second nature. Hopefully, you've starred all problems that challenged you and kept a running list of their page numbers in the front of your book. Good luck with your continued review as you refine your skills!

SUMMING IT UP

- Remember these facts about lines and angles:

  - **Complementary angles** have a sum of 90°.

  - **Supplementary angles** have a sum of 180°.

  - **Vertical angles** are congruent.

  - **Parallel lines** intersected by a transversal create the following types of congruent angle pairs: corresponding angles, alternate interior angles, and alternate exterior angles.

  - Any obtuse and acute angle formed by parallel lines cut by a transversal will be supplementary.

- Remember these facts about triangles:

  - The **triangle inequality theorem** states that the sum of any two sides of a triangle must be greater than the third side.

  - The **Pythagorean theorem** states that for any right triangle with legs a and b and hypotenuse c, $a^2 + b^2 = c^2$.

  - In all triangles, the shortest side is always opposite the smallest angle and the longest side is always opposite the largest angle.

  - **30-60-90 triangles** have a special side ratio: the hypotenuse is twice the length of the shortest leg and the longer leg is $\sqrt{3}$ times the shortest leg.

  - **45-45-90 triangles** have a special side ratio: the hypotenuse is $\sqrt{2}$ times the length of the congruent legs.

  - The measure of exterior angle of a triangle is equal to the sum of the two remote interior angles.

  - If $\triangle ABC$ and $\triangle XYZ$ are similar, their corresponding angles are congruent and their corresponding sides will be proportional: $\dfrac{a}{x} = \dfrac{b}{y} = \dfrac{c}{z}$.

- Remember these facts about polygons:

  - The sum of the interior angles of a polygon with n sides is $(n-2) \times 180°$.

  - The measure of an interior angle of a regular polygon with n sides is $\dfrac{(n-2) \times 180°}{n}$.

- Remember these facts about circles:

  - A line is tangent to a circle, it intersects the circle at only *one* point; it will be perpendicular to the radius that terminates at the point of intersection.

  - Two radii that intersect to create the vertex at the center of the circle form a **central angle**. A central angle has the same measure as its intercepted arc.

- An **inscribed angle** is formed by two intersecting chords and has its vertex on the circumference of the circle. An inscribed angle has a measure that is half its intercepted arc.

- When two chords intersect within a circle, the products of their segments are equal.

- Remember these facts about areas and perimeters:
  - The perimeter and area of a square with side length s are $P = 4s$ and $A = s^2$.

  - The perimeter and area of a rectangle with length l and width w are $P = 2l + 2w$ and $A = l \times w$.

  - The area of a triangle with base b and height h is $A = \dfrac{1}{2}b \cdot h$.

  - The area of a parallelogram with base b and height h is $A = b \cdot h$.

  - The area of a trapezoid with bases b_1 and b_2, and height h is $A = \dfrac{1}{2}(h)b_1 + b_2$.

  - The circumference and area of a circle with radius r are $C = 2\pi r$ and $A = \pi r^2$.

  - In a circle with radius r, the length of an arc formed by a central angle θ is
  $\text{Arc Length} = 2\pi r \times \dfrac{\theta}{360}$.

- Remember these facts about surface area:
  - The surface area of a cube with side length s is $SA = 6s^2$.

  - The surface area of a rectangular prism with length l, width w, and height h is $SA = 2lw + 2lh + 2wh$.

  - The surface area of a cylinder with radius r and height h is $SA = 2\pi rh + 2\pi r^2$.

- Remember these facts about volume:
  - The volume of a cube with side length a is $V = a^3$.

  - The volume of a rectangular box with side lengths l, w, and h is $V = l \times w \times h$.

  - The volume of a cylinder with radius r and height h is $V = \pi r^2$.

- Remember these facts about transformations:
  - After a clockwise rotation of 90°, coordinate pair (x, y) will become $(y, -x)$.

  - After a counterclockwise rotation of 90°, coordinate pair (x, y) will become $(-y, x)$.

  - After a rotation of 180°, coordinate pair (x, y) will become $(-y, -x)$.

- Remember these facts about trigonometric relationships:
  - In a right triangle with an acute angle θ, $\sin\theta = \dfrac{\text{opposite}}{\text{hypotenuse}}$.

  - In a right triangle with an acute angle θ, $\cos\theta = \dfrac{\text{adjacent}}{\text{hypotenuse}}$.

- In a right triangle with an acute angle θ, $\tan\theta = \dfrac{\text{opposite}}{\text{adjacent}}$.
  - The following inverse trig ratios can be used to solve for an angle θ in a right triangle:

$$\theta = \arcsin\left(\frac{\text{opposite}}{\text{hypotenuse}}\right), \theta = \arccos\left(\frac{\text{adjacent}}{\text{hypotenuse}}\right), \theta = \arctan\left(\frac{\text{opposite}}{\text{adjacent}}\right).$$

- Remember these facts about circle trigonometry:
  - To convert an angle from radian measure into degrees, replace π with $180°$ and evaluate the expression.
  - To convert an angle from degrees to radian measure, multiply the angle by $\dfrac{\pi}{180}$, reduce the constants, and keep pi as π.

- Polar coordinate (r, θ) is equivalent to $(r \cdot \cos\theta, r \cdot \sin\theta)$ in the standard (x, y) coordinate plane.

- Remember these facts about graphing trigonometric functions:
  - $y = \cos\theta$ is an even function. It is symmetric over the y-axis, and $\cos\theta = \cos(-\theta)$.
  - $y = \sin\theta$ is an odd function. It is symmetric over the origin, and $\sin(-\theta) = -\sin\theta$.
  - Given the functions $y = A\sin(B\theta - C) + D$ and $y = A\cos(B\theta - C) + D$, the amplitude is A, the frequency is B, the phase shift is $\dfrac{C}{B}$, and the vertical shift is D.

- Remember these facts about graphing trigonometric identities:
  - The **Pythagorean identity** from the unit circle states $\cos^2\theta + \sin^2\theta = 1$, and from that come the identities $\cos\theta = \sqrt{1 - \sin^2\theta}$ and $\sin\theta = \sqrt{1 - \cos^2\theta}$.
  - The **double angle formulas** for sine and cosine are $\sin(2\theta) = 2\sin\theta\cos\theta$ and $\cos(2\theta) = \cos^2\theta - \sin^2\theta$.

- Remember these facts about the laws of sines and cosines:
  - The **law of sines for non-right triangles** with sides a, b, and c and angles A, B and C states that $\dfrac{a}{\sin A} = \dfrac{b}{\sin B} = \dfrac{c}{\sin C}$.
  - The **law of cosines for non-right triangles** with sides a, b, and c and $\angle C$ states that $c^2 = a^2 + b^2 - 2ab\cos C$.

CHAPTER 6
ACT® READING:
SOCIAL STUDIES/NATURAL
SCIENCES PASSAGES

OVERVIEW

- About Social Studies/Natural Sciences Passages

- Main Idea/Central Theme Questions

- Detail Questions

- Vocabulary-in-Context Questions

- Function Questions

- Summing It Up

The ACT Reading test is always the third one you'll see on test day, after Math and before Science. You'll have 35 minutes to answer 40 multiple-choice questions that are attached to related text passages. The section is designed to test your reading comprehension skills—can you understand a passage presented to you to pick out its meaning and most important details?

The Reading test is divided into four thematic subsections, and each of these is worth 25 percent of your Reading score:

Theme	Potential Content Areas	
Social Studies	anthropology archaeology biography business economics education	geography history political science psychology sociology
Natural Science	anatomy astronomy biology botany chemistry ecology geology	medicine meteorology microbiology natural history physiology physics technology zoology
Literary Narrative/Prose Fiction	**Literary Narrative:** short stories novels memoirs personal essays	**Prose Fiction:** short stories novels
Humanities	architecture art dance ethics film language	literary criticism music philosophy radio television theater

In each of these subsections, there will be a passage (or two shorter, related passages) followed by a set of 10 multiple-choice questions. In cases where there are two passages in the section, the questions may deal with one or both of the passages. The Reading test doesn't test your ability to memorize grammar rules, vocabulary, or specific ideas—rather, it checks your ability to read and interpret on the fly and use your own knowledge to make decisions about the text. In terms of difficulty, the passages are usually set around the level you'd see in your first year of college.

NOTE: Because there are only four total passages on the Reading test, each test will include either a Literary Narrative OR a Prose Fiction passage. You should be prepared for both types, but you won't see both within the same test. Think of them as the Superman/Clark Kent of the ACT.

The ACT Reading test doesn't require you to be an expert in any of the content areas or demand that you be able to define obscure vocabulary words on cue. Rather, it tests your ability to read a piece of text that you (probably) haven't seen before and make conclusions based on context and facts presented in the passages. You can expect the questions to involve any of these skills:

- Identifying and understanding main ideas
- Locating and interpreting details within a passage
- Making comparisons within the passage
- Identifying and understanding relationships within the passage (sequence of events, the flow of ideas, cause-and-effect relationships)
- Determining the meaning of words, phrases, and sentences from the context of the passage
- Making inferences about the themes and details presented in the passage
- Analyzing the author's/narrator's voice (tone and purpose)

In this chapter, we'll cover the hardest passage and question types you're likely to see in the Social Studies and Natural Sciences passages. The next chapter will go over the most challenging question types for the Literary/Narrative Prose Fiction and Humanities passages.

Now that you know the basics of what to expect in this section, let's get started!

ABOUT SOCIAL STUDIES/NATURAL SCIENCES PASSAGES

The ACT Reading test score is broken into two subscores: Social Studies/Natural Sciences and Literary Narrative/Prose Fiction and Humanities (basically, the latter are grouped together as kind of an arts & literature subheading, like in the game Trivial Pursuit). However, each of the four subsections of the Reading test is worth the same amount toward your score, so there's no need to give any subsection more priority than the others. All of the questions are weighted the same, and there is no set pattern of difficulty (e.g., the questions about Passage 4 won't necessarily be more difficult than the questions about Passage 2).

READING STRATEGIES

As in all sections of the ACT, you're working against the clock, so you should know your strengths ahead of time and find a method that works best for you. For example, if you're strongest in social studies, as a rule, tackle that passage and question set first before going back to the others. This way, you can breeze through your strong points, then go back and have time for the others. The last thing you want to do is spend most of your time on a problematic passage, only to run out of time when you get to the other, potentially easier passages. The best way to find your strengths/preferences is to do several timed practice tests and see which passages hung you up and which ones you breezed through.

 Taking timed, full-length practice tests is the best way to identify your strengths and weaknesses. Knowing where you need extra time will help you focus your prep energies where they're needed most.

Active Reading

Even though time will be short, you'll want to read each passage. The first time through (before you read any of the questions), feel free to make notes. While you're reading, underline any details that seem important or challenging vocabulary words. Also make a note of the main idea and themes and mark any details that support those main points. As you read, ask yourself, "What is the purpose of this passage? What is it trying to say?" and mark any important-seeming details that point to the overall purpose.

After you've gone through the passage once and made your notes, move down to the questions following the passage.

Close Reading

Once you move on to the questions, you'll go back to the passage for closer reading. This will be directed by what the questions are specifically asking you to determine. Unlike in the English test, there won't be specific underlined words or phrases that need to be fixed directly. Rather, you can expect that the questions will be more general about a line, paragraph, or passage as a whole.

For example:

According to Paragraph 4, what was the main reason for the ship's voyage?

In lines 13–15, what did the author most likely mean when she said, "The rain in Spain, it falls mainly on the plain?"

The author believes that the causes for the dinosaurs' extinction included all of the following EXCEPT:

The cues in the questions will help you zero in on the right section of the passage to figure out the answer. For questions that ask about the passage as a whole, rely on your notes (mental or otherwise) from your first pass through the text. This is why it's important to take stock of any clear details on that first read; it can help guide you right back to the sections you'll need to answer the question.

 To practice for ACT reading, go out of your way to read unfamiliar texts or documents. While you're reading, make notes and think about things like the main idea, the purpose of the writing, and the meaning of challenging vocabulary. This will help your brain start thinking quickly and analytically.

Let's try it with a sample annotated passage. Some active reading highlighting has been done here to point out key sentences that should help you to identify main ideas; keep them in mind as we go through the passage together.

The Gettysburg Address

Fourscore and seven years ago our fathers brought forth on this continent a new nation, conceived in liberty and dedicated to the proposition that all men are created equal.

Now we are engaged in a great civil war, testing whether that
5 nation or any nation so conceived and so dedicated can long endure. We are met on a great battlefield of that war. We have come to dedicate a portion of that field as a final resting-place for those who here gave their lives that that nation might live. It is altogether fitting and proper that we should do this.

10 But in a larger sense, we cannot dedicate, we cannot consecrate, we cannot hallow this ground. The brave men, living and dead who struggled here have consecrated it far above our poor power to add or detract. The world will little note nor long remember what we say here, but it can never forget what they did here. It is for us the living
15 rather to be dedicated here to the unfinished work which they who fought here have thus far so nobly advanced. It is rather for us to be here dedicated to the great task remaining before us—that from these honored dead we take increased devotion to that cause for which they gave the last full measure of devotion—that we here
20 highly resolve that these dead shall not have died in vain, that this nation under God shall have a new birth of freedom, and that government of the people, by the people, for the people shall not perish from the earth.

The more advanced questions on the ACT Reading test will ask you to take information from the passage that isn't clearly stated. You'll be asked to make generalizations, draw inferences, or use more complex parts of the passage to answer questions. Let's take a walk through the general question types and see how the tougher versions of them might pop up on test day. Throughout the chapter, there will be eight Reading test questions like the ones you'll see on test day.

MAIN IDEA/CENTRAL THEME QUESTIONS

Main idea questions are common on the ACT—they ask you to identify or infer the main topic of the reading passage (or the quick summary of what the passage is about). In some passages, the main idea will be clear. For example, in a passage about baseball, well, the main idea is likely to be baseball—and that'll be clear right in the first paragraph. More challenging passages will have a main idea that is less obvious. When you're reading the passage, the main topic will be the answer to the question, "what is the author's main point in this passage?" In complex passages, this may require some detective work on your part.

For example, in the Gettysburg Address sample passage, the reader needs to infer (from statements throughout the speech) that President Lincoln is speaking to commemorate a specific Civil War battle. Which lines actually tell you that information?

Let's look at Paragraph 1:

> Fourscore and seven years ago our fathers brought forth on this continent a new nation, conceived in liberty and dedicated to the proposition that all men are created equal.

Nothing in this paragraph tells you specifically what the speaker (in this case, President Abraham Lincoln) is talking about overall. It gives background, but for *what* is still unclear. Let's move on to Paragraph 2:

> Now we are engaged in a great civil war, testing whether that nation or any nation so conceived and so dedicated can long endure. We are met on a great battlefield of that war. We have come to dedicate a portion of that field as a final resting-place for those who here gave their lives that that nation might live. It is altogether fitting and proper that we should do this.

Now we're getting somewhere. The sentence that begins by saying *We have come to dedicate a portion of that field as a final resting-place* (lines 6–8) tells you why Lincoln is giving the speech. From there, you need to confirm that this is, in fact, the main idea of the speech. Let's also take a quick look at Paragraph 3 to make sure there's either supporting information or no potentially conflicting topics.

> But in a larger sense, we cannot dedicate, we cannot consecrate, we cannot hallow this ground. The brave men, living and dead who struggled here have consecrated it far above our poor power to add or detract. The world will little note nor long remember what we say here, but it can never forget what they did here. It is for us the living rather to be dedicated here to the unfinished work which they who fought here have thus far so nobly advanced. It is rather for us to be here dedicated to the great task remaining before us—that from these honored dead we take increased devotion to that cause for which they gave the last full measure of devotion—that we here highly resolve that these dead shall not have died in vain, that this nation under God shall have a new birth of freedom, and that government of the people, by the people, for the people shall not perish from the earth.

The good news is that this paragraph doesn't put up any conflicting topics. Lincoln is still talking about commemorating the battleground. However, this paragraph does make it challenging to confirm that as the main idea. The first sentence of Paragraph 3 (lines 10–11) may give you pause: *But in a larger sense, we cannot dedicate, we cannot consecrate, we cannot hallow this ground.* Doesn't that statement run contrary to what seemed to be the main idea? If you look at the sentence directly following that one (lines 11–13), you realize that Lincoln is speaking in a more metaphorical way: *The brave men, living and dead who struggled here have consecrated it far above our poor power to add or detract.*

If the main idea isn't immediately apparent, be prepared to find it anywhere in the passage—and once you zero in on it, check to make sure there's no conflicting information in the passage.

 It's important to be as specific as possible when identifying a main idea. If you're torn between two answer choices, err on the side of the more specific answer.

In addition to the passage's main idea, you may also be asked about individual paragraphs' main ideas. If that's the case, the process is still the same—just on a smaller scale. You would still skim the paragraph to answer the question, "what is the author's main point here?", and then identify any supporting points. Note that the main idea of a given paragraph isn't necessarily the same as the main idea of the whole passage. You would be treating the paragraph as its own mini-passage to get the answer. Be sure to read the question carefully to know exactly what you're looking for.

CENTRAL THEMES

The more advanced ACT Reading questions may ask you to identify the central theme(s), not just the main idea.

Remember, there's a difference between the *main idea* (the topic of the passage or paragraph, or what it's about) and the *central theme* (the message or lesson of the passage or paragraph). Some students skip right past that nuance in the rush to answer the question in the allotted 35 minutes, and so this is an element you really want to watch out for on test day. One of the most important areas to review as you prep for the ACT is determining a passage's (or paragraph's) main idea vs. its central theme. You're probably already very familiar with how to name the basic topic of any given piece of writing, and we've already reviewed how to find main ideas that aren't immediately obvious. To up your ACT Reading test game, let's focus on the central themes.

Most high-difficulty central theme questions will ask you to identify themes in passages that range from challenging to highly complex. They'll expect you to be able to take a complicated passage and do two things:

1. Infer at least one theme.

2. Locate and summarize key supporting details for those themes.

Let's go back to the Gettysburg Address example, and see how best to approach these questions.

The Gettysburg Address

Fourscore and seven years ago our fathers brought forth on this continent a new nation, conceived in liberty and dedicated to the proposition that all men are created equal.

Now we are engaged in a great civil war, testing whether that
5   nation or any nation so conceived and so dedicated can long endure. We are met on a great battlefield of that war. We have come to dedicate a portion of that field as a final resting-place for those who here gave their lives that that nation might live. It is altogether fitting and proper that we should do this.

10   But in a larger sense, we cannot dedicate, we cannot consecrate, we cannot hallow this ground. The brave men, living and dead who struggled here have consecrated it far above our poor power to add or detract. The world will little note nor long remember what we say here, but it can never forget what they did here. It is for us the living
15   rather to be dedicated here to the unfinished work which they who fought here have thus far so nobly advanced. It is rather for us to be here dedicated to the great task remaining before us—that from these honored dead we take increased devotion to that cause for which they gave the last full measure of devotion—that we here
20   highly resolve that these dead shall not have died in vain, that this nation under God shall have a new birth of freedom, and that government of the people, by the people, for the people shall not perish from the earth.

Which of the following is a central theme of the passage?

A.   The Civil War was long and difficult.
B.   It's important to memorialize history and the sacrifices that were made.
C.   Coming together to celebrate a pivotal battle in the Civil War.
D.   It's most important to learn from history so that the sacrifices made for it are meaningful.

To answer this kind of question, first check to see if you can rule out any of the answer choices right away, based on your reading. Instead of thinking "what is the author's main point?" (as with main idea questions), you'll want to consider, "what is the bigger message of this passage or paragraph?" If the main idea is the subject of the passage, then the theme is the concept(s) behind the subject.

Going back to the question, first look at the answer choices. Choice A is too vague, so you can rule that one out right away. Choice B is possible—Paragraph 3 discusses the sacrifices made by those who died at Gettysburg. Choice C is another one you can rule out: this is the main idea (the subject) of the passage, but not really a message or idea. Choice D is also possible, because it aligns with the information in Paragraph 3. So which one is correct? If you need to go back and do a quick skim of the paragraph to differentiate, do it here. Otherwise, look at the differences between the choices. Choice B is technically an idea, but choice D is more specific: it builds on choice B by explaining how the sacrifices should be meaningful. **The correct answer is D.**

For nonfiction passages such as those for Social Studies and Natural Sciences, the main ideas and themes are often fairly straightforward. If you're prepared to search and do quick comparisons of ideas, you'll be well-equipped to tackle the toughest main idea and central theme questions. The most important skill is being able to differentiate between the two, especially in passages that have sophisticated language or complicated ideas.

Use the sample passage to answer a practice question on your own.

· ·

The Gettysburg Address

Fourscore and seven years ago our fathers brought forth on this continent a new nation, conceived in liberty and dedicated to the proposition that all men are created equal.

Now we are engaged in a great civil war, testing whether that
5   nation or any nation so conceived and so dedicated can long endure. We are met on a great battlefield of that war. We have come to dedicate a portion of that field as a final resting-place for those who here gave their lives that that nation might live. It is altogether fitting and proper that we should do this.

10   But in a larger sense, we cannot dedicate, we cannot consecrate, we cannot hallow this ground. The brave men, living and dead who struggled here have consecrated it far above our poor power to add or detract. The world will little note nor long remember what we say here, but it can never forget what they did here. It is for us the living
15   rather to be dedicated here to the unfinished work which they who fought here have thus far so nobly advanced. It is rather for us to be here dedicated to the great task remaining before us—that from these honored dead we take increased devotion to that cause for which they gave the last full measure of devotion—that we here
20   highly resolve that these dead shall not have died in vain, that this nation under God shall have a new birth of freedom, and that government of the people, by the people, for the people shall not perish from the earth.

Which of the following statements supports the author's theme of rebirth?

- **F.** We have come to dedicate a portion of that field as a final resting-place for those who here gave their lives that that nation might live.
- **G.** The brave men, living and dead who struggled here have consecrated it far above our poor power to add or detract.
- **H.** The world will little note nor long remember what we say here, but it can never forget what they did here.
- **J.** We are met on a great battlefield of that war.

The correct answer is F. The author mentions "birth" several times through the passage, but it's not only those sentences that support that theme. Choice F is correct because it juxtaposes the deaths on the battlefield with the purpose of coming to that same spot to heal and move on as a nation. You can eliminate choice G because it deals only with death. Choices H and J are too vague—neither connects to either a birth or death theme. So you want to choose the option that pulls together the elements of the theme. Choice F is the only option that accomplishes that purpose.

DETAIL QUESTIONS

Detail questions deal with the nitty-gritty information in a passage. In these, the test will usually ask you to identify a specific detail in a passage or paragraph. These questions are the most straightforward ones you'll see on the ACT Reading test—it's really just about retrieving information and connecting it to the best answer choice. However, like all of the question types, there are easy detail questions and hard ones. An easy one might ask you to find a very clear detail that supports the main idea of the passage. Trickier ones will take a few different paths:

- The **needle-in-a-haystack** detail: You will need to find a major or minor detail that's buried in a long or dense part of the passage.

- The **hiding-in-plain-sight** detail: You will need to identify a detail that's subtly stated.

None of these will be readily apparent in your initial read of the passage, so you'll need to be able to zero in on them as you're going through the questions. They're more difficult because they may be obscure details that aren't directly related to the main topic or theme of the passage, so you need to hunt for them.

THE NEEDLE-IN-A-HAYSTACK DETAIL

Some questions may direct you to a particular paragraph or line, and that makes it much easier to zip over to that spot, read the text, and answer the question. Others leave it more open-ended, referring to "the passage" or just not specifying where the information can be found. For those questions, start by figuring out what information the question is asking you to find. Next, eliminate any blatantly wrong answer choices—e.g., ones that contradict information you remember from the passage or don't seem related at all.

Finally, once you've narrowed down the answer choices, take key words or ideas, and scan to find them in the passage. After you've located that information, choose the answer that fits best.

 Always, always read the question carefully. The more difficult ACT Reading test questions may have very subtle meanings.

Let's look at a sample Natural Sciences passage.

How Is Water Conserved?

There are many technologies and methods to conserve water. Some of them are appropriate for individual households or businesses; others are suitable for large-scale applications. There are also ways to use nonfresh-water sources, such as greywater and desalinated
5 water, in place of fresh water.

Among the most effective technologies for water conservation are water-efficient plumbing fixtures and appliances. Low-flow aerators limit the amount of water coming out of a faucet by blocking a portion of the mouth of the faucet. The water that flows out of the
10 faucet is separated into several different streams instead of a single, solid one. Some models add pressurized air to the stream of water, allowing the faucet to emit less water while maintaining high water pressure.

Modern appliances—including dishwashers, water heaters, and
15 washing machines—are designed with water conservation in mind. These appliances use significantly less water than older models. Moreover, replacing older appliances with newer, water-efficient ones greatly cuts down on cost and water use.

Water-efficient toilets are another effective way to reduce water
20 consumption. Dual-flush toilets have two different settings: one for solid waste, the other for liquid waste. Older toilets use about 5 gallons of water for each flush, but new ones may use only 1.6 gallons per flush for solid waste and less than 1 gallon for liquid waste. Waterless urinals also save water.

25 Water that is not suitable for drinking may be used for other purposes, such as watering plants or flushing toilets. Known as greywater, this water is recycled from showers, bathroom sinks, washing machines, and drinking fountains. Rainwater can be collected as runoff and used for the same purposes as greywater. Plumbers
30 must install additional pipes and storage tanks to keep greywater and rainwater separate from drinking water.

Wastewater—water that has already been used and collected through sewer systems—may be used for non-drinking purposes after being treated. This water, known as reclaimed water, is processed
35 at a wastewater treatment plant to remove contaminants. Often, reclaimed water is cleaner than drinking water, but it is almost always limited to use in landscaping. Many cities use reclaimed water to maintain parks, golf courses, and other outdoor facilities.

Households and businesses can look to green landscaping
40 practices to cut down on their water use. Landscaping is water intensive, but a technique known as xeriscaping uses significantly less water than the amount required for traditional landscaping. Xeriscaping uses native plants that do not require as much water and minimizes the number of plants in a landscape. For example, a
45 common practice in xeriscaping is replacing grass either with plants that do not need much water or with rock gardens. Xeriscaping may also use water-efficient sprinkler systems that operate at times other than peak sunlight hours to reduce evaporation.

A needle-in-a-haystack question might look like this:

According to the passage, what kind of water is recycled from showers and drinking fountains?

A. Drinking water
B. Greywater
C. Rainwater
D. Wastewater

This is a detail that has little to do with the main topic of the passage (how to conserve water), so the answer might not be obvious to you after your initial reading of the passage. The following series of questions can help you to pinpoint the answer.

Question 1: *What is the question asking?* This question is pretty direct in its purpose: You need to find what specific kind of water is recycled from showers and drinking fountains.

Question 2: *Can you eliminate any of the choices?* In this list, that's rainwater (choice C). The question itself tells you that the water is recycled from showers and drinking fountains, and we know rainwater comes from the sky. (This is about the extent of direct science knowledge you'll need for this section of the exam.) One down!

Question 3: *Where is the information?* In this case, "showers and drinking fountains" jump out. You can take those back and skim the passage. Both terms come up in Paragraph 5, so that tells you you're in the right spot.

Question 4: *Which answer choice fits?* Now take a quick look at the information in that very sentence where you found the keywords: *Known as greywater, this water is recycled from showers, bathroom sinks, washing machines, and drinking fountains.* That directly answers the question, so you can confidently pick choice B and move on. If you want to be doubly sure, and have a few extra seconds, you can double-check the definition of *wastewater* (choice D) in the next paragraph.

THE HIDING-IN-PLAIN-SIGHT DETAIL

Going back to the sample water conservation passage, a hiding-in-plain-sight question might look like this:

According to the passage, which of the following is NOT an appropriate use for rainwater?

- **F.** landscaping
- **G.** watering plants
- **H.** drinking
- **J.** flushing toilets

Again, let's analyze, using our series of questions.

> **Question 1:** *What is the question asking?* This question is asking you to not only find the appropriate use(s) for rainwater, but also to rule out one of the answer choices definitively.
>
> **Question 2:** *Can you eliminate any of the choices?* If you remember from your initial reading of the passage what the uses for rainwater are (or what they *aren't*, given that this is the focus of the question), great! Mark your choice and skip ahead to the next question on the test. If you don't quite recall that information, then move on to the next question.
>
> **Question 3:** *Where is the information?* "Rainwater" is the key word here, so you'll be looking directly for that word in the passage. Skim the passage superfast, hunting for your keyword, and you'll see that it doesn't appear until paragraph 5.
>
> **Question 4:** *Which answer choice fits?* The paragraph tells you that rainwater is basically the same as greywater, which can be used for landscaping, choice F; watering plants, choice G; and flushing toilets, choice J. That leaves drinking, choice H, which is confirmed by the first lines of the paragraph: *Water that is not suitable for drinking may be used for other purposes, such as watering plants or flushing toilets. Known as greywater....*

Questions like this one are advanced because they ask you to juggle several different details and make a judgment call on which one answers the question at hand. Again, it's extremely important to make sure you fully understand what the question is asking, so that you don't get tricked by "close enough" or "almost" answer choices.

Now use the sample passage to answer two practice questions on your own.

．．

How Is Water Conserved?

There are many technologies and methods to conserve water. Some of them are appropriate for individual households or businesses; others are suitable for large-scale applications. There are also ways to use nonfresh-water sources, such as greywater and desalinated
5   water, in place of fresh water.

Among the most effective technologies for water conservation are water-efficient plumbing fixtures and appliances. Low-flow aerators limit the amount of water coming out of a faucet by blocking a portion of the mouth of the faucet. The water that flows out of the faucet is
10 separated into several different streams instead of a single, solid one. Some models add pressurized air to the stream of water, allowing the faucet to emit less water while maintaining high water pressure.

Modern appliances—including dishwashers, water heaters, and washing machines—are designed with water conservation in mind.
15 These appliances use significantly less water than older models. Moreover, replacing older appliances with newer, water-efficient ones greatly cuts down on cost and water use.

Water-efficient toilets are another effective way to reduce water consumption. Dual-flush toilets have two different settings: one for
20 solid waste, the other for liquid waste. Older toilets use about 5 gallons of water for each flush, but new ones may use only 1.6 gallons per flush for solid waste and less than 1 gallon for liquid waste. Waterless urinals also save water.

Water that is not suitable for drinking may be used for other
25 purposes, such as watering plants or flushing toilets. Known as greywater, this water is recycled from showers, bathroom sinks, washing machines, and drinking fountains. Rainwater can be collected as runoff and used for the same purposes as greywater. Plumbers must install additional pipes and storage tanks to keep greywater
30 and rainwater separate from drinking water.

Wastewater—water that has already been used and collected through sewer systems—may be used for non-drinking purposes after being treated. This water, known as reclaimed water, is processed at a wastewater treatment plant to remove contaminants. Often,
35 reclaimed water is cleaner than drinking water, but it is almost always limited to use in landscaping. Many cities use reclaimed water to maintain parks, golf courses, and other outdoor facilities.

Households and businesses can look to green landscaping practices to cut down on their water use. Landscaping is water
40 intensive, but a technique known as xeriscaping uses significantly less water than the amount required for traditional landscaping. Xeriscaping uses native plants that do not require as much water and minimizes the number of plants in a landscape. For example, a common practice in xeriscaping is replacing grass either with plants
45 that do not need much water or with rock gardens. Xeriscaping may also use water-efficient sprinkler systems that operate at times other than peak sunlight hours to reduce evaporation.

According to the passage, which type of water is often the cleanest?

A. Drinking water
B. Greywater
C. Reclaimed water
D. Xeriscaping water

The correct answer is C. Paragraphs 5 and 6 discuss the different types of water and their various uses, so it's best to start there. Choice D is incorrect because xeriscaping water is not a water type discussed in the passage, so you can eliminate that one right away. The passage doesn't specifically tell you how clean greywater (choice B) is or isn't, so rather than make a leap, it's better to eliminate this choice too. Choice A seems like the correct answer because the passage explicitly states that reclaimed water isn't allowed to be used for drinking water, except for a minor detail buried in Paragraph 6: reclaimed water is typically cleaner than drinking water, despite the segregation of the water types. So choice C is correct.

All of the following technologies help conserve water EXCEPT:

F. Dual-flush toilets
G. Low-flow aerators
H. Older toilets
J. Landscaping techniques like xeriscaping

The correct answer is H. This one is complicated because the details are spread all throughout the passage. Choices F, G, and J are all mentioned as water-conserving technologies, but Paragraph 4 tells you that older toilets have been replaced by newer toilets that use four times less water.

VOCABULARY-IN-CONTEXT QUESTIONS

Remember how we stated that the ACT Reading test doesn't test specific vocabulary? It turns out that statement has a bit of an asterisk attached to it. You'll never be asked to give the exact meaning of a word, it's true—but you *will* be asked to figure out the meaning of a word or phrase based on the context of the sentence, paragraph, or passage. The ACT uses vocabulary as a test of your reasoning skills and your ability to make decisions based on information you're given.

Because the vocabulary questions test your process as much as words you already know, there's no set list of words you can memorize as a slam dunk. What you *can* do ahead of test day to boost your comprehension skills is study commonly confused words (like the list from Chapter 2) so that you're not stymied by subtle differences in tougher questions. It's also a good idea to brush up on your idioms, because the ACT often includes commonly used idioms. Otherwise, it's best to focus your prep on how to approach vocabulary questions regardless of whether you already know the meanings of the words involved or not.

 One of the best things you can do to prep for a top ACT score is to **read, read, read!** The more varied the materials you read, the more familiar you'll become with different types of writing and how to process them.

Lower-difficulty ACT questions will ask you directly about words in the passage or to paraphrase the meaning or give a synonym for a particular word in the passage.

For example:

> *As it is used in line 32, the word* franchise *most nearly means:*

> *Based on the theme of the passage as a whole,* salient *most nearly means:*

These are pretty straightforward. If you don't recognize the word or its meaning by sight, skim the passage until you find the noted line or paragraph and look at the surrounding words. At that point, the meaning will be clear to you, or you'll at least be able to eliminate some of the answer choices.

 Make sure you're careful to pick the answer choice that most closely matches the context in the passage. The ACT often uses words that have multiple meanings or subtle differences in meaning to trip you up.

The more advanced vocabulary-in-context questions will focus on a few different areas:

- Analyzing the relationship between word/phrase choices and meaning or tone in complicated passages

- Interpreting the meaning of technical jargon or figurative language in a passage

- Interpreting the meaning of a paragraph or passage by using a particular word or phrase

Ideally, you'd be able to do these things in passages ranging from simple to complex. In the next chapter, we'll focus on figurative language and other elements found in literature (and Humanities) passages. To prepare you for the most advanced Reading test questions, let's walk through the vocabulary-in-context question types using a complex Natural Science passage.

The Einstein Theory of Relativity

The total eclipse of the sun of May 29, 1919, resulted in a striking confirmation of the new theory of the universal attractive power of gravitation developed by Albert Einstein, and thus reinforced the conviction that the defining of this theory is one of the most important
5   steps ever taken in the domain of natural science. In response to a request by the editor, I will attempt to contribute something to its general appreciation in the following lines.

For centuries Newton's doctrine of the attraction of gravitation has been the most prominent example of a theory of natural science.
10 Through the simplicity of its basic idea, an attraction between two bodies proportionate to their mass and also proportionate to the square of the distance; through the completeness with which it explained so many of the peculiarities in the movement of the bodies making up the solar system; and, finally, through its universal validity,
15 even in the case of the far-distant planetary systems, it compelled the admiration of all.

But, while the skill of the mathematicians was devoted to making more exact calculations of the consequences to which it led, no real progress was made in the science of gravitation. It is true that the
20 inquiry was transferred to the field of physics, following Cavendish's success in demonstrating the common attraction between bodies with which laboratory work can be done, but it always was evident that natural philosophy had no grip on the universal power of attraction. While in electric effects an influence exercised by the matter
25 placed between bodies was speedily observed—the starting-point of a new and fertile doctrine of electricity—in the case of gravitation not a trace of an influence exercised by intermediate matter could

ever be discovered. It was, and remained, inaccessible and unchangeable, without any connection, apparently, with other
30 phenomena of natural philosophy.

Einstein has put an end to this isolation; it is now well established that gravitation affects not only matter, but also light. Thus strengthened in the faith that his theory already has inspired, we may assume with him that there is not a single physical or chemical
35 phenomenon—which does not feel, although very probably in an unnoticeable degree, the influence of gravitation, and that, on the other side, the attraction exercised by a body is limited in the first place by the quantity of matter it contains and also, to some degree, by motion and by the physical and chemical condition in which it
40 moves.

It is comprehensible that a person could not have arrived at such a far-reaching change of view by continuing to follow the old beaten paths, but only by introducing some sort of new idea. Indeed, Einstein arrived at his theory through a train of thought of great
45 originality.

This is a very dense passage—a description of a complicated scientific theory written in very formal language. Lots of five-dollar words in there, some of which may not even be familiar to you. As you make your way through the passage, don't stress out about the size or complexity of the words—try to use the context to get a general sense of what the passage is about. With a passage like this, if it helps you to make notes, feel free to jot down a few general words summarizing each paragraph (you can do this right on your test booklet). That way, when you go back to answer questions, you can use your own guidelines instead of having to wade back through all of the dense sentences.

For Natural Sciences passages, it's also important to remember that you're not responsible for keeping track of (or understanding) the actual science involved. No one expects you to know Einstein's theory of relativity inside and out, for instance. You're supposed to focus on the information actually conveyed in the passage and what it means in a larger sense. It's the writing, not the science.

Here's an example of a marked-up passage:

The Einstein Theory of Relativity

The total eclipse of the sun of May 29, 1919, resulted in a striking confirmation of the new theory of the universal attractive power of gravitation developed by Albert Einstein, and thus reinforced the conviction that the defining of this theory is one of the most important steps ever taken in the domain of natural science. In response to a request by the editor, I will attempt to contribute something to its general appreciation in the following lines.

Einstein's confirmed, most important scientific discovery

For centuries Newton's doctrine of the attraction of gravitation has been the most prominent example of a theory of natural science. Through the simplicity of its basic idea, an attraction between two bodies proportionate to their mass and also proportionate to the square of the distance; through the completeness with which it explained so many of the peculiarities in the movement of the bodies making up the solar system; and, finally, through its universal validity, even in the case of the far-distant planetary systems, it compelled the admiration of all.

Newton's theory popular, but replaced

But, while the skill of the mathematicians was devoted to making more exact calculations of the consequences to which it led, no real progress was made in the science of gravitation. It is true that the inquiry was transferred to the field of physics, following Cavendish's success in demonstrating the common attraction between bodies with which laboratory work can be done, but it always was evident that natural philosophy had no grip on the universal power of attraction. While in electric effects an influence exercised by the matter placed between bodies was speedily observed—the starting-point of a new and fertile doctrine of electricity—in the case of gravitation not a trace of an influence exercised by intermediate matter could ever be discovered. It was, and remained, inaccessible and unchangeable, without any connection, apparently, with other phenomena of natural philosophy.

No scientific proof of gravity

Einstein has put an end to this isolation; it is now well established that gravitation affects not only matter, but also light. Thus strengthened in the faith that his theory already has inspired, we may assume with him that there is not a single physical or chemical phenomenon—which does not feel, although very probably in an unnoticeable degree, the influence of gravitation, and that, on the other side, the attraction exercised by a body is limited in the first place by the quantity of matter it contains and also, to some degree, by motion and by the physical and chemical condition in which it moves.

Only an original idea could have led to breakthrough

It is comprehensible that a person could not have arrived at such a far-reaching change of view by continuing to follow the old beaten paths, but only by introducing some sort of new idea. Indeed, Einstein arrived at his theory through a train of thought of great originality.

Einstein proved gravity affects everything

Having these notes can make it easier to comb back through the passage for any questions where you're not given a specific line reference.

VOCAB/WORD CHOICE AND MEANING

In a complex passage like "The Einstein Theory of Relativity," where the language is very sophisticated, word choice is an important part of conveying the meaning of the overall passage. It's worth noting the author's general style when approaching vocabulary questions. For example, this author uses complex syntax in several places, using a "not" construction to make a positive statement. For example: *[W]e may assume with him that there is not a single physical or chemical phenomenon—which does not feel … the influence of gravitation* is one such sentence and means "all scientific phenomena are affected by gravitation." Another sentence: *It is comprehensible that a person could not have arrived at such a far-reaching change of view by continuing to follow the old beaten paths.* This one translates into, "Far-reaching discoveries are a result of taking a new path." Noticing any quirks in syntax and translating them into your own words can help with vocabulary-related questions.

Try a vocabulary/word choice question that pertains to meaning.

• •

Which of the following phrases best expresses the author's opinion of Einstein's theory?

A. Well established
B. One of the most important steps ever taken in the domain of natural science
C. The most prominent example of a theory of natural science
D. Inaccessible and unchangeable

The correct answer is B. Overall, the author supports the validity of Einstein's theory. For this question, it's important to know the gist of the passage, as that can help you eliminate answer choices right away. Choices A, B, and C are all positive phrases. Choice D is not, so it does not fit with the author's opinion of Einstein's theory. That one's out. To evaluate the rest, go back to try to find each phrase in context, so you can see how they speak to the broader meaning. Choice A is a possibility—"well established" *sounds* like an endorsement, right? Not so fast … the ACT is notorious for slipping in "almost" answer choices. Choice B is much clearer, and if you track down the original location (Paragraph 1), you see that it states the author's support for Einstein. Choice C is incorrect because when you go back to the passage, you discover that it's talking about the old theories, not Einstein's, so it doesn't answer the question. That leaves you with choices A and B still, and when in doubt, always pick the answer choice that more fully answers the question.

• •

JARGON AND TECHNICAL LANGUAGE

Especially in a Natural Science passage, you may be asked to determine the meaning of technical, academic, or domain-specific language (also known as *jargon*). The ACT doesn't require you to know the ins and outs of various academic fields in order to be able to identify vocabulary definitions in context (or their effect on the passage as a whole). As with other types of ACT vocabulary, a question will ask you to take the information given to you in the passage to make a decision about the word. Let's look at a section (paragraphs 3 and 4) from the Einstein passage.

> But, while the skill of the mathematicians was devoted to making more exact calculations of the consequences to which it led, no real progress was made in the science of gravitation. It is true that the
> 20 inquiry was transferred to the field of physics, following Cavendish's success in demonstrating the common attraction between bodies with which laboratory work can be done, but it always was evident that natural philosophy had no grip on the universal power of attraction. While in electric effects an influence exercised by the matter
> 25 placed between bodies was speedily observed—the starting point of a new and fertile doctrine of electricity—in the case of gravitation

not a trace of an influence exercised by intermediate matter could ever be discovered. It was, and remained, inaccessible and unchangeable, without any connection, apparently, with other
30 phenomena of natural philosophy.

Einstein has put an end to this isolation; it is now well established that gravitation affects not only matter, but also light. Thus strengthened in the faith that his theory already has inspired, we may assume with him that there is not a single physical or chemical
35 phenomenon—which does not feel, although very probably in an unnoticeable degree, the influence of gravitation, and that, on the other side, the attraction exercised by a body is limited in the first place by the quantity of matter it contains and also, to some degree, by motion and by the physical and chemical condition in which
40 it moves.

This passage uses a lot of language that would be second nature to a physicist or an academic from the author's time. Paragraph 3 is especially dense, given that it talks the most about the theory itself and how it works. While you're reading the passage for the first time, you don't need to worry too much about the specific wording or what *all* of the words mean—again, just try to keep the gist of the passage in mind. If the ACT wants you to deal with a particular word or phrase, it'll direct you back there via the questions, so it's not worth puzzling over every subject-specific vocabulary word on your first trip through the passage.

Although the ACT often uses the phrase *most nearly* in vocabulary questions, don't take that to mean "close enough." Always make sure that your answer is fully supported by the passage.

These questions will look a lot like the more basic vocabulary questions, but will ask you to suss out a subject-specific meaning. An example:

Line 32 suggests that *matter* most nearly means which of the following?

- **F.** Physical substance
- **G.** A topic
- **H.** Significance
- **J.** Incident

This question is challenging because it calls on you to identify the scientific definition of *matter* and separate it from the multiple meanings of the word. If you're not a physics whiz, don't worry! Try plugging in the answer choices for sentences that contain *matter* in the passage.

...it is now well established that gravitation affects not only *physical substance*, but also light.

...it is now well established that gravitation affects not only *a topic*, but also light.

...it is now well established that gravitation affects not only *significance*, but also light.

...it is now well established that gravitation affects not only *an incident*, but also light.

Of these, only the first option really makes any sense. **The correct answer is F.**

When choosing an answer, never make the choice based on something that sounds like it *could* be true, if only you had more information. Always pick the answer choice that is fully backed up by the passage.

This kind of vocabulary question often deals with figurative language in a passage, which we'll discuss more in Chapter 7.

Now, use the sample passage to answer two practice questions on your own.

. . . .

The Einstein Theory of Relativity

The total eclipse of the sun of May 29, 1919, resulted in a striking confirmation of the new theory of the universal attractive power of gravitation developed by Albert Einstein, and thus reinforced the conviction that the defining of this theory is one of the most important
5 steps ever taken in the domain of natural science. In response to a request by the editor, I will attempt to contribute something to its general appreciation in the following lines.

For centuries Newton's doctrine of the attraction of gravitation has been the most prominent example of a theory of natural science.
10 Through the simplicity of its basic idea, an attraction between two bodies proportionate to their mass and also proportionate to the square of the distance; through the completeness with which it explained so many of the peculiarities in the movement of the bodies making up the solar system; and, finally, through its universal validity,
15 even in the case of the far-distant planetary systems, it compelled the admiration of all.

But, while the skill of the mathematicians was devoted to making more exact calculations of the consequences to which it led, no real progress was made in the science of gravitation. It is true that the

20 inquiry was transferred to the field of physics, following Cavendish's
success in demonstrating the common attraction between bodies
with which laboratory work can be done, but it always was evident
that natural philosophy had no grip on the universal power of
attraction. While in electric effects an influence exercised by the matter
25 placed between bodies was speedily observed—the starting point of
a new and fertile doctrine of electricity—in the case of gravitation
not a trace of an influence exercised by intermediate matter could
ever be discovered. It was, and remained, inaccessible and
unchangeable, without any connection, apparently, with other
30 phenomena of natural philosophy.

Einstein has put an end to this isolation; it is now well established
that gravitation affects not only matter, but also light. Thus
strengthened in the faith that his theory already has inspired, we
may assume with him that there is not a single physical or chemical
35 phenomenon—which does not feel, although very probably in an
unnoticeable degree, the influence of gravitation, and that, on the
other side, the attraction exercised by a body is limited in the first
place by the quantity of matter it contains and also, to some degree,
by motion and by the physical and chemical condition in which
40 it moves.

It is comprehensible that a person could not have arrived at
such a far-reaching change of view by continuing to follow the old
beaten paths, but only by introducing some sort of new idea. Indeed,
Einstein arrived at his theory through a train of thought of
45 great originality.

Throughout the passage, the author most likely uses the word *natural* to:

- **A.** emphasize the artificiality of Einstein's theory.
- **B.** contrast the old way of thinking about science with the new way of thinking about science.
- **C.** disprove Einstein's theory by suggesting it's unnatural.
- **D.** prove Einstein's theory.

The correct answer is B. The author uses *natural* several times throughout the passage, always in reference to previous theories and philosophies about how gravitation worked. This sets up a comparison between the old, "natural" ways of approaching science and the new one embraced by Einstein's modern approach. Choice B is the best option. Choices A and C are not supported by the passage—nowhere is the author trying to discredit Einstein's theory. Choice D is incorrect because the passage also doesn't support the idea that the author is testing the theory itself—just discussing the importance of it to the scientific community.

In line 35, ph*enomenon* most nearly means which of the following?

F. A flash in the pan
G. A cultural event
H. A naturally occurring event
J. A miracle

The correct answer is H. You can eliminate choice G right away—the passage is about a scientific advancement, not a cultural one. The others are slightly trickier. Choice F is incorrect because the author clearly thinks Einstein's theory is a scientific solution for the ages, and "flash in the pan" suggests something that is temporary. That leaves choices H and J. Choice J is tempting because the author clearly supports Einstein's theory, but there's no indication that the author thinks that there's a spiritual element; he has restricted the rest of the passage to a purely scientific point of view. That leaves choice H, which makes the most sense when you plug it into the sentence.

. . . .

FUNCTION QUESTIONS

After detail questions, function questions make up the next biggest block of ACT Reading test questions. Function questions ask you what a particular word, phrase, sentence, or paragraph does within the passage. Development questions are a variation on function questions—they ask you to figure out how the given information relates to the structure of the passage as a whole (i.e., how the author uses it to develop a theme or idea). Instead of vocabulary in context, think of function and development questions as action in context.

When answering function and development questions, the main question to keep in your mind is, "how does this text serve the purpose of the overall paragraph or passage?" Purpose is the driving force behind function questions at all levels of difficulty.

To analyze development and function questions, use the same series of questions as you would for detail questions:

- What is the question asking?

- Can you eliminate any of the choices?

- Where is the information?

- Which remaining answer choice fits?

FUNCTION QUESTIONS

Here are some of the types of function questions you're likely to see on test day:

> *The main purpose of the third paragraph is to:*
>
> *The poem in lines 50–60 is used in this passage to support the idea that:*
>
> *The author uses the fourth paragraph (lines 27–33) primarily to:*
>
> *The author likely included the information in paragraph 6 (lines 90–102) to:*
>
> *In relation to the first paragraph's earlier description of the nightmare, the narrator's comments in lines 10–13 primarily serve to:*

One of the most important things to remember with function questions is that the passage is rarely a self-contained whole—it's an excerpt of a larger piece of writing. There may not be a logical 1, 2, 3 structure, with a neat template of opening, supporting details, and closing. You don't have access to the entire piece, so you can't make determinations about any themes, ideas, or arguments that aren't presented. However, you should still treat the passage like a standalone piece of writing and work only with the information you have. Be sure not to make assumptions or leaps in logic based on what might be in the book, but not in the passage on the test. Be prepared to find subtler forms of organization and relationships in the passage that may not be apparent on first glance.

DEVELOPMENT QUESTIONS

Development questions aren't quite as common on the ACT Reading test, but they do come up. You should be ready to answer them using challenging or complex passages.

The main difference is that development questions usually ask a bigger question of, "what happens in this paragraph?" Take a look at some of the types of development questions you're likely to see on test day:

> *The author develops the fourth paragraph mainly through:*
>
> *Which of the following best describes the structure of the passage?*
>
> *In terms of the passage as a whole, one of the main functions of the third paragraph is to suggest that:*
>
> *In terms of developing the narrative, the last paragraph primarily serves to:*

Rather than focus on how specific information supports or informs the purpose of the passage, development questions address how the structure of the passage itself (paragraph placement, flow of ideas throughout) supports the main topic and ideas in the passage.

The more advanced function and development questions will ask you to make these determinations about passages that are complex or where the information is subtly stated. Let's look at a sample passage.

The Prince

All the States and Governments by which men are or ever have been ruled, have been and are either Republics or Princedoms. Princedoms are either hereditary, in which the sovereignty is derived through an ancient line of ancestors, or they are new.

5   New Princedoms are either wholly new, as that of Milan to Francesco Sforza; or they are like limbs joined on to the hereditary possessions of the Prince who acquires them, as the Kingdom of Naples to the dominions of the King of Spain. The States thus acquired have either been used to live under a Prince or have been free; and
10   he who acquires them does so either by his own arms or by the arms of others, and either by good fortune or by merit.

Of Republics I shall not now speak, having elsewhere spoken of them at length. Here I shall treat exclusively of Princedoms, and, filling in the outline above traced out, shall proceed to examine how
15   such States are to be governed and maintained. I say, then, that hereditary States, accustomed to the family of their Prince, are maintained with far less difficulty than new States, since all that is required is that the Prince shall not depart from the usages of his ancestors, trusting for the rest to deal with events as they arise. So that if an
20   hereditary Prince be of average address, he will always maintain himself in his Princedom, unless deprived of it by some extraordinary and irresistible force; and even if so deprived will recover it, should any, even the least, mishap overtake the usurper. We have in Italy an example of this in the Duke of Ferrara, who never could have with
25   stood the attacks of the Venetians in 1484, nor those of Pope Julius in 1510, had not his authority in that State been consolidated by time. For since a Prince by birth has fewer occasions and less need to give offence, he ought to be better loved, and will naturally be popular with his subjects unless outrageous vices make him odious.
30   Moreover, the very antiquity and continuance of his rule will efface the memories and causes which lead to innovation. For one change always leaves a dovetail into which another will fit.

In the third paragraph, the author mentions the Duke of Ferrara primarily to:

A. show how princedoms are always better than republics.

B. illustrate how princes cause innovation.

C. explain how princes rule forever.

D. suggest that even weak princes can stay in power by not upsetting the status quo.

The four-question process for answering these question types is pretty similar to the one for answering detail questions.

Question 1: *What is the question asking?* Start by rephrasing the question in your own words. The question is asking you to figure out what role the Duke of Ferrara plays in supporting the main idea of the paragraph. It may *seem* like the question is asking you to decide why the author picked this particular example, but unless you have a psychic connection to Niccolo Machiavelli, there's no way for you to know why this particular example was chosen. What you can do, however, is determine what the Duke of Ferrara detail supports in the passage.

Question 2: *Can you eliminate any of the choices?* Right away, you can get rid of choice C. The second paragraph tells you that some republics result from the end of princedoms, so that undermines the idea that princedoms last forever. It's a subtle detail crammed into a dense paragraph, but the more advanced ACT Reading test questions want you to be able to account for information from different parts of the passage.

Question 3: *Where is the information?* The question directs you to Paragraph 3, so that means you can restrict your investigation to how the detail relates to the paragraph on its own. However, because you need to figure out how the given information (the Duke of Ferrara) fits, you need to look at the whole paragraph, not just the Duke of Ferrara reference.

Question 4: *Which answer choice fits?* While you were reading or skimming the passage initially, you should have made some notes (mental ones or jotted-down ones) about the main ideas of the essay and the paragraphs. For the third paragraph, the main idea is that princes should have an easier time staying in power, because they come by that power through heredity, not conflict.

Which of the answer choices supports that idea? Choice A is problematic because there's nothing in the paragraph that suggests the author believes that princedoms are better than republics. If the information isn't in the paragraph or anywhere in the passage, eliminate the choice. Choice B is a possibility, because "innovation" comes up at the end of the paragraph—but if you look closer, the author is saying the opposite of choice B: that princes represent the kind of stability that prevents innovation. Choice C has already been eliminated because it goes against information in the passage. Choice D works; the Duke of Ferrara is explicitly described as "weak" despite his role and is mentioned as an example of "always maintain[ing] himself in his Princedom, unless deprived of it by some extraordinary and irresistible force," as the author states in the previous sentence. **The correct answer is D.**

Now, use the sample passage to answer two practice questions on your own.

. . . .

The Prince

All the States and Governments by which men are or ever have been ruled, have been and are either Republics or Princedoms. Princedoms are either hereditary, in which the sovereignty is derived through an ancient line of ancestors, or they are new.

5   New Princedoms are either wholly new, as that of Milan to Francesco Sforza; or they are like limbs joined on to the hereditary possessions of the Prince who acquires them, as the Kingdom of Naples to the dominions of the King of Spain. The States thus acquired have either been used to live under a Prince or have been free; and
10 he who acquires them does so either by his own arms or by the arms of others, and either by good fortune or by merit.

Of Republics I shall not now speak, having elsewhere spoken of them at length. Here I shall treat exclusively of Princedoms, and, filling in the outline above traced out, shall proceed to examine how
15 such States are to be governed and maintained. I say, then, that hereditary States, accustomed to the family of their Prince, are main- tained with far less difficulty than new States, since all that is required is that the Prince shall not depart from the usages of his ancestors, trusting for the rest to deal with events as they arise. So that if an
20 hereditary Prince be of average address, he will always maintain himself in his Princedom, unless deprived of it by some extraordinary and irresistible force; and even if so deprived will recover it, should any, even the least, mishap overtake the usurper. We have in Italy an example of this in the Duke of Ferrara, who never could have with-
25 stood the attacks of the Venetians in 1484, nor those of Pope Julius in 1510, had not his authority in that State been consolidated by time. For since a Prince by birth has fewer occasions and less need to give offence, he ought to be better loved, and will naturally be popular with his subjects unless outrageous vices make him odious.
30 Moreover, the very antiquity and continuance of his rule will efface the memories and causes which lead to innovation. For one change always leaves a dovetail into which another will fit.

The author develops the third paragraph through:

F. detailing how republics are different from princedoms.
G. stating that princedoms are easier to maintain than republics.
H. comparing Italy to the rest of the world.
J. giving a real-life examples of a prince.

The correct answer is J. The author uses the example of a real-life prince (the Duke of Ferrara) and the threats he faced to illustrate that maintaining the status quo is often the easiest way for a prince to maintain power. Choice F is incorrect because the author explicitly says he's not going to discuss republics in this passage. Choice G is incorrect because although this is a supporting detail, it has little to do with the author's development of the larger idea. Choice H is incorrect because there's no information given about other countries, just a specific Italian example, so the passage doesn't support that choice.

The statement, "The States thus acquired have either been used to live under a Prince or have been free; and he who acquires them does so either by his own arms or by the arms of others, and either by good fortune or by merit" was likely included to emphasize:

- **A.** the superiority of princedoms.
- **B.** the risk undertaken by princes who take power rather than being born to it.
- **C.** the risk undertaken by princes who are born into power.
- **D.** the success of princedoms in Italy.

The correct answer is B. One of the main topics of this passage is the idea that princes who inherit their title and stay away from conflict are safer than those who seize power via conflict. Choice A is incorrect because it's too general, and there's nothing in the passage that directly supports that as a theme. Choice D is incorrect because the statement is not specific to Italy. Choices B and C are the two left standing, but are opposite—it's important to read closely to confirm which one fits the text. The sentence directly mentions *he who acquires them [States]*, so you know the author is not talking about natural-born princes. Choice B is correct.

In the second paragraph, what purpose does the use of the word *limbs* (line 6) serve?

- **F.** It emphasizes the conflict between hereditary princedoms and acquired princedoms.
- **G.** It suggests that countries have human rights.
- **H.** It illustrates the usefulness of acquiring other countries.
- **J.** It describes the relationship between the King of Naples and the King of Spain.

The correct answer is H. Choice F is incorrect because *limbs* actually refers to territories acquired by hereditary princes, so the idea of conflict here is incorrect. Choice G is incorrect because the passage doesn't support the idea that countries are living beings with rights. Choice H is correct because *limbs* sets a specific picture of how these acquired territories function for the acquiring country. Choice J is incorrect because although it does describe the relationship, choice H answers the question more fully.

SUMMING IT UP

- **The ACT Reading test is designed to assess your reading comprehension skills and your ability to look below the surface in complex pieces of writing.** It's divided into two subsections, the Social Studies/Natural Sciences passages and the Literary Narrative/Prose Fiction and Humanities passages. All four passages on the ACT Reading test will be followed by 10 multiple-choice questions.

- **The Social Studies and Natural Sciences passages make up half of the ACT Reading test and feature nonfiction passages, which often have very technical or formal writing styles.** The emphasis in these passages is finding specific information in the passages or identifying supporting details within complicated blocks of text.

- **The most difficult main idea and central theme questions will ask you to identify the main idea (the topic) or the central theme (the message) in passages where the information is buried deep in the passage.** You will be expected to infer themes that aren't directly stated, and locate/summarize details that support those themes.

- **Advanced detail questions will ask you to put together several streams of information to find the right information.** You may need to dig those details out of dense, technical passages or call attention to a detail that is subtly stated in a complex piece of writing.

- **Challenging vocabulary-in-context questions will ask you to look beyond basic word meanings and call for you to look at the effects of the vocabulary on the meaning of the passage.** These questions will include figuring out the meanings of technical-speak or jargon based on context, as well as figurative language used by the author.

- **Function questions ask you to figure out what purpose a particular word, phrase, or line is serving within a paragraph or passage.** Development questions, which are a type of function question, are bigger-picture questions that ask you to identify how a sentence or detail supports the passage as a whole.

CHAPTER 7
ACT® READING:
LITERARY NARRATIVE/
PROSE FICTION AND
HUMANITIES PASSAGES

OVERVIEW

- About Literary Narrative/Prose Fiction and Humanities Passages

- Paired Passages

- Inference Questions

- Relationship Questions

- Summing It Up

In Chapter 6, we reviewed the toughest question types you'll see on the Social Studies and Natural Sciences passages on the ACT Reading test. Now it's time to dive into the other half of the Reading test: the Literary Narrative/Prose Fiction and Humanities passages.

Why are there five passage types listed when you know there are only four passages on the test, you ask? If you'll recall from the ACT Reading overview in Chapter 6, the ACT will test you on either Literary Narrative OR Prose Fiction. Think of it as kind of a literature super-passage. On test day, it'll be either a Humanities passage and a Literary Narrative passage or a Humanities passage and a Prose Fiction passage—never all of the above. What does that mean for you? Bottom line: it means that you need to be prepared for all potential passages on the ACT. (No skimping on Literary Narrative prep, then crossing your fingers and hoping for Prose Fiction—sorry!) You're an advanced student, so you know the drill. If you spend time on all five potential ACT Reading passage types before test day, you're much less likely to have unpleasant surprises.

ABOUT LITERARY NARRATIVE/PROSE FICTION AND HUMANITIES PASSAGES

The Literary Narrative, Prose Fiction, and Humanities passages are grouped together under a single subscore because they're tested slightly differently than the Social Studies and Natural Sciences passages. Social Studies and Natural Sciences tend to present straightforward nonfiction facts, and the related questions tend to focus on specific details and information that can be directly backed up in each passage. Literary Narrative, Prose Fiction, and Humanities passages are approached from a more perspective-oriented way—the questions focus more on issues like tone, the narrator's perspective, and the writer's intent.

The Prose Fiction passage is usually an excerpt from a novel or short story, one you likely haven't read in your high school classes. Literary Narrative passages may include non-fiction as well—think stylized nonfiction, like an autobiography, personal essay, or memoir, instead of history. The Literary Narrative/Prose Fiction passage can be anywhere from 350–1,000 words.

The Humanities passage is nonfiction prose as well and can be excerpted from any of these topic areas (essentially, philosophy and the arts):

- Architecture
- Art
- Dance
- Ethics
- Film
- Language

- Literary criticism
- Music
- Philosophy
- Radio
- Television
- Theater

Humanities passages are nonfiction like the social studies passages, but they tend to be more literary in nature (while social studies passages tend to be more historical or political).

Like the other ACT Reading passages, each passage is followed by 10 multiple-choice questions. However, there is one area where the Literary and Narrative/Prose Fiction and Humanities format differs from the other two passages: sometimes the selection will be comprised of two shorter passages for comparison, instead of one long passage. If there's a case where there are two passages, the questions will likely ask you to compare and contrast the two mini-passages. For example, the Prose Fiction passage may have two shorter works by the same author or two pieces that are similar in theme.

In this chapter, we'll cover the hardest passage and question types you're likely to see in the Literary Narrative/Prose Fiction and Humanities passages. Throughout the chapter, there will be eight Reading test questions like the ones you'll see on test day. Now that we've covered the basics of what to expect on this section, let's get started!

PAIRED PASSAGES

Paired passages are a particular hazard of the Literary Narrative, Prose Fiction, or Humanities selections. There's nothing stopping the ACT from using two shorter passages in the Social Studies or Natural Sciences passages, but in practice, they almost always pop up as a Literary Narrative/Prose Fiction or Humanities passage. In the paired passages, instead of one long passage there will be two shorter ones, approximately 40–50 lines a piece (sort of like mini-passages). The good news is that the number of questions doesn't change—it's the same 10 questions that you'd see for any other single passage.

The main difference is that you have two separate pieces of writing to read and process in the same amount of time in which you'd usually tackle one passage. The questions on paired passages are divided into three kinds: questions about Passage A, questions about Passage B, and questions that ask you to compare or contrast Passages A and B. In terms of strategy, it really depends on how you work through questions best—in order or jumping around. However, with the paired passages, you might find it easier to attack the single-passage questions first, then move on to the questions that will make you go back and forth between the mini-passages.

Don't forget that even with two shorter passages, you're still facing the same group of 10 multiple-choice questions for that particular section. Don't get too bogged down in focusing on the two passages because you still need to answer the same number of questions regardless of the passage breakdown.

Answering the Passage A OR Passage B questions first has an added advantage: it familiarizes you further with both passages, which could make it easier when you need to go between the two to answer questions about both. Also, because the passages are shorter and likely less complex than the long single passages, it could make keyword hunts easier.

The Passage A OR Passage B questions will be pretty straightforward and like most ACT Reading test questions. The Passage A + Passage B questions are the biggest challenge in paired passages, so it makes the most sense to focus your prep on those combo questions. The goal is to be able to draw logical conclusions from anywhere in the two mini-passages (not just generalizations about each one) and be able to connect them in a meaningful way.

Passage A + Passage B questions for Literary Narrative or Prose Fiction passages will usually concern the tones, characters, or themes of the mini-passages. Passage A + Passage B questions for Humanities mini-passages may ask you to compare information or details between the two and how each writer approaches the information.

Let's take a look at a sample set of paired passages.

Passage A is excerpted from the travel memoir *Life on the Mississippi* by Mark Twain.

Passage A

After a close study of the face of the pilot on watch, I was satisfied that I had never seen him before; so I went up there. The pilot inspected me; I re-inspected the pilot. These customary preliminaries over, I sat down on the high bench, and he faced about and went on with his
5   work. Every detail of the pilot-house was familiar to me, with one exception—a large-mouthed tube under the breast-board. I puzzled over that thing a considerable time; then gave up and asked what it was for.

"To hear the engine-bells through."

10   It was another good contrivance which ought to have been invented half a century sooner. So I was thinking, when the pilot asked—

"Do you know what this rope is for?"

I managed to get around this question, without committing myself.

15   "Is this the first time you were ever in a pilot-house?"

I crept under that one.

"Where are you from?"

"New England."

"First time you have ever been West?"

20   I climbed over this one.

"If you take an interest in such things, I can tell you what all these things are for."

I said I should like it.

"This," putting his hand on a backing-bell rope, "is to sound the
25   fire-alarm; this," putting his hand on a go-ahead bell, "is to call the texas-tender; this one," indicating the whistle-lever, "is to call the captain"—and so he went on, touching one object after another, and reeling off his tranquil spool of lies.

I had never felt so like a passenger before. I thanked him, with
30   emotion, for each new fact, and wrote it down in my note-book. The pilot warmed to his opportunity, and proceeded to load me up in the good old-fashioned way. At times I was afraid he was going to rupture his invention; but it always stood the strain, and he pulled through all right. He drifted, by easy stages, into revealments of the

35 river's marvelous eccentricities of one sort and another, and backed them up with some pretty gigantic illustrations. For instance—

"Do you see that little boulder sticking out of the water yonder? Well, when I first came on the river, that was a solid ridge of rock, over sixty feet high and two miles long. All washed away but that."
40 [This with a sigh.]

I had a mighty impulse to destroy him, but it seemed to me that killing, in any ordinary way, would be too good for him.

Passage B is excerpted from the novel *Heart of Darkness* by Joseph Conrad.

Passage B

The sun set; the dusk fell on the stream, and lights began to appear along the shore. The Chapman light–house, a three–legged thing erect on a mud–flat, shone strongly. Lights of ships moved in the fairway—a great stir of lights going up and going down. And
5 farther west on the upper reaches the place of the monstrous town was still marked ominously on the sky, a brooding gloom in sunshine, a lurid glare under the stars.

"And this also," said Marlow suddenly, "has been one of the dark places of the earth."

10 He was the only man of us who still "followed the sea." The worst that could be said of him was that he did not represent his class. He was a seaman, but he was a wanderer, too, while most seamen lead, if one may so express it, a sedentary life. Their minds are of the stay–at–home order, and their home is always with them—the ship; and
15 so is their country—the sea. One ship is very much like another, and the sea is always the same. In the immutability of their surroundings the foreign shores, the foreign faces, the changing immensity of life, glide past, veiled not by a sense of mystery but by a slightly disdainful ignorance; for there is nothing mysterious to a seaman unless it be
20 the sea itself, which is the mistress of his existence and as inscrutable as Destiny. For the rest, after his hours of work, a casual stroll or a casual spree on shore suffices to unfold for him the secret of a whole continent, and generally he finds the secret not worth knowing. The yarns of seamen have a direct simplicity, the whole meaning of which
25 lies within the shell of a cracked nut. But Marlow was not typical (if his propensity to spin yarns be excepted), and to him the meaning of an episode was not inside like a kernel but outside, enveloping the tale which brought it out only as a glow brings out a haze, in the likeness of one of these misty halos that sometimes are made visible
30 by the spectral illumination of moonshine.

Both passages have a clear topic in common—a novice sailor learning from a more experienced one. Beyond that, it's up to you to be able to find connections (or comparison points). As you read through the passages initially, be sure to make a note of any similarities you find, in addition to the usual reading hallmarks of big themes, main supporting points, and the like.

Let's look at an example Passage A + Passage B question based on the passages.

Which of the following statements most accurately compares the tone of each passage?

- **A.** Passage A is humorous, while Passage B is philosophical.
- **B.** Passage A is philosophical, while Passage B is humorous.
- **C.** Both passages are informational and clinical.
- **D.** Passage B is angry, while Passage A is cynical.

As with other question types, you'll want to follow a process for each question. However, because the Literary Narrative/Prose Fiction and Humanities passages are working with figurative language and literary elements rather than straight-up information, the question of "where is the exact information?" is less important. It can be difficult to trace tone or inferred themes to a single specific word or phrase—it's more of a collective conclusion based on the entire passage(s). So there's a slightly modified process for these questions:

> **Question 1:** *What is the question asking?* Look for words like "compared to," "comparison," and "in contrast" to help you nail down what information you're seeking.

> **Question 2:** *Can you eliminate any of the choices?* Eliminating answer choices is even more important with paired passage questions, because if any part of an answer choice is incorrect, the whole thing is incorrect. This is more complicated when you need to verify the information in two different places.

> **Question 3:** *Which answer choice fits?* Remember, there's only one unquestionably correct answer, as with every other question on the ACT. Make sure that you're choosing the answer that works fully.

Going back to the example question:

> **Question 1:** *What is the question asking?* You'll need to correctly identify the tone of Passage A and also the tone of Passage B. Passage A is a fairly lighthearted conversation between the narrator and the ship's pilot. Passage B is a more serious and philosophical look at sailing and those involved in it. Both excerpts feature a character who likes to "spin yarns," but that's more of a character detail than a tone issue.

> **Question 2:** *Can you eliminate any of the choices?* Here's an interesting one because choices A and B are opposites of one another, so one is clearly incorrect—but which one? Passage A is less formal than Passage B—it's a straight conversation between the two men, with the narrator's tongue-in-cheek commentary running throughout. (It even ends with the narrator

jokingly wishing death on the pilot, even though there's no indication from the rest of the passage that he means it.) There's very little philosophical thinking going on. In Passage B, however, a large part of the third paragraph is devoted to a larger exploration of life at sea: *In the immutability of their surroundings, the foreign shores, the foreign faces, the changing immensity of life, glide past, veiled not by a sense of mystery but by a slightly disdainful ignorance; for there is nothing mysterious to a seaman unless it be the sea itself, which is the mistress of his existence and as inscrutable as Destiny.* So Passage A is the humorous one, while Passage B is the philosophical one. You can then eliminate choice B. Similarly, you can likely rule out choice C as well, because you've already identified differences in tone between the passages, so it's not likely that a question asking you to compare them is going to be answered by a statement that "both passages are ___." So you can tentatively eliminate choice C as well, but make sure you verify in the next question.

Question 3: *Which answer choice fits?* Choice A is looking pretty good, based on the assessment of the passages' overall tones. Choices B is out, as we determined in Question 2. Choice C is also out, because neither passage is informational (conveying facts) or clinical (devoid of voice). Choice D is also out because although you can make an argument for Passage A being somewhat cynical (mocking), there's nothing in Passage B that shows anger—and here, you should remember that you need all parts of an answer to hold up. **The correct answer is A.**

Now use the sample paired passages to answer practice questions on your own.

. . . .

Passage A

After a close study of the face of the pilot on watch, I was satisfied that I had never seen him before; so I went up there. The pilot inspected me; I re-inspected the pilot. These customary preliminaries over, I sat down on the high bench, and he faced about and went on with his
5   work. Every detail of the pilot-house was familiar to me, with one exception—a large-mouthed tube under the breast-board. I puzzled over that thing a considerable time; then gave up and asked what it was for.

"To hear the engine-bells through."

10   It was another good contrivance which ought to have been invented half a century sooner. So I was thinking, when the pilot asked—

"Do you know what this rope is for?"

I managed to get around this question, without committing myself.

15 "Is this the first time you were ever in a pilot-house?"

I crept under that one.

"Where are you from?"

"New England."

"First time you have ever been West?"

20 I climbed over this one.

"If you take an interest in such things, I can tell you what all these things are for."

I said I should like it.

"This," putting his hand on a backing-bell rope, "is to sound the
25 fire-alarm; this," putting his hand on a go-ahead bell, "is to call the texas-tender; this one," indicating the whistle-lever, "is to call the captain"—and so he went on, touching one object after another, and reeling off his tranquil spool of lies.

I had never felt so like a passenger before. I thanked him, with
30 emotion, for each new fact, and wrote it down in my note-book. The pilot warmed to his opportunity, and proceeded to load me up in the good old-fashioned way. At times I was afraid he was going to rupture his invention; but it always stood the strain, and he pulled through all right. He drifted, by easy stages, into revealments of the
35 river's marvelous eccentricities of one sort and another, and backed them up with some pretty gigantic illustrations. For instance—

"Do you see that little boulder sticking out of the water yonder? Well, when I first came on the river, that was a solid ridge of rock, over sixty feet high and two miles long. All washed away but that."
40 [This with a sigh.]

I had a mighty impulse to destroy him, but it seemed to me that killing, in any ordinary way, would be too good for him.

Passage B

The sun set; the dusk fell on the stream, and lights began to appear along the shore. The Chapman light–house, a three–legged thing erect on a mud–flat, shone strongly. Lights of ships moved in the fairway—a great stir of lights going up and going down. And
5 farther west on the upper reaches the place of the monstrous town was still marked ominously on the sky, a brooding gloom in sunshine, a lurid glare under the stars.

"And this also," said Marlow suddenly, "has been one of the dark places of the earth."

10   He was the only man of us who still "followed the sea." The worst
that could be said of him was that he did not represent his class. He
was a seaman, but he was a wanderer, too, while most seamen lead,
if one may so express it, a sedentary life. Their minds are of the stay–
at–home order, and their home is always with them—the ship; and
15   so is their country—the sea. One ship is very much like another, and
the sea is always the same. In the immutability of their surroundings
the foreign shores, the foreign faces, the changing immensity of life,
glide past, veiled not by a sense of mystery but by a slightly disdainful
ignorance; for there is nothing mysterious to a seaman unless it be
20   the sea itself, which is the mistress of his existence and as inscrutable
as Destiny. For the rest, after his hours of work, a casual stroll or a
casual spree on shore suffices to unfold for him the secret of a whole
continent, and generally he finds the secret not worth knowing. The
yarns of seamen have a direct simplicity, the whole meaning of which
25   lies within the shell of a cracked nut. But Marlow was not typical (if
his propensity to spin yarns be excepted), and to him the meaning
of an episode was not inside like a kernel but outside, enveloping
the tale which brought it out only as a glow brings out a haze, in the
likeness of one of these misty halos that sometimes are made visible
30   by the spectral illumination of moonshine.

Based on the two passages, which pair of phrases best compares Twain's relationship
to the pilot and the Passage B narrator's relationship with Marlow?

- **A.**   Teacher vs. student
- **B.**   Dishonest vs. honest
- **C.**   Interested student vs. casual listener
- **D.**   Unhappy vs. pleasant

The correct answer is C. Choice A is incorrect because in Passage A, the narrator is
clearly engaging the pilot, asking questions and taking notes—so the narrator isn't the
teacher. Choice B is incorrect because both narrators suggest that their respective subjects (the pilot and Marlow) like to exaggerate (or spin a "spool of lies" in Passage A's
case). Choice C is correct because again, Twain's narrator is going out of his way to
interview the pilot, while Marlow is speaking up out of nowhere, with no obvious
prompting from the narrator. Choice D is incorrect because even though Twain's narrator
jokes about killing the pilot, there's no indication that the interaction is an unhappy one.
(And in fact, the narrator is eager for more information from the pilot.)

Unlike the author of Passage A, the author of Passage B makes significant use of:

- **F.**   first-person descriptions.
- **G.**   humorous commentary.
- **H.**   dialogue.
- **J.**   philosophical speculation.

The correct answer is J. Choice F is incorrect because both passages are told from a
first-person perspective. Choice G is incorrect because Passage A is the one that takes

a more humorous, tongue-in-cheek tone. Choice H is incorrect because Passage A is also the one that makes more use of dialogue, while Passage B only has one line of dialogue that is then described and analyzed by the narrator. Choice J is correct because Passage B's narrator speculates on the meaning and perspective of Marlow's words, trying to give it a philosophical context of what life is like for seamen. Passage A is much more focused on the conversation between the narrator and the pilot, and the narrator is most interested in focusing on the pilot's own words.

Compared to the narrator in Passage A, the narrator in Passage B is:

- **A.** more interested in the physical aspects of life on a boat.
- **B.** more likely to believe the yarns of the old sailor.
- **C.** less likely to believe the yarns of the old sailor.
- **D.** more interested in the history of sea life.

The correct answer is D. Choice A is incorrect because it is the Passage A narrator who asks direct questions about what the instruments on the boat do, and he takes notes as an active observer. In Passage B, there's no discussion of anything having to do with the boat itself. Choice B is incorrect because both narrators note the sailors' tendency to exaggerate. Choice C is incorrect because again, both narrators seem to make the same bemused note about how sailors exaggerate stories—there's no real contrast there. Choice D is correct because each narrator has a different purpose. In Passage A, the narrator is trying to learn about how everything on the boat works. In Passage B, the narrator is more interested in the life and perspective of a seaman.

INFERENCE QUESTIONS

Inference questions ask you to take information from the passage (or a specific line or paragraph) and draw a conclusion about what that information means. Unlike function and development questions, these won't ask you to make decisions about what purpose a particular word, phrase, or section has in relation to the whole passage. Instead, inference questions call for you to use your judgment to draw conclusions about what the author is indirectly saying. If you see phrases like, "it can be reasonably inferred that …" or "suggests that …" in a question, it's likely an inference question. Basically, an inference question is the indirect version of a detail question.

Inference questions may pop up in any ACT Reading passage, but they're most often used—and most challenging—in the Literary Narrative, Prose Fiction, and Humanities passages. This is because the information presented in these passages isn't always as straightforward as the data or interpretations presented in Social Studies or Natural Science passages. That means the reader (meaning you) has to work harder to determine what the writer is actually trying to say. By the end of your ACT prep, it could reasonably be inferred that you may never want to see an inference question again. Yet they're very important if you want to maximize your ACT Reading score, so infer we will.

Some examples of inference questions you might see on test day:

It can be reasonably inferred from the passage that the narrator's motivation is:

The narrator's use of exaggeration in the second paragraph suggests that he felt that:

By her statements in lines 42–47, the narrator is most nearly suggesting that:

The conflict mentioned in the third paragraph is best described by which of the following statements?

Inference questions can ask you to infer any number of things: meaning (as in vocabulary), theme, purpose, tone, function, or the author/narrator's intentions. The ACT doesn't require you to be psychic about what an author meant to say, but you should be able to find information to support your answer choice in the passage. The most advanced inference questions on the ACT will be attached to complex passages and will require you to decode information and make conclusions based on several different spots in a sophisticated piece of text.

 When answering an inference question, you have to *trust the passage*—in other words, approach the question knowing that the details in the passage will prove your inference, and therefore one of the answer choices, is correct.

Let's take a look at a sample Humanities passage and explore how inference questions might factor in on test day. This is excerpted from Ralph Waldo Emerson's philosophy essay, "Beauty."

Beauty

A nobler want of man is served by nature, namely, the love of Beauty.

The ancient Greeks called the world κοσμος [kosmos], beauty.
Such is the constitution of all things, or such the plastic power of the
5   human eye, that the primary forms, as the sky, the mountain, the
tree, the animal, give us a delight in and for themselves; a pleasure
arising from outline, color, motion, and grouping. This seems partly
owing to the eye itself. The eye is the best of artists. By the mutual
action of its structure and of the laws of light, perspective is produced,
10 which integrates every mass of objects, of what character soever,
into a well colored and shaded globe, so that where the particular
objects are mean and unaffecting, the landscape which they compose,
is round and symmetrical. And as the eye is the best composer, so
light is the first of painters. There is no object so foul that intense
15 light will not make beautiful. And the stimulus it affords to the sense,
and a sort of infinitude which it hath, like space and time, make all

matter gay. Even the corpse has its own beauty. But besides this general grace diffused over nature, almost all the individual forms are agreeable to the eye, as is proved by our endless imitations of
20 some of them, as the acorn, the grape, the pine-cone, the wheat-ear, the egg, the wings and forms of most birds, the lion's claw, the serpent, the butterfly, sea-shells, flames, clouds, buds, leaves, and the forms of many trees, as the palm.

For better consideration, we may distribute the aspects of Beauty
25 in a threefold manner.

1. First, the simple perception of natural forms is a delight. The influence of the forms and actions in nature, is so needful to man, that, in its lowest functions, it seems to lie on the confines of commodity and beauty. To the body and mind which have been cramped
30 by noxious work or company, nature is medicinal and restores their tone. The tradesman, the attorney comes out of the din and craft of the street, and sees the sky and the woods, and is a man again. In their eternal calm, he finds himself. The health of the eye seems to demand a horizon. We are never tired, so long as we can see far enough.

35 But in other hours, Nature satisfies by its loveliness, and without any mixture of corporeal benefit. I see the spectacle of morning from the hill-top over against my house, from day-break to sun-rise, with emotions which an angel might share. The long slender bars of cloud float like fishes in the sea of crimson light. From the earth, as a shore,
40 I look out into that silent sea. I seem to partake its rapid transformations: the active enchantment reaches my dust, and I dilate and conspire with the morning wind. How does Nature deify us with a few and cheap elements! Give me health and a day, and I will make the pomp of emperors ridiculous. The dawn is my Assyria; the sun-set
45 and moon-rise my Paphos, and unimaginable realms of faerie; broad noon shall be my England of the senses and the understanding; the night shall be my Germany of mystic philosophy and dreams.

Not less excellent, except for our less susceptibility in the afternoon, was the charm, last evening, of a January sunset. The
50 western clouds divided and subdivided themselves into pink flakes modulated with tints of unspeakable softness; and the air had so much life and sweetness, that it was a pain to come within doors. What was it that nature would say? Was there no meaning in the live repose of the valley behind the mill, and which Homer or Shakespeare
55 could not reform for me in words? The leafless trees become spires of flame in the sunset, with the blue east for their back-ground, and the stars of the dead calices of flowers, and every withered stem and stubble rimed with frost, contribute something to the mute music.

The inhabitants of cities suppose that the country landscape is
60 pleasant only half the year. I please myself with the graces of the
winter scenery, and believe that we are as much touched by it as by
the genial influences of summer. To the attentive eye, each moment
of the year has its own beauty, and in the same field, it beholds, every
hour, a picture which was never seen before, and which shall never
65 be seen again. The heavens change every moment, and reflect their
glory or gloom on the plains beneath. The state of the crop in the
surrounding farms alters the expression of the earth from week to
week. The succession of native plants in the pastures and roadsides,
which makes the silent clock by which time tells the summer hours,
70 will make even the divisions of the day sensible to a keen observer.
The tribes of birds and insects, like the plants punctual to their time,
follow each other, and the year has room for all. By water-courses,
the variety is greater. In July, the blue pontederia or pickerel-weed
blooms in large beds in the shallow parts of our pleasant river, and
75 swarms with yellow butterflies in continual motion. Art cannot rival
this pomp of purple and gold. Indeed the river is a perpetual gala,
and boasts each month a new ornament.

But this beauty of Nature which is seen and felt as beauty, is
the least part. The shows of day, the dewy morning, the rainbow,
80 mountains, orchards in blossom, stars, moonlight, shadows in still
water, and the like, if too eagerly hunted, become shows merely, and
mock us with their unreality. Go out of the house to see the moon,
and 't is mere tinsel; it will not please as when its light shines upon
your necessary journey. The beauty that shimmers in the yellow
85 afternoons of October, who ever could clutch it? Go forth to find it,
and it is gone: 't is only a mirage as you look from the windows of
diligence.

This is a long and fairly complex passage. Also, because it's a personal opinion essay
exploring philosophical ideas, there aren't many specific data points to hang on to. Your
approach for passages like this should be to make notes (mental or pencil) on the usual
suspects: topic, main themes, any points that seem to be supporting those. You should
also make notes on general tone and imagery … think of them as breadcrumbs to find
your way back through when you're working on the questions.

So, what kind of advanced inference questions can you expect with a passage like this?
You'll likely be asked to draw conclusions about themes or the author's purposes. Let's
take a look at how to tackle these with an example.

From the passage, it can reasonably be inferred that the author believes which of the following?

F. Natural beauty is superior to artificial beauty.
G. Outdoor beauty can only be found in summer.
H. One can only find beauty in nature.
J. Beauty doesn't exist in nature without humans.

First, it's important to note that the question itself doesn't give you any landmarks—no line references, or even a paragraph reference to orient you to the right spot. This means you'll need to make a general assessment, rather than a pinpoint statement. Let's go back to our questions for analyzing Literary Narrative/Prose Fiction and Humanities passages.

Question 1: *What is the question asking?* This question is asking you to make a conclusion about the author's perspective and rephrase it.

Question 2: *Can you eliminate any of the choices?* Eliminating choices is very difficult with such a general question unless there's an obviously wrong answer. Quickly skim the choices to see if any of them just feel wrong based on your initial read. In this case, choice J is a red flag—the author spends a lot of time talking about natural beauty that has nothing to do with humans, so this is unlikely to be the answer.

Question 3: *Which answer choice fits?* Try reading the first sentence of each paragraph in a long passage like this one. Doing so can be helpful in helping you ballpark where each answer choice might be found. For example, the first sentence of the fourth paragraph is, "First, the simple perception of natural forms is a delight." Hmm, that seems very similar to choice F, doesn't it? Let's look at some other first sentences. Paragraph 5: "But in other hours, Nature satisfies by its loveliness, and without any mixture of corporeal benefit." This one suggests that nature is beautiful without human intervention—which is the opposite of choice J. The first sentence of the seventh paragraph: "The inhabitants of cities suppose that the country landscape is pleasant only half the year." This doesn't directly relate to any of the answer choices, but it does tell you that the paragraph is about seasonal beauty, so it's a prime candidate to find information about choice G. In the paragraph, the author talks about year-round beauty, so that basically eliminates choice G. That leaves choice H. There's nothing in the passage that especially supports or refutes this one—but remember, if you don't see evidence in the passage, you don't have evidence to back up your answer. It's too vague. This leaves F as the best answer choice in the field. **The correct answer is F.**

One way to approach very general inference questions is to work through the other big-picture questions first. That way, you've got a good sense of what's going on in the passage, and that might uncover insights that will help you answer the question.

Now use the sample passage to answer two inference questions on your own.

. . . .

Beauty

A nobler want of man is served by nature, namely, the love of Beauty.

The ancient Greeks called the world κοσμος [kosmos], beauty. Such is the constitution of all things, or such the plastic power of the
5   human eye, that the primary forms, as the sky, the mountain, the tree, the animal, give us a delight in and for themselves; a pleasure arising from outline, color, motion, and grouping. This seems partly owing to the eye itself. The eye is the best of artists. By the mutual action of its structure and of the laws of light, perspective is produced,
10 which integrates every mass of objects, of what character soever, into a well colored and shaded globe, so that where the particular objects are mean and unaffecting, the landscape which they compose, is round and symmetrical. And as the eye is the best composer, so light is the first of painters. There is no object so foul that intense
15 light will not make beautiful. And the stimulus it affords to the sense, and a sort of infinitude which it hath, like space and time, make all matter gay. Even the corpse has its own beauty. But besides this general grace diffused over nature, almost all the individual forms are agreeable to the eye, as is proved by our endless imitations of
20 some of them, as the acorn, the grape, the pine-cone, the wheat-ear, the egg, the wings and forms of most birds, the lion's claw, the serpent, the butterfly, sea-shells, flames, clouds, buds, leaves, and the forms of many trees, as the palm.

For better consideration, we may distribute the aspects of Beauty
25 in a threefold manner.

1. First, the simple perception of natural forms is a delight. The influence of the forms and actions in nature, is so needful to man, that, in its lowest functions, it seems to lie on the confines of commodity and beauty. To the body and mind which have been cramped
30 by noxious work or company, nature is medicinal and restores their tone. The tradesman, the attorney comes out of the din and craft of the street, and sees the sky and the woods, and is a man again. In their eternal calm, he finds himself. The health of the eye seems to demand a horizon. We are never tired, so long as we can see far enough.

35   But in other hours, Nature satisfies by its loveliness, and without any mixture of corporeal benefit. I see the spectacle of morning from the hill-top over against my house, from day-break to sun-rise, with emotions which an angel might share. The long slender bars of cloud float like fishes in the sea of crimson light. From the earth, as a shore,

40 I look out into that silent sea. I seem to partake its rapid transformations: the active enchantment reaches my dust, and I dilate and
conspire with the morning wind. How does Nature deify us with a
few and cheap elements! Give me health and a day, and I will make
the pomp of emperors ridiculous. The dawn is my Assyria; the sun-set
45 and moon-rise my Paphos, and unimaginable realms of faerie; broad
noon shall be my England of the senses and the understanding; the
night shall be my Germany of mystic philosophy and dreams.

Not less excellent, except for our less susceptibility in the
afternoon, was the charm, last evening, of a January sunset. The
50 western clouds divided and subdivided themselves into pink flakes
modulated with tints of unspeakable softness; and the air had so
much life and sweetness, that it was a pain to come within doors.
What was it that nature would say? Was there no meaning in the live
repose of the valley behind the mill, and which Homer or Shakespeare
55 could not reform for me in words? The leafless trees become spires
of flame in the sunset, with the blue east for their back-ground, and
the stars of the dead calices of flowers, and every withered stem and
stubble rimed with frost, contribute something to the mute music.

The inhabitants of cities suppose that the country landscape is
60 pleasant only half the year. I please myself with the graces of the
winter scenery, and believe that we are as much touched by it as by
the genial influences of summer. To the attentive eye, each moment
of the year has its own beauty, and in the same field, it beholds, every
hour, a picture which was never seen before, and which shall never
65 be seen again. The heavens change every moment, and reflect their
glory or gloom on the plains beneath. The state of the crop in the
surrounding farms alters the expression of the earth from week to
week. The succession of native plants in the pastures and roadsides,
which makes the silent clock by which time tells the summer hours,
70 will make even the divisions of the day sensible to a keen observer.
The tribes of birds and insects, like the plants punctual to their time,
follow each other, and the year has room for all. By water-courses,
the variety is greater. In July, the blue pontederia or pickerel-weed
blooms in large beds in the shallow parts of our pleasant river, and
75 swarms with yellow butterflies in continual motion. Art cannot rival
this pomp of purple and gold. Indeed the river is a perpetual gala,
and boasts each month a new ornament.

But this beauty of Nature which is seen and felt as beauty, is
the least part. The shows of day, the dewy morning, the rainbow,
80 mountains, orchards in blossom, stars, moonlight, shadows in still
water, and the like, if too eagerly hunted, become shows merely, and
mock us with their unreality. Go out of the house to see the moon,

and 't is mere tinsel; it will not please as when its light shines upon your necessary journey. The beauty that shimmers in the yellow
85 afternoons of October, who ever could clutch it? Go forth to find it, and it is gone: 't is only a mirage as you look from the windows of diligence.

By referring to "the tradesman, the attorney" (line 31), it can reasonably be inferred that the author's purpose in the essay is to:

F. make everyone go outside.
G. show that humans can be inspired by the beauty of nature.
H. show that city-dwellers have no appreciation for natural beauty.
J. show that humans are destroying natural beauty with their city ways.

The correct answer is G. Choice F is incorrect because the author doesn't take a particular stand on what people should do—he talks generally about natural beauty and its ability to make people feel better. Choice G is correct because this reference to an individual (Emerson is referring to the attorney as a tradesman) who lives in the artificial chaos of the city suggests that nature's beauty is available to anyone who seeks it. Choice H is incorrect because the author is saying the opposite—that anyone can find beauty outside of the artificial world. Choice J is incorrect because there's no information that supports any kind of accusation of ruining beauty.

Based on the passage, it can reasonably be inferred that the author's purpose is:

A. comparing and contrasting different kinds of beauty.
B. exploring the beauty is his own backyard.
C. preventing others from experiencing nature's beauty for themselves.
D. joining him on a nature walk.

The correct answer is A. The author mentions in lines 24–25 that for better consideration, we may distribute the aspects of Beauty in a threefold manner. This suggests that even if you don't see the comparison points in this excerpt, he plans to compare the different aspects of beauty. Even within the excerpt, he's comparing natural beauty with "the din and craft of the street," so there are several levels of beauty comparison going on. Choice A is the best answer of the group. Choice B is incorrect because the author specifically mentions that all natural forms are beautiful, so this isn't limited to what he himself can see. Choice C is incorrect because in the fourth paragraph, the author emphasizes that anyone can and should enjoy beauty. Choice D is incorrect because there's no invitation, implied or otherwise, in the passage.

RELATIONSHIP QUESTIONS

Relationship questions make you draw conclusions about characters, themes, or events in a passage and determine how they're related. The ACT is primarily concerned with two kinds of relationships in the passages:

1. Sequence of events
2. Cause-and-effect

On easier questions, both of these may be fairly clear—either the passage will be laid out in an approximately chronological way or events will be directly related to other events. Where things get a little trickier is the complex passages or where the information is much more subtly written.

Let's take this excerpt from Jane Austen's novel *Emma* as an example for identifying relationships in a complex passage.

> Emma Woodhouse, handsome, clever, and rich, with a comfortable home and happy disposition, seemed to unite some of the best blessings of existence; and had lived nearly twenty-one years in the world with very little to distress or vex her.
>
> 5   She was the youngest of the two daughters of a most affectionate, indulgent father; and had, in consequence of her sister's marriage, been mistress of his house from a very early period. Her mother had died too long ago for her to have more than an indistinct remembrance of her caresses; and her place had been supplied by an
> 10   excellent woman as governess, who had fallen little short of a mother in affection.
>
>   Sixteen years had Miss Taylor been in Mr. Woodhouse's family, less as a governess than a friend, very fond of both daughters, but particularly of Emma. Between them it was more the intimacy of
> 15   sisters. Even before Miss Taylor had ceased to hold the nominal office of governess, the mildness of her temper had hardly allowed her to impose any restraint; and the shadow of authority being now long passed away, they had been living together as friend and friend very mutually attached, and Emma doing just what she liked; highly
> 20   esteeming Miss Taylor's judgment, but directed chiefly by her own.
>
>   The real evils, indeed, of Emma's situation were the power of having rather too much her own way, and a disposition to think a little too well of herself; these were the disadvantages which threatened alloy to her many enjoyments. The danger, however, was
> 25   at present so unperceived, that they did not by any means rank as misfortunes with her.
>
>   Sorrow came—a gentle sorrow—but not at all in the shape of any disagreeable consciousness.—Miss Taylor married. It was Miss Taylor's loss which first brought grief. It was on the wedding-day of

30 this beloved friend that Emma first sat in mournful thought of any continuance. The wedding over, and the bride-people gone, her father and herself were left to dine together, with no prospect of a third to cheer a long evening. Her father composed himself to sleep after dinner, as usual, and she had then only to sit and think of what *35* she had lost.

The event had every promise of happiness for her friend. Mr. Weston was a man of unexceptionable character, easy fortune, suitable age, and pleasant manners; and there was some satisfaction in considering with what self-denying, generous friendship she had always *40* wished and promoted the match; but it was a black morning's work for her. The want of Miss Taylor would be felt every hour of every day. She recalled her past kindness—the kindness, the affection of sixteen years—how she had taught and how she had played with her from five years old—how she had devoted all her powers to attach and *45* amuse her in health—and how nursed her through the various illnesses of childhood. A large debt of gratitude was owing here; but the intercourse of the last seven years, the equal footing and perfect unreserve which had soon followed Isabella's marriage, on their being left to each other, was yet a dearer, tenderer recollection. She had *50* been a friend and companion such as few possessed: intelligent, well-informed, useful, gentle, knowing all the ways of the family, interested in all its concerns, and peculiarly interested in herself, in every pleasure, every scheme of hers—one to whom she could speak every thought as it arose, and who had such an affection for her as *55* could never find fault.

How was she to bear the change?—It was true that her friend was going only half a mile from them; but Emma was aware that great must be the difference between a Mrs. Weston, only half a mile from them, and a Miss Taylor in the house; and with all her advantages, *60* natural and domestic, she was now in great danger of suffering from intellectual solitude. She dearly loved her father, but he was no companion for her. He could not meet her in conversation, rational or playful.

The evil of the actual disparity in their ages (and Mr. Woodhouse *65* had not married early) was much increased by his constitution and habits; for having been a valetudinarian all his life, without activity of mind or body, he was a much older man in ways than in years; and though everywhere beloved for the friendliness of his heart and his amiable temper, his talents could not have recommended him at *70* any time.

Her sister, though comparatively but little removed by matrimony, being settled in London, only sixteen miles off, was much beyond her daily reach; and many a long October and November evening

must be struggled through at Hartfield, before Christmas brought
75 the next visit from Isabella and her husband, and their little children,
to fill the house, and give her pleasant society again.

Let's look at chronological events in this passage. In this excerpt, the point where the narrator starts the story is not necessarily where the events start. When the chronology is unclear and you're tasked with answering a question about the order in which events happen, it can be helpful to make quick margin notes as you're reading through the passage. So let's say the question is:

Whose wedding came first in the passage?

    A. Emma's
    B. Miss Taylor's
    C. Isabella's
    D. Mr. Woodhouse's

You can look at the passage logically and skim for mentions of weddings or marriages. Emma is single and lives at home with her father, so you can eliminate choice A right away. The first actual marriage mentioned is Emma's sister's. The next is Miss Taylor's, which occurred well after the sister married and moved out of the house. But the sneaky one is Mr. Woodhouse's marriage—the author drops in mention of his marriage in the eighth paragraph (lines 64–65) as a reference to Mr. Woodhouse's age. Mr. Woodhouse's wedding preceded both Emma's sister's and Miss Taylor's wedding. **The correct answer is D.**

The most challenging ACT questions may require you to sift for "blink and you'll miss it" details, so always be extra sure of what the question is asking and what keywords you can use to look for it.

It's also important to note that more complex passages may lay out information in a sequence based on priority or significance, rather than factual order of events. The excerpt from *Emma* does this—it unfolds the information to illustrate Emma's current state of mind, rather than listing the events like:

    1. Emma's mother passes away, leaving her father, sister, and governess as her only family.
    2. Emma's sister Isabella gets married and moves away.
    3. Miss Taylor gets married and moves away.
    4. Emma is now lonely as a result.

Instead, the passage starts midstream, after Miss Taylor's wedding, and unspools details in a way that shows how Emma arrived at this crisis in her young life.

Now let's look at some cause-and-effect elements from the passage. Cause-and-effect questions ask about the logical relationship between two characters, events, or arguments in a passage. In literary writing, authors often make subtle connections to establish a broader theme or create additional associations. On the ACT Reading test, these questions usually have key words and phrases like *in order to, due to, the reason for, because,* and similar phrases. Basic cause-and-effect questions will ask you to look for something directly stated in the passage. The more advanced questions will have you look for more subtle connections or ones that are implied rather than discussed head-on.

Some examples of cause-and-effect questions would be:

The passage indicates that Mary was unhappy because:

According to the passage, the reason for the party was most nearly:

The passage suggests that Aaron Burr's main reason for dueling with Alexander Hamilton was:

As with the sequence relationships, the most challenging cause-and-effect questions will take two paths: questions that make you dig for the information in a given passage, and questions that ask for clear cause-and effect-relationships to be identified in highly complex passages. Author Jane Austen was famous for the complicated relationships in her books, so let's take another look at *Emma* for a cause-and-effect question.

> Emma Woodhouse, handsome, clever, and rich, with a comfortable home and happy disposition, seemed to unite some of the best blessings of existence; and had lived nearly twenty-one years in the world with very little to distress or vex her.

5   She was the youngest of the two daughters of a most affectionate, indulgent father; and had, in consequence of her sister's marriage, been mistress of his house from a very early period. Her mother had died too long ago for her to have more than an indistinct remembrance of her caresses; and her place had been supplied by an
10   excellent woman as governess, who had fallen little short of a mother in affection.

> Sixteen years had Miss Taylor been in Mr. Woodhouse's family, less as a governess than a friend, very fond of both daughters, but particularly of Emma. Between them it was more the intimacy of
15   sisters. Even before Miss Taylor had ceased to hold the nominal office of governess, the mildness of her temper had hardly allowed her to impose any restraint; and the shadow of authority being now long passed away, they had been living together as friend and friend very mutually attached, and Emma doing just what she liked; highly
20   esteeming Miss Taylor's judgment, but directed chiefly by her own.

> The real evils, indeed, of Emma's situation were the power of having rather too much her own way, and a disposition to think a little too well of herself; these were the disadvantages which threatened alloy to her many enjoyments. The danger, however, was
25   at present so unperceived, that they did not by any means rank as misfortunes with her.

> Sorrow came—a gentle sorrow—but not at all in the shape of any disagreeable consciousness.—Miss Taylor married. It was Miss Taylor's loss which first brought grief. It was on the wedding-day of

30   this beloved friend that Emma first sat in mournful thought of any
continuance. The wedding over, and the bride-people gone, her
father and herself were left to dine together, with no prospect of a
third to cheer a long evening. Her father composed himself to sleep
after dinner, as usual, and she had then only to sit and think of what
35   she had lost.

The event had every promise of happiness for her friend. Mr.
Weston was a man of unexceptionable character, easy fortune, suitable
age, and pleasant manners; and there was some satisfaction in considering with what self-denying, generous friendship she had always
40   wished and promoted the match; but it was a black morning's work
for her. The want of Miss Taylor would be felt every hour of every day.
She recalled her past kindness—the kindness, the affection of sixteen
years—how she had taught and how she had played with her from
five years old—how she had devoted all her powers to attach and
45   amuse her in health—and how nursed her through the various illnesses of childhood. A large debt of gratitude was owing here; but
the intercourse of the last seven years, the equal footing and perfect
unreserve which had soon followed Isabella's marriage, on their being
left to each other, was yet a dearer, tenderer recollection. She had
50   been a friend and companion such as few possessed: intelligent,
well-informed, useful, gentle, knowing all the ways of the family,
interested in all its concerns, and peculiarly interested in herself, in
every pleasure, every scheme of hers—one to whom she could speak
every thought as it arose, and who had such an affection for her as
55   could never find fault.

How was she to bear the change?—It was true that her friend
was going only half a mile from them; but Emma was aware that
great must be the difference between a Mrs. Weston, only half a mile
from them, and a Miss Taylor in the house; and with all her advantages,
60   natural and domestic, she was now in great danger of suffering from
intellectual solitude. She dearly loved her father, but he was no
companion for her. He could not meet her in conversation, rational
or playful.

The evil of the actual disparity in their ages (and Mr. Woodhouse
65   had not married early) was much increased by his constitution and
habits; for having been a valetudinarian all his life, without activity
of mind or body, he was a much older man in ways than in years; and
though everywhere beloved for the friendliness of his heart and his
amiable temper, his talents could not have recommended him at
70   any time.

Her sister, though comparatively but little removed by matrimony,
being settled in London, only sixteen miles off, was much beyond
her daily reach; and many a long October and November evening

must be struggled through at Hartfield, before Christmas brought
75 the next visit from Isabella and her husband, and their little children,
to fill the house, and give her pleasant society again.

According to the passage, what does Emma perceive as her biggest source of unhappiness?

A. Miss Taylor getting married and moving away
B. Emma's father's inability to relate to her
C. Emma's tendency to have things her own way and her self-centeredness
D. Emma's sister's living in London

This is left very general—no line reference or even a paragraph reference. The attack plan for questions like this is similar to other ACT Reading test questions:

> **Question 1:** *What is the question asking?* It's important to read this one carefully—if you move fast, you could come away thinking that the question is asking you what Emma's biggest source of unhappiness is. In reality, it's asking you what Emma *thinks* her biggest source of unhappiness is. It's a subtle difference, but it produces an entirely different answer. (And remember, only one answer can be correct here.)

> **Question 2:** *Can you eliminate any of the choices?* There aren't any obvious false ones here, but from your first reading of the passage, you might recall that Emma is closer to Miss Taylor than her father or her sister Isabella, so you can tentatively cross out choices B and D. That leaves choices A and C.

> **Question 3:** *Which answer choice fits?* The narrator clearly states that Emma's biggest problem is really her own personality quirks. However, remember Question 1. Emma herself clearly believes that Miss Taylor's absence is her biggest problem, as suggested in sentences like, "The want of Miss Taylor would be felt every hour of every day." **The correct answer is A.**

Now use the excerpted passage to answer some relationship questions on your own.

· ·

Emma Woodhouse, handsome, clever, and rich, with a comfortable home and happy disposition, seemed to unite some of the best blessings of existence; and had lived nearly twenty-one years in the world with very little to distress or vex her.

5 She was the youngest of the two daughters of a most affectionate, indulgent father; and had, in consequence of her sister's marriage, been mistress of his house from a very early period. Her mother had died too long ago for her to have more than an indistinct remembrance of her caresses; and her place had been supplied by an
10 excellent woman as governess, who had fallen little short of a mother in affection.

Sixteen years had Miss Taylor been in Mr. Woodhouse's family, less as a governess than a friend, very fond of both daughters, but particularly of Emma. Between them it was more the intimacy of
15 sisters. Even before Miss Taylor had ceased to hold the nominal office of governess, the mildness of her temper had hardly allowed her to impose any restraint; and the shadow of authority being now long passed away, they had been living together as friend and friend very mutually attached, and Emma doing just what she liked; highly
20 esteeming Miss Taylor's judgment, but directed chiefly by her own.

The real evils, indeed, of Emma's situation were the power of having rather too much her own way, and a disposition to think a little too well of herself; these were the disadvantages which threatened alloy to her many enjoyments. The danger, however, was
25 at present so unperceived, that they did not by any means rank as misfortunes with her.

Sorrow came—a gentle sorrow—but not at all in the shape of any disagreeable consciousness.—Miss Taylor married. It was Miss Taylor's loss which first brought grief. It was on the wedding-day of
30 this beloved friend that Emma first sat in mournful thought of any continuance. The wedding over, and the bride-people gone, her father and herself were left to dine together, with no prospect of a third to cheer a long evening. Her father composed himself to sleep after dinner, as usual, and she had then only to sit and think of what
35 she had lost.

The event had every promise of happiness for her friend. Mr. Weston was a man of unexceptionable character, easy fortune, suitable age, and pleasant manners; and there was some satisfaction in considering with what self-denying, generous friendship she had always
40 wished and promoted the match; but it was a black morning's work for her. The want of Miss Taylor would be felt every hour of every day. She recalled her past kindness—the kindness, the affection of sixteen years—how she had taught and how she had played with her from five years old—how she had devoted all her powers to attach and
45 amuse her in health—and how nursed her through the various illnesses of childhood. A large debt of gratitude was owing here; but the intercourse of the last seven years, the equal footing and perfect unreserve which had soon followed Isabella's marriage, on their being left to each other, was yet a dearer, tenderer recollection. She had
50 been a friend and companion such as few possessed: intelligent, well-informed, useful, gentle, knowing all the ways of the family, interested in all its concerns, and peculiarly interested in herself, in every pleasure, every scheme of hers—one to whom she could speak every thought as it arose, and who had such an affection for her as
55 could never find fault.

How was she to bear the change?—It was true that her friend was going only half a mile from them; but Emma was aware that great must be the difference between a Mrs. Weston, only half a mile from them, and a Miss Taylor in the house; and with all her advantages, natural and domestic, she was now in great danger of suffering from intellectual solitude. She dearly loved her father, but he was no companion for her. He could not meet her in conversation, rational or playful.

60

The evil of the actual disparity in their ages (and Mr. Woodhouse had not married early) was much increased by his constitution and habits; for having been a valetudinarian all his life, without activity of mind or body, he was a much older man in ways than in years; and though everywhere beloved for the friendliness of his heart and his amiable temper, his talents could not have recommended him at any time.

65

70

Her sister, though comparatively but little removed by matrimony, being settled in London, only sixteen miles off, was much beyond her daily reach; and many a long October and November evening must be struggled through at Hartfield, before Christmas brought the next visit from Isabella and her husband, and their little children, to fill the house, and give her pleasant society again.

75

The passage suggests that Emma's relationship with her father was distant due to:

F. her closer relationship with Miss Taylor.
G. his preference for her sister Isabella.
H. the early death of her mother.
J. the large difference in their ages and personalities.

The correct answer is J. Choice F is incorrect because although the narrator suggests that Emma and Miss Taylor's relationship is *close* to a mother-daughter relationship, there's no indication that Emma values this parental relationship over her father. Choice G is incorrect because there's nothing in the passage that suggests Isabelle is the favorite daughter. Choice H is incorrect because there's no indication that Emma is angry or blames her father for the early loss of her mother (further suggested by lines like, "Her mother had died too long ago for her to have more than an indistinct remembrance of her caresses"). Choice J is correct because the passage provides the most evidence for this option, with statements like, "He could not meet her in conversation, rational or playful," (lines 62–63) and "The evil of the actual disparity in their ages (and Mr. Woodhouse had not married early) was much increased by his constitution and habits" (line 64).

According to the passage, which of the following events has happened most recently?

A. Emma's mother's death
B. Isabella's wedding
C. Mrs. Weston moving away
D. Isabella's visit from London

The correct answer is C. Choice A is easily expendable—it's clear at several points in the passage that Emma's mother passed away many years ago. Choice B is a little murkier, but the second paragraph suggests that Isabella's marriage left Emma and Miss Taylor living at home, prior to Miss Taylor's wedding. Choice D is incorrect because Isabella's visit is something that Emma is looking forward to and hasn't yet happened (the question uses the past tense). So choice C is the most recent event that happened—but you need to be careful because Mrs. Weston is actually another way for the author to refer to Miss Taylor, so if you missed that detail in the passage you might skip right over the correct answer.

Based on the passage, which event caused Emma to experience her first crisis?

    F.   Miss Taylor's engagement
    G.   Miss Taylor's wedding day
    H.   Her sister's wedding
    J.   Her father's habit of going to bed right after dinner

The correct answer is G. It's not until the sixth paragraph (lines 29–31) that the author specifically mentions that "it was on the wedding-day of this beloved friend that Emma first sat in mournful thought of any continuance." This question requires you to take note of all the possible things that are causing Emma's grief and put them in order to make sure that the timing answers the question. Choice F is incorrect because the seventh paragraph mentions that previously, Emma had supported and "promoted" the relationship between Miss Taylor and Mr. Weston. Choice H is incorrect because although Emma clearly wishes her sister were closer, the relationship with Miss Taylor is presented as the more important one in this excerpt. Choice J is incorrect because the father's lack of socializing is presented as a reason for why Emma's father isn't an ideal friend, but in itself it isn't an event that causes Emma to be depressed.

· ·

Now that you've had practice with some of the toughest ACT Reading concepts that may come your way on test day, you're in great shape! The more you practice, the more you'll be able to navigate the most challenging questions, and the more naturally the close reading strategies will become. Taking lots of practice tests is key, but don't forget to read, read, read material from all sorts of genres and practice your literary deconstruction skills as well. Good luck!

SUMMING IT UP

- **The Literary Narrative, Prose Fiction, and Humanities passages make up half of the ACT Reading test.** Unlike the Social Studies and Natural Sciences passages, which tend to contain hard information, the Literary Narrative/Prose Fiction and Humanities passages focus on more figurative elements and bigger themes in the writing.

- **Paired passages are among the most difficult ACT Reading passages**, because you need to be able to track down information in two different passages and make coherent conclusions about and comparisons between themes and characters. The most efficient way to attack these is to answer the single-passage questions first, then work on the questions that require you to look at both passages.

- **Inference questions ask you to use passage context and your own judgment to draw conclusions about the passage.** Inference questions can be found at all difficulty levels and in all passage types, but the most advanced ones can usually be found in complex Literary Narrative/Prose Fiction and Humanities passages. For inference questions, make sure your answer choice is *fully* supported by the passage. Don't let "most nearly" questions trick you into a "close enough" answer.

- **Relationship questions ask you to draw conclusions about underlying information in a passage**: sequence of events, cause-and-effect relationships, and how characters or themes are connected. As you read the passage, try to keep track of what happens when and what relationships the characters have so that you can easily go back and find evidence in the passage.

- **Always, always read the question carefully so that you know what it's asking.** The most advanced questions may throw in subtle cues or wordings that could lead you straight to the wrong answer choice.

CHAPTER 8
DATA REPRESENTATION:
INTERPRETING AND APPLYING
EXPERIMENTAL RESULTS

OVERVIEW

- About Data Representation Questions

- Data Representation: Getting Advanced

- Summing It Up

Data Representation questions make up at least one third of the ACT Science test, usually comprising 30–40 percent of the total number of questions you'll see in this section. These questions are easy to pick out because you will always be provided with an introductory paragraph, followed by a graph or table. It will be your job to read through the experimental details, identify the tested variables, comprehend and interpret the data on display, and draw conclusions from the provided data.

Such skills are required for all Data Representation questions, and as such, they will receive some attention in this chapter. However, we're aiming for the sky here and want to be able to conquer the most difficult questions that could show up on the ACT Science test. In order to accomplish this, we will additionally discuss strategies for overcoming an array of obstacles that elevate the difficulty of the passages and questions you might see.

ABOUT DATA REPRESENTATION QUESTIONS

Since you aren't expected to be an expert in every science field covered on the ACT, you can expect the written introduction for a Data Representation question set to provide you with enough details and key terminology so that you will be able to figure out what is actually happening scientifically. Beyond this introductory paragraph (or paragraphs), the most important part of a Data Representation question set will be the figures. As the name "Data Representation" indicates, these question types will primarily focus on your ability to analyze data. A standard Data Representation passage will be followed by five questions that will test your ability to:

- Understand data

- Analyze data tables and graphs

- Draw conclusions based on those data tables and graphs
- Assess the validity and reliability of the data
- Consider future experimental directions that can be taken based on the data

Practicing questions of this type will increase your familiarity with the different kinds of Data Representation passages and questions you might see, and by the time you're ready to take the exam, you will be comfortable with the format and have some idea of how to approach any kind of experimental topic, data table, or graph you might come across.

To start off, we will briefly review the skills we've just mentioned that are essential for answering any Data Representation question, but then we'll delve more deeply into how you can approach the very toughest questions you might encounter on the ACT Science test.

ELEMENTS OF A DATA REPRESENTATION QUESTION

Regardless of the kind of scientific topic or data you're dealing with, the first thing you need to do when you encounter a Data Representation passage is identify the scientific question that is being asked. Sometimes, this question will be stated directly in the introductory text, but often you may have to use the provided figure to determine the question of interest. After all, if you don't know the purpose of a particular experiment, how can you extract meaningful patterns and conclusions from its data?

Here are a few examples of the language an ACT Science passage will use when presenting a scientific question:

> A group of students wanted to test the effect of pressure on the rate of oxygen consumption in a combustion reaction.

> A scientist decided to determine the frequency of earthquakes in Kenya at various distances from the equator.

> A student measured the rate of pea plant growth for plants grown at several different temperatures.

The written introduction is placed first in the passage with good reason: You should always start here before attempting to analyze data. The introduction will give you details that might not necessarily be included in the provided tables or graphs, and the scientific question is usually included here.

Additionally, the introductory text might include a hypothesis, an educated prediction about the outcome of an experiment. You may not always find a clear scientific question or hypothesis in the text itself, however; often, this means the ensuing questions will ask you to determine one or both of these based on the data. Most of the time, you will see at least one of these statements in the introduction.

If it is presented in the passage, here's what a hypothesis might look like:

The student predicted that larger planetary size would result in lower measured body weights of humans due to differences in gravitational acceleration.

A greater mass of product was expected to be generated as the limiting reagent concentration increased for a given chemical reaction that runs to completion.

 As you peruse the introduction, it may help to underline or circle key words that you'll want to refer back to later when you're answering the questions.

As you assess a passage, you will also want to keep an eye out for and identify the independent variable and the dependent variable. The **independent variable** is the experimental condition that the scientist alters during the experiment, and the **dependent variable** is the experimental condition that the scientist is measuring.

The students measured the UV-vis signal at 500 nm using a spectrophotometer. (dependent variable)

A group of scientists wanted to study the effect of average weekly temperature (independent variable) on the population of Plant X (dependent variable) in a given forest plot area.

You might also want to make note of any **constants**, which are conditions that remain the same in all experimental trials, as well as **controls**. A **positive control** gives an expected positive result for the phenomenon of interest, while a **negative control** gives an expected negative result for the phenomenon of interest. Controls are used as points of comparison for the experimental trials and help to minimize the effects of outside variables. For example, if one is testing the effect of a potential antibiotic on bacterial growth on a plate, a positive control would be a plate containing an antibiotic known to kill the bacteria, while a negative control would be a plate containing no antibiotic at all.

Let's see what this would look like in a passage:

A scientist wanted to study the effect of a pesticide on pea plant growth. She grew three pea plants at the same temperature and with equivalent amounts of sunlight and water. The first plant received a high concentration of pesticide, the second plant received a low concentration of pesticide, and the third plant received no pesticide.

The third plant is the negative control because the pesticide is absent, and the plant should grow normally. The temperature, amount of sunlight, and amount of water are all constants because they are identical among all experimental runs.

If the written introduction does not clearly identify these variables, or if there is unfamiliar terminology in the text, any figure you're given can help you out tremendously. A well-constructed data table will provide the independent and dependent variables in the headers, while a well-constructed graph or scatterplot will provide these variables on the axes. The y-axis (the vertical axis) will usually be the dependent variable, while the x-axis (the horizontal axis) will usually be the independent variable. While it is certainly useful to understand the written introduction to help you to understand the specifics of the experiment, the diagrams and figures often provide more than enough information to give you a solid foundation upon which to begin your data analysis.

For example, take a look at this graph, in which scientists examined 313 children in Madagascar and plotted their left ventricular mass index (LVMI) as a function of their body mass index (BMI). The BMI percentile is the independent variable. It appears on the x-axis. The LVMI is the dependent variable. It appears on the y-axis and is the variable that is being measured with respect to the BMI.

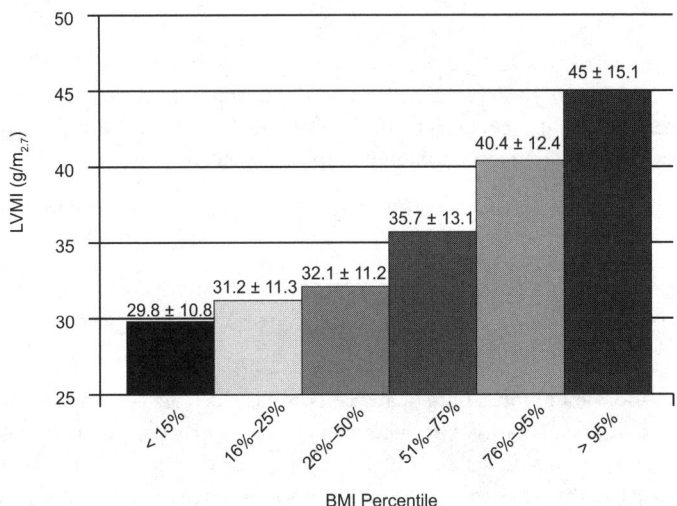

Figure 1

IMAGES IN DATA REPRESENTATION QUESTIONS

Every Data Representation passage you encounter will include a data table or a graph to analyze. While data tables are often straightforward with labeled headers and column organization, graphs are much more varied in terms of how they present data. With occasional exceptions (i.e., a pie chart), a graph consists of a horizontal x-axis and a vertical y-axis (and rarely, for 3D graphs, a z-axis that emerges from the page directly at you).

Most of the graphs you see on the ACT Science test will be linear functions, which are straight lines, or exponential functions, which are curved lines. Linear functions that increase from left to right have positive slopes, while those that decrease from left to right have negative slopes. A perfectly horizontal line has a slope of zero, while a perfectly vertical line is usually described as "undefined" or "infinite." Less commonly seen on the ACT Science test are parabolas (u-shaped graphs) and hyperbolas (curved graphs that approach, but never quite reach, invisible asymptote lines).

Questions based on provided graphs may ask you to identify dependent or independent variables, or you may even be given a data table and asked to predict the shape of the corresponding graph.

Let's look at an example.

· ·

Consider the data table below.

Table 1	
Variable X	**Variable Y**
0	3
1	6
2	12
3	24
4	48

With respect to Variable X, Variable Y:

    A.   increases linearly.
    B.   decreases linearly.
    C.   increases exponentially.
    D.   decreases exponentially.

The correct answer is C. The values of Variable Y increase as the values of Variable X increase, allowing us to rule out choices B and D right away. The values of Variable Y do not increase by the same number per Variable X interval, so the data does not exhibit a linear increase. The numbers do double per Variable X interval. Therefore, the data increases exponentially.

· ·

DRAWING CONCLUSIONS

Once you've analyzed the data table or graph and determined its purpose, you will almost always be required to use the figure to answer questions or draw conclusions. For this reason, it is important to make note of patterns and trends as you examine the provided data. Questions might ask you to describe trends, use any observed patterns to predict results that have not been provided, or apply the data to a different but relevant situation.

For example, look at the following question.

. . . .

A group of students wanted to look at the relationship between pressure and temperature in a gas sample. Using an enclosed, constant-volume container, the students added a known quantity of argon gas. The students then adjusted the container to a range of temperatures and measured the pressure at each temperature. The data is displayed in Figure 1.

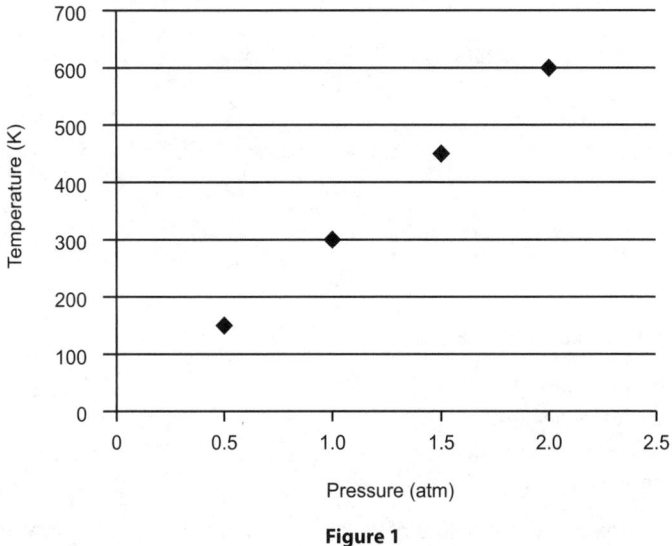

Figure 1

Which of the following conclusions can be drawn based on the presented data?

F. Increasing the pressure of a constant-temperature gas system results in a volume increase.

G. Increasing the pressure of a constant-temperature gas system results in a volume decrease.

H. Increasing the temperature of a constant-volume gas system results in a pressure increase.

J. Increasing the temperature of a constant-volume gas system results in a pressure decrease.

The correct answer is H. The volume remained constant, which allows for the elimination of choices F and G. Between choices H and J, choice J is correct because it describes the trend as a positive correlation in which temperature increases as pressure increases.

. . . .

 Trends in data tend to be fairly straightforward, as the test makers want to test your analytical ability, not confuse you.

Aside from recognizing patterns and drawing conclusions, may also be asked to critically assess the validity and reliability of the presented data. Such analyses are based more in statistics than in scientific content, but you won't have to be a math genius to tackle these kinds of questions.

The two main ways you can assess data validity are by examining accuracy and precision. **Accuracy** describes how close a particular number or measurement agrees with a known value or standard. For example, if a scientist measures the mass and volume of a given liquid to determine its density at 25°C, the scientist can compare his or her final calculated density to actual known values determined by other scientists in the past. Numerically, one can express accuracy using a percent error calculation:

$$\text{Percent Error} = \left| \frac{\text{Known Value} - \text{Measured Value}}{\text{Known Value}} \right| \times 100\%$$

If several trials of the same experiment are performed, the measured value you should use here is the mean, or average, value of the trials:

$$\text{Average} = \frac{\text{Sum of Values from All Trials}}{\text{Number of Trials}}$$

In many scientific experiments, however, you will not know an actual value, so you may not always be able to determine accuracy, as scientific research aims to discover new information that is currently undiscovered. As such, known values are not always available.

See if you can answer a question of this type.

· ·

A student performs a chemical reaction with known amounts of reactants. Based on the masses he uses, he uses stoichiometry to calculate a theoretical yield of 40 g, the yield of product that would be obtained if the reaction ran to completion perfectly, without any errors. He performs the experiment twice and obtains 25 g and 35 g of product in the trials. What is the percent error for this experiment?

A. 10%
B. 25%
C. 55%
D. 75%

The correct answer is B. The first step is to find the average product mass between the two trials:

$$\text{Mean} = \frac{25\,g + 35\,g}{2} = 30\,g.$$

The second step is to calculate the percent error:

$$\% \text{ Error} = \frac{40\,g - 30\,g}{40\,g} \times 100\% = 25\%.$$

. . . .

While you may not always be able to determine accuracy, you *can* always determine precision when several trials are performed of the same experiment. **Precision** describes how close the measured values in a repeated set are to each other. You can often tell if data is precise simply by looking at it. If the numbers you measure for several trials of the same experiment are close to another, your data is probably precise. On the other hand, if the numbers don't agree and are not close to one another at all, the data is probably not precise.

Obtaining consistent numbers when you repeat the same experiment multiple times is important because it confirms that your result is not simply a fluke. Precision can be measured numerically by calculating standard deviation, which indicates how far a set of measured numbers are from their average and is therefore a measure of data precision. While you will certainly not have to calculate standard deviations, you should know that a low standard deviation indicates higher precision, while a high standard deviation indicates a lower one. Data is often considered to be more valid when they are precise, namely when the standard deviation is as low as possible. A trial in a set of the same repeated experiment that yields a very different result from the rest is called an **outlier**; you can usually conclude that an error occurred in this trial because the result was so different from the others, and questions may ask you to predict an error that might have caused the outlier.

Take a look at the following example.

. . . .

All of the following data sets have the same mean value of 50. Which data set will have the smallest standard deviation?

    F.   25, 50, 75
    G.   40, 50, 60
    H.   10, 70, 70
    J.   44, 52, 54

The correct answer is J. The data set with the smallest standard deviation would be the most precise and would therefore have a set of numbers that are very close to one another. The data set in which the numbers are closest together is the data set in choice J.

. . . .

Aside from assessing accuracy and precision, you may be asked to assess data validity in other ways. For example, you might be asked to identify potential design flaws in the experiment or chosen mode of data presentation, or you might be asked to predict the effect an error would have on the results (or to predict an error that might lead to a certain result).

Almost always, one scientific research experiment will pose additional questions for exploration, and new experiments can then be performed either as an extension of the original experiment or to test an entirely new variable related to the topic of interest. Data Representation questions may ask you to suggest an additional experiment by stating a goal, and your job will be to choose the answer that will accomplish this provided goal. Remember, it is always important to identify the dependent and independent variables for the noted goal so that you can choose the answer choice that correctly uses these variables. As such, process of elimination is a great strategy for these types of questions because you can rule out answers that change the wrong conditions or take the wrong measurements.

DATA REPRESENTATION: GETTING ADVANCED

Now that the basics are out of the way, let's get to the main reason you're here—to get to the tough stuff. ACT Data Representation passages and questions will vary in difficulty with regard to both topic and question types, and our goal here is to prepare you for the most challenging obstacles you could face when answering Data Representation questions on the ACT Science test. Here, we will focus on five key features of tricky Data Representation passages and questions: two of these features apply to the content of the passage itself, while three pertain to the question types.

The main challenging features in the passage content you'll often see are:

- An unfamiliar topic or unfamiliar terminology
- Unusual graph types or graphical organization

Tricky Data Representation questions may ask you to:

- Use multiple figures to answer one question
- Locate information in unusual places
- Use one figure to get multiple kinds of data

We will now focus on each of these features and demonstrate, through the use of sample passages, how to tackle each type of obstacle.

Unfamiliar Topic or Terminology

The test makers at ACT, Inc., insist that no advanced knowledge of science topics is required to do well on the ACT Science test. And this is mostly true. The passages themselves will give you most of the information you need to answer the questions that have been posed. Data Representation questions primarily focus on your ability to read data tables and graphs, and anything you cannot discern from the figures can usually be determined by reading the introductory passage.

However, each test generally has a few questions that will require outside knowledge. For instance, it would be helpful and save you a lot of time on the exam if you are familiar with the following:

- The phases of matter (solid, liquid, and gas)
- Basic atomic structure (protons, neutrons, and electrons) in chemistry
- The concepts of kinetic and potential energy in physics
- The three rock types (igneous, metamorphic, and sedimentary) in Earth science
- The basic characteristics of the four classes of biomolecules (proteins, carbohydrates, lipids, and nucleic acids) and the functions of cellular organelles in biology

As you strategize and study for the ACT, review your class notes on these topics (without going too in-depth) before the exam in case any of these topics happen to appear. But know that the vast majority of the questions on the exam can be answered with the material provided.

Which brings us to the issue at hand: unfamiliar scientific content. What happens when you encounter a passage full of terminology that is completely over your head or that discusses subject matter you've never heard of before? This could happen to you, no matter how much studying you've done in advance, but there are plenty of strategies you can employ to make sure you can maximize your understanding of this new and unfamiliar topic area.

The first (and perhaps most important) action you should take is to stay calm. Allowing yourself to become flustered and frustrated will not help you at all. Encountering an unfamiliar topic or science word does not necessarily mean you are stuck and won't be able to figure out what is happening in the passage. Oftentimes, the passage will simply provide you with the definition of an unfamiliar word. In that case, you're good to go!

But we're focusing on the most challenging kinds of questions you'll encounter, so let's say there is no provided definition. This is where your reading comprehension and logic skills come into play. More often than not, you will be provided with enough information in the passage or in the figure to determine the definition of an unfamiliar word or grasp a concept you've never seen before. In other scenarios, you may encounter an unfamiliar word whose definition is not needed to answer the question. For example, a passage may provide a bar graph with experimental fluorescence intensity data for five different biomolecules, and an ensuing question may ask you which molecule has the strongest fluorescence signal. In this example, you can answer the question by looking at the graph; you don't even need to know what fluorescence is or how it works.

Let's look at a sample ACT question that illustrates this concept.

. . . .

A student wanted to use UV-visible spectroscopy on Molecule X to determine a suitable wavelength at which to measure absorbance as an indicator of concentration changes of the molecule. The spectrum is shown in Figure 1:

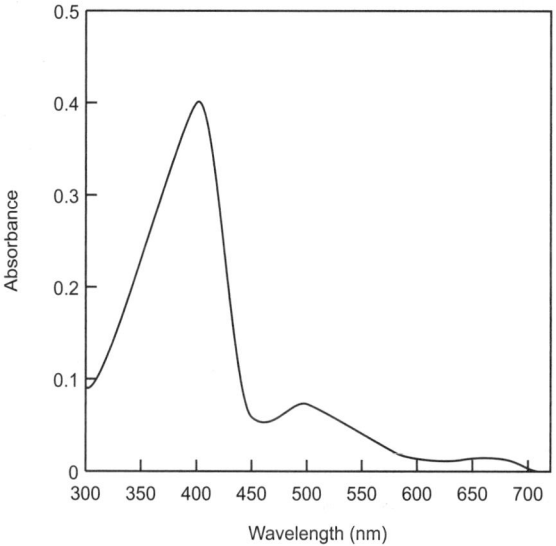

Figure 1

Which wavelength would be least useful for detection of Molecule X?

- **A.** 300 nm
- **B.** 400 nm
- **C.** 500 nm
- **D.** 700 nm

The correct answer is D. Even if you don't understand UV-visible spectroscopy or molecular absorbance of light, the text and graph provide enough information to answer the question. The text indicates that absorbance is proportional to concentration and can be used to detect molecule concentrations. To find the molecule that is least effective for Molecule X detection, you simply need to find the wavelength among the choices that gives the smallest absorbance. Choices A, B, and C are wavelengths that provide absorbance of varying values, but the absorbance is essentially zero at 700 nm, so this is the correct answer.

. . . .

When you do need to grasp a particular topic or term, your reading comprehension skills will come in handy. Look at the words you do understand and summarize them in a way that makes sense to you. Feel free to jot down notes in the margins as you read to make sure you remember important information. Check out the data table or graph in order to get a better idea of what the scientists are altering and measuring in the experiment.

Most important, though, don't let an out-of-left-field topic or term befuddle you. Just use text cues to make an educated guess about a word you don't know. Even if you do come across a rare word that completely baffles you, it is unlikely that more than a question or two will rely on its definition. Most passages will give you all the information you need to answer the questions; the tough part is keeping calm so you can piece together what you do know and understand.

For example, check out the passage introduction below:

· ·

> Gradient centrifugation can be used to concentrate virus particles based on their specific density as a means of separation from other particles of different densities. A scientist wanted to isolate virus particles using a discontinuous CsCl gradient, with a high-density CsCl layer on the bottom and a low-density CsCl layer at the top. The scientist added her viral particles to the gradient and spun it in a centrifuge, resulting in the particles moving through the gradient accordingly. The scientist's viral particles were collected in a band at the sharp interface between the layers.

Based on the location of collected viral particles within the discontinuous gradient, it can be concluded that the density of the viral particles:

    F.   is equal to that of the low-density CsCl.
    G.   is equal to that of the high-density CsCl.
    H.   is higher than either CsCl layer.
    J.   falls between those of the low-and high-density CsCl.

The correct answer is J. Centrifugation pushes solutions toward the bottom of a tube, with more dense solutions pushed further down. Even if you didn't know this, the passage indicates that gradient centrifugation separates particles by density, so a band of particles between high- and low-density CsCl would indicate that the density of the particles falls between the densities of the high- and low-density CsCl.

· ·

Unusual Graphs

In general, scatterplots, bar graphs, and line graphs will be the most frequent kinds of graphs you will see throughout the ACT Science test. These graphs are fairly straight-forward, in that the independent variable occupies the x-axis, and the dependent variable occupies the y-axis. But we're focusing on the most challenging questions you might encounter on the ACT Science test. So what if you come across a graph that isn't so simple to understand?

Sometimes, scientists decide to use a unique kind of graph because it suits their data better than standard graph types. For example, if a biologist has collected an array of invertebrate organisms from a stream, sorted them into their various phyla, and calculated their relative abundances, the biologist may wish to use a pie chart to represent his data because he is working with percentages that add up to a total of 100 percent. A pie chart is unusual because there are no axes, so you cannot rely on the figure itself to determine the dependent and independent variables. Perhaps a geologist has analyzed the masses of elements within three different rock samples and wants to convey in her graph the total mass of each rock as well as the masses of the contributing elements; she might opt to use a stacked bar graph to suit her needs. Sometimes, a scientist might create a completely original kind of graphic to suit his or her needs. You might consequently come across figures that initially make little sense to you.

Often, the more complicated or strange a data representation may look, the more explanation you will receive in the written portion of the passage. But since this is not always the case, you will need to be observant to comprehend the data you've been given. When you encounter an unfamiliar type of graph, pay attention to the legend and any labels that appear on the graph. You will be hard-pressed to find a graph that is completely devoid of labels of any kind, so be sure to use the labels that are there. Even if a graph lacks axes, labels can provide hints to what the dependent and independent variables might be. For example, referring back to the aforementioned pie chart to convey invertebrate relative abundances, if you notice that the wedges have labels like "Annelid" and "Cnidarian," that would be a tip-off that each wedge represents a different invertebrate phylum. Since each wedge has a different label, you can conclude that the phylum is the independent variable.

Let's dive deeper into the test to take a look at a sample passage and test-like questions that might accompany it. Work your way through the questions, and then check out the detailed explanations that follow.

This is a biology passage that focuses on DNA, mRNA, and genetic analysis.

· ·

A wide array of factors influence the ability of plants to tolerate environmental stresses. Cotton, a plant native to tropical and subtropical zones, is relatively resistant to stress, but because it undergoes a long growth period, its quality and production decline because it must in the process endure various abiotic stresses like extreme high temperatures, salt stress, and cold waves.

A group of scientists treated numerous *Gossypium barbadense* cotton plants with various stresses. The scientists then constructed a cDNA library, using reverse transcriptase, to convert abundant mRNA produced to cDNA. Finally, the scientists determined the sequences of the various cDNA fragments, called expressed sequence tags (ESTs), produced. With the sequences in hand, the scientists used a gene database to compare the sequences with known genomes from *G. barbadense* (*Gb*) and three other species of cotton (*Ga*, *Gh*, and *Gr*) to see which species might possess the same genes that responded to stress. The numbers of sequences found in each species are shown in Figure 1. Numbers in overlapping ovals show genes present in more than one species.

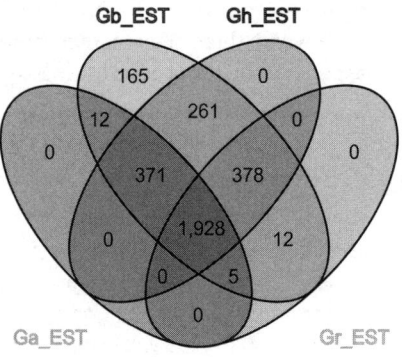

Figure 1

The scientists then ran a database search, based on sequence comparisons with related genes, to determine for each EST its associated cellular component, its molecular function, and the biological process with which it is likely involved. Finally, for each EST determined to be involved in typical stimulus response activities, the scientists found the specific stimulus response with which each is involved. Their findings are shown in Figure 2.

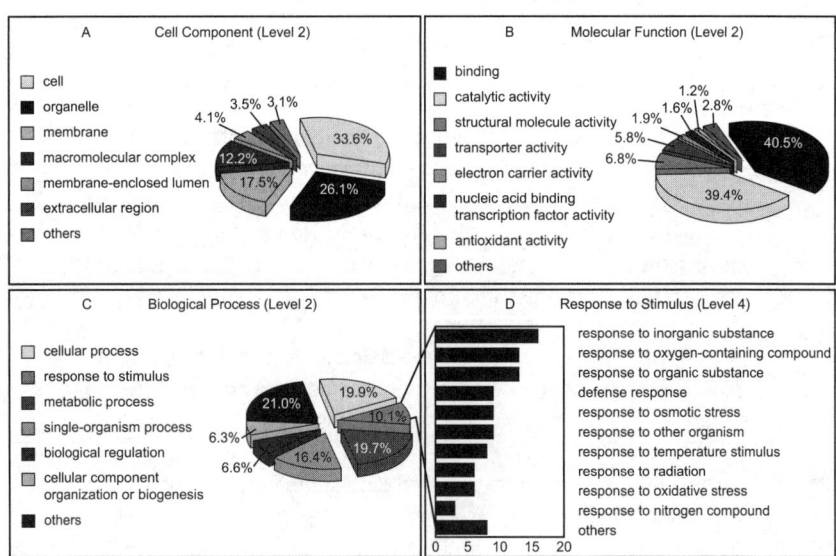

Figure 2

Finally, the scientists ran RT-PCR on a few of the EST-based genes to see if they are expressed under five different types of stress (CK, ABA, PEG, NaCl, and cold) and five different stress levels (0 = low stress, 8 = high stress). Their data is shown in Figure 3, in which bright bands indicate high expression levels.

Expression of selected cotton genes under stress

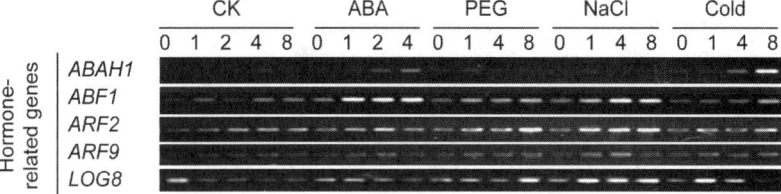

Figure 3

Which of the following choices best states the scientific question posed in this set of experiments?

A. What cellular functions are performed by the greatest percentage of genes in the *G. barbadense* genome?

B. What are the identities and functions of genes up-regulated under stress conditions in *G. barbadense*?

C. Which type of stress is most counterproductive to *G. barbadense* development?

D. Which hormones are produced under stress conditions in *G. barbadense*?

The correct answer is B. The passage states that the cDNA ESTs used throughout this study were produced from the mRNA generated when the cotton was exposed to various stresses. The passage does not explicitly tell you that mRNA overproduction is the same as gene up-regulating, but this is where some background knowledge comes in—since mRNA is used as the template to build proteins from amino acids in the ribosomes during translation, you can deduce that gene expression is being tested here. Even if you didn't know that, however, there are clues throughout the passage that could tip you off to this. Most prominently, the passage states that "the scientists used a gene database to compare the sequences with known genomes from *G. barbadense* (*Gb*) and three other species of cotton (*Ga*, *Gh*, and *Gr*) to see which species might possess the same genes that responded to stress." Even if the concepts of mRNA, reverse transcriptase, and cDNA described in the passage make no sense to you, this line indicates that the obtained sequences refer to genes that responded to stress, which would be the genes up-regulated in response to stress. Choice A is incorrect because it refers to all genes in the *G. barbadense* genome, when this study really focuses only on genes involved in stress response. Choice C is incorrect because the different stress types are not really compared other than in Figure 3, and even there the comparison among stress types is not the focus. Choice D is incorrect because hormones are not specifically tested, even though Figure 3 specifically focuses on hormone-related genes.

According to Figure 1, which pair of cotton species has the greatest number of ESTs exclusively common to just the two of them?

F. *Ga* and *Gb*
G. *Ga* and *Gh*
H. *Gb* and *Gh*
J. *Gb* and *Gr*

The correct answer is H. Figure 1 is essentially a very complex Venn diagram and is clearly a figure specifically tailored to this passage. Based on the passage, the numbers in overlapping ovals tell you how many ESTs the involved species have in common. Therefore, to answer this question, you have to look at each section of the diagram that has two overlapping ovals and choose the highest number. Fortunately, you can take advantage of the fact that this is a multiple-choice question and focus on the four provided choices. Based on the choices given, the *Gb/Gh* overlap has the highest number, 261. Choices F, G, and J are incorrect because their respective overlap values are 12 (*Ga/Gb*), 0 (*Ga/Gh*), and 12 (*Gb/Gr*).

Which of the following subgroups is the smallest, among the ESTs identified in *G. barbadense*?

A. Genes associated with the extracellular region
B. Genes with binding as their main molecular function
C. Genes involved in cellular component organization or biogenesis
D. Genes involved in responding to inorganic substance stimuli

The correct answer is D. This question actually incorporates something we will cover later, the use of multiple figures for the same question, but in this case, the comparison is among percentages, so that aspect of the question is not as tricky. The challenge here comes in actually reading the pie charts and bar graph correctly. Choices A, B, and C are fairly straightforward, in that you can simply view the pie charts and record the percentages: 3.5%, 40.5%, and 6.3%. Among these three options, 3.5% is the lowest number. However, you have to be careful about what you're looking at when considering choice D, which specifically refers to genes involved in responding to inorganic substance stimuli, a function that appears in Figure 2D. At first glance, you'll notice that the given percentage, 16%, is higher than the 3.5% and 6.3% values for choices A and C, respectively. However, note that Figure 2D is a subset of the 10.1% wedge in Figure 2C; that is, the sum of all of the percentages in Figure 2D is 100%. That means that the overall percentage of genes that function to respond to inorganic substances is actually 16% of the 10.1% wedge in Figure 2C, or approximately 1.6% overall. This percentage is lower than any of the other options and is therefore the correct answer.

In the RT-PCR experiment, the dependent variable is the:

F. stress level.
G. type of environmental stress.
H. gene expression level.
J. gene type.

The correct answer is H. Here, we have to deal with yet another unusual mode of data display. This is RT-PCR data; while Figure 1 is a data table of sorts and Figure 2 is a series of graphs, Figure 3 provides collected data directly. Most of the experiments you encounter will be much simpler and straightforward, but since we're looking to acquaint you with the toughest kinds of questions you'll see, it is important to get some practice reading actual data in case you happen to encounter something like this. Fortunately, if you do have to deal with real data, you'll be given information about how to use and analyze it; in most cases, you won't have to understand much about how the experiment works. In this case, you don't have to know anything about RT-PCR, other than what is given. The passage text states that the purpose of the RT-PCR experiment was to test gene expression levels, and that bright bands indicate high expression levels. The question asks you to identify the dependent variable in this experiment. Choices F, G, and J all represent independent variables in this experiment; these are all conditions that the scientists are varying. The dependent variable is what is being measured, and since the purpose of this experiment is to look at band brightness as an indicator of gene expression level, choice H is the correct answer.

• •

USING MULTIPLE FIGURES TO ANSWER ONE QUESTION

Now that we've covered challenging passage content, we will move on to challenging question types. Some Data Representation questions are straightforward and have a single data table or graph to analyze. Others are more complex and include two figures that convey different but related data. Passages with multiple figures are not especially unusual, but questions that follow these passages can get tricky if they ask you to relate the figures to one another to make a comparison or draw a conclusion. Question 3 from the previous sample passage touched upon this question type, but here we're going to focus on strategies dealing with multiple figures that provide different kinds of data or are of different types.

As with any Data Representation passage, you would approach two-figure passages the same way you would approach one-figure passages: by treating each figure as its own entity, analyzing each one separately. Your approach to a question that asks you to relate two figures should be very similar. Even when a question wants you to make a connection between two separate figures, you should still take the time to look at each individual figure and note its variables. What variable is being altered in each figure? What variable is being measured? Are there any distinctive patterns in the figure? Then, after you've clearly determined what each individual figure is conveying, briefly note the take-home message of each figure; in other words, what was the main reason the scientist decided to construct this figure? What does the scientist want his or her readers to take away from it? Once you've analyzed each figure separately, look at the take-home message for each and think about how these statements connect with one another. This will generally lead you to the correct answer.

A useful strategy you can employ if you are struggling to connect two figures in order to answer a question is the synthesis technique. Synthesizing several different figures essentially means to take data from each figure and construct either a data table or graph that incorporates the data, resulting in a new figure you can use for analysis. This takes some extra time, but if you're struggling to connect two figures, this is a great way to integrate the data from both sources. If you're synthesizing two graphs with a lot of data points each, you can always save time by choosing a few representative data points and using those in your synthesis. The synthesis technique is particularly useful when you encounter two figures that have the same dependent or independent variable.

Let's take a look at a test-like example of how this might be presented.

A medical researcher wanted to examine the correlation between total cholesterol levels and weight. He was given data for four patients as shown in Figure 1 and Table 1.

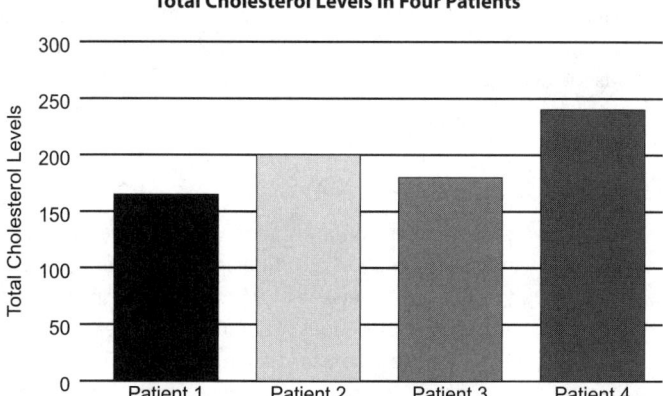

Figure 1

Table 1	
Patients	Weight (lbs.)
Patient 1	120
Patient 2	150
Patient 3	200
Patient 4	285

Since the goal here is to correlate total cholesterol level and weight, these two variables should be plotted in the same table or on the same kind of graph so that you can visualize their relationship. For instance, you could plot the data together on the same double bar graph and clearly see how it relates:

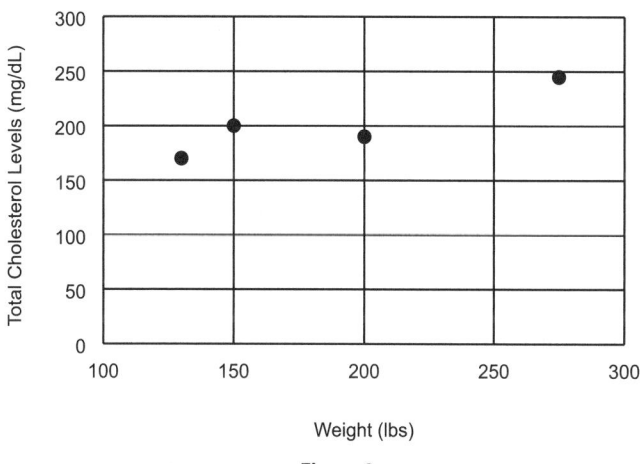

Weight (lbs)

Figure 2

Based on this synthesized graph that relates your two variables of interest, you can see that total cholesterol level generally increases as weight increases.

FINDING INFORMATION IN UNEXPECTED PLACES

If pressed for time when tackling a Data Representation passage, test takers may tend to skip the introduction and jump right to the figures, under the assumption that the questions will focus on the visuals. In general, this is actually true. Data Representation questions are intended to test you on your ability to analyze figures, so this is not a bad strategy. However, if you encounter a question that completely baffles you, there are a few unexpected places you might look as you skim through the information again; specifically, those places are the introductory text, the figure legends, and the figure captions.

The introductory text provides the basis for the data you are going to analyze and is important for setting the stage for the data and questions to follow. Because you have 35 minutes to answer 40 questions, you may not pay much attention to the introduction, or you might skip it altogether. And if the ensuing data is straightforward enough, this is a perfectly fine strategy. But if you reach a question that you simply cannot figure out from the figures, skim through the introduction again.

For instance, a condition such as a constant may not be completely obvious if you're

The main purpose of the introduction is to introduce the topic of interest and experimental details, which usually will include some mention of independent variables, dependent variables, constants, etc.

simply looking at a data table or graph, because a constant doesn't change during an experiment and isn't measured. This is exactly the kind of question that might require you to look back at the introduction, where constants may be listed outright, or you may have to predict an implied constant based on procedural details.

Figure legends are also an extremely useful source of information. Not all graphs will have figure legends, but if they do, they often provide useful information about the independent variable. For instance, a line graph may test a variety of conditions and plot all of the lines on the same set of axes; here, you should check out the figure legend to be 100 percent clear about what each line represents.

Figure captions are also very useful. Not all figures will have captions, but if they do, they may include key words that can tip you off to a concept or detail about the figure that is not plainly obvious from the visual itself. For example, in the previous sample about expressed sequence tags, if you skipped all of the text and jumped right to the visuals, it may be obvious that Figure 2 is displaying cellular functions, but you may not be clear on what these functions are actually referring to. The caption includes the buzzword "ESTs" that lets you know that the figure is describing a functional analysis of the collected ESTs in the experiment.

USING ONE FIGURE TO ACQUIRE MULTIPLE KINDS OF DATA

A Data Representation question may ask you to use a figure to obtain several kinds of data, and this can get tricky because there are a few forms in which this kind of question may appear. The most straightforward version is a graph that simply contains two kinds of data to analyze.

For example, you might see a bar graph with a line graph overlay, with each graph type having its own y-axis and therefore its own dependent variable. In this case, you have a single set of axes that provides information about two distinct data sets. Another version of this question type can occur if you have a more complicated graph type that incorporates several kinds of data into a single plot. An example is a stacked bar, in which you have an overall bar that gives you a total value for a particular condition, but then the stacked bars that comprise that overall bar could further break down that total into component values. Another example might be a bar graph in which you have two or more tested independent variables, as in Figure 1, in which both agar type and antibiotic presence are tested as independent variables.

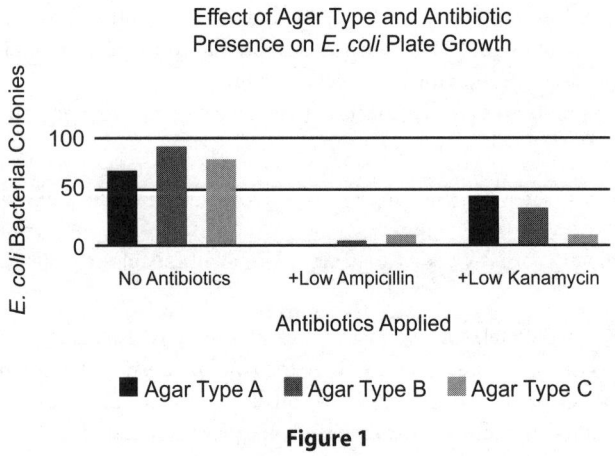

Figure 1

When approaching a graph that contains multiple kinds of data, even if those data types may not seem to be especially related, the easiest strategy to employ is to treat each data type individually. If there are two or more distinct dependent or independent variables, note the patterns and try to draw a conclusion from each. Then, once you've nailed down the take-home message from each kind of data, you can start to make connections between them in an attempt to answer the relevant question that has been posed. This next question set is based on an Earth science passage that focuses on the effects of a major earthquake on the surrounding vegetation.

· ·

An earthquake in south central Chile in February of 2010 caused a 2.0-m coseismic uplift that dramatically modified the coastal landscape. Over the course of two years, a group of scientists studied the response of the land and vegetation to the major earthquake. The group focused on three distinct zones of similar sizes in the region (the seawall, the revetment, and the beach), choosing four sites from each category. They first tracked species richness by counting the average number of species in each zone type at the start of data collection in February 2012, as well as the average number of species for all zone types throughout the sampling period (Figure 1 (a and b)). They then tracked changes in the average area per zone type that contained vegetation Figure 1 (c).

Species richness and vegetation coverage over a two-year collection period
(F = February, A = April, Au = August, O = October, J = June, Ju = July, and N = November)
(Error bars represent standard deviations.)

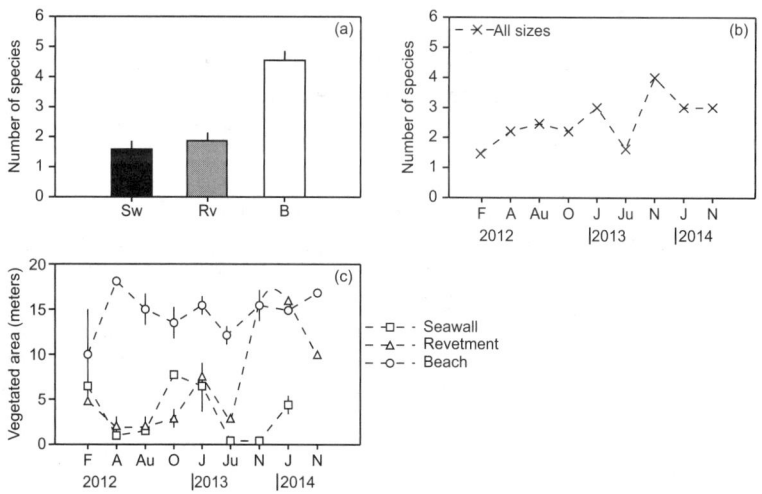

Figure 1

The scientists then explored the specific plant types that were most commonly seen in the various zone types at the start of data collection in February 2012, calculating the average cover (in decimal fraction of total zone area) of total plants and three specific plant species. The data is displayed in Figure 2 (a, b, and c).

Total land coverage of all plants and three common plant types
(Error bars represent standard deviations.)

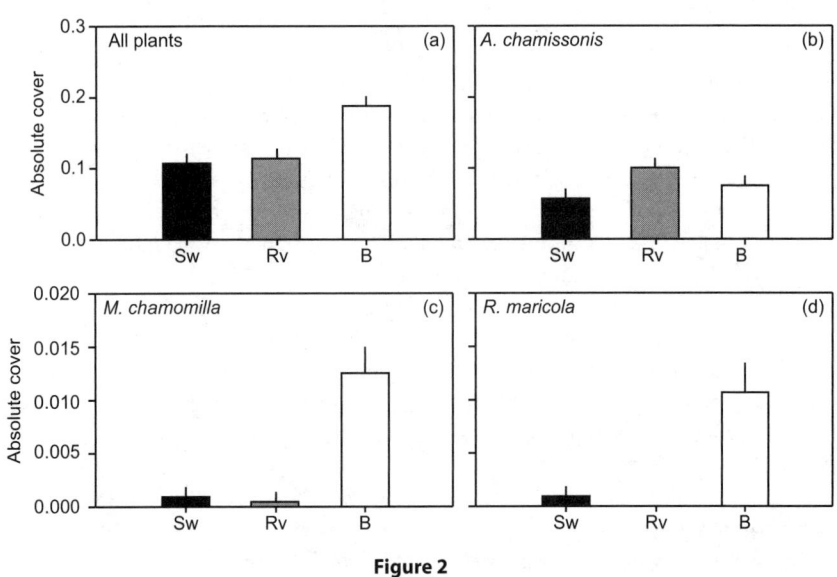

Figure 2

Finally, the scientists tracked the total coverage of three representative plant species over their designated time course to observe changes in post-earthquake recovery times. The data is shown in Figure 3.

Changes in plant populations over the experimental time course
(Error bars represent standard deviations.)

Source: http://journals.plos.org/ plosone/article?id=10.1371/journal.pone.0124334 (open access)

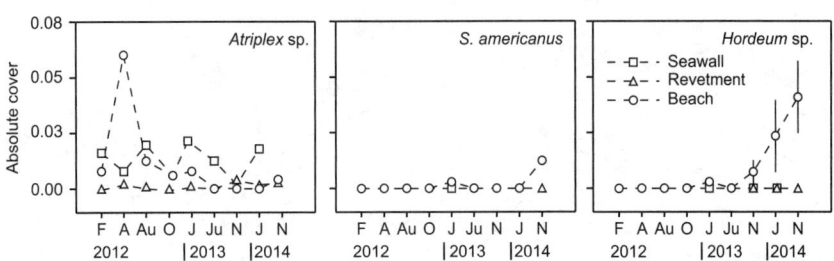

Figure 3

In the zone type that exhibited the greatest plant biodiversity after the earthquake, during which month was the smallest area of land covered by vegetation?

A. February 2012
B. April 2012
C. July 2013
D. November 2013

The correct answer is A. This question requires you to use information in an unusual location (the figure caption) as well as analyze two different graphs to determine an answer. The figure caption provides the key for the different months on the x-axis, which are not all intuitive since several months begin with the same letter. The real challenge, though, is figuring out how to use the graphs in conjunction with one another. The first step is to work with the first half of the question stem and determine which zone type exhibited the greatest plant biodiversity after the earthquake, which according to Figure 1a, is the beach zone because it had the greatest number of plant species. Next, you must determine the month during which this zone exhibited the smallest amount of vegetation cover. Be careful not to use Figure 1b, as this figure is not zone-specific. Instead, refer to Figure 1c and look specifically at the line marked with circles, as this refers to the beach zone. The lowest value can be found in February 2012, so this is the correct answer. Note that the other answer choices refer to absolute and local minima for the other zones, so if you missed the first step, you might have answered incorrectly.

According to Figure 2, which plant type covered the greatest land area, on average, in the beach zones?

F. *A. chamisonnis*
G. *Hordeum sp.*
H. *M. chamomilla*
J. *R. maricola*

The correct answer is F. This question asks you to use two separate graphs to extract information. This question requires a different approach than the previous question, however, because the two graphs you're using represent the same kind of data, whereas the previous question referred to two completely different graphs and data types. This question is tricky, however, because you can't simply look at the bar sizes; just looking at the bar sizes might lead you to believe that *M. chamomilla* has the highest absolute cover of the three plants in Figure 2. The key is to notice that the Figures 2c and 2d graphs use a different y-axis than Figures 2a and 2b. As such, the small-looking beach bar for *A. chamissonis* actually represents an absolute cover value that nearly reaches 0.1, while the larger-looking beach bars for *M. chamomilla* and *R. maricola* don't even pass 0.015. Therefore, the correct answer is choice F, rather than choices H or J. For completeness, note that choice G is represented in Figure 3, not Figure 2.

Which of the following statements accurately descriptions trial precision for the experiments depicted in Figure 3?

A. As mean values increased per trial set, precision also increased for the sets.
B. Trial sets that yielded lower mean values tended to be more precise.
C. In general, the trial sets were consistently imprecise regardless of mean values.
D. All trials were extremely precise and equally precise.

The correct answer is B. This question requires you to read the figure caption as confirmation that the error bars represent standard deviations, which can in turn be used as indicators of precision. This question also requires you to look at a single set of graphs and extract two kinds of information from them: mean values and precision, in the form of standard deviation/error bar values. On one hand, you need to look at the values marked on the graph itself, but you must also estimate the error bar sizes. This is where the synthesis method may come in handy; you could choose three or four points on any of the graphs and record the absolute cover and error bar size for each in a data table. You could always eyeball it and figure it out that way, but performing a quick synthesis by constructing your own data table could make it less confusing and more manageable. In general, larger mean values resulted in larger error bars, which indicates lower precision. That means that choice A is exactly the opposite of the correct answer, while choice B is correct. Choices C and D indicate that the error bars were the same throughout the graphs, which is not true.

In terms of comparing this earthquake plant response to earthquake plant responses in other environments of different sizes, a weakness of Figure 1c is:

F. the exclusion of an "actual" value to which results can be compared.
G. the lack of a consistent gap between *x*-axis major time values.
H. the measurement of actual areas rather than percent coverage.
J. the absence of error bars for each of the data points.

The correct answer is H. This question asks you to analyze the validity of Figure 1c in terms of applicability and validity. Choice F is incorrect because there is no "actual" value for this kind of experiment; the scientists were not trying to determine a specific universal property or value. Choice G is incorrect because, while the unequal gaps may make the graph a bit less straightforward, it does not stand in the way of results comparisons with other related data collections. Choice J is incorrect because error bars actually are present. Choice H is correct; by providing actual areas rather than percentages (like Figure 2 does in the form of decimals), Figure 1c would be difficult to compare to other related data for regions of different sizes.

SUMMING IT UP

- **Data Representation passages present you with a graph, table, or figure that describes some kind of scientific experiment or phenomenon.** Each Data Representation passage is accompanied by approximately five questions that ask you to understand the presented data, draw conclusions based on the presented data, analyze or construct graphical figures, assess the validity of presented data, and consider future work based on the presented data.

- When faced with a Data Representation question, first identify the scientific question before you attempt to analyze the data. It will also benefit you to identify the **hypothesis, independent** and **dependent variables, constants**, and **controls**.
  - When you identify independent and dependent variables, you are able to use process of elimination to answer questions about experimentation—you can rule out answers that change the wrong conditions or take the wrong measurements.

- Always **keep patterns and trends in data in mind** as you read a passage and accompanying figures—you will almost always be required to draw a conclusion based on all the information presented.

- In a graph, the **y-axis (the vertical axis) will usually be the dependent variable**, while **the x-axis (the horizontal axis) will usually be the independent variable**.

- **Accuracy** describes how close a particular number or measurement agrees with a known value or standard. **Precision** describes how close the measured values in a repeated set are to each other. Precision can be measured numerically by calculating standard deviation, or how far a set of measured numbers are from their average.

- A very different result from the rest is called an **outlier**, which usually indicates an error in a trial of the experiment.

- **Almost every question on the ACT Science test can be answered with the material provided**—you need to bring in very little outside knowledge. You need to be able to interpret only what you are presented. Every passage and data set gives enough information to determine definitions of unfamiliar vocabulary or unfamiliar scientific methods.

- When you encounter an unfamiliar kind of graph, pay attention to the **legend** and any **labels** that appear on the graph.

- **Approach two-figure passages the same way you would approach one-figure passages:** by treating each figure as its own entity, analyzing each one separately. If you are having trouble connecting two figures in order to answer a question, you can take data from each figure and construct either a data table or graph that incorporates the data, resulting in a new figure you can use for analysis.

CHAPTER 9
RESEARCH SUMMARIES:
ASSESSING EXPERIMENTAL
DESIGN AND
ANALYZING RESULTS

OVERVIEW

- About Research Summaries Questions
- Research Summaries: Getting Advanced
- Summing It Up

Research Summaries are the most common question type that you'll find on the ACT Science test, and with good reason. Research Summaries, which comprise 45–55 percent of the test, take you through the entire scientific process, from asking a scientific question, through developing the experiment, to analyzing the obtained results. Of the three main types of questions you will encounter on the ACT Science test, Research Summaries most resemble the kind of writing you will find in the real world of science research, whether you're looking through a scientific journal, a magazine, or even a textbook.

Fortunately, many of the skills you use to answer Data Representation questions are very much applicable to Research Summaries, because both question types ask you to analyze data. Both question types cover the same general disciplines of biology, chemistry, physics, and earth/space sciences (as do any questions you will come across on the ACT Science test). The key difference between Data Representation passages and Research Summaries is that you will be asked to put more thought into the experiment itself, namely its design, functionality, and validity. Research Summaries usually will give you more background information about the experimental design, and questions may additionally emphasize topics that are more relevant to design than data analysis, such as the variables and controls discussed in the previous chapter. You may be asked to apply scientific principles to explain why a procedure was done, or you may be asked to consider ways to improve the protocol. In addition, questions will still ask you to analyze data and draw conclusions, so you'll be able to use the skills here that we already covered in our examination of Data Representation questions.

ABOUT RESEARCH SUMMARIES QUESTIONS

Like Data Representation passages, Research Summaries will usually begin with a written introduction to provide background information about the scientific topic of interest, including vocabulary words, key relevant principles, and specific details. Then you will be given a fairly detailed description of the experiment, from which you should be able to ascertain the independent variable, dependent variable, and control variables. Since these passages emphasize experimental design and the full scientific method more than Data Representation passages do, you will often see longer written portions in these passages, though you may also be given images to help you visualize the experimental setup. Finally, you will be provided with the data obtained in the experiment, which can include a table, a graph, a written description of results, or some combination of these. You may also be given conclusions that were drawn, although you will often be asked to do this part yourself; you may even be asked to use the data to support or refute a provided conclusion, so take provided conclusions with a grain of salt.

Here's what a Research Summary passage will look like:

> A student wants to investigate the relationship between the period and length of a simple pendulum. The student sets up a simple pendulum with a 50-cm string and a 50-g weight hanging at the end of it. The student lifts the weight toward him at a 15° angle from the vertical and releases it. He uses a stopwatch to measure the period time, that is, the time it takes for the pendulum weight to complete a full oscillation, swinging to the other side and then returning at its maximal height. The student then adjusts the length of the string to 60 cm and repeats the experiment. He adjusts the string length again to 70, 80, 90, and 100 cm, measuring the period time at each string length. His data is shown in Figure 1:

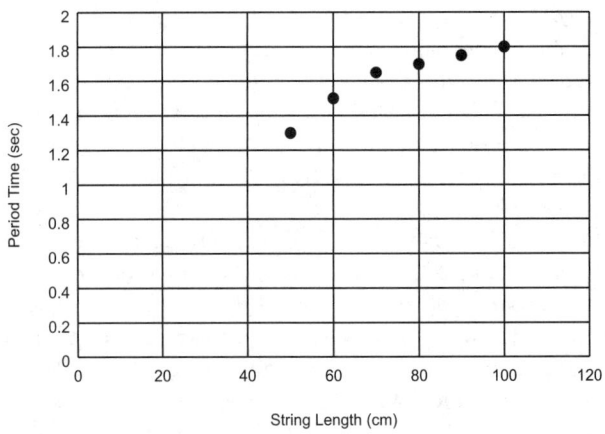

Figure 1

Questions that accompany Research Summaries cover more ground than simple data analysis, so these passages usually have more associated questions, most commonly five or six, which will test you on an array of skills: identifying the scientific question, formulating hypotheses, proposing experiments or alternative experimental methods, analyzing data, and using data to draw conclusions. Your proficiency in most (or all) of these areas could be covered on each Research Summary you encounter, so it is important to be familiar with each. Since we have already discussed several of these topics, we will review them briefly before getting to the tough stuff.

For any given scientific experiment, it is important to identify the scientific question, or purpose, as described in the previous chapter:

- Why was this experiment performed?
- What is being varied (i.e., the independent variable)?
- What is being measured (i.e., the dependent variable)?
- Why is this topic significant?

The scientific question provides the reason for designing an experiment, so without a clear and specific question in mind, it will be very difficult to come up with a logical way to address it. Background information is especially useful for fleshing out a scientific question because it may familiarize you with related work in the field or with the scientific principle itself. Since you can't exactly do your own background research during the test, Research Summaries will do it for you, and if the scientific question has not been stated outright, the background information (as well as the experiment and data) can help you to determine what it is.

For example, let's look at the pendulum passage. Based on both the introductory text and the graph itself, we can see that the student is varying the length of the string and measuring the period time of the pendulum. The variable that is altered is the independent variable, so the string length is the independent variable. The variable that is measured is the dependent variable, so the period time is the dependent variable. Constants are variables that stay the same throughout the experiment. The mass of the weight at the end of the string is a constant because it never changes at any point during this experiment. Other constants include the string material and the angle from which the weight is released during each run (15° from the vertical).

 Identifying the scientific question as soon as possible will help you to focus on the kinds of conclusions you will need to draw from the data that follows.

You may also be asked to identify or develop a hypothesis or an educated prediction of the outcome for a given experiment. Questions about hypotheses may be extremely straightforward if the hypothesis is stated somewhere in the passage. You may also be asked to choose an appropriate hypothesis based on the text. Hypotheses are based on cause and effect and, as such, are often (but not always) written in the "If . . ., then . . ."

format. Hypotheses require you to combine logic and background knowledge to predict what will happen, but usually the key to choosing an appropriate hypothesis lies in the correct identification of the independent and dependent variables.

Remember that hypotheses are predictions, not actual results, so hypotheses do *not* have to match the data obtained later in the experiment.

If a hypothesis correctly identifies the variables but makes an incorrect prediction, that's perfectly fine and still very much valid—it happens all the time in the real world! In fact, when an experiment gives an unexpected result, it simply opens the door to new experiments to explain why the unusual result was obtained. After obtaining data, you can go back and indicate whether or not the data supports your original hypothesis, but hypotheses are simply attempts to make predictions and do not always match the obtained results.

Once you have worked through any questions related to the scientific question and hypothesis, you will almost always encounter at least one or two questions related to the experimental design, which focuses on the actual methods and techniques used to investigate the scientific question.

Questions testing the scientific question and experimental design will read something like this, based on the pendulum passage:

Which of the following statements provide the scientific question of this experiment?

What is a reasonable hypothesis one might develop to predict the outcome of this experiment?

An example of a constant in this experiment is:

You may recognize the techniques used in an experiment, but many times, the methods will be completely new to you. Fortunately, you will be given enough detail about the experimental design and variables to determine what is happening in the experiment.

Research Summaries will usually involve simple, straightforward techniques. Of course, the examples we look at in these chapters will be more complex because we want to acquaint you with the toughest challenges you might face on the Science test, but the vast majority of experiments you encounter in Research Summaries will not be incredibly difficult. Even if a method or technique is over your head, you will be given enough background information to figure out what is happening.

Questions about the experimental methods can take on a number of forms. On one hand, these questions can be straightforward and ask you to identify variables and controls or to answer simple recall questions about the experiment or relevant scientific principles.

For example, the following question is based on the pendulum passage.

· ·

The purpose of keeping the release angle constant throughout this experiment is to:

A. modify two distinct independent variables in this experiment.

B. keep all nonvariable conditions the same throughout the experiment so that the different runs can be compared to one another.

C. cancel out the effect of gravity on the downward movement of the pendulum weight on both sides of its oscillatory motion.

D. provide a control trial to which all other trials may be compared.

The correct answer is B. It is important to maintain constants throughout the experiment so that only the variables of interest are changed, allowing for each of the runs to be compared to one another.

· ·

Other questions may require you to get below the surface by asking you to critique the experiment, suggest possible improvements to the given experiment, suggest an alternative experimental method altogether to address the same scientific question, or recommend a logical next step to take experimentally as a follow-up.

Try this question, also based on the previous passage.

· ·

Which of the following experimental changes would improve the validity of the obtained results?

F. Perform multiple experimental trials for each string length.

G. Perform the same experiment at different altitudes.

H. Use a weight of increased mass.

J. Convert the time measurements to minutes.

The correct answer is F. Increasing the number of trials always improves validity. Performing the experiment at different altitudes introduces a new independent variable, which doesn't help to improve the validity of the obtained results. Changing the mass of the weight doesn't affect pendulum time at all and won't be a useful improvement. Converting time units from seconds to minutes isn't an experimental improvement; it is simply a choice in data analysis that won't change anything about the results or their validity.

· ·

Remember, you won't be expected to know specialized techniques off the top of your head, so questions based on experimental design are really testing your proficiency in reading comprehension, logic, and critical assessment.

After reading through the experimental details, you will be given data to analyze. Those same skills you used with Data Representation questions for interpreting data and drawing conclusions will apply here to your data analysis:

- Understanding the provided data
- Analyzing and constructing graphs
- Drawing reasonable conclusions based on data
- Assessing the validity of data
- Determining future experimental directions based on the results

Be sure to review Chapter 8 if you'd like to delve into these topics again.

RESEARCH SUMMARIES: GETTING ADVANCED

You will encounter many of the same kinds of tough passages and questions in Research Summaries as in Data Representation questions. As such, consider this section as a sort of addendum to the previous chapter, in that you should still use the skills we discussed in Chapter 8; what we will discuss now are a few additional tools you can add to your arsenal.

Two of these new tools apply to the passage content, and two apply to the kinds of questions you might encounter. With regard to passage content for Research Summaries, you might come across these:

- Unfamiliar techniques
- Technical jargon

With regard to questions, the most challenging questions (in addition to the kinds of questions discussed in Chapter 8) address the following:

- Unexpected results
- Criticizing your source material

As a reminder, the vast majority of the ACT Science Research Summaries will be straightforward and relatively simple. But we're here to emphasize the most challenging kinds of passages you might see, so this section is intended to help you conquer those passages that are at the highest level of difficulty.

Unfamiliar Techniques

We've already discussed and practiced strategies for dealing with new topics and terminology. In Chapter 8, we talked about how reading comprehension and logic skills can allow you to make educated guesses about topics or vocabulary words with which you may not be familiar. Here, we will extend this discussion to include experiment-based principles that may be new to you. Specifically, we will focus on dealing with new experimental principles and techniques, as well as detection modes and units.

When it comes to figuring out how new techniques work, reading comprehension and logic are still absolutely critical skills to hone. In addition, pay attention to prefixes, suffixes, and root words in new vocabulary, as they can tip you off to the meaning of an unfamiliar word.

For example, consider the technique *UV spectroscopy*, a commonly used technique in physical and biological chemistry. As a college-bound high school student, you may have no idea what it is. This technique would never just appear as a random phrase—there will always be some background information and actual context. But let's look at the phrase itself and see if we can extract some meaning from it. The first word in the technique name is *UV*. *UV* is not an obscure abbreviation; it means "ultraviolet," in reference to light. Sunlight falls within the appropriate wavelength range and is ultraviolet light by definition. But even if you didn't know the meaning of *UV*, the rest of the technique name provides additional hints about its function. Look at the term *spectroscopy*. The first part of the word, *spectro-*, looks and sounds a lot like *spectrum*, which refers to the entire range of wavelengths of light and provides an additional clue that this technique deals with light. *UV* merely specifies the wavelength range upon which the technique focuses. Now check out the second part of the word: *-scopy*. This suffix looks and sounds like *scope*, which refers to an instrument that allows you to view something, like a telescope or a microscope. Putting all of these clues together, we can predict that *UV spectroscopy* is a technique that allows us to visualize the full set of light wavelengths in the UV range.

However, you don't have to be a word guru to deal with unfamiliar techniques (although it certainly doesn't hurt if you can guess what a technique is for, based simply on its name). Using reading comprehension and logic, as discussed in Chapter 8, is incredibly useful for figuring out what a technique does. Look for key words that you understand. Use the background information to rationalize the methods. Check out the kind of data that is collected in the figures, and identify the measurement that is being taken during the experiment. Even if you still don't think you understand a technique, at least make an educated guess about what is going on—you will likely not even need to understand all of the intricacies in order to answer the questions.

Here's an example.

Circular dichroism (CD) spectroscopy is a technique that is used to track changes in a biomolecule's secondary structure. The secondary structure refers to the motifs, such as helices and parallel sheets in proteins, that occur in biomolecules, and tracking changes in the CD spectra of a biomolecule under different conditions indicates which structural changes are taking place as a result of those conditions.

A scientist wanted to test the effect of nimustine, a DNA-binding molecule, on the secondary structure of DNA using circular dichroism spectroscopy. She first recorded a spectrum of free DNA, with no nimustine added. She then added nimustine in increasing molar ratios: 1/20, 1/40, and 1/80 DNA/nimustine. The CD spectrum is shown in Figure 1.

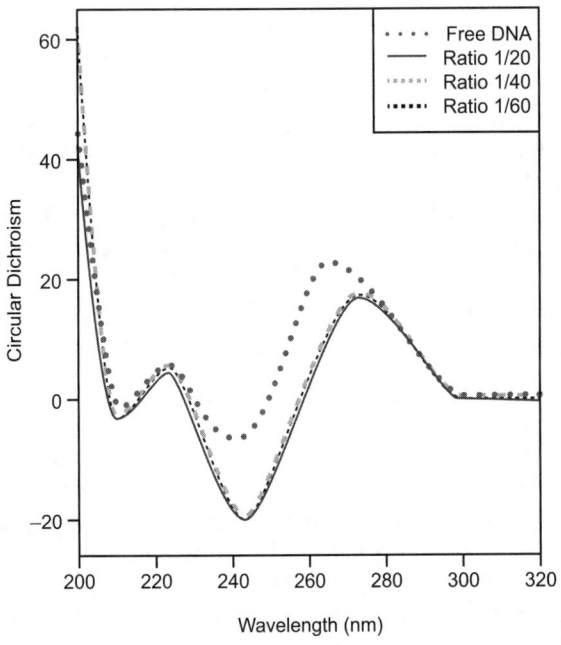

Figure 1

Which transition caused the largest change in secondary structure?

   A.   Free DNA to 1/20

   B.   1/20 to 1/40

   C.   1/40 to 1/80

   D.   There is no difference among the transitions.

The correct answer is A. The spectra for all samples that include nimustine are similar, but the spectra for the sample of free DNA is markedly different than the others throughout the range of wavelengths. This means that there is probably a large secondary structure change as soon as any nimustine is added.

. . . .

Circular dichroism spectroscopy is a very complicated technique in which certain regions of the spectrum represent particular motifs, and peak shifts indicate how motifs change, etc. You don't have to know any of that. All you really have to know about the technique to answer the question is that more dramatic changes in the spectrum indicate more dramatic changes in DNA structural conformation. There are several lines in the introductory text that can tip you off to this. One such line is: "[T]racking changes in the CD spectra of a biomolecule under different conditions indicates which structural changes are taking place as a result of those conditions." This line tells you that spectral changes correspond with conformational changes, and while it hints that there is more to it than that conceptually, you don't have to know any more than the basics to get the right answer to this question.

An additional hitch you might face here is if you encounter an unfamiliar mode of detection or measurement unit. Let's say a technique measures *phosphorescence* or pressure in *kilopascals*. With regard to mode of detection, stick with those same reading comprehension skills. The written portion of the passage will almost certainly drop some hints about what is being detected or measured in an experiment.

 For unfamiliar units, there won't be any intense mathematics on the ACT Science test, so you won't have to do unit conversions with units you may know nothing about.

In many cases, as long as you understand what is being measured, you can practically ignore units other than as cues to point you toward the correct data to answer the question.

Technical Jargon

Dealing with technical jargon is different from dealing with unfamiliar terms. Technical jargon can include words that look confusing but are really not worth wasting your time on. A common example of this is species names in biology-based passages. If a passage is focusing on several kinds of bacteria, you may be given their scientific names and see crazy-looking words like *Escherichia coli* (*E. coli*) or *Staphylococcus aureus* (*S. aureus*). These are not words you'll have to analyze or understand in any way, but if you come across them in a passage, you may get flustered because they seem so intense.

A good strategy to use if this happens is to abbreviate them so they are less confusing. For example, any time you see a version of *Escherichia coli* or *E. coli*, replace it in your head (or even on the page) with "EC" to keep it short and simple. Technical jargon can make even the simplest concepts seem more difficult than they are.

Other common instances where technical jargon can make simple concepts seem unnecessarily complicated are gene or protein names (biology), chemical or molecular names (chemistry), astronomical nomenclature (earth/space sciences), and physical laws (physics). Try not to get hung up on words that do not contribute to your understanding of the scientific principle on hand—just come up with your own shorthand version of each word to simplify them as much as possible!

Let's take a look at a passage and some sample test-like questions.

· ·

Antitumor drugs like temozolomide add a methyl group to the O6-position of guanosine in the DNA of cancer cells, marking the cells for destruction. However, elevated levels of the DNA repair enzyme O6-methylguanine DNA methyltransferase (MGMT) reverses this action, disrupting the effect of the drug. Consequently, measuring MGMT levels in cancer patients can help to determine whether or not drugs like temozolomide will be effective in certain patients.

A group of scientists wanted to devise a way to measure MGMT levels directly, so they produced a fluorescent probe that targets MGMT without disrupting enzymatic activity or destroying the enzyme. When MGMT removes the methyl from guanosine, the probe binds to MGMT, lights up, and is detected as fluorescence intensity.

To test the effectiveness of the probe, the scientists incubated 10 nM MGMT with two different inhibitors, BG and PaTrin-2, at a wide range of concentrations for 10 minutes at 37°C in buffer at pH 7.8. Both BG and PaTrin-2 inhibit MGMT activity by blocking its active site. All incubations were performed in the same total liquid volume. The scientists then added the probe to each mixture at a concentration of 10 nM and detected the fluorescence intensity. They "normalized" their data by comparing it to a positive control trial that contained no inhibitor and therefore should detect the full concentration of MGMT. They repeated each trial three times. Their data is shown in Figure 1, with error bar standard deviations:

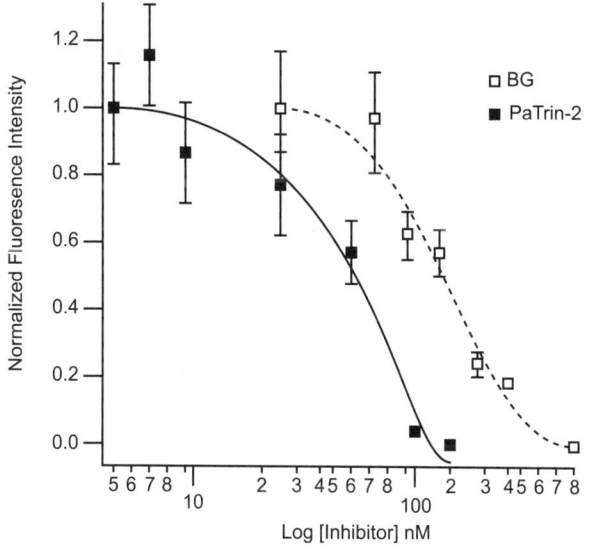

Figure 1

The scientists then tested the probe *in vivo* in real cells. They used TK6+ cells, which have high MGMT levels, and TK6– cells, which have low MGMT levels. They added the same amount of probe to each cell type, and they again performed each measurement three times.

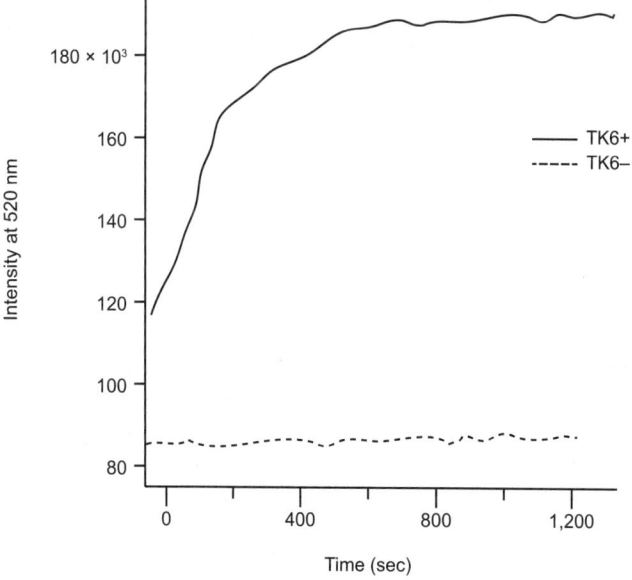

Figure 2

Which of the following scientific questions best encompasses the purpose of this set of experiments?

F. How do increasing concentrations of the BG and PaTrin-2 inhibitors affect MGMT levels in TK6 cells?

G. What is the effect of the fluorescent probe concentration on MGMT levels in TK6 cells?

H. Is the fluorescent probe capable of BG and PaTrin-2 binding and detection *in vitro* and *in vivo*?

J. Can the fluorescent probe detect active MGMT levels *in vitro* and *in vivo*?

The correct answer is J. Now that we've waded through the jargon, figuring out the scientific question simply requires that you understand how all of these different molecules relate to one another. Choice F gives BG and PaTrin-2 concentrations as the independent variable, with MGMT as the dependent variable. The inhibitors are used in this experiment only as a means of exhibiting varied MGMT levels for fluorescence detection, and they are involved only in the first half of the experiment, which has its data presented in Figure 1. Choice G refers specifically to TK6 cells, which are relevant only to the second experiment, which has its data displayed in Figure 2, but more important, the independent variable is incorrectly listed as the fluorescent probe concentration, when this value is actually a constant for all experiments performed. Choice H is incorrect because it indicates that the fluorescent probe binds the inhibitors, which contradicts the information given in the introduction. Choice J is correct because both of these experiments aim to determine whether or not the fluorescent probe can functionally detect MGMT concentrations *in vitro* and *in vivo*. Even if you weren't able to narrow it down using this line of reasoning, a careful look at the introduction hints at the answer; the first paragraph indicates that the purpose of the experiments is "to devise a way to measure MGMT levels directly," and the second paragraph begins with the phrase "To test the effectiveness of the probe," which had just been described as the means of MGMT binding and detection.

A constant in the experiment depicted in Figure 1 is the:

A. concentration of MGMT detected by the probe.

B. use of TK6 cells.

C. inhibitor concentration.

D. incubation temperature.

The correct answer is D. A constant in an experiment is something that is the same for every trial. Choice A is incorrect because while the initial concentration of MGMT was the same for every trial, the concentration of MGMT detected by the probe varied because the inhibitors blocked MGMT activity, thereby preventing its detection by the probe. Choice B is incorrect because TK6 cells were used in the Figure 2 experiment, not the Figure 1 experiment. Choice C is incorrect because inhibitor concentration is the independent variable in this experiment. The incubation temperature, 37°C, was the same for all trials and is a constant in this experiment.

A valid negative control for the experiment depicted in Figure 1 could be a:

    F. run with enough of either inhibitor to completely block MGMT activity.

    G. run that includes MGMT but does not use any inhibitors or the fluorescent probe.

    H. run that includes MGMT and the fluorescent probe but no inhibitors.

    J. run that includes the buffer solution only.

The correct answer is F. According to the passage, the positive control for this experiment was a run that contained probe and MGMT, but no inhibitors. This is a positive control because it would give the expected phenomenon: a fluorescence signal when MGMT is definitely present and active. A negative control, therefore, should be a run in which MGMT may or may not be present, but in which MGMT should not be active. The fluorescent probe would be present, but no fluorescence should be observed because MGMT is inactive. Adding enough inhibitor to completely block MGMT activity, as described in choice F, would satisfy these criteria and would be a useful negative control. Choice G is incorrect because the probe must be present. Choice H is incorrect because this is identical to the positive control run described in the passage. Choice J is incorrect because there is again no probe present.

As a follow-up experiment, the scientists wish to test the functional robustness of the probe, at low and high MGMT concentrations, with respect to temperature *in vivo*. Which of the following experiments would sufficiently test this scientific question?

    A. Repeat the experiment depicted in Figure 1 at low and high temperatures.

    B. Repeat the experiment depicted in Figure 2 at low and high temperatures.

    C. Repeat the experiment depicted in Figure 1 at low and high MGMT concentrations.

    D. Repeat the experiment depicted in Figure 2, except add either BG or PaTrin-2 at very low concentrations.

The correct answer is B. Choices A and C are incorrect because the Figure 1 experiment occurs *in vitro*. If you don't know what *in vitro* means, the passage states outright that the Figure 2 experiment occurs *in vivo*, so that would alert you to the fact that you should be focusing on the Figure 2 experiment. Choice D is incorrect because adding inhibitor does not vary temperature (the proposed independent variable) in any way. Choice B is correct because this experiment would allow you to repeat the Figure 2 experiment at high and low temperatures; comparing your results to Figure 2 would then tell you whether the responsiveness of the probe to MGMT has changed at the new tested temperatures.

· ·

The previous passage could be considered both a biology and chemistry passage because it includes elements of both. This passage is full of jargon and abbreviations, so it's important to keep everything straight. MGMT is the enzyme that the probe is detecting. BG and PaTrin-2 are inhibitors that halt MGMT activity. TK6+ and TK6− are cell types. The fluorescent probe is the new entity that the scientists have synthesized. The passage also includes the concept of fluorescence and fluorescence intensity.

In fluorescence, electrons in a molecule are excited by a given wavelength of light, and when they return to their original energy levels, an emission wavelength can be detected. If you already knew this, then this passage will be very easy to understand. But if you didn't know it, you're still in great shape, because you don't actually have to understand fluorescence to understand its purpose here. The scientists are adding a probe to different mixtures; when MGMT is present, the probe binds to it and creates light, which is detected as fluorescence activity. This information is stated outright at the end of the first paragraph. Understanding the specifics of fluorescence is therefore not necessary for understanding its usefulness in this particular experiment.

UNEXPECTED RESULTS

An important thing to remember when you're thinking about scientific experiments is the fact that they are indeed "experiments," which by definition are used to test new hypotheses or confirm known information. In the former case, the testing of new hypotheses, you theoretically go into an experiment not knowing how it will turn out. As such, the results are intended to show you something you don't already know. You may have a pretty good idea of how the experiment, in theory, *should* turn out, but technically the experiment will be teaching you something new. In the latter case, you might perform an experiment to support an idea or concept that is already known or has already been tested in the past. In either case, however, you might not get exactly the results you might expect.

Some of the greatest discoveries happened because experiments didn't go exactly as planned. Spencer Silver was attempting to develop an ultra-strong adhesive in 1968 when he accidentally made a weak, reusable adhesive that Arthur Fry later developed into the Post-it® note.

If you're testing a new hypothesis, you could get unexpected results, and these could lead to a cool new discovery. If you get unexpected results when testing something that has previously been tested or is considered to be "known" information, perhaps something went wrong in your experiment, but alternatively, you might have also found something new or righted a wrong, effectively changing the "known."

The point here is that experimental results do not always come out the way you might expect. When you read through a Research Summary and then look at the results, it is important to analyze the data as presented. Even if the results seem incorrect or potentially flawed, your goal here is to analyze the data you have been given.

Try this question on your own.

· ·

A student folded construction paper of three different colors (white, green, and black) in half the long way and taped them in place to create pockets. The student collected three thermometers and made sure all three read the same temperature to start. He then placed one thermometer into each pocket, placed the pockets in the same area of his porch with the same intensity of sunlight exposure, and took a temperature reading every ten minutes for thirty minutes. His data is shown in Table 1:

Table 1			
Time (min.)	Temperature (°C)		
	White Paper	Green Paper	Black Paper
0	28.0	28.0	28.0
10	31.2	32.2	30.0
20	33.3	34.1	30.2
30	35.1	36.3	31.8

Based on the collected data, which color absorbed heat from the sun most rapidly?

F. White
G. Green
H. Black
J. All colors absorbed heat equally.

The correct answer is G. Based on the data, the values for green paper increased the fastest, followed by the white paper. According to the data in the table, the black paper absorbed heat the most slowly. You probably know from experience that darker colors absorb heat more quickly, so this data does not appear to be correct. However, the questions must be answered based on the data, and in this case, the data indicates that the green paper absorbed heat more quickly than the white or black paper.

· ·

In short, don't read through an experiment and skip the results section because the expected results seem obvious. Remember that the questions you will be asked require you to analyze the data in front of you, and if you don't look at the provided data, you might not answer the questions correctly. Data included on the ACT Science test, for the most part, will be exactly what you might expect, but because we're focusing on challenging questions and potential tricks, this is a possible pitfall that you now know to look out for. So pay attention to the numbers and don't assume a result without looking closely at the data first!

CRITICIZING THE SOURCE MATERIAL

A concept that can be difficult to grasp, even when questions directly address it, is the idea that you can criticize your source material. Students often become so accustomed to learning from textbooks and other sources of "known" information that they assume that what they're reading is true and never question it.

On the ACT Science test, especially with regard to Research Summaries, you are essentially reading a very short journal article that describes scientific research. This means that someone else devised and carried out an experiment, and then presented the results of that experiment. Scientific research, however, does not always go as planned, even in published journal articles; while published articles are reviewed by peer scientists for completeness, articles can still make it through the publication process with inherent flaws that reviewers might have missed. The same applies to Research Summaries.

In general, Research Summaries will be fairly simple and straightforward, with no major issues in terms of experimental design, but sometimes you'll get a Research Summary passage or two that are missing a control trial, or that used a technique for the wrong purpose, or that published outlier data because there were not enough trials performed, among others. If you notice that something is missing from the experimental design or results, there is a good chance you will have to address it in the questions. Even if you don't notice anything obvious on the first read-through, you still may be asked to critically assess what you have just read.

When you have to critically assess a given Research Summary, there are two possible directions that these questions can take. On the one hand, the Research Summary might be fine, allowing you to select the answer choice that indicates that everything is valid. More often than not, however, if you are asked a question about something that is not quite right with an experimental design or result, there is probably something worth criticizing.

If you haven't picked up on the flaw on your first or even your second read-through, it's perfectly fine! This is where you can take advantage of the fact that the ACT Science test is a multiple-choice test. Check out each of the answer choices you've been given and choose the one you feel is the strongest.

For instance, if a question asks you to identify a flaw in the experiment, consider each of your answer choices and decide if the answer choice is:

1. a flaw that should be corrected,
2. a detail that may not be ideal, but ultimately isn't important to the experiment or result, or
3. even a flaw at all. This will help you to narrow down your options and select the best answer choice.

Now try another sample question set on your own. The questions are based on a physics passage that describes a relatively simple experiment. The questions are more challenging, however, because they ask you to analyze and criticize the experiment.

A group of students wanted to investigate the effect of the mass at the end of a spring on the time period over which the spring oscillates. The students constructed the experimental setup shown in Figure 1.

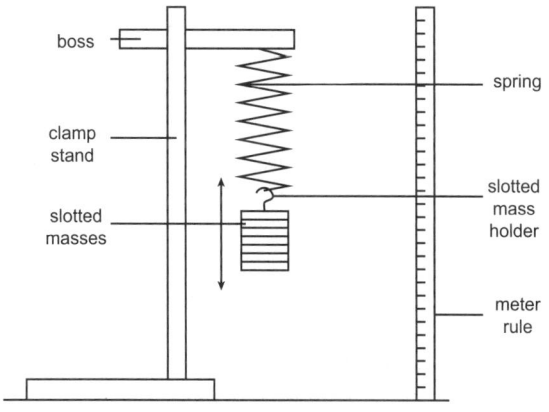

Figure 1

The students positioned a meter stick next to the spring for control of the oscillation amplitude. On the slotted mass holder, the students used 100 g for the first set of trials. Per trial, the students pulled the mass holder down by 5 cm, based on the meter stick, and released the spring, using a stopwatch to measure the time required for the spring to complete ten oscillations. One oscillation time period is defined by the students as the time it takes for the end of the spring to return to its equilibrium point after moving upward and downward one time each. The 100-g experiment was performed two additional times.

This set of experiments was repeated for three other masses: 400 g, 700 g, and 1 kg. The oscillation times were compiled in Table 1.

	Time required for 10 oscillations (sec.)				Avg. time of
Mass (g)	Trial 1 (sec.)	Trial 2 (sec.)	Trial 3 (sec.)	Average (sec.)	1 oscillation (sec.)
100	1.40	1.28	1.28	1.32	0.132
400	4.40	4.52	4.42	4.45	0.445
700	7.80	7.85	7.67	7.77	0.777
1000	12.12	11.99	11.95	12.02	1.202

Table 1

The students noted that the whole setup, including the base, shook uncontrollably for the trials with the 1-kg mass, but they still managed to acquire their measurements for time required for the ten oscillations per trial.

The students measured the time period of ten oscillations rather than directly measuring the time period of a single oscillation because:

- **A.** the upper and lower limits of the oscillation would have been more difficult to discern based on only one oscillation.
- **B.** the spring constant varies more over the course of a single oscillation than over the course of ten oscillations.
- **C.** the time period of ten oscillations is significantly higher and easier to measure than that of one oscillation.
- **D.** the relationship between time period and mass varies dramatically from trial to trial based on only one oscillation.

The correct answer is C. Choice A is incorrect because, if anything, the first oscillation will be the largest and easiest to measure. Choice B is incorrect because the spring constant, per its name, is a constant for a given spring and will not change during an experiment. Choice D is incorrect because if the relationship between time period and mass varies dramatically from trial to trial based on only one oscillation, it would not be useful to calculate an average time period for one oscillation; also, if you have any background knowledge of springs, you would know that this statement is simply untrue. Choice C is correct because most of the average time periods calculated per single oscillation are less than 1.00 seconds, and it would be extremely difficult to measure this with a stopwatch. Using the time period of ten oscillations gives a larger and more manageable time period to measure.

The graph that best conveys the trend in average oscillation time as a function of mass, according to the data, is:

F.

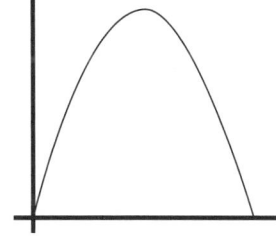

G.

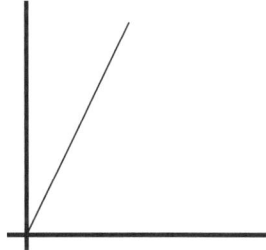

H.

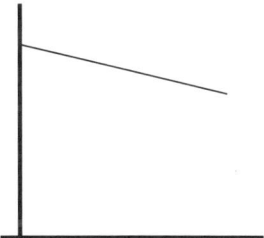

J.

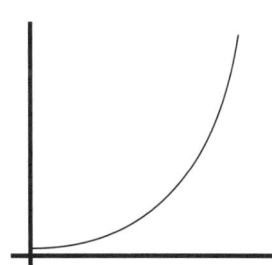

The correct answer is G. Based on the data, the increase in mass results in a corresponding and constant increase in average oscillation time period, which would result in a linear graph. Choice F is incorrect because the time periods do not increase and then decrease as mass increases, as this graph indicates. Choice H is incorrect because it indicates that the time period decreases as mass increases. Choice J is where this actually gets challenging, because if you have any background knowledge of springs, you would know that this is actually the result that *should* have been obtained.

Mathematically and physically, oscillation time is actually linearly proportional to $\sqrt{mass}$, not mass as a straight quantity. However, you have to analyze the data you've been given, and the data is linear.

Which of the following improvements to the experiment would remedy the shaking described for some of the trials during the experiment?

    A.   Fasten the boss more tightly and securely to the clamp stand.
    B.   Use a larger spring for all of the trials.
    C.   Perform the experiment at a lower temperature.
    D.   Limit the tested mass range to masses below 700 g.

The correct answer is D. Choice A may initially seem like a good answer because tightening pieces of the setup would eliminate shaking within the setup itself. However, the passage indicates that the entire setup, including the base, is shaking, so based on the image shown in Figure 1, simply tightening the connection between the boss and clamp stand more tightly will not eliminate the shaking. Choice B is incorrect because a larger spring would, if anything, increase shaking because the mass shaking occurred at higher masses. Choice C is incorrect because temperature is irrelevant here. Choice D is correct because, of the tested trials, only the 1-kg (1,000 g) mass caused shaking, so limiting the tested masses to an upper limit of 700 g would eliminate shaking.

The students realized after the experiment that the ceiling fan automatically turned on and off throughout the experiment. The constant that would most be affected by this environmental condition is:

    F.   the spring constant.
    G.   the amplitude of oscillation.
    H.   acceleration due to gravity.
    J.   friction due to air resistance.

The correct answer is J. The presence of intermittent ceiling fan action would alter air resistance and therefore affects the results by influencing friction of the spring. Choice F is incorrect because the spring constant remains constant regardless of mass and would not be influenced by the ceiling fan disturbance. Choice G is incorrect because the amplitude of oscillation, controlled through the use of the ruler, would not be affected by the ceiling fan disturbance. Choice H is incorrect because gravitational acceleration is always constant at 9.8 m/s^2.

. . . .

SUMMING IT UP

- **Research Summaries present you with background information, a description of experimental methods, and the associated data for a particular research project.** Within this question type, you will be asked to put more thought into the experiment itself—its design, functionality, and validity.

- Each Research Summary passage is accompanied by approximately five questions that test your ability to **identify the scientific question or purpose; develop a relevant hypothesis; propose an experiment or suggest an alternative method; analyze data**; and **draw conclusions based on the provided data.**

- As in Data Representation questions, it is important to **identify the scientific question, or purpose, when you first read a passage.** Research Summaries do all of the research for you; if the scientific question has not been stated outright, the background information and data can help you determine what it is.

- Questions about hypotheses may be extremely straightforward (if the hypothesis is stated somewhere in the passage), or you may be asked to select the correct hypothesis based on the text. Usually, **the key to choosing an appropriate hypothesis lies in identifying the independent and dependent variables.**

- **You will likely see at least one or two questions related to the experimental design**—the actual methods and techniques used to investigate the scientific question. Some might be straightforward and ask you to identify variables and controls or answer simple recall questions about the experiment or relevant scientific principles; others might ask you to critique the experiment and its methods or suggest logical next steps.

- **Questions based on experimental design are really testing your proficiency in reading comprehension, logic, and critical assessment.**

- **When faced with unfamiliar vocabulary and terminology, pay attention to prefixes, suffixes, and root words—they can tip you off to the meaning of a new word.** Don't let long, scientific words fluster you. Replace them in your mind with abbreviations so they're less confusing. The ACT is testing your knowledge of process and reading comprehension, not tricky terminology.

- **Experimental results do not always come out in the obvious way.** Always analyze the data as presented—don't let your expectations color your analysis. Even if the results seem incorrect or potentially flawed, your goal is to analyze *only* the data you have been given.

- **Be on the lookout for flaws in experiments—don't assume that what you have been presented is 100% correct and flawless experimental design.** If you notice that something is missing from the experimental design or results, there is a good chance you will have to address it when answering the questions.

CHAPTER 10
CONFLICTING VIEWPOINTS:
INTERPRETING AND RELATING
ARGUMENTS

OVERVIEW

- About Conflicting Viewpoints Questions
- Conflicting Viewpoints: Getting Advanced
- Summing It Up

The smallest portion of the ACT Science test, about 15–20 percent, is composed of Conflicting Viewpoints questions. Conflicting Viewpoints are a different kind of beast than the Data Representation and Research Summaries. Instead of presenting you with experimental procedures and data that resemble research articles from scientific journals, Conflicting Viewpoints present you with the kind of information you might find in a short communication in a scientific journal or a perspective piece in a science magazine.

Conflicting Viewpoints passages present you with at least two viewpoints about a given topic, and the questions that follow ask you to analyze the pros and cons of each. Beyond that, you will be asked to recall details from the passages and relate the passages to one another.

As you can probably tell from this description alone, Conflicting Viewpoints passages take on an entirely different style than the rest of the ACT Science test. In fact, they are more similar to reading comprehension passages found elsewhere on the test. Fortunately, the benefit of reading comprehension evaluations is that you are generally given most or all of the information you need to answer the questions in the passages themselves. You won't have to bring a whole lot of background knowledge to the table.

ABOUT CONFLICTING VIEWPOINTS QUESTIONS

Conflicting Viewpoints passages themselves are usually viewpoints, summaries, or hypotheses that describe the same science topic or field. These passages may also take the form of scientists tackling simple experimental questions in different ways and presenting their findings.

Regardless of the content, you will usually be presented with two viewpoints, though sometimes you may see three. The questions that follow then ask you to analyze each viewpoint individually before relating the viewpoints to each other. With regard to content in this portion of the test, it is important to distinguish between hypotheses and theories. As noted in Chapter 8, a **hypothesis** is an educated guess about the outcome of an experiment or phenomenon based on background or logic. While the term *theory* is often used synonymously with *hypothesis*, it is actually a slightly different concept; a **theory** usually has more substantial data and observations as support. In short, a theory is a more corroborated hypothesis. Examples of theories include the theory of evolution and the Big Bang theory; there is a lot of evidence to support both of these theories, but neither is considered to be concrete scientific fact.

Examples of Famous Hypotheses

- **The Expanding Earth Hypothesis:** The existence of continental drift and underwater mountain ranges indicates that Earth is gradually growing, as new mountains are created as continents move further and further apart.

- **The Phlogiston Hypothesis:** Now out of favor, this hypothesis proposed that all combustible objects released a tasteless, colorless, odorless substance called phlogiston when they caught fire; once burned, objects were thought to have returned to their true "calx" form.

Examples of Famous Theories

- **The Theory of Heliocentrism:** This theory proposed that Earth and the other planets revolved around the sun.

- **The Special Theory of Relativity:** This theory, according to Albert Einstein, proposed that the laws of physics are the same for all nonaccelerating frames of reference, and that the speed of light in a vacuum is the same for any observer, irrespective of the motion of the light source.

Conflicting Viewpoints passages will usually start with a short paragraph to introduce the topic of interest, which you should jot down so you know what main idea to hone in on as you read the viewpoints. This introductory paragraph will then be followed by the viewpoints themselves. It is helpful to continue taking notes as you read, jotting down the main idea of each viewpoint, key supporting data, and any important vocabulary words. Once you've read through the viewpoints, take a look at the questions. The questions will often evaluate your ability to:

1. Recall details from each viewpoint
2. Relate the viewpoints to each other by comparing or contrasting
3. Make inferences and use real or hypothetical data to support or refute the viewpoints

Questions that ask you to recall details from each viewpoint is easily the most straight-forward question type you will encounter when working on a Conflicting Viewpoints passage. This is reading comprehension at its most basic, as you must simply look back at the passage and find the answer you are looking for.

Here's what these questions might look like:

> According to Article 1, the best preventative diet for avoiding colon cancer consists of:

> The main argument of Article 2 is:

> What does the second article suggest is the main cause of global climate change in the present day?

PAY ATTENTION TO WHAT INFO GOES WITH EACH PASSAGE

There are a few ways you can get tripped up on these kinds of questions. Perhaps the most common way is by mixing up the viewpoints. If a question asks you for the main argument of Viewpoint 1, there is a very good chance that one of the incorrect distractor answers will be the main argument of Viewpoint 2, just in case you didn't read carefully enough and looked at the wrong viewpoint.

READ THE QUESTION STEM CAREFULLY

Another way you might stumble on a basic recall question is by not answering the question posed. This may seem obvious, but under a time crunch, you might decide to look for key words or phrases or choose an answer that is obviously related to the viewpoint of interest. Some of the distractors might be completely irrelevant, but usually most of the distractors you see will be very much relevant to the viewpoint of interest. Make sure you're choosing the choice that correctly answers the question, not just a choice that makes a correct statement.

For instance, if someone asks you which planet in the solar system has the hottest surface, and you respond that Jupiter is the largest planet in the solar system, your response is a true statement but it is not the answer to the question. (For the record, Venus has the hottest surface due to the greenhouse effect caused by its dense atmosphere.)

Relying on key words is also a crutch to avoid if you can—just because an answer choice includes a relevant vocabulary word does not mean that it is the correct answer choice. Distractors like these occur frequently in Conflicting Viewpoints questions and throughout the ACT Science test, so be careful!

COMPARING AND CONTRASTING

Questions that follow Conflicting Viewpoints will often ask you to compare and contrast the two viewpoints. Often, you will be able to find statements in the viewpoints that directly state the same idea and can therefore be a point of comparison between the viewpoints.

The same goes for differences, as you will probably be able to find direct statements of opposing ideas in the viewpoints.

For example, Article 1 might argue in favor of the phlogiston hypothesis, which indicates that an undetectable chemical substance called phlogiston is released from any burning object, and when the object is done burning, it has returned to its true form. Supporting this argument might be the assertion that most fires are very similar in appearance. Meanwhile, Article 2 might support the oxygen theory of combustion, which asserts that oxygen gas combines with substances as they burn. Supporting evidence here might include the fact that some metals actually gain mass as they burn, which both supports the idea that another substance is involved in combustion and refutes the idea that a substance (like phlogiston) is released.

A point of comparison between the two arguments is the idea that all burning objects are united by a characteristic chemical reaction.

A point of contrast between the two arguments is the chemical process itself. The phlogiston hypothesis argues for the release of a chemical, phlogiston, while the oxygen theory of combustion argues for the input of a chemical, oxygen.

Where Conflicting Viewpoints can get tricky, though, is when you have to think about implied ideas. For example, Viewpoint 1 might directly state that there is no connection between carbon dioxide and global warming, while Viewpoint 2 might show a graph with a strong positive correlation between atmospheric carbon dioxide levels and average global temperature over time. While Viewpoint 2 has not stated it directly, you can imply that Viewpoint 2 is attempting to demonstrate that there *is* a connection between carbon dioxide levels and global warming, making this a key difference between the viewpoints.

USING DATA TO MAKE INFERENCES

The final question type you will see following Conflicting Viewpoints are those that ask you to make inferences and use real or hypothetical data to support or refute the viewpoints. These two concepts are interrelated because they both involve drawing conclusions and making connections that are not explicitly spelled out in the viewpoints themselves.

Questions that ask you to make inferences might ask you to draw a conclusion based on the evidence presented in the viewpoint or predict how the author of the viewpoint would feel about a given statement.

For example, if a particular viewpoint argues that there is no connection between carbon dioxide levels and global warming, a question might ask you how the author of that viewpoint would feel about the statement that global warming can be remedied by limiting the burning of fossil fuels globally. Since the viewpoint is arguing that there is no connection between carbon dioxide levels and global warming, you would have to fill in the blanks and conclude that the author would disagree with the statement. Burning fossil fuels results in the release of carbon dioxide into the atmosphere, and if the author believes that carbon dioxide does not affect global warming, then the author would also believe that limiting the burning of fossil fuels will have no effect whatsoever on global warming.

Inference-based questions might also ask you to draw connections between the passages that are not explicitly spelled out. For instance, if Viewpoint 1 argues in favor of symbiogenesis, the theory that eukaryotes originated from a symbiosis between unicellular organisms, and Viewpoint 2 argues that eukaryotic mitochondria and chloroplasts are remarkably similar to cyanobacteria, you may be asked whether or not these two viewpoints are compatible with one another. Even though these two viewpoints may not be arguing the same point, they can still be compatible because Viewpoint 2 actually provides evidence that can be used to support Viewpoint 1 since cyanobacteria are unicellular organisms, and plastids like mitochondria and chloroplasts are found exclusively in eukaryotic cells.

In addition to demonstrating inference as it pertains to relating separate viewpoints, this example also illustrates the fact that Conflicting Viewpoints are not always necessarily "conflicting" in the traditional sense; a set of Conflicting Viewpoints may be considered "conflicting" because they are not arguing the same point, but they still may be compatible with one another.

Finally, a common inference-based question type for Conflicting Viewpoints passages is the use of real or hypothetical data. If you are presented with two passages, you may be presented in a question a piece of data, which may or may not be real, and you will be asked whether the piece of data supports one, both, or neither of the passages. Questions like these require you to think outside the box a bit and consider new information as it relates to information you already have.

Give this question a try.

. . . .

Continental drift was discovered by Alfred Wegener around 1912. The theory of plate tectonics was developed about half of a century later. According to this theory, the crustal plates, which are juxtaposed and interlocked with each other to form plate boundaries, mountain ranges, and oceanic trenches, move relative to one another due to the ever-changing surface of Earth. These changes are caused by the formation of crust and the resulting interaction with the mantle of the planet. All of the major continents were a supercontinent, Pangaea, millions of years ago, but the buildup of heat beneath the supercontinent caused rifts and splitting, forming new sub-continents between which oceans formed. This feature of the theory describes continental drift.

Which of the following pieces of evidence least supports the theory of plate tectonics?

A. The pattern of magnetic material on the sea floor is indicative of magma forcing its way up to the surface and cooling the material into minerals.
B. Similar fossils were found in western Africa and eastern South America.
C. Satellite technology shows changing distances between two lasers on Earth that are located on different continents.
D. Convection provides less energy than is required for plate movement.

The correct answer is D. Choice A supports the idea of mountain ranges forming under the sea due to crustal plate movement. Choice B supports the concept of Pangaea because the same organisms occur on coasts that would have been adjacent on Pangaea. Choice C indicates that the distances between laser points on continents are changing. Choice D indicates that not enough energy is provided by convection to explain plate movement.

· ·

CONFLICTING VIEWPOINTS: GETTING ADVANCED

Conflicting Viewpoints can range from absurdly simplistic to unexpectedly advanced in terms of content, but regardless of the kinds of viewpoints you see, *you will have most of the information in front of you to answer the questions.* Repeat that to yourself if you ever get overwhelmed by scientific information.

 Even the most difficult topics will not be unmanageable, as you'll have plenty of clues throughout the passage to help you answer questions.

In addition to the aforementioned skills and question types, there are three other obstacles you may face in the most difficult Conflicting Viewpoints passages on the ACT Science test:

1. High-level content
2. More than two viewpoints
3. Experimental data

After we go through these points, we will go through two sample passages to demonstrate the strategies we have discussed throughout this chapter. For the sake of looking at a diverse array of questions and subject matter, our sample passages will each be accompanied by four questions, but please note that on the real ACT Science test, every Conflicting Viewpoints passage will be accompanied by seven questions. This is constant; there are never more or less than seven questions following any Conflicting Viewpoints passage.

High-Level Content

As with any other type of passage or question on the ACT Science test, the difficulty is always elevated when the topic of the passage or question is unfamiliar. Fortunately, when it comes to Conflicting Viewpoints passages, most of your gaps in understanding can be filled in through reading comprehension.

Vocabulary words that are completely obscure will usually be defined, but more often than not, you will come across at least a few other words that are new to you, especially in viewpoints that describe a topic with which you are not familiar. Sometimes, but certainly not always, a visual may be provided to enhance your understanding of the topic. While in Data Representation passages you can often get away with skimming the text and focusing on the figures, the meaty content of Conflicting Viewpoints passages is in the text, particularly in the viewpoints themselves, so this is not a section in which you will want to skip the text or skim through too quickly.

Take a look at the following example.

> The population of finches diversified quickly with respect to beak size via adaptive radiation, thanks to a rainy season that followed a lengthy dry season. Due to the availability of water, a wide array of seeds were available to the finches, and a wide array of beak sizes emerged in the population. This rapid diversification of finch beak size strongly influenced the diversity of the finches long-term.

In this example, the term "adaptive radiation" can be defined based on surrounding clues. The population "diversified rapidly," indicating that adaptive radiation occurs over a relatively short period of time. The description of the newly available water indicates that this rapid diversification was caused by an environmental change that had made available a new resource. The result of adaptive radiation is a population with a diverse, wide array of beak sizes.

Regardless of the scientific content, however, the important initial take-home from each viewpoint with which you are presented is the argument. This is generally the first sentence of a given viewpoint, though this may not always be the case. Make sure at the very least you understand the argument each viewpoint is trying to make, and then you can delve into the evidence and additional content. Even if the topic is over your head, you should be able to extract the main argument or theory or hypothesis from any viewpoint you read, and this should generally be the first thing you do any time you encounter a viewpoint in these kinds of passages.

More Than Two Viewpoints

Viewpoints can vary in length; some will be short and sweet, while others will provide you with plenty of evidence or supporting details. This may look especially intimidating on a passage that includes three passages rather than two. Typically, Conflicting Viewpoints passages have two viewpoints, but we're talking about the highest level of complexity here, and a Conflicting Viewpoints passage that contains three viewpoints certainly meets that requirement.

You can pretty much treat a three-viewpoint passage the same way you would treat a two-viewpoint passage: identify the thesis, take notes on key terms or concepts, and then move on to the questions. However, dealing with three viewpoints rather than two elevates the level of difficulty because you have more information to keep straight. This is where note-taking becomes especially important, because you want to be sure you're attributing the correct details to the appropriate passages. As noted earlier, incorrect answer choices will include key words from all of the passages, and if you don't keep your details straight, you may find yourself mixing up passages and selecting incorrect answers.

Given your limited time, viewpoints that appear in trios tend to be shorter and less in-depth than viewpoints that appear in pairs. They will not be as extensive because you have more content to get through. On the whole, two-viewpoint Conflicting Viewpoints passages and three-viewpoint Conflicting Viewpoints passages are generally similar in length. So if you encounter a three-viewpoint Conflicting Viewpoints passage as you work through the ACT Science test, just stay calm and treat it exactly as you would any other Conflicting Viewpoints passage—just take a little more care to stay organized and keep your details straight.

EXPERIMENTAL DATA

When experimental data appears in Conflicting Viewpoints passages, it is usually not in the form of tables or graphs. Many of the experimental data you will see in Conflicting Viewpoints passages will be qualitative. Other provided experimental results may be quantitative, but in useful, digestible nuggets—you generally won't see long lists of numbers or extremely complex organizational charts.

When you're given quantitative data, it will usually be in a small dose and in sentence form, such as:

> The concentration of dissolved oxygen in the lake decreased by 17% from 2015 to 2016.

> The number of predators who visited the test site decreased from 20 to 15, or by 25%, when the pesticides were added to the area.

When you see experimental data in Conflicting Viewpoints passages, it is generally presented to you as a means of supporting the argument provided by a viewpoint. In other words, the author of the viewpoint is giving you the data as a means to an end—whatever data you are given is intended to help show why the author's argument seems valid. You generally won't have to do any in-depth data analysis or even really draw your own conclusions; when experimental data is provided to you in these passages, that work is usually already done for you, and the data is given in a context that demonstrates why the author felt the need to include it. As indicated earlier, the Conflicting Viewpoints portion of the ACT Science test has a whole different feel than Data Representation or Research Summaries passages because you are really being tested on your ability to understand, analyze, and relate science-based arguments. The inclusion of experimental data is there to strengthen the provided argument, not to give you numbers to analyze.

As such, it is important that you do not spend too much time overanalyzing or over-thinking data you might come across in Conflicting Viewpoints passages.

A twist on the inclusion of experimental data can occur in the questions that follow a Conflicting Viewpoints passage, where you might be asked to consider real or hypo-thetical data with respect to the two viewpoints you just read. Such a question might look like this:

> *Scientists determine that Earth's lower mantle contains a highly iron-rich metal. Which viewpoint(s) is/are supported by this piece of evidence?*

When faced with questions like this, consider each provided piece of data and ask yourself if it fits in with the main argument of the described viewpoint:

- Does it support the argument the viewpoint is making?
- Does it refute the argument?
- Does it reinforce or contradict anything you read in the viewpoint?

These are the questions you should ask yourself if you have to consider newly provided real or hypothetical experimental data in light of the viewpoints.

As opposed to experimental data presented in Data Representation and Research Summaries passages, experimental data in Conflicting Viewpoints passages look more like the data you might find in a science magazine or newspaper rather than in a scientific journal. Instead of being presented with a huge amount of raw data, you will usually be given the most important take-home results.

Try out the following question set. This earth/space sciences passage provides two viewpoints that speculate on the cause of the K-T extinction of the dinosaurs.

· ·

The Cretaceous-Paleogene extinction event, also known as the K-T extinction, was the mass extinction of about three-quarters of the plant and animal species on Earth, including all non-avian dinosaurs, which occurred over a relatively short period of time approximately 66 million years ago. Scientists generally agree that the time period around which the K-T extinction of dinosaurs occurred was charac-terized by global climate change and short-term environmental disturbances. The climate of the planet generally changed from warm and mild to cooler and more varied. Short-term disturbances included poisonous gas emission, acid rain, and cooling, which collectively contributed to the longer-term consequence that is the greenhouse effect. During the K-T extinction, 75% of all organisms, marine and terrestrial, invertebrate and vertebrate, went extinct, likely due to the change in climate, and the K-T boundary in numerous locations is characterized by a thin layer of clay that is high in iridium content, a rare metal that is similar to platinum.

Two of the main viewpoints that attempt to explain the cause of the K-T extinction are provided below:

The Intrinsic Gradualist Viewpoint

Intrinsic gradualists argue that the cause of the K-T extinction was intrinsic, or caused by the earth itself, and gradual—several million years, to be specific. Two main concepts contribute to the intrinsic gradualist argument to explain the K-T extinction: plate tectonics and volcanic activity. According to the hypothesis of plate tectonics, continental drift was causing major changes at the K-T boundary. The oceans were receding from land, experiencing a regression. These changes would effectively lead to a less mild climate in consequence. While there is geological evidence that numerous enormous tectonic events took place during the Mesozoic era, no extinction events have yet been tied to these disturbances with certainty. Simultaneously, the action of plate tectonics would lead to increased volcanic activity, which indeed appeared to be characteristic of the late Cretaceous period. Over the course of several million years of increased volcanic activity, the abundance of dust and soot would block out the sunlight, contributing to the climate change. The Deccan traps, which can be seen today in India at the K-T boundary, serve as evidence for the massive streams of lava spewed from volcanic eruptions during the Late Cretaceous period. The release of volcanic gases, especially sulfur dioxide, would have contributed to the climate change. Furthermore, the chemical composition of these rocks in India indicates that they originated in the mantle of the earth, which is relatively iridium-rich.

The Extrinsic Catastrophic Viewpoint

Extrinsic catastrophists argue that the K-T extinction was caused by factors that were extrinsic, or not of earthly origin, and catastrophic, or rather sudden in nature over a short period of time. Among the main proponents of this viewpoint are the father-son duo of Luis and Walter Alvarez, who posed the Alvarez Hypothesis. According to this hypothesis, a massive extraterrestrial object collided with the earth, and its impact stirred up a tremendous amount of dust, causing the climatic change. Lending support to this hypothesis is the fact that asteroids and related extraterrestrial bodies have higher iridium concentrations than the earth's crust, resulting in the observed iridium layer at the K-T boundary. There is currently no evidence of a confirmed crater, which would be approximately 65 million years old and is predicted to have been about 100 km in diameter, but more recent evidence found a potential candidate for a crater on the Yucatan Peninsula of Mexico at *Chicxulub*. In addition, shocked quartz was found in the rocks at the K-T boundary, an indication of a powerful shock wave that was able to rearrange the crystal structure of quartz grains. Additional supporting evidence includes the discovery of widespread glass spheres of *impact ejecta*, ejected molten rock that solidified upon cooling into droplets, as well as a soot layer that likely resulted from widespread forest fires following from the impact.

Based on the Alvarez Hypothesis, the prehistoric food chain was most significantly disrupted globally by the:

   F. abundance and regularity of volcanic eruptions.
   G. halt of photosynthesis due to the enshrouding dust cloud.
   H. immediate death of land animals due to physical impact by the extraterrestrial body.
   J. increase in average global temperature.

The correct answer is G. The key phrase "Alvarez Hypothesis" should immediately point you to the second viewpoint, which attributes the K-T extinction to a sudden catastrophic extraterrestrial impact. Choice F is incorrect because both viewpoints recognize the regularity of volcanic eruptions, but the Alvarez Hypothesis does not attribute the extinction to the volcanic activity. Choice H is incorrect because the extraterrestrial body, according to the second viewpoint, is estimated to be about 100 km in diameter, which means that the physical impact would not have been the main cause of organismal death globally—the immediate *effects* of this impact caused most of the organismal death on a global scale. Choice J is incorrect because the introduction states that the average global temperature actually declined around the time of the K-T extinction. Choice G is correct because the Alvarez Hypothesis indicates that the extraterrestrial impact would have stirred up a massive dust cloud that caused climate change. By inference, one can determine that this dust cloud blocked the sunlight, which would have halted photosynthesis in plants and prevented energy distribution throughout the food chain.

Based on the provided information, the two viewpoints agree on:

   A. the source of iridium found in the clay.
   B. the briefness of the punctuated time period over which the K-T extinction took place.
   C. *Chicxulub* as the most likely point of impact for the massive extraterrestrial collision that caused the K-T extinction.
   D. the regularity of volcanic activity at the K-T boundary.

The correct answer is D. Choice A is incorrect because both viewpoints provide different explanations for the iridium source; the first viewpoint claims that the iridium comes from Earth's mantle, while the second viewpoint claims that the iridium comes from extraterrestrial bodies. Choice B is incorrect because the first viewpoint emphasizes a gradual, long-term extinction rather than the short, punctuated one described in the second viewpoint. Choice C is incorrect because only the second viewpoint argues that an extraterrestrial collision caused the K-T extinction. Choice D is correct. The first viewpoint explicitly mentions volcanic activity as the source of the extinction. While the second viewpoint does not attribute the extinction to the volcanic activity, the mention of widespread *impact ejecta* indicates regular volcanic activity because the impact disturbed molten rock that solidified upon cooling. In order for the rock to be molten in the first place, there must have been volcanic activity.

The fossil record suggests that mass extinctions are periodic, occurring roughly every 26 million years, and astronomers suggest that the Oort cloud of comets crosses the path of our solar system every 26 million years. The correlation between these two pieces of evidence supports:

    F. the intrinsic gradualist viewpoint only.
    G. the extrinsic catastrophist viewpoint only.
    H. both viewpoints.
    J. neither viewpoint.

The correct answer is G. The periodic mass extinctions, aligned with periodic extraterrestrial disturbance, points directly at the second viewpoint, as it would seem that the impact of comets from the Oort cloud are the cause of these mass extinctions. These pieces of evidence in no way support a more gradual cause of the observed extinctions, as the correlation in time period between the extinction events and Oort cloud path interference suggests that the comets are causing the observed extinctions.

Which of the following scientific advancements would most help to provide more solid evidence to support or refute both viewpoints?

    A. A reliable means of dating rocks or fossils that are millions of years old
    B. The ability to simulate the effect of constant volcanic activity on local organismal survival
    C. A valid technique for predicting the distance traveled by *impact ejecta* based on droplet shape and size
    D. Genomic data for prehistoric marine organisms for phylogenetic comparison to marine organisms observed today

The correct answer is A. Carbon dating is very limited in scope and is not useful for rocks that are millions of years old. The passage alludes to this idea by noting that all fossil or rock dates are approximates. Logically, however, a complete, dated fossil record would help to demonstrate whether species gradually died out due to the climate change, or whether species died out suddenly due to extreme climate changes resulting from an extraterrestrial impact. Choices B and C are incorrect because they are not relevant to providing information about the extinction time period, even though both could potentially provide very interesting data. Choice D would provide useful information about marine organismal evolution based on DNA sequences, but this would not provide much evidence to support or refute the provided arguments.

This is a biology passage that discusses the effects of genes and hormones as they pertain to a predisposition to autism spectrum disorders.

Three scientists discussed the genetic mechanisms that predispose a child to autism spectrum disorders (ASD), and each argued for a different mechanism as the primary cause of genetic predisposition to autism, focusing on the neural system. Lesions in the neural system may be localized or distributed. Localized lesions, caused by genetic mutations, may lower functionality of one component of the circuit and effectively damage other nearby components, whereas distributed lesions result in system-wide neural disarray. There are numerous sources of evidence for genetic legions that disturb specific brain connections, such as the corpus callosum; in the case of the corpus callosum, experimental evidence has shown that its size is smaller in individuals with ASD relative to the total brain volume than in unaffected individuals.

Scientist A

The main source of genetic predisposition to ASD lies in evolutionary-driven expansion of cerebrum and cerebellar size. As the mammalian brain has evolved, it has increased in size morphologically. The human brain is approximately three times larger than that of a chimpanzee. Additionally, the prefrontal cortex of humans, which is the center for complex thinking, planning, and decision-making, is significantly larger compared with those of apes, monkeys, and less evolved mammals. Shortly after birth, individuals with ASD demonstrate increased brain volume and head circumference, especially in the frontal lobes. This difference has been attributed to FGF signaling. Mice with a defect in Fgf17 were found to be viable but have a subtle reduction in prefrontal cortex size, indicating that the lesion of one signal gene, Fgf17, related to brain size can disrupt the functions of the neural systems required for ASD. Similar experimental results were seen for Fgf8.

Scientist B

The main source of genetic predisposition to ASD lies in the balance of excitation and inhibition (E/I balance). The E/I balance refers to the relative contributions of excitatory and inhibitory synaptic outputs that correspond to a neuronal event. Molecular lesions that affect excitatory and inhibitory synapses can disrupt neural systems and cause some forms of ASD. The high prevalence of epilepsy in individuals with ASD suggests an increase in the excitatory/inhibitory ratio. Experiments with mice showed that when inhibition is blocked using drugs, cortical activity becomes epileptic, and neurons lose their selectivity to different stimuli.

Furthermore, the Dlx genes regulate the development and function of forebrain-inhibitory neurons. Lesions in the Dlx genes, in consequence, can weaken the forebrain-inhibitory tone and increase the excitatory/inhibitory ratio.

Scientist C

There is approximately a 4:1 ratio of ASD-affected boys relative to ASD-affected girls. Therefore, the main source of genetic predisposition to ASD lies in the hormone levels. There are several ASD-susceptible genes on the X chromosome, so direct genetics cannot explain the prevalence of ASD in males. Male:female hormonal differences, namely brain concentrations of androgens and estrogens, may cause the ASD bias. Such hormones drive sex-specific behaviors, regulate cell survival and neuronal connectivity and function, and can also modify the E/I balance. Therefore, sex steroid levels may be a major contributor to ASD genetic predisposition.

Which of the following observations, if true, would be consistent with the viewpoints of Scientists B or C, but not necessarily that of Scientist A?

F. ASD is primarily caused by post-translational protein modifications.

G. The excitatory/inhibitory balance is a consistent key marker for the presence or absence of ASD.

H. FGF signaling is the genetic system that plays the most significant role in ASD genetic predisposition.

J. Female hormones are more likely than male hormones to direct an individual toward development of ASD.

The correct answer is G. The viewpoints of Scientists B and C both point to the excitatory/inhibitory balance as a main indicator for ASD. Scientist B indicates that disturbance of this balance is caused by genes, while Scientist C indicates that disturbance of this balance is caused by hormones. Choice F is incorrect because this statement takes the genetics out of the picture completely and indicates that protein modifications provide the most critical contribution to ASD development. Choice H is incorrect because it is completely consistent with the viewpoint of Scientist A, which is the opposite of what the question asks. Choice J is incorrect because hormones are not relevant to the viewpoints of Scientists A and B; furthermore, the viewpoint of Scientist C indicates that the sex ratio of ASD-affected individuals is 4:1 males:females, which means that male hormones, not female hormones, would direct an individual toward ASD development in order to be consistent with the viewpoint of Scientist C.

Lesion development as a genetic cause of ASD is a critical component of the theories of:

A. Scientists A and B only.

B. Scientists A and C only.

C. Scientists B and C only.

D. all three scientists.

The correct answer is A. The viewpoints of Scientists A and B specifically talk about genes that, if afflicted by lesions, can lead to ASD development. No lesions come into play in the hormone-geared viewpoint presented by Scientist C.

Hypothetical evidence shows that in ASD-afflicted individuals, male hormones consistently and strongly downregulate the expression of Fgf17. This new piece of evidence would:

    F.   confirm the ASD-related genes and mode of regulation posed by Scientist A.

    G. confirm that Scientist A identified the appropriate genes related to ASD but instead confirm the mode of regulation posed by Scientist B.

    H. confirm that Scientist A identified the appropriate genes related to ASD but instead confirm the mode of regulation posed by Scientist C.

    J.   wholly refute the viewpoints of Scientists A and C in terms of relevant genes and modes of regulation.

The correct answer is H. Scientist A attributed defects in Fgf17 to ASD development, but it was Scientist C who proposed that sex hormones might drive the development of ASD. Therefore, based on this hypothetical data, Scientist A would have identified the relevant gene system, but Scientist C proposed the correct regulatory mode. Choice F is incorrect because Scientist A attributed Fgf17 defects to lesions rather than hormones. Choice G is incorrect because Scientist B also indicated that lesions cause ASD development. Choice J is incorrect because the hypothetical data support components of the viewpoints of both Scientist A and Scientist C.

Which of the following statements best describes the compatibility of the three viewpoints with regard to ASD genetic predisposition contribution?

    A. The viewpoints of Scientists A and B are compatible with one another, but neither is compatible with that of Scientist C.

    B. The viewpoints of Scientists A and C are compatible with one another, but neither is compatible with that of Scientist B.

    C. The viewpoints of Scientists B and C are compatible with one another, but neither is compatible with that of Scientist A.

    D. All three viewpoints are compatible with one another and could be simultaneous contributors to ASD genetic predisposition.

The correct answer is D. Even though all three viewpoints pose different regulated genes and modes of regulation for ASD genetic predisposition, none of the viewpoints include any arguments or evidence that would exclude any of the other viewpoints. As such, all three are compatible and could play roles in ASD genetic predisposition.

SUMMING IT UP

- **Conflicting Viewpoints passages make up 15–20 percent of the exam** and present you with at least two viewpoints in the form of arguments, hypotheses, theories, etc., that describe the same science topic or field.

- **Each Conflicting Viewpoints passage is accompanied by exactly seven questions** that ask you to recall details from the passage, compare and contrast the viewpoints in the passage, make inferences in order to draw conclusions about the authors' views, connect the viewpoints to one another, or decide whether or not real or hypothetical data would support or refute the viewpoints.

- Within Conflicting Viewpoints, it is important to distinguish between hypotheses and theories. A **hypothesis** is an educated guess about the outcome of an experiment or phenomenon based on background or logic; a **theory** usually has more substantial data, evidence, and observations as support.

- **Conflicting Viewpoints passages will begin with an introduction that presents the topic of interest**—take note, so you know the main idea before you read the two or three different viewpoints.

- **Conflicting Viewpoints do not always necessarily have different points of view**; a set of Conflicting Viewpoints may be considered "conflicting" because they are not arguing the same point, but they still may be compatible with one another.

- **Conflicting Viewpoints questions may ask you to recall details from each viewpoint:** these are basic reading comprehension questions—must simply look back at the passage to find the answer you are looking for.
  - **Do not mix up the viewpoints**, and make sure you know which point of view and information goes with which passage.

- **Conflicting Viewpoints questions may ask you to make inferences:** these questions might require you to draw a conclusion based on the evidence or predict how the author of a viewpoint would feel about a given statement.

- **Conflicting Viewpoints questions are often not accompanied by figures, so this is not a section in which you will want to skip the text or skim through too quickly.** Make sure you understand the argument each viewpoint represents. Even if the topic is over your head, the first thing you should do is extract the main argument, theory, or hypothesis from any viewpoint you read.
  - Double-check to **make sure you're choosing the choice that correctly answers the question**, not just a choice that makes a correct statement.

- **Treat a three-viewpoint passage the same way you would treat a two-viewpoint passage**: identify the thesis, take notes on key terms or concepts, and then move on to the questions. Take notes to make sure you are certain which information goes with which viewpoint.

- As with all ACT Science test questions, **you have all the information you need to answer the questions in front of you**. Stick to what is in the passages!

CHAPTER 11:
THE ACT® WRITING TEST

OVERVIEW

- Why You Should Take the ACT® Writing Test
- Test Overview
- How the ACT® Writing Test Is Scored
- The ACT® Writing Test: A Closer Look
- Planning Your Essay
- Writing a Perfect-Scoring Essay
- Reviewing Your Essay
- Practice Essay Prompt One
- Practice Essay Prompt Two
- Summing It Up

We know you're on the hunt for nothing less than a perfect score on the ACT—even on the optional ACT Writing test.

As you make your way through this chapter, you'll encounter a comprehensive overview of the ACT Writing test, including how it's structured and scored and what official ACT essay readers are looking for in an essay that deserves a perfect score; proven test-taking strategies; expert advice for honing your writing abilities, attacking essay prompts, and using your time effectively to plan and construct an essay that will earn a perfect score; and effective writing practice and review with targeted sample prompts and model essays to compare your work against, all designed with a *singular purpose:* to help you craft an essay that demonstrates a masterful command of all four writing proficiency domains that your work will be judged upon—and earn a perfect score!

WHY YOU SHOULD TAKE THE ACT® WRITING TEST

Even though the ACT Writing test is an *optional* component of the ACT, you're not just an average student, and you're certainly not looking to take any shortcuts—either on the ACT or in your academic career—and you want the official ACT essay readers and college admissions personnel to know that you're an elite student with serious writing skills, which are fundamental to success in every academic discipline.

As you know, the competition to get into top colleges and universities is fierce. At these elite institutions, there will be very little differentiating serious applicants—*everyone* will have great grades and killer application packages. Sometimes, admissions decisions will come down to the *smallest* details, the tiniest differentiating factors between applicants. A perfect score on the ACT Writing test just might be the factor that gives you the edge over the competition!

As you thoroughly research your target schools, make sure you know their individual admissions requirements regarding ACT Writing test scores. You have a few options:

- Contact schools directly.
- Ask your high school counselor for information.
- Use the College Writing Test Requirements Search Tool on the official ACT website (***https://actapps.act.org/writPrefRM/***) to see which schools require or recommend that you take the ACT Writing test.

 ALERT: The ACT Writing test does not impact your scores on other ACT subject area tests or your overall composite score. However, the *only* way to receive an English Language Arts (ELA) test score is by taking the optional ACT Writing test.

Here's the bottom line: Taking the ACT Writing test signals college admissions officers that you're confident in your writing ability and you're eager to showcase your skills. You've spent your entire academic career meeting challenges head on, achieving success, and leading the pack. Approach the ACT Writing test with the same mindset, and get ready to earn a perfect score!

TEST OVERVIEW

The ACT Writing test is a 40-minute essay exam designed to:

- Assess your English language writing capabilities
- Gauge your ability to respond thoughtfully and persuasively to a provided topic
- Measure your analytical ability
- Test your ability to develop ideas using logical reasoning and craft a well-structured piece of argumentative writing

In order to achieve a perfect score on the ACT Writing test, you'll need to utilize the entire breadth and scope of writing knowledge you've acquired throughout your academic career, including the core tenets of English language writing conventions, to craft a compelling argumentative essay in response to a provided essay prompt.

Remain Aware of the World Around You!

The range of essay topics that you could potentially encounter on test day is nearly limitless. Although you're being tested on your ability to craft an effective argument-based piece of writing, not to simply present facts, your knowledge of the topic in question will certainly enhance your ability to do so. Make an effort to stay informed and current on a wide range of issues and current events, especially those that receive a great deal of serious media attention and coverage.

A strong understanding of a wide range of topics and a firm grasp of core writing fundamentals will be your two most potent weapons when attacking the ACT Writing test!

As you've undoubtedly figured out through various successful academic endeavors, diligent practice is the key to success in every class and subject area. Writing is no different. The best preparation for writing an essay that earns the highest possible score is—you guessed it—writing practice. In addition to the writing assignments you'll tackle in your classes, make the most of your time between now and test day to polish your writing abilities.

Take full advantage of the effective practice you'll find in this book. You'll get to practice writing using essay prompts that are similar to what you might see on test day later in this chapter. You'll also get to analyze sample top-scoring essays to help you evaluate your own writing and determine what you need to work on to get a perfect score!

The ACT Writing test can be taken on all six of the official national test dates (which includes the United States, US territories, Canada, and Puerto Rico), as well as the five official international test dates and special or arranged test dates (visit the official ACT website for additional test scheduling information).

The test is taken using a pencil (remember to bring a few sharpened, nonmechanical #2 pencils with you), and you'll write your essay on paper provided to you by the test administrator. If you require specific test accommodations, please visit the official ACT website for additional information.

ACT WRITING TEST ENHANCEMENTS

In your hunt for a perfect score on the ACT Writing test, you've likely done your research and have discovered that the test has undergone some changes recently. This chapter covers everything you need to know to ace the current test format.

Although at its core the ACT Writing test is still designed to assess your writing abilities, the official test developers have made a few recent enhancements of which you should be aware:

- **Increased time for essay planning and writing:** Previously, test takers had 30 minutes to plan and write their essays. Test takers now have 40 minutes to do so. Students who get a perfect score on the ACT Writing test come to the test comfortable and familiar with developing an effective essay within the given time frame. Your study plan between now and test day should invariably include practice with organizing, structuring, and crafting a polished essay within the time allotted.

- **More comprehensive scoring:** The ACT Writing test now includes scoring in four specific writing proficiency domains: **Ideas and Analysis, Development and Support, Organization,** and **Language Use and Conventions** (more detail on these domains is provided later in this chapter).

- **Scores received:** You'll receive a Writing score and a scaled English Language Arts (ELA) score (ranging from 1–36, similar to the other test sections on the ACT). Additional scoring information appears later in this chapter.

- **More guidance and structure for essay planning:** The test now features prewriting guidance for structuring and crafting a written response. Students who earn a perfect score on the ACT don't ignore or gloss over any helpful information provided—they take full advantage of it to help them reach their goal of achieving a perfect score. Your approach to the writing test should follow the same path.

- **Wider range of subjects:** Previous essay prompts focused mainly on school-based subject matter. Now, essay prompts will draw from a wider array of engaging subjects and topical issues. As mentioned, your best strategy for achieving a perfect score on the test is to stay up to date on a wide array of news stories and current events as you practice writing.

- **Broader topic perspectives provided:** Test takers will get three diverse perspectives on the issue provided in the essay prompt, allowing for a more multifaceted analytical engagement. Use these perspectives, including aspects you agree with and aspects you don't agree with, to help you develop an engaging, perfect-scoring essay.

- **More reflective of real-world topic discussion:** Previously, students provided a response to the issue provided in the prompt. Now, their responses are built alongside, and in dialogue with, varying perspectives. As stated, a perfect-scoring essay will factor in these diverse perspectives to create a comprehensive written response.

HOW THE ACT® WRITING TEST IS SCORED

The ACT Writing test is designed to provide a comprehensive assessment of your abilities on a range of fundamental writing proficiency domains. You'll have the opportunity to respond to a writing prompt based on a carefully chosen topic, which will be presented alongside three distinct perspectives, each of which will be suggestive of a certain way of thinking about the issue.

A high-scoring essay will meet the following basic criteria:

- Analyze and evaluate the perspectives given
- State and develop your own perspective on the issue
- Explain the relationship between your perspective and those given

As you plan and structure your written response, your unique perspective on the issue can fully agree with any of the three perspectives provided, agree partially, or be completely distinct. An essay that achieves a perfect score will demonstrate a well-developed, clear, and confident position on the issue with relevant contextual support and use careful analysis, solid reasoning, sound ideas, and compelling examples.

THE FOUR WRITING PROFICIENCY DOMAINS

Your essay will be scored by two separate (and highly experienced) certified ACT essay readers in four specific writing proficiency domains. Let's take a closer look at each domain so you'll have a better understanding of what it will take to earn a perfect score on test day.

 In order to achieve a perfect score on the ACT Writing test, you'll need to get a score of 6 on *each* of the four tested writing proficiency domains.

1. Ideas and Analysis

This domain measures how well you can critically analyze a provided prompt and diverse array of perspectives on a given topic. A perfect-scoring essay will demonstrate an excellent understanding of the topic and provide a compelling, relevant argument that reflects your distinct perspective.

An essay that receives a score of 6 in this domain will demonstrate:

- Effective critical engagement with perspectives
- Nuance and purpose-driven precision
- Excellent depth and contextual insight on the topic
- Thoughtful analysis of the prompt issue(s) and implications of the writer's perspective

2. Development and Support

This domain assesses your ability to craft an effective written argument with sound ideas, solid reasoning, a clear rationale, and thoughtful support. A perfect-scoring essay will demonstrate a clear flow of thoughts that reflect a solid stance on the issue(s) provided in the prompt, with compelling support in defense of your perspective.

An essay that receives a score of 6 in this domain will demonstrate:

- A deep and insightful level of effective idea development to promote understanding
- The use of skilled reasoning and relevant and varied support to strengthen perspective

3. Organization

This domain measures your ability to carefully and thoughtfully organize your ideas to create a convincing, coherent, and well-structured essay. A perfect-scoring essay will be a clear, on-target, and purposeful piece of argumentative writing that demonstrates a solid understanding of essay structure and an effective flow of ideas—from introduction to conclusion.

An essay that receives a score of 6 in this domain will demonstrate:

- A skilled ability to capably organize ideas into a cogent piece of writing
- An effective and insightful central narrative theme that unifies the text
- A thorough understanding of standard essay structure and flow, including effective transitions between sentences and thoughts

A perfect-scoring essay demonstrates the value of starting and ending strong. Don't underestimate the importance of making a strong first impression on ACT essay readers with a killer introduction and leaving them wanting more with an unforgettable conclusion.

4. Language Use and Conventions

This domain measures your ability to effectively utilize English-language writing principles, including spelling, vocabulary, grammar, syntax, and language mechanics. A perfect-scoring essay will be a clear, polished, and effective piece of writing that reflects a mastery of language use and conventions.

An essay that receives a score of 6 in this domain will demonstrate:

- Skillful deployment of standard English language principles
- Excellent use of varied and engaging vocabulary and sentence structures
- A clear, authoritative, and effective voice and tone
- Few or no errors in grammar, mechanics, and syntax

SCORING YOUR ESSAY: AN INSIDE LOOK

The two readers who will be scoring your essay will provide a score from 1–6 in each of the four writing proficiency domains. Your total domain score for each of the four areas will be the sum of the two scores and will range from 2–12 (if the scores of the two readers in any domain area differ by more than one point, a third reader will be used to resolve the discrepancy).

Your domain scores will reflect the essay readers' impressions of your abilities as follows:

Score 6: Your essay demonstrates a highly effective skill level in this domain area.

Score 5: Your essay demonstrates a well-developed skill level in this domain area.

Score 4: Your essay demonstrates an adequate skill level in this domain area.

Score 3: Your essay demonstrates some developing ability in this domain area.

Score 2: Your essay demonstrates a weak or inconsistent skill level in this domain area.

Score 1: Your essay demonstrates a deficient skill level in this domain area.

The essay readers will calculate your individual domain scores based on the following ACT scoring rubric:

Score Level	Score 6
Ideas and Analysis	**Essay demonstrates:** • Effective critical engagement with perspectives • Nuance and purpose-driven precision • Excellent depth and contextual insight on the topic • Thoughtful analysis of the prompt issue(s) and implications of the writer's perspective
Development and Support	**Essay demonstrates:** • A deep and insightful level of effective idea development to promote understanding • Skilled reasoning and use of relevant and varied support to strengthen perspective
Organization	**Essay demonstrates:** • A skilled ability to capably organize ideas into a cogent piece of writing • An effective and insightful central narrative theme that unifies the text • A thorough understanding of standard essay structure and flow, including effective transitions between sentences and thoughts
Language Use and Conventions	**Essay demonstrates:** • Skillful deployment of standard English language principles • Excellent use of varied and engaging vocabulary and sentence structures • A clear, authoritative, and effective voice and tone • Few or no errors in grammar, mechanics, and syntax

Score Level	Score 5
Ideas and Analysis	**Essay demonstrates:** • Productive critical engagement with perspectives • Purpose-driven precision • Depth and contextual insight on the topic • Commendable analysis of the prompt issue(s) and acknowledgment of the implications of the writer's perspective
Development and Support	**Essay demonstrates:** • A commendable level of idea development to deepen understanding • Solid reasoning and use of relevant and varied support to strengthen perspective
Organization	**Essay demonstrates:** • A solid ability to capably organize ideas into a cogent piece of writing • A solid central narrative theme that unifies the text • A commendable understanding of standard essay structure and flow, including effective transitions between sentences and thoughts
Language Use and Conventions	**Essay demonstrates:** • Commendable deployment of standard English language principles • Strong use of varied and engaging vocabulary and sentence structures • A capable and effective voice and tone • Few or no errors in grammar, mechanics, and syntax

Score Level	Score 4
Ideas and Analysis	**Essay demonstrates:** • Critical engagement with perspectives • Noticeable clarity and purpose • Insight on the topic • Analysis of the issue(s) in the essay prompt
Development and Support	**Essay demonstrates:** • A good level of idea development that provides clarity • Good reasoning and use of relevant and varied support to strengthen perspective
Organization	**Essay demonstrates:** • An ability to organize ideas into a coherent piece of writing • A central narrative theme that demonstrates a real effort to unify the text • A good understanding of standard essay structure and flow, including evidence of clear transitions between sentences and thoughts
Language Use and Conventions	**Essay demonstrates:** • A good use of standard English language principles • Use of varied and engaging vocabulary and sentence structures • A good attempt to establish voice and tone • Some errors in grammar, mechanics, and syntax, which may occasionally impede meaning

Score Level	Score 3
Ideas and Analysis	**Essay demonstrates:** • A limited engagement with perspectives • Noticeable clarity and purpose • Some discernible insight on the topic • Some analysis of the issue(s) in the essay prompt
Development and Support	**Essay demonstrates:** • Some general but simplistic idea development • Some evidence of reasoning in an attempt to clarify argument
Organization	**Essay demonstrates:** • An attempt to organize ideas into a piece of writing with a basic structure • A grouping of ideas in some logical order • An attempt to provide a structure and flow between sentences and thoughts that the reader can follow
Language Use and Conventions	**Essay demonstrates:** • An attempt to deploy standard English language principles, with occasional errors • An attempt to display some varied range of vocabulary and sentence structures, though errors are present • A discernible voice and tone, though largely hard to discern • Noticeable errors in grammar, mechanics, and syntax that impede meaning

Score Level	Score 2
Ideas and Analysis	**Essay demonstrates:** • A weak engagement with perspectives • Limited clarity and purpose • Deficient insight on the topic • Poor analysis of the issue(s) in the essay prompt
Development and Support	**Essay demonstrates:** • Weak or deficient idea development • An effort to offer reasoning in an attempt to clarify argument, though largely ineffective or off target
Organization	**Essay demonstrates:** • A weak organization of ideas and deficient structure • Ideas are weakly ordered, adversely affecting comprehensibility • A largely ineffective attempt at providing sound structure and flow between sentences and thoughts
Language Use and Conventions	**Essay demonstrates:** • A deficient attempt to deploy standard English language principles, with several noticeable errors • A weak or deficient vocabulary range and basic, often flawed, sentence structures • A weak, ineffective voice and tone, largely hard to discern • Several obvious errors in grammar, mechanics, and syntax that strongly impede meaning

Score Level	Score 1
Ideas and Analysis	**Essay demonstrates:** • No engagement with perspectives • Lack of clarity and purpose • No insight on the topic • Lack of analysis of the issue(s) in the essay prompt
Development and Support	**Essay demonstrates:** • An absence of appropriate idea development • No appropriate or discernible effort to offer reasoning in an attempt to clarify argument
Organization	**Essay demonstrates:** • No organization of ideas and a lack of basic structure • A lack of thoughtful order of ideas, severely affecting comprehensibility • An absent attempt at providing sound structure and flow between sentences and thoughts
Language Use and Conventions	**Essay demonstrates:** • No attempt to deploy standard English language principles, with serious errors • A very basic and often erroneous use of vocabulary, and many serious errors in sentence structure • A largely absent or indistinct voice and tone • Serious and widespread errors in grammar, mechanics, and syntax that profoundly impact meaning and comprehension

Your overall subject-level writing score is determined from your domain scores and will be reported on a scale of 1–36. You'll also receive a scaled English Language Arts (ELA) score ranging from 1–36. If you decide to take the ACT Writing test, your score reports will be released approximately five to eight weeks after your test date.

> The colleges that you decide to release your ACT score report to will also be able to view your complete essay. Keep this in mind as you craft your essay.

THE ACT® WRITING TEST: A CLOSER LOOK

Let's deconstruct and analyze each piece of the ACT Writing test and essay, so you'll be well-informed and prepared to reach your goal of a perfect score.

THE ACT ESSAY PROMPT

You'll be given a prompt from which to craft a thoughtfully constructed, well-written, and compelling essay that reflects your perspective on the issue(s) provided. The essay prompt can be based on a myriad of topics, so the best way to prepare for a perfect score is to *be prepared for anything*.

As you start to tackle the essay prompt, make sure you read it *at least* twice.

- Your first read-through should focus solely on digesting the information provided. Make sure you know exactly what the issue being presented is and what questions and ideas you are being asked to address in your essay response. Don't rush into furiously writing your essay without first knowing what it should cover!

- Your second read-through should confirm that you're completely clear on the essay task at hand and should also be an opportunity to start preliminary brainstorming, including ideas that you plan to include in your essay.

> *Don't* race off into writing your essay after reading the prompt. If you want to achieve a perfect score, your essay will include a critical analysis of the three perspectives provided alongside the essay prompt and task.

Here's a sample essay prompt, in the format you'll encounter on test day:

The Focus of Education: STEM vs. STEAM

In recent years, there has been a concerted effort by some educational policymakers to reposition the focus of academic curricula to a STEM model, an acronym that stands for science, technology, engineering, and math. Proponents believe that these four core academic areas reflect the primary knowledge bases that individuals will most need to be successful and vital in the twenty-first century, and that less resources should be allocated to the arts, history, and physical education, as their importance will decrease in our technology-focused world.

Critics of this approach contend that a STEAM model (science, technology, engineering, arts, and math) is a better, more comprehensive model, one that reflects the value and contributions that the arts make—both at an individual level and at every level of society including education, culture, and shaping the future.

Given the limited resources available and America's desire to reassert its commitment to education so that its citizens are prepared to tackle the challenges of the twenty-first century and succeed on a global scale, it is worth examining the debate regarding educational models, as well as exploring additional ideas for shaping policy in this area.

High-scoring test takers will carefully read, analyze, and consider the entire essay prompt before moving forward. Notice that the prompt includes conflicting viewpoints, designed to help stimulate your thinking on the issue provided. You'll likely find a format similar to this in your Writing test prompt. This prompt serves as the foundation for the perspectives you will encounter next, and it should get you thinking about your own opinion on the topic. A perfect-score essay will reflect a deep and thorough understanding of the topic and will address it within a well-structured written response. The test readers will certainly be looking to make sure that you do this, and your scores will reflect how successful you are.

After reading the prompt at least twice, don't go into full essay planning mode just yet. Consider taking a few notes during and immediately after your second read-through if something important or relevant crosses your mind that would fit well into your essay or that would help you structure and organize your response.

Think critically about the sample prompt. You're being asked to analyze the relative merits and disadvantages of two specific education models (STEM and STEAM). You're given some general thoughts from various proponents and critics regarding which primary knowledge bases are most essential, information that you can utilize to support or argue against. Start building your own perspective on the issue at hand, and assess how the information provided aligns with your thoughts.

Again, the questions toward the end of the prompt will help you structure the body of your essay. An in-depth review of the questions in this sample prompt make it clear that you'll need to discuss which education model represents the best directional approach and wiser focus for preparing individuals for global-scale success in the twenty-first century. A perfect scoring essay will not only take a multifaceted approach and include your thoughts on the potential advantages and disadvantages of each of the two models provided, it will go one step further and explore curriculum ideas that fall outside these two models.

A Key to Success: Observe Issues from Many Sides

Great debaters are typically successful on the ACT Writing test. Why? Because they have a great deal of practice arguing their points of view on a wide range of topics.

Make it a habit to sharpen your debating skills in preparation for test day. Stay aware of issues and current events that people are talking about, and make it a point to engage others in conversations (and debates) about them as often as possible.

Getting comfortable arguing your perspective on a range of issues is valuable practice—and one of these issues just might be the foundation for your essay prompt when you take the ACT Writing test!

Once you have carefully analyzed the essay prompt, have thoughtfully considered the ideas presented in it, and perhaps have written down your preliminary thoughts and ideas, you're ready to move on to the three perspectives provided.

THE ACT ESSAY PERSPECTIVES

You will also be given three varying perspectives on the issue provided in the essay prompt. If you're aiming for a perfect score, you'll need to carefully consider each of these three perspectives as you plan—and eventually construct—your essay, and your final piece of writing should reflect a thoughtful analysis of each, integrated with your own well-developed perspective.

As you analyze the three perspectives, think about how each complements or detracts from *your* thoughts on the issue. Continue to brainstorm all sides of the issue as your distinct perspective develops. The ideas flowing through your mind at this stage will likely serve to structure the fundamental core of your written response.

Reading the various perspectives provided alongside the essay prompt will undoubtedly get your argumentative and creative wheels turning. This is a great opportunity to take some quick notes and capture your thoughts.

At this stage, your brainstorming notes might be a simple list of various ideas that you think may prove useful later on when you're planning your essay. Or, you might be the type of student who needs to add more structure to the notes. Consider making some general columns in which your notes can be added. A few suggestions:

- Make columns for "My Perspective," "Competing Perspectives," and "Miscellaneous Ideas," and use these general categories to organize your thoughts.

- Make columns that correspond to the basic structural elements of essays: "Introduction," "Body Paragraphs," and "Conclusion," and use these categories to manage your ideas.

Choose a strategy that works best for you. If you're vying for a perfect score, the last thing you want to have happen on test day is to complete the Writing test only to realize that you left out key points in your final essay.

Let's take a look at three perspectives on "The Focus of Education: STEM vs. STEAM":

Read and carefully consider these perspectives. Each suggests a particular way of thinking about the notion of instituting a STEM- or STEAM-based curriculum model.

PERSPECTIVE ONE

Schools nationwide, and at every grade level, should strictly follow a STEM curriculum model. The direction that the twenty-first century is taking has become quite clear in its early decades—the primacy of science and technology in every facet of society is apparent—and education programs should be able to shift and pivot to accurately reflect society. However, educational institutions are forced to deal with severe limitations in money, time, and resources. Making sure that the limited resources that are available are used in the wisest and most beneficial areas, those that will most benefit students as they become the workers and innovators of the future—locally, nationally, and globally—is the best way to position the United States for future success.

PERSPECTIVE TWO

A collective failure to acknowledge the importance of the arts in education is both tragic and dangerous—for future generations and society at large. Providing students with a deep and comprehensive education in science, technology, engineering, and mathematics is important to prepare them for success beyond the classroom, but there is clearly both room and importance for tempering this model with an education in the liberal arts. It isn't wise to assume that there won't be a need or place for the arts in the future, and demonstrating or advocating a collective "devaluing" of the arts, or history, or music doesn't bode well for society. In order to create a future that allows individuals to fully flourish, express themselves, and grow and live in a world where there's room for wonderful innovations in technology and the arts, a STEAM model is the wisest approach.

PERSPECTIVE THREE

Mandating a rigid educational model for every student, at every level, is confining at best—and potentially stifling. A "one size fits all" approach to life is rarely beneficial to the individuals who make up the "all," and this is true in education as well. While it's true that there are benefits to both STEM and STEAM models, a truly progressive society that's eager to refocus education for the future should allow students to individually tailor their academic experiences to match their unique interests and goals. In recent years, there has been a growing concern over the general lack of focus and attention students give to school; perhaps if they had a greater opportunity to create learning programs that engage them, they'd be more inclined to give school the attention it deserves—and all facets of society will benefit as a result.

As you read these perspectives, think carefully about how each point of view might complement—or counter—your own perspective on the issue of utilizing a STEM vs. STEAM education model. Again, it may be a good idea to take some notes and capture your thoughts on each perspective.

If you're of the mindset that the STEM model is clearly the superior approach, you'll likely start thinking about how your ideas align with those in Perspective One and begin formulating an argument why Perspective Two represents a flawed way of thinking. Perhaps you think the STEAM model is the more logical approach; if so, you'll likely take the opposite approach. If you think there are merits to both models, or if you have a completely different notion regarding the focus of education in the twenty-first century, you may align most closely with Perspective Three and argue against the narrow focus of Perspectives One and Two.

Regardless of which perspective best aligns with your specific way of thinking, if you're aiming for a perfect score, you'll need to take a nuanced, multifaceted approach and analyze all three perspectives in your essay. Don't forget—a truly great argumentative essay not only fiercely supports a specific point of view, it also capably acknowledges and addresses alternate and competing viewpoints.

 Remember—a great piece of writing that fails to *fully* address the essay prompt and task will not earn you great scores on test day.

Now that you've fully digested the essay prompt and carefully considered each of the three perspectives provided and have some idea about how they all align with your specific perspective (and perhaps have some helpful notes that will serve you well when planning and structuring your essay), you're ready to move forward.

The ACT Essay Task

Be sure to read the essay task *carefully*—the test readers will be checking to make sure your essay capably addresses the task provided, and a perfect-scoring essay simply cannot leave any aspect of the task unaddressed.

Read the following essay task for "The Focus of Education: STEM vs. STEAM":

Essay Task

Write a cohesive, logical essay in which you evaluate multiple perspectives on the STEM vs. STEAM education model. In your essay, be sure to:

- Examine and assess the perspectives given

- Declare and explain your own perspective on the issue

- Discuss the relationship between your perspective and those given

Your perspective may be in full or partial agreement, or in total disagreement, with any of the others. Whatever the case, support your ideas with logical reasoning and detailed, persuasive examples.

Okay—you've read the essay prompt and considered your take on the issue alongside the three perspectives provided, and you're fully aware of the essay task at hand. At this point, you likely have some cogent ideas that you'd like to incorporate into your writing. The next step is to move forward and structure your essay!

PLANNING YOUR ESSAY

The first thing to acknowledge about essay planning is that there's no single, proven method that works for everyone. You've undoubtedly written a variety of effective essays during your academic career and have learned which strategies work for you and which don't. Do you like to write an outline or plan in your head? How do you like to brainstorm ideas? There's no reason to "reinvent the wheel" for the ACT—use the writing strategies that have proven to work well for you in the past as you aim for a perfect test score!

Although your essay will be unique and reflect your own distinct perspective on the issue provided in the prompt, an effective piece of argumentative essay writing should follow the basic structure of Introduction, Body, and Conclusion.

INTRODUCTION

The introduction of your essay is your opportunity to make a strong and lasting impression on the essay readers. Use your essay opening to grab the reader's attention, confidently introduce your thoughts on the topic, and explain why you think it's an important issue worth exploration. Consider the following tools for starting your essay:

- A memorable and relevant quote from a noted figure
- An emotional and impassioned connection between you and the central issue of the essay prompt
- An intriguing question posed to your readers

When handled effectively, a strong introduction can really keep readers interested in what you have to say. Conversely, a weak introduction can be a challenge to overcome and can make it difficult for you to earn a perfect score.

Make every opportunity to introduce the central idea or thesis of your essay as early as possible. With limited time to craft your essay, you should make readers aware of your main idea quickly and allow yourself ample time to develop adequate and convincing support in the body of your essay.

BODY

The body paragraphs of your essay—and any essay that achieves a perfect score—should include the following:

- A thoughtful analysis of the essay prompt and task
- Effective idea development that supports your central thesis
- A comprehensive analysis of the three perspectives provided and how they complement or contrast with your own distinct perspective

A high-scoring essay will be an in-depth, well-rounded, and memorable piece of writing that covers an array of viewpoints (including opposing ones!) while strengthening your own central thesis.

CONCLUSION

Starting your essay strong with an effective introduction that makes an exceptional initial impression in the minds of official ACT readers is important, but just as important is ending your essay with an unforgettable conclusion—especially if you're gunning for a perfect score.

Make sure the conclusion of your essay does the following:

- Neatly ties up the ideas you've provided in your essay
- Reasserts the importance and value of your central position on the topic
- Includes relevant and insightful ideas for further exploration

Consider utilizing the strategies mentioned earlier for creating a powerful introduction when developing your essay's conclusion. A memorable and relevant quote, an emotional personal connection that demonstrates your passion toward the main issue, or a provocative question can help you conclude on a high note.

Brainstorming and Taking Notes

As previously suggested, taking notes as you brainstorm can be an effective initial strategy as you prepare to structure, organize, and develop your essay. *Don't* waste time crafting grammatically perfect, well-constructed sentences out of your notes. Remember, the clock is ticking as you take the test, and if your goal is a perfect score, you'll need to make the most of the time allotted for every section of the exam.

Your notes should simply be a rough collection of relevant thoughts that arise as you analyze the essay prompt, perspectives, and task. These early notes can serve in the following key ways:

- They can be developed into the polished, carefully organized, and compelling ideas that will make up your essay.
- They can stimulate your thinking about new ideas for your piece.
- They can help you avoid forgetting to include key information and ideas in your essay, which could potentially get lost as you work to finish your essay in the time allotted.
- They can help you prune out unnecessary or superfluous ideas that won't serve to strengthen your piece.

Your notes don't have to include only the things you may want to include in your final essay. They can also include relevant questions you'd like to explore (and eventually answer!), ideas about structure and organization, and general writing notes to yourself.

We suggest you spend *no more than 10 minutes* brainstorming, taking notes, and planning your essay before you start writing your first draft. This is where practice before test day comes in handy. Get comfortable with a time formula that works best for you; determine if the "10 minutes planning/30 minutes writing and editing" approach works for you, and don't be afraid to tweak it if necessary!

 Students who get perfect ACT test scores are more than just smart—they have practiced and gotten comfortable with working in test-like conditions, including timing, through diligent practice and are equipped with confidence on test day!

Let's take a look at a sample brainstorming list for "The Focus of Education: STEM vs. STEAM." The following list mirrors the basic structural elements of an essay: introduction, body paragraphs, and conclusion. Remember, how you approach brainstorming and note taking should reflect the strategies that have worked for you thus far in your academic career. There's no need to change what works for you!

Introduction Ideas

- *STEAM is a better educational model*
- *Discuss the power of education, to highlight issue importance (give quote?)*
- *Why issue is so important at this moment in history?*
- *Discuss local, national, global implications, for present and future*
- *How have the arts enriched/changed my life?*

Body paragraph ideas

- *Why is STEAM a better model than STEM?*
- *Advantages of liberal arts education*
  - *More well-rounded students*
  - *Culture and arts to feed our souls and enhance society*
  - *Arts provide richness and meaning to life*
- *Negatives of a world devoid of arts*
- *Acknowledge importance of STEM (learning for future innovation, etc.)*
- *Discuss "real" educational problem—lack of sufficient money and resources*
  - *How should this be addressed?*
- *How would I influence policy if given the opportunity?*
  - *What would I change or keep the same?*

Conclusion ideas

- *Advantages/disadvantages/realistic limitations facing education/focus*
- *Supplement school learning with home learning—"H" in STEAM?*
- *Reiterate importance of this issue, for all of us and future generations*

You can see that by using this method, an essay response is already starting to take shape. The list includes thoughts that can be further developed into effective essay sentences, as well as questions to help stimulate new ideas.

Consider your notes your initial essay blueprint or outline, which you can refer to as needed when you move past the brainstorming phase and begin writing. Your notes can help keep you on track and ensure that all of your ideas are incorporated into your final essay.

After you've taken approximately 10 minutes to develop a general plan or outline for your essay, take a deep breath and pick up your pencil—because you're ready to start writing your first draft.

WRITING A PERFECT-SCORING ESSAY

Students aiming for a perfect score on the ACT should approach the exam with a comprehensive study plan between now and test day—including essay writing practice.

Now that you know what to expect on the ACT Writing test and have a solid initial plan of attack—including a critical analysis of the essay prompt, perspectives, and task, as well as brainstorming, outlining, and taking notes—you're ready to dive into essay writing practice. Find a quiet place to work, get a pencil and some paper, set a timer for 40 minutes, and let's get started.

We're going to use "The Focus of Education: STEM vs. STEAM" to practice developing, writing, and polishing an ACT-worthy essay.

Take the first 10 minutes to reread the material provided and think about this issue. Use the following space to brainstorm ideas that will help you construct your final work, or feel free to use a separate notebook or scratch paper.

Remember, the key to effective practice is to be honest and serious about using the time allotted to complete this section of the test. You'd likely be able to develop an impressive and high-scoring essay on nearly any topic if given unlimited time to write— the key on the ACT Writing test is to be able to do just that in 40 minutes.

Brainstorming ideas for:
"The Focus of Education: STEM vs. STEAM"

Introduction

_____
_____
_____
_____
_____
_____
_____
_____
_____
_____

Body Paragraphs

_____
_____
_____
_____
_____
_____
_____
_____
_____
_____

Conclusion

_____
_____
_____
_____
_____
_____
_____
_____

Okay, so you've used approximately 10 minutes to brainstorm, outline, and construct a solid list of relevant ideas, related thoughts, and questions for further exploration, which will help form the core of your essay—consider this time well spent!

A few quick reminders that bear repeating, because when the clock is ticking and stress levels are high, we often forget the most fundamental things first. Although your essay will be unique and reflect your distinct perspective on the issue provided in the prompt, an effective piece of argumentative writing should follow basic structural tenets including an introduction, supporting body paragraphs, and a conclusion. Make sure your essay thoroughly addresses the prompt and task. If it doesn't, your goal of earning a perfect essay score will remain out of reach.

Defend Your Viewpoint

One important note that hasn't been covered yet: Don't be afraid to be provocative. Too often, students choose to write from a perspective on the essay task that they *think* the official ACT readers will want to read, even if it doesn't match their actual beliefs. This could result in an essay that lacks passion and conviction and may adversely affect the final score.

Don't be afraid to write from a perspective that may seem controversial—your essay will be judged on how well you develop and support your ideas, not on whether or not the readers agree with your point of view.

Now it's time to use your remaining 30 minutes to craft and edit your essay on "The Focus of Education: STEM vs. STEAM." What's the most effective way to use this time? Again, this is completely up to you and how you like to work, but we suggest you take 20–25 minutes to write your first essay draft, and 5–10 minutes to edit your work, making sure it's polished and free of errors.

Make sure your writing environment is quiet and free from distractions and you have enough pencils and paper and an accurate timer. Best of luck!

Editing Your Essay

Once you've written a competent first draft of your essay, ideally, you'll have 5–10 minutes left on the clock to review and polish your work. This isn't a lot of time, so you'll have to make the most of every minute left available to you, especially if getting a perfect score is your goal. Remember, one of the four primary domains that your essay is going to be scored on is Language Use and Conventions, so you'll want to convince the official readers that your essay demonstrates the following:

- Skillful deployment of standard English language principles. When you edit your essay, make sure that your work follows sound principles of English language writing, including essay format.

- Excellent use of varied and engaging vocabulary and sentence structures. Does your work demonstrate a masterful command of vocabulary and use of compelling and varied sentence types? Essays that receive a perfect score do, so make sure your essay does when you're reviewing it.

- A clear, authoritative, and effective voice and tone. Your final essay should be a confident, passionate, and convincing assertion of your perspective on the topic provided.

- Few or no errors in grammar, mechanics, and syntax. Nothing is sadder than an essay that's full of great ideas, but also full of misspellings and grammatical errors, which will likely prevent you from getting a perfect score. The editing phase is the ideal time for you to make sure your work is free from errors in grammar, mechanics, and syntax.

ACT Writing Test: Use Your Time Wisely

Use this guide to make the most of your time on test day:

Total test time: 40 minutes
Brainstorming: 10 minutes
Essay writing: 20–25 minutes
Editing and revising: 5–10 minutes

REVIEWING YOUR ESSAY

Now that you've written and edited your essay and your 40 minutes are up, we know what you're thinking: *How did I do? Does my essay deserve a top score? Are there areas I need to improve on between now and test day to ensure that my goal of getting a perfect score is within reach?*

Don't Let Passion Prevail!

On test day, you may encounter a topic that you feel passionately about. You are eager to pour your vast wealth of knowledge on the subject onto the pages provided in an effort to dazzle and impress the test readers—until the test time is up and you're left with an unpolished, disorganized piece of work.

Remember, this is a test of your ability to craft a well-organized, argumentative piece of writing that reflects a mastery of English language mechanics and conventions, not an opportunity to show off how much you know on a given subject. Even if you encounter the *perfect* essay task on test day, step back for a moment, relax, and don't forget to pace yourself properly, allowing yourself time to carefully plan, organize, structure, develop, and polish your writing into an effective piece of work in 40 minutes.

A great way to get a sense of your own work is to compare it to a sample essay response that received top scores in each of the four writing domains. When you review the sample response, think about how your essay stacks up against this one. When performing your analysis, consider things that this sample essay does particularly well, and how your essay compares in each of the primary writing domains. Feel free to take notes, and use them to continue to dissect, analyze, and ultimately improve your writing as you pursue your quest for a perfect score.

SAMPLE ESSAY—SCORE 6

Ideas and Analysis:	Score = 6
Development and Support:	Score = 6
Organization:	Score = 6
Language Use and Conventions:	Score = 6

Nelson Mandela once said, "Education is the most powerful weapon which you can use to change the world." Throughout history, the progressive march of nations worldwide has been fueled by improved access to education and continued refinement to educational models and processes, which makes instinctual sense; as a nation evolves, so should its method and model for educating it's people. The 21st century, thus far a heady mix of rapid technological and social progression, has left the United States at a true inflection point. The entrenched educational models we utilize to stimulate and expand the minds of future leaders and innovators feel outdated, and out of step with the pace of our current technological era. To make a complicated issue even more challenging, resources for system-wide educational overhaul remain woefully limited. Regardless, great nations become great in times of adversity, when challenges are met and overcome, with real forward progress as lasting proof of wise decisions having been made precisely when decisions were needed.

I believe that the best education has no walls beyond those in the classroom. The hungry minds of our nation should be nourished with the full range of "fruits" that this great nation has to offer. In this regard, a STEAM-based model offers the best of both worlds: a solid education in science, technology, engineering, and math—the fields that will continue to drive progress and innovation through this century and beyond; and the arts—the fields that allow us to learn from our collective and individual experiences and histories, celebrate life and our distinct, varied cultures and feed our souls through creative expression in art, writing, music, film, and more. If a STEM education allows us to build our houses, the "A" in STEAM allows us to make them homes, to bring richness and meaning to our lives. Who could argue that a model that's missing any of these is a step forward?

Although if pressed I'd choose a STEAM over a STEM educational model, I contend that the true issue at the heart of our nation's "educational problem" is the fact that we have to choose in the first place. A truly progressive nation should place a higher value on education and find a way to provide the resources needed to ensure that we don't have to choose. If I were in the position to influence educational policy, this would be my highest priority. My efforts would be geared toward making the argument that funds given to education should not be looked at as an expense but rather as an investment—in all of our futures.

Until this happens, educational policymakers need to make the most of available, albeit limited, resources. This means that hard choices need to be made; a focus on the STEM-centric model with time allocated for core liberal arts curricula—in history, English, and elective programs that engage students by letting them pursue the areas they're most interested in—seems like a wise approach given the circumstances.

However, I strongly believe that an additional letter should be added to the acronym—an "H" for home. Educational administrators and policymakers need to do a better job of spreading the message that learning doesn't just need to happen in the classroom. Teachers need to work with families and parents to spread the message that learning at school can, and should, be supplemented by learning at home. This way, no subject gets shortchanged. In sum, if part of our educational focus is to spread the message that learning is an ongoing, lifelong process that occurs in all of the rooms that we find ourselves in throughout our lives, we'll all be better off—and the pace of progress in all areas of life will be more of a confident march than a tentative stroll.

The following is an analysis of the sample essay in each of the four domains on which your ACT essay will be scored. Use this to identify areas of strength and weakness in your own writing, which will help you structure an effective essay writing skills improvement plan and get ready for a perfect score on test day.

Scoring Explanation

Ideas and Analysis: Score = 6

This essay offers an engaging, nuanced, and thoughtful analysis of the issue of STEM vs. STEAM and takes it a step further—the writer expands on the issue and provides ideas on what he or she perceives to be core problems regarding the direction and focus of education today ("A truly progressive nation should place a higher value on education, and find a way to provide the resources needed to ensure that we don't have to choose"); the idea to add a greater focus on learning outside of the classroom was a particularly insightful addition. The overall result is an in-depth, multifaceted, and carefully considered argument.

Development and Support: Score = 6

The writer of this essay provides an exceptional level of development and support to bolster his or her argument—from the opening quote from Nelson Mandela regarding the transformative power of education to the stirring salvo at the conclusion highlighting the role learning plays in dictating the pace of global progress. The writer establishes his preference for an all-inclusive educational model and develops a stirring case for why it's a wise choice. The overall level of sophistication and depth in the writing greatly supports the writer's perspective and leads to a persuasive argument.

Organization: Score = 6

It's clear the writer of this essay has a strong command of the basic principles of essay structure and was able to effectively deploy them in service of his or her position on the essay prompt. A strong introduction, well-reasoned review of both sides of the prompt, additional insight on the core issues facing education, and holistic approach to idea generation results in a very successful essay.

Language Use and Conventions: Score = 6

An impressive display of vocabulary and varied word choice throughout the piece, use of engaging analogies (i.e., comparing STEM vs. STEAM to a house vs. a home) and sophisticated sentences and transitions clearly indicate a high level of writing proficiency. The writer was able to infuse a great deal of passion into his or her essay and captures the reader's attention from beginning to end. The essay is largely free from errors, resulting in a highly polished and provocative piece.

Take a Step Beyond

When crafting your essay, think about "above and beyond" ideas that can enhance your work. Take "The Focus of Education: STEM vs. STEAM" exercise as an example. The sample essay effectively addresses the essay prompt and task—but doesn't stop there. The author introduces the notion of adding an "H" for home to the acronym, stressing the importance of education continuing at home. Fresh, innovative thinking about the essay task—as long as it doesn't veer off topic—can really impress official ACT essay readers.

Hopefully, you now have a better sense of where your own writing skill levels are and what you need to do between now and test day to get ready to achieve a perfect score. Now, you'll have the opportunity to practice writing two additional essays and review your work against high-scoring samples. Use these opportunities for additional practice and skills assessment to your advantage, and you'll be well on your way to achieving your ultimate ACT goal—a perfect score.

Bottom line: You're a student who's no stranger to academic success or to writing essays based on a given subject. Get plenty of practice with the ACT Writing test format and timing, utilize your best and most proven writing strategies, and remain keenly aware of the primary domains on which your work will be scored and you'll put yourself in the best position possible to achieve your goal of getting a perfect score!

PRACTICE ESSAY PROMPT ONE

Utilize the following sample ACT Writing test essay prompts to practice and build your skills in preparation for test day. Each includes a model high-scoring essay and scoring analysis, to help you gauge your own writing.

Credit Cards for College Students

Recent decades have witnessed a concerted effort by major credit card companies to market and provide a targeted line of credit products, including credit cards, to college students nationwide. These credit cards allow students to make various purchases when cash isn't readily available. Student credit cards also come with a variety of terms that students and their parents should be aware of, including varying credit limits and APRs (annual percentage rates), which can often be altered by the parent financial institutions and can greatly affect the ultimate costs of purchases made. Given that most students will have a sizable student loan to repay after graduation, it is worth examining the ethics of marketing and providing credit cards to college students.

Read and carefully consider these perspectives. Each suggests a particular way of thinking about the availability of student credit cards.

PERSPECTIVE ONE

Student credit cards represent the worst aspects of consumer capitalism and should no longer exist. They are deliberate and calculated attempts to transform impressionable young individuals into lifetime users of credit, to the detriment of their own long-term financial well-being. Uninformed students get lured into credit card agreements with murky and confusing terms that only favor the heartless financial behemoths that supply them, and the result is all too common: Students use them irresponsibly and are left with colossal debt, damaged credit histories, and an unhealthy reliance on credit cards, while the credit card–issuing companies make huge profits.

Perspective Two

College is an important time of life for young adults to develop the skills needed to become responsible adults, and this includes exhibiting sound and healthy financial behavior. Student credit cards represent good tools for students to practice using credit responsibly, develop good habits regarding money and spending, and establish credit histories, which is often necessary for future loans and major purchases. Individuals of all ages learn from trial and error, successes as well as missteps, and credit cards allow students opportunities to adopt a greater understanding of money management and budgeting and work towards financial independence.

Perspective Three

Like many things in life, student credit cards represent potentially positive opportunities that are also fraught with potential hazards. Just because something has the potential for misuse doesn't mean that it shouldn't be allowed—medicines, automobiles, and kitchen knives wouldn't be allowed under that metric. College is a time for individual exploration and development, in preparation for the world of adulthood, which doesn't include a safety net, and having the opportunity to learn how to build and use credit is a worthy experience, even if mistakes are made along the way. However, this doesn't mean that an unregulated connection between credit card companies and students should be allowed to exist. This should be a heavily regulated system that protects students from hidden, unclear, and predatory money-making tactics from credit card companies and should require the involvement of parents or guardians.

The Essay Task

Write a cohesive, logical essay in which you consider multiple perspectives on the issue of credit cards for college students. In your essay, be sure to:

- examine and assess the perspectives given
- declare and explain your own perspective on the issue
- discuss the relationship between your perspective and those given

Your perspective may be in full or partial agreement, or in total disagreement, with any of the others. Whatever the case, support your ideas with logical reasoning and detailed, persuasive examples.

Sample Essay—Score 6

Ideas and Analysis:	Score = 6
Development and Support:	Score = 6
Organization:	Score = 6
Language Use and Conventions:	Score = 6

What credible journey to adulthood doesn't include lessons learned from failure and success? College is meant to be a time of personal exploration, an opportunity to explore, learn, and grow, to learn what we're capable of and what kinds of lives we hope to lead—which often comes through trial and error, new trails blazed in bold experiments, retrenchments, and, hopefully, wisdom. This includes acquiring the financial responsibility of a seasoned adult, which most of us simply aren't born with.

Credit cards for college students represent good opportunities for burgeoning adults to build essential money management and budgeting skills, and, if regulated carefully, can represent positive experiences, even if they include mistakes made and lessons learned. College students are typically thrown into adulthood after they graduate, get jobs, and move into their own living spaces, often without a safety net. Is this the right time for them to start developing sound financial skills? I contend that the ideal time to get comfortable using credit and to start establishing a credit history is within the guided structure of college.

The argument against marketing credit cards to this impressionable and largely unseasoned demographic is certainly compelling. It's not unheard of for college students to behave irresponsibly and to make decisions that don't always represent their best interests. Furthermore, the deceptive and nefarious practices of massive credit card companies, all designed to maximize profits, are well known and documented. However, a carefully regulated system can help offset some of the fears connected with issuing credit cards to students. Unmovable ceilings on credit limits, reasonable interest rates, and mandatory parental or guardian approval should be hardwired into the system. Recent advances in technology can help keep students from abusing credit cards—updates and warnings via apps or text messages can help monitor credit usage and keep students on track.

I also think colleges should seriously consider implementing mandatory classes in financial literacy and money management, including how to use credit cards and budget effectively. Today's world is fraught with economic challenges for young adults who are eager to achieve and maintain financial independence and discover ways to create long-term financial security. Institutions of higher education, which obtain a great deal of money from students, often in the form of loans that students will have to learn how to properly budget for upon graduation, should feel a responsibility to offer education programs that focus on developing positive financial habits—including how to use and build credit responsibly. Effective financial education programs will serve the dual purpose of helping students use credit cards effectively while in college, as well as preparing young adults for responsible, independent, and secure adulthood.

> *Although some additional levels of regulation regarding student credit cards should be put into place, things that have the potential to be abused, like credit cards, aren't automatically evil and shouldn't be banned. A free and progressive society shouldn't feel the responsibility to shield people from all potential dangers—it simply isn't a rational approach to life and wouldn't allow individuals to learn from their mistakes. There is a freedom to being given the room to succeed—and fail—and in that space we are tested and have opportunities to become the best versions of ourselves.*

SCORING EXPLANATION

Ideas and Analysis: Score = 6

This essay reflects an in-depth understanding of the issues involved in the student credit card debate, and its author provides a multifaceted written response with an exemplary level of analysis. The author covers the gamut of prospective advantages to practicing and building sound financial behaviors in young adulthood (*"I contend that the ideal time to get comfortable using credit and to start establishing a credit history is within the guided structure of college."*) and the dangers of government intrusion to abolish potential risk (*"There is a freedom to being given the room to succeed—and fail—and in that space we are tested and have opportunities to become the best versions of ourselves."*). The author wisely acknowledges opposing viewpoints and effectively uses it as a springboard to promote his or her thoughts regarding the need for additional systemic regulation and financial education programs. The result is a bold and memorable piece of argumentative writing that hits its target.

Development and Support: Score = 6

This essay represents a firm grasp of efficacious idea development and support for the author's point of view that student credit cards, if properly and carefully regulated and accompanied by education that promotes financial literacy, represent positive opportunities for young adults to build responsible money managements skills in preparation for impending adulthood (*"Credit cards for college students represent good opportunities for burgeoning adults to build essential money management and budgeting skills, and, if regulated carefully, can represent positive experiences, even if they include mistakes made and lessons learned."*). Support for this perspective is built on a solid foundation of idea analysis on both sides of the issue, and the resulting essay not only offers a compelling argument for allowing college students to have access to credit cards, it takes a bold step further—arguing for the merits of allowing all individuals to gain wisdom and experience through personal exploration, success, and failure.

Organization: Score = 6

The author of this piece clearly understands how to structure and organize his or her thoughts into an effective and convincing essay that more than meets the task at hand. It starts with a provocative question to readers (*"What credible journey to adulthood doesn't include lessons learned from failure and success?"*), analyzes both sides of the debate while building a convincing argument in favor of student credit cards in the body paragraphs, blends in new ideas to improve the system (*"Effective financial education programs will serve the dual purpose of helping students use credit cards effectively while in college, as well as preparing young adults for responsible, independent, and secure adulthood."*), and concludes with a passionate plea for allowing individuals the freedom to discover, explore, succeed, fail, learn, and grow. This is an engaging and memorable essay that takes full advantage of sound organizational strategy.

Language Use and Conventions: Score = 6

An essay full of strong, compelling ideas can lose credibility and effectiveness if it is full of poor grammar, weak transitions, and embarrassing typos. This essay represents just the opposite—strong ideas with sound development and organization that's girded by an excellent display of language use and conventions. A great deal of passion and careful thought comes through in the author's writing, and it seems evident that the author made a real effort to polish and craft his or her writing, as it is largely free of errors, resulting in a high score.

PRACTICE ESSAY PROMPT TWO

Prisoner Rights and National Security

News headlines across the globe contain horrific stories involving terrorism—activities both carried out and thwarted—and it seems that no nation, community, or demographic can consider itself safe from potential acts of violence. Countries that are eager to reduce the levels of threats and acts of terrorism incurred by its citizenry have either used or considered using "enhanced interrogation techniques"—which some call torture—against prisoners with known or suspected ties to terrorism, in an effort to obtain potentially valuable information that can prevent future acts of terrorism.

Considering the toll that terrorist attacks have taken on society, the question of whether the use of enhanced interrogation techniques on a prisoner in the name of national security is an infringement on that person's rights or a justifiable action in an effort to obtain valuable information is surely going to be hotly debated both now and in the foreseeable future.

Read and carefully consider these perspectives. Each suggests a particular way of thinking about the issue of prisoner rights and national security.

PERSPECTIVE ONE

"Enhanced interrogation techniques" is just a sanitized euphemism for torture and should never be tolerated. Even considering its possible use signals that a nation or law enforcement agency is too close to crossing a moral boundary, which can never be uncrossed—just as any crime can never be undone, an infringement on a prisoner's basic rights, even if done in the name of national security, forever weakens the very foundation that a free and just nation is built upon. Basic human rights aren't things that should be decided upon or legislated; they are inalienable, undeniable—and should be unmovable.

PERSPECTIVE TWO

A progressive and free democracy must recognize the reality of the world around it, including dangers and threats that are constantly looming and must place the security of its populace—both within its borders and abroad—among its most important and sacred responsibilities. If using torture against prisoners will help keep people safe and secure, then it is a tool that should be utilized. Imagine the following scenario: there is legitimate and verified intelligence indicating that an elementary school is targeted to be blown up by a known group of terrorists in the next few days. If there is a prisoner with known ties to this terrorist group, who has boastfully intimated that he has information about the attack, enhanced interrogation techniques should be used against him in an effort to protect the students and teachers at that school.

The modern world is a complex place, with a complicated network of inter-twined and enmeshed political systems that make having concrete, unmoving public policy seem short-sighted and limiting. A nation's policy regarding the use of enhanced interrogation techniques must bend and flex with the changing world—a world in which the threat of terrorism is a growing concern in the hearts and minds of people around the world. Enhanced interrogation techniques aren't things to be used lightly, or flippantly; rather, there should be discussion and consensus among like-minded nations regarding its use, its use should be made open and public with clear evidence supporting it, and it should always be considered a last resort that should only be used when there is a high degree of certainty that it will help prevent a threat to a nation's security, after all other efforts have been exhausted.

THE ESSAY TASK

Write a unified, coherent essay in which you evaluate multiple perspectives on the issue of prisoner rights and national security. In your essay, be sure to:

- examine and assess the perspectives given
- declare and explain your own perspective on the issue
- discuss the relationship between your perspective and those given

Your perspective may be in full or partial agreement, or in total disagreement, with any of the others. Whatever the case, support your ideas with logical reasoning and detailed, persuasive examples.

Sample Essay—Score 6

Ideas and Analysis:	Score = 6
Development and Support:	Score = 6
Organization:	Score = 6
Language Use and Conventions:	Score = 6

Winston Churchill once proclaimed that "the treatment of crime and criminals mark and measure the stored-up strength of a nation and are the sign and proof of the living virtue in it." Churchill uttered these words in a different era and world and made this procla- mation within a different mix of global powers, policies, and dangers, so we're forced to wonder about the strength and bond that holds together his claim. Should they stand resolute and unwavering in the face of global terrorism? When the safety of a nation, and its people, are threatened, which of its foundations are movable and changeable to face these threats?

At first glance, these feel like murky and complicated questions. But are they really? The structure of a building is absolute; its foundation cannot be altered to meet the changing weather if it's to remain standing. The roots of a tree must remain firmly planted if it's to survive. And just as human life requires a working brain and a beating heart to go on, the beating heart of a nation and what it stands for must not flinch, shift, or disappear when tested. This includes the use of enhanced interrogation techniques, which I'll refer to as torture because that is what it is, even in the most dire of circumstances. The way free and fair nations treat criminals is among the truest tests of their determination and resolve to stand by the principles at its very roots, even in the face of terrorism.

Let's revisit the scenario where there is legitimate and verified intelligence indicating that an elementary school is targeted to be blown up by a known group of terrorists in the next few days, and we are on the hunt for quick information from a prisoner with known ties to the group. Let's imagine we tortured the prisoner for information. The following scenarios are certainly feasible following whatever unjust and inhuman treatment is taken upon the prisoner:

In order to make the torture stop, the prisoner provides information, but it ultimately proves to be useless, sending law enforcement down a fruitless rabbit hole. The lines of justice were crossed for nothing.

Perhaps the prisoner lies and provides information that another person is going to carry out the attack—an innocent person. Law enforcement goes after the innocent person. How far do they go to interrogate this innocent person in the name of national security?

Maybe the prisoner has no useful information and provides nothing to law enforcement despite repeated torturing. How long does the torture go on for?

Where lines are drawn and when it's appropriate to consider crossing them is always a slippery slope, one that ethical people—and nations—must confront whenever making tough moral decisions. Where torture is involved, there's no coming back once the line is crossed, and once a line is crossed, it makes it easier to keep going further, perhaps to a point where morals and ethics don't exist.

Evil should never be met on its own terms. It is the test of free and just societies to combat evil with righteousness and with the tools of justice and ethical law enforcement that have served to build and defend free nations—if for no other reason than to show all evildoers that there is a better way. If we choose to meet evil with evil, the outcome has already been decided—we've all lost.

SCORING EXPLANATION

Ideas and Analysis: Score = 6

This written response provides a confident and engaging argument against the use of enhanced interrogation techniques in any circumstance, even in the name of national security. It begins with a compelling quote from Winston Churchill that perfectly supports the essay author's point of view and offers a wealth of engaging ideas on the issue—the scenarios of tried and failed uses of prisoner torture, and their potential consequences, represent a thoroughly impressive and multifaceted analysis of both sides of the debate and are particularly effective. The author takes the opportunity to conclude this piece of writing with a memorable thought regarding how just societies should face evil (*"If we choose to meet evil with evil, the outcome has already been decided—we've all lost."*), no doubt leaving a lasting mark in the minds of readers.

Development and Support: Score = 6

The author of this piece has a masterful command of effective idea development and galvanizes his or her abilities in support of a very clear and unwavering perspective on torturing prisoners in instances of national security and the slippery slope that is reached when choosing to meet evil on its own terms. An effective argument such as this one does not simply advocate for its position; it acknowledges other perspectives (*"When the safety of a nation, and its people, are threatened, which of its foundations are movable and changeable to face these threats?"*) and—when truly successful—is able to use this to both strengthen his or her position and weaken opposing viewpoints. The author acknowledges the weightiness of this issue and does not equivocate in his or her belief on the right path forward. The end result is a sophisticated and nuanced argument that would be hard for any reader—supporter or not—to ignore.

Organization: Score = 6

This piece of argumentative writing reflects an adherence to the tenets of effective essay writing structure. It includes an engaging introduction that grabs readers' attention (proclamation by Winston Churchill), effective body paragraphs that support the author's perspective while weakening opposing points of view (*"Where torture is involved, there's no coming back once the line is crossed, and once a line is crossed it makes it easier to keep going further, perhaps to a point where morals and ethics don't exist."*), and a compelling conclusion that makes it hard not to ponder the issue long after reading this essay (*"It is the test of free and just societies to combat evil with righteousness, and with the tools of justice and ethical law enforcement that have served to build and defend free nations—if for no other reason than to show all evildoers that there is a better way.*"), which is truly the mark of an effective argument.

Language Use and Conventions: Score = 6

The level of sophistication displayed in the vocabulary and word choice used in this essay is both impressive and effective and serves to make an already compelling argument even stronger. The author of this piece clearly has a deep and thorough understanding of how to craft a passionate and convincing argument with a masterful command of the core tenets of language use and conventions. It appears to have been carefully considered, constructed, and edited and more than meets the essay task at hand.

SUMMING IT UP

- **Analyze and understand all of the prompt material**: Befor you start writing, analyze the instructions, the essay prompt, the perspectives, and the essay task *carefully*. Be sure you fully understand the issues presented in the prompt material and know *exactly* what you're being asked to write about.

- **Use what you know**: Since you won't know what essay prompt topic you'll encounter, the best way to prepare is to stay aware of issues and current events taking place around you and in the world. Be ready to draw upon your wealth of knowledge and experience to help you develop a well-rounded essay response with sufficient real-world support.

- **Use your time wisely**: Practice planning and writing essays in the time provided (40 minutes), using an approach that you've practiced before test day (we recommend 10 minutes of brainstorming, 20–25 minutes of writing, and 5–10 minutes of editing). Come to test day with a good idea of a writing pace that works for you.

- **Plan carefully**: Instead of writing furiously to get as much down on the pages before the end of the test, take a few minutes to think critically about the issue and plan. Creating an outline can help you properly structure your essay and save you time in the long run.

- **Write purposefully**: Establish a clear perspective (thesis statement) and craft compelling, well-structured sentences that support your argument and address the essay prompt and perspectives provided, as well as the implications and potential consequences of your ideas.

- **Structure your work effectively**: Don't forget that the structure and polish of your final essay is being scored alongside the quality and content of your ideas. Make sure that your essay adheres to the rules of proper essay structure, with an introduction, body paragraphs, and conclusion that stay on target.

- **Efficiency and clarity are crucial**: Avoid redundancy in your final essay—creating an efficient and economical piece of writing that stays on task, eloquently covers your points, and highlights your distinct perspective is the best approach on test day.

- **Avoid tired, overused words and phrases**: If you're vying for a perfect score, be mindful of your writing decisions—use varied, creative word choices and sentence structure throughout your piece in an effort to dazzle your readers.

- **Edit your work**: Save a few minutes to review and edit your work after writing your essay. Think about the four writing domains that your essay will be scored on as you review your work:
    - Does your essay present a wealth of compelling ideas and nuanced analysis in response to the prompt?
    - Are the ideas in your essay fully developed, and do they contain sufficient support to bolster your perspective?
    - Is your essay well-structured and organized?
    - Does your writing adhere to established English language principles and mechanics, avoiding common test-day essay mistakes including sentence fragments, run-ons, reliance on passive voice, and inappropriate pronoun shifts?
    - Have you proofread your essay (sweeping for errors, proper word choice, grammar, sense, and sentence usage)?

- **Practice makes perfect**: Use the time you have between now and test day to practice writing essays on a variety of subjects. Choose a topic that's getting a lot of news attention or, better still, work with a writing partner who'll help you choose writing topics and who can also review your work. If you can find a reader who's capable of reviewing your work along the four ACT test domains and providing helpful critical feedback, that's even better!

NOTES

NOTES

NOTES

NOTES

NOTES

NOTES

NOTES

NOTES